Mother worship

BL
325
.M6
M67

# Studies in Religion

Charles H. Long, *Editor*
The University of North Carolina at Chapel Hill

James J. Preston, Editor

# Mother Worship

## Theme and Variations

The University of North Carolina Press

Chapel Hill

Frontispiece: Black madonna of Tindari

Library of Congress Cataloging in Publication Data

Main entry under title:

Mother worship.

   (Studies in religion)
   Includes index.
   Contents: Introduction / James M. Freeman—The
Virgin of Guadalupe and the female self-image /
Ena Campbell—The Tonantsi cult of the eastern
Nahua / Alan R. Sandstrom—[etc.]
   1. Mother-goddesses—Addresses, essays, lectures.
2. Women and religion—Addresses, essays, lectures.
3. Mary, Blessed Virgin, Saint—Cult—Addresses,
essays, lecture.  I. Preston, James, 1941–
II. Series: Studies in religion (Chapel Hill, N.C.)
BL325.M6M67    306'.6    81-3336
ISBN 0-8078-1471-7    AACR2

*For Carolyn*

# Contents

# Illustrations

# Preface

Mother worship has not previously been examined crossculturally by contemporary anthropologists. Earlier studies of female deities were based on secondhand data derived from questionable sources. This is a volume of studies conducted by anthropologists and other scholars who have collected impressive original data based on extensive field research. Though mother worship is a significant aspect of religion, it is rarely discussed in the literature. Thus, the collection of essays presented here represents a unique and valuable contribution to religious studies.

This book is concerned with a wide variety of manifestations of female sacred images. It is recognized that not all female deities are primarily mother figures. Nevertheless, a survey of the literature on the topic reveals that even the most nonnurturant goddesses are considered "mother deities" by their devotees, because the term "mother" stands for more than simple nurturance. The essays in this collection attest to the great variety of forms taken by the divine feminine. It is hoped that the new material offered here will inspire other scholars to conduct further research on this surprisingly under-investigated subject. No single scholar could have written a book of this kind: mother worship is far too complex for such a grand synthesis. Yet perhaps the present volume will bring us closer to the kind of synthesis needed for the study of religion to advance to a higher level of sophistication.

Each scholar has brought a unique set of questions to the diverse aspects of mother worship reported here. The essays have been carefully selected to represent a variety of methodological approaches in different cultures and religions. They are not intended to provide a geographical survey of mother worship, an undertaking that would require several volumes. The papers have been organized by geographical region only to provide the reader with easy comparisons of deities with similar historical roots or common cultural contexts. The collection does not cover Australia, the Pacific, East Asia, or South American cultures, in which female deities are sometimes well represented. Nor does it include certain major world religions, such as Protestantism, Islam, or Shinto. These omissions are intentional. Instead of collecting an encyclopedia of articles on mother worship, the editor has selected certain major regions where this phenomenon flourishes in order to reveal the enormous variation of such female divinities even within a single location. Thus, the volume concentrates on two major focuses of mother worship, the madonna complex in Europe and Mexico, and the Great Goddess of South Asia. For contrast, selections from Southeast Asia and Africa have been included.

*Mother Worship* has been edited with the general educated reader in mind. It is also expected to appeal to scholars in the history of religions, sociology, psychology, women's studies, literary criticism, and anthropology. Anyone who is interested in symbolism and religion will find the volume a refreshing exploration into the great complexity and amazing tenacity of the divine feminine. The anthropological approach of the authors provides the reader with rich comparative data in specific cultural contexts on a fascinating, yet little-researched, aspect of human religion.

The impulse for *Mother Worship* came from a session entitled "Anthropological Inquiries into Mother Worship" chaired by Professor James Preston at an American Anthropological Association meeting (San Francisco, 1975). This session was heavily attended, attracted considerable press coverage, and became the point of reference for an ongoing scholarly dialogue. The volume has taken several years to complete. Many valuable papers had to be omitted owing to lack of space or in order to avoid unnecessary duplication. All but two of the essays were specially prepared for the present volume. The studies represent the most current anthropological research on the topic.

It takes many people to bring a collection of this kind to completion. I wish to acknowledge particularly the help of James Freeman, Alan Sandstrom, and Ena Campbell, who encouraged me to undertake the task of editing *Mother Worship*. Their contributions to the symposium in San Francisco as discussants and critics were largely responsible for instigating this final product. I also wish to thank Leonard Moss, Barbara Myerhoff, and Pauline Kolenda for helpful guidance in preparing the manuscript. Several drafts of the volume were painstakingly produced with the secretarial skills of Robin Whitbeck, Carol

Deming, Gloria Hall, and Hilda Mercun. Their assistance was greatly appreciated. I am also grateful to Ron Embling for his advice and careful preparation of graphic materials. Lastly, I am indebted to the State University of New York for support of this project.

James J. Preston

# Introduction:
# The Crosscultural Study
# of Mother Worship
## by James M. Freeman

The image of the mother has engaged humans for countless centuries. The earliest extant artistic representations of the mother are images of female organs in the Dordogne Caves of France, now about 27,000 years old, and the European venus figurines of some 20,000 to 24,000 years ago, probably associated with fertility. Since that time, in cultures throughout the world, the image of the mother has appeared as a central theme in art, myths, and dramatic performances. Novelists, poets, artists, psychologists, historians of religion, anthropologists, and many others have studied and speculated about the meaning of mother worship. Some investigators have looked for and stressed what they believe to be universal characteristics of the mother; others have focused on specific manifestations in particular cultures.

Quite possibly, mother worship reflects or is derived in part from the deep biopsychological bond that infants develop with an adult, usually, but not invariably, the mother. The emotional character of this bond varies widely for different persons, who have different personalities, experience different life situations, and come from different cultures; but infants throughout the world develop attitudes of love, hate, and fear toward those individuals who provide both gratification and frustration of their physical and emotional needs, and who thus appear both nurturant and withholding. Significantly, many of the articles in this book dwell on ambivalent attitudes about the mother, who is seen as having both power and a dual nature—that of the nurturing creator and the terrifying destroyer.

Whatever its biopsychological underpinnings may be, mother worship varies considerably in different cultural settings. The articles in this book describe an astonishing variety of themes, symbols, rituals, and attitudes focused on mother worship, that are not predictable or even intelligible without a consideration of the cultural backgrounds in which they occur.

These articles do not cover all possible approaches, but through the use of anthropological perspectives, they inform us superbly about aspects of mother worship that we might otherwise overlook. When an event occurs in a particular culture, anthropologists and those who use anthropological perspectives usually ask one or more of the following questions: (1) How is the event related to the setting in which it occurs? The setting may be biological, ecological, psychological, economic, social, cultural-symbolic, or a combination of these, but in all cases the emphasis is on describing the contexts of events, the ways they are related, and the ways they change over time. (2) Do similar events exist in other cultures, and if so, what accounts for these similarities? If similar events are absent, what accounts for their absence? (3) What events are universal, what accounts for their universality, and what do these events tell us about the human condition?

All these questions receive attention in this book. Some essays focus on a single culture or group; others stress comparisons within cultures that have dual or multiple traditions; some compare cultures that have had historical contact; and some focus both on a particular culture and on possible universal or near-universal themes associated with mother worship.

Quite often, anthropologists live among the people whom they study, and this experience enables them to acquire an appreciation and understanding of conceptions of reality and life-styles from the points of view of the people themselves. Many of the articles presented here are based on original firsthand field research. They present rich contextual studies that deepen our understanding of the varieties of mother worship throughout the world. From them we learn that mother worship is neither a simple phenomenon nor one that appears with equal intensity, application, or significance in all cultures or even within cultures.

Nevertheless, several themes recur throughout the book: (1) the ambivalent character of the mother as nurturer and destroyer; (2) the mother or mother goddess as a central cultural symbol that both contains multiple meanings in different contexts and serves as a unifying symbol for widely divergent elements of a culture; (3) the mother goddess associated with a regional or national political power; (4) the origins of mother goddesses or feminine principles; (5) the relationship between images of the mother or mother goddess and idealized women's roles and values, and conceptions of femaleness and maleness; (6) the role of mother goddesses as agents of change, revolution, and modernization; (7) nongoddess symbols of maternity; (8) syncretic goddesses whose characteristics originate from two or more different cultural traditions; (9) the relation of the mother goddess to religious conflicts between institutionalized church religions and pagan folk religions; (10) ties to social classes, castes, or identifiable groups within a culture.

The essays also question some cherished ideas, such as the assumption that the ideological denigration or subordination of the feminine is necessarily associated with the actual subordination of females. Also questioned here is the notion that traditional religious beliefs and institutions are incompatible with modernization and inevitably crumble before it. Other ideas are challenged: (1) that mother goddesses and mother worship are absent or unimportant in Southeast Asia, Russia, and Africa; (2) that mother worship is not indigenous and has no continuity throughout European history; (3) that saints such as Brigid of Ireland are historical persons; (4) that the coloration of the black madonnas is accidental; (5) that European mother goddess paganism inevitably gives way to Christianity. All these erroneous assumptions become clarified by the studies presented in this unique volume.

The arrangement of the articles by geographical area highlights both the continuities and the internal variations within these areas. The section on the New World contains two essays that, although different in their approaches, complement each other. In her thematic article on the Virgin of Guadalupe, Ena Campbell emphasizes the role of this Hispanic-Indian syncretic mother goddess as a national symbol for Mexico that has served as an agent of revolution and change. Campbell also relates the Virgin of Guadalupe, who symbolizes the chaste virgin mother, to ideals of feminine purity, women's roles, and views of Mexican women as having moral superiority over males; and she investigates whether the positive aspect of the mother is a compensation for the subordination of women in Mexico. After describing defects in the views on mother goddesses of E. O. James, Erich Neumann, and Raphael Patai, Campbell suggests that throughout the world mother goddesses are dominant in cultures that polarize male and female roles, and that mother goddess worship stands in inverse relationship with high secular female status.

Whereas Campbell discusses Mexico as a whole, Alan Sandstrom focuses on approximately five hundred Nahua Indians in east central Mexico. These people worship Tonantsi, the Indian version of the Virgin of Guadalupe. Sandstrom views Tonantsi as a central cultural symbol that has multiple meanings and unifies apparently disparate elements of Nahua culture, but he emphasizes those aspects of the goddess intelligible only to those who understand Nahua views of the world. In describing an important ritual featuring Tonantsi, Sandstrom shows how rituals serve as transactions—as strategies for maximizing the acquisition of specific rewards. The central concerns of people are with rainfall for crops, diseases, and crop fertility; accordingly, rituals focus on these themes.

Mother goddess syncretism occurs not only in Mexico, but also in Europe, and four of the five articles on Europe focus on syncretic goddess figures. Leonard Moss and Stephen Cappannari investigate one link between pre-Christian pagan goddesses and Christian madonnas. Nearly one hundred black-visaged madonnas are found throughout the world. What accounts for these black faces? Some match the physiognomy and skin pigmentation of indigenous populations; others have turned black over time because of a variety of physical factors; but about thirty European black madonnas, who are renowned as miracle workers, remain unexplained by the first two reasons. Citing archeological, historical, and literary evidence, Moss and Cappannari conclude that these figures are pre-Christian fertility and earth goddesses associated with powers of death and darkness, with an overlay of Roman Catholicism that enables them to be reinterpreted as madonnas.

Donál Ó Cathasaigh describes another Pagan-Christian syncretism, Ireland's Cult of Brigid. Saint Brigid, the patroness of Ireland, is not a historical person, but a Celtic mother goddess whose pagan imagery associated with sexuality has become sublimated in favor of the image of the Virgin Mother of Christ. The cult of Brigid is related to ancient spring fertility rites celebrating lactation and the abundance of milk products; the pilgrimage associated with Saint Brigid retains elements of Druidic ritual. The Celtic goddess of poetry, healing, and the metal arts has been transformed into the Christian patroness of learning, healing, and the domestic arts.

The superimposition of the madonna on pagan goddesses does not always occur without conflict. Tullio Tentori describes recent unsuccessful attempts of the Roman Catholic church to force devotees of a ritual held near Naples, Italy, to conform to idealized church doctrine. The festival of the Madonna of the Arch originated in a pagan Great Mother spring initiation rite involving possession, trance, and exorcism, which to this day remain central to worship of the madonna. Church leaders, opposing pagan rites in Christian shrines as a contamination of authentic Christianity, have tried to suppress the popular cult activities of the Madonna of the Arch. Tentori contends that the popular rituals appeal to downtrodden and exploited persons who compensate by putting their trust in the madonna. Consequently, attempts to purify the cult are contradictory and will heighten conflict, for they involve transforming an existential mode of religious expression of the subordinate classes into a functional instrument of the system run by those who are dominant. Tentori claims that the tension between official religion and living syncretic religion is ancient and ever present, stemming from conditions in which the downtrodden use religion as a vehicle to liberate themselves from human exploitation and want. The attempts of the church to modify folk cults are doomed to failure without the economic and social liberation of the followers of these cults.

Joanna Hubbs focuses on themes of the feminine in Russian religion, folk custom and lore, literature, and social structure. She traces themes of a great female divine power from Neolithic cultures of 5000 B.C. through contemporary Russian folk art and film. Even though the new Soviet woman is subjugated and regulated to serve men and the state, the gravitational pull toward the maternal soil remains. Russians use maternal images in describing their love for Russia, and they continue to practice pagan as well as Christian rites linked closely with feminine power; all this, claims Hubbs, reveals the deeply rooted presence of images of the feminine in Russia today.

The final article on Europe is concerned with the resurgence of Marianism in the nineteenth and early twentieth centuries. Edith and Victor Turner draw attention to the significant pilgrimage dimension of mother worship in the contemporary world. Particularly important here is the relationship of the Virgin Mary to a powerful miracle tradition. Although industrialization seems to be breaking down regional pilgrimages to local saints, Marian devotion has flourished. A common characteristic of this new florescence of Marianism is a vision in which Mary delivers an important message to humankind "to repent and be saved." The Turners illustrate this modern form of Marianism with two major French pilgrimage sites, La Salette and Lourdes. In each case, despite considerable skepticism, an intense form of mother worship becomes newly manifested in the modern world.

Four of the five articles on south Asia focus on different regions of India, demonstrating the great cultural diversity of the Indian sub-continent. Jacob Pandian describes and assesses the significance of Kannagi, the heroine of a famous literary masterpiece, "Epic of the Ankle Bracelet," and the central symbol of south Indian Tamil society. The goddess Kannagi stands as an ideal of chastity, a basic cultural symbol that has remained potent for two thousand years in spite of many structural changes in Tamil society. Chastity among the Tamils does not connote asexuality, but rather sacred power, and as the Epic of Kannagi shows, chastity is also associated with justice. The story of Kannagi presents elements that draw into a unitary culture the diverse Tamils, who today number forty million. The Kannagi symbol effectively mediates among different domains of Tamil cultural experience, such as family, language, politics, and ethnicity, and between ideals and existing sociopolitical structures. The concept of chastity and purity in Tamil culture serves as a vehicle for cultural revivalism and resistance to the integration of Tamil culture with the Hindi-speaking cultures of northern India. The Kannagi symbol, in short, distinguishes Tamil culture from the rest of India.

Unlike the Tamils, the Bengalis of eastern India have, not one dominant mother goddess, but several who are termed mothers. As Ralph Nicholas shows in his survey of mother goddesses in eight villages, the Bengalis are particularly distinctive in their attachment to mother goddesses. Different castes and individuals worship different goddesses. The most widely worshiped are Durga, the protective aspect of the mother, and Shitala, the symbol of maternal punishment. Durga, usually represented in anthropomorphic form as a beautiful goddess who tramples and spears a Buffalo Demon, is worshiped in each high caste house, particularly in the Autumn. Nicholas observes that to men she symbolizes an idealized woman who is sexually desirable and yet, as their mother, sexually forbidden. Shitala, the goddess of diseases and smallpox, is a crudely formed lump of stone worshiped collectively by a village, usually in the spring. Historically, Shitala worship grew strong after a severe epidemic two centuries ago. Shitala is beautiful, but often poses as an ugly hag. These images of the mother are rooted deeply in the Bengali psyche; the most fundamental mother of all, says Nicholas, is the land, which gives birth to people. Persons born in the same village—in the same earth—are considered related, much as are siblings born from the same womb.

James Preston focuses on the relationship between mother goddess worship and modernization in the Orissan city of Cuttack, located south of Bengal in eastern India. Using data on the recent spectacular rise of a formerly minor temple devoted to the worship of the mother goddess Chandi, Preston questions those who assume that modernization and modern urbanization inevitably lead to the collapse of traditional religious institutions. He provides an example of the vitality and adaptability of Indian religion to changing environments. Preston documents how this temple has recently attracted rich merchants who give it large donations and support. The temple priests have adapted to the needs of an emerging urban elite. The shrine has become what Preston calls an "urban commercial temple," tied to the growing citywide popular celebrations of the goddess Durga; and it fits the psychological needs of individuals attempting to cope with new stresses, competition, dislocation, and alienation in the city. The goddess Chandi has become an important agent of change.

Pauline Kolenda reports on the smallpox goddess of a northern Indian village of some five thousand persons. Like Nicholas, Kolenda observes that smallpox is associated with the angry mother; the disease, with its seeming arbitrariness of recovery or death, is linked with the irrational volatility of the deity's rage. People give gifts to the goddess to appease her. The goddess represents some of the northern Indian images of femininity and female power: a person who is capricious, unpredictable, powerful, and dissatisfied, and who causes illness and death to please herself. According to the villagers, capriciousness of the goddess, not personal sin, is the cause of the illness. A person afflicted with smallpox is believed to be possessed; the pustules are said to be the goddess's teeth, and gifts are given to the goddess to persuade her to leave the body of the afflicted person. Kolenda describes numerous attributes linked to the smallpox goddess —purity and pollution; barrenness; the anger and envy of a childless woman who possesses the evil eye and becomes a malevolent ghost after death; heat; anger; feminine malevolence; and divine power. The smallpox goddess is not a mother—she longs to be one, as do envious barren women.

The last South Asian article, which focuses on Sri Lanka, describes not a goddess, but the central symbol of milk. As A. J. Weeramunda observes, Sinhalese villagers know of a mother goddess called Pattini, but she lacks nurturant and maternal attributes; furthermore, she symbolizes meanings opposite those of milk. The symbol of milk is related to ties of kinship, maternal inheritance, classifications of flora, and many rituals, as the basic sacred meal. Pattini is seen as aggressive and vindictive. She is a Buddhacized goddess who is also an ascetic. Pattini is, in fact, the Tamil goddess Kannagi described by Jacob Pandian, transformed to fit Sinhalese culture. In his description of the Sinhalese milk overflowing ceremony, Weeramunda considers why the symbol of milk rather than that of a mother goddess becomes the central concept. Milk is rooted in the social concerns of villagers; the goddess Pattini is removed from them. Milk bridges many dimensions of mother symbolism: the nurturant quality of the mother, the sap of milk trees, matrilineal kinship links, bodily health, and certain egalitarian principles. The symbol of milk is positive; that of Pattini is negative, destructive. Milk rituals remain popular, whereas Pattini rituals, associated with infectious diseases, are declining, possibly owing to the success of modern health programs. Whatever the reasons, milk remains a central symbol articulated and developed in particular ways that give Sinhalese culture its distinctive character.

Two articles in this book explore facets of mother worship in Southeast Asia, one considering Bali and the other, Burma and Thailand. In his discussion of Rangda the Witch, who figures prominently in the traditional world view, ritual, and myth of the Balinese, Philip McKean demonstrates how Rangda has become involved in the growing tourist industry of Bali. The crucial question addressed by McKean is whether the Balinese can retain their sense of the sacred while commercializing once-sacred forms in secular tourist performances. In ritual performances, Rangda, an angry, destructive, vengeful widow and witch, is opposed by Barong, a protecting and beneficent dragon who wards off disease and misfortune. The performances, done by masked dancers, many of whom go into trance, may continue throughout the night. The Balinese distinguish between religious and commercial performances: for tourists, the masks used are not sanctified with special offerings; trance states are simulated, not genuine; and the main purpose is to attract spectators for a profit, not to disclose a sacred reality. McKean believes that this compartmentalization so far has been successful in Bali because Rangda and Barong are rich cultural symbols that reach many aspects of Balinese life: they contain psychological elements of the Great Mother, maximize cultural resources by attracting tourists, and articulate basic sociopolitical conflicts and tensions, both traditional and modern.

Many people might deny that Burma and Thailand have anything resembling a Great Goddess; John Ferguson, by contrast, insists that the Great Goddess is at the center of Theravada Buddhism as the matron of suffering, the fundamental cause of all mankind's sorrows. The Buddha's life is a rejection of the Great Goddess, but a hidden tribute to her—a negative validation. The Buddha's renunciation of the worldly life, symbolized by the goddess, is a renunciation not of what he hates, but of what he loves too much. The famous middle path then is seen as a complex compromise. Drawing on many other themes, Ferguson contends that the goddess herself not only is involved in the Buddha's enlightenment, but directly makes it possible. Buddhist imagery contains many mother goddess themes, including the notion that merit for a boy's first entrance into monkhood accrues to the boy's mother, so that renunciation of the mother simultaneously is a tribute to her. The monkhood itself is seen as a sacrifice to the earth mother to ensure water for crops. Theravada Buddhism, Ferguson suggests, is built upon a preexisting mother worship tradition. Although the image of woman is negative and subordinate to that of man in religious matters, Ferguson notes that the women of Thailand and Burma are among the world's most liberated females. Burmese women control much of the nation's material wealth, inherit equally with their brothers, are active and successful in business ventures. Thai women have an active role in commercial activities, work equally with men, and appear to be social equals. Ideology is not replicated in social roles or actual behavior. The situation Ferguson describes—the high social status of Burmese and Thai women, in contrast to their ideological subordination—appears to be the inverse of the pattern Campbell describes—the low status of Mexican women, in contrast to their high ideological valuation through mother goddess worship.

The final article is concerned with three cultural groupings in western Africa: the Akan, Yoruba, and Ibo. Daniel McCall's basic question is under what conditions an earth goddess might be expected to appear and flourish. His analysis leads him to question Durkheim's assumptions about the coherence of religious forms and social structures if they are viewed from a static, nonchanging perspective. However, McCall claims that, by adding a time dimension, he can vindicate Durkheim's basic assumptions. McCall presents a hypothetical reconstruction based on the notion that mother goddess worship is dominant in primary Neolithic cultures, but comes under attack and is pushed into the background with the development of increased social stratification, kingship, and urbanization. McCall's view also leads him to claim that West Africa is an integral part of complex and widely dispersed cultural traditions that began with the development of food-producing societies in Southwest Asia, and were subsequently overlain with other traditions that included urban influences.

In a concluding chapter, James Preston summarizes earlier literature on the phenomenon of mother worship, suggesting new theoretical issues raised by contemporary scholarship. Here he notes common patterns of goddess symbolism in world cultures and stresses significant cultural differences. In a discussion of the relationship between the symbols of mother and the empirical reality of mothers, Preston discovers four typical patterns as revealed in crosscultural data. Whereas, in some cases, mother symbolism is a direct reflection of the role of women as mothers in the real world, in other instances goddess symbols are inversely related to their human counterparts. Two important questions reveal the other two prominent patterns: Why is mother symbolism conspicuously absent in some religions? And what explains the new interest in mother worship among contemporary scholars? Preston concludes with a discussion of the mother-infant bond and its relationship to anxiety, consciousness, and the phenomenon of mother worship.

The articles in this book demonstrate the importance of fine-grained studies in many cultures; for without such studies we could never grasp the myriad ways in which people redefine and elaborate the basic biopsychological relationship of mother and child. These studies therefore point to the importance of focusing not only on possible human universals, but also on more specific questions that guide our understanding of the ways people in particular cultures use and combine symbols of the mother. As these studies show convincingly, the symbols of the mother that people use are neither idle nor haphazard elements, but active forces that work for people, bring desired ends, unify people, lead to change, and disclose in a variety of ways inescapable aspects of our human condition, as well as our attempts to comprehend and transcend it.

Mother
Worship

# ONE

Mother Worship
in the New World

# 1

## The Virgin of Guadalupe
## and the Female Self-Image:
## A Mexican Case History
### by Ena Campbell

Given the strong monotheism of Western culture the presence of a
female principle is an anomaly in the Christian triad, where the an-
thropomorphized divine principle is a male "God the Father," "God
the Son," and "God the Holy Spirit." Adoration of the Virgin Mother
has played a central role in both folk and orthodox religious expressions. Consequently it has often been necessary for prelates of the
Roman Catholic church to exercise strong supervision over the worship of Mary.[1] The Virgin Mother has been enhanced in many communities throughout the world. She is Our Lady of Covadonga, protectress of the Spanish nation. The Polish people have long revered
her as Czestochawa. Millions of pilgrims flock to her shrine at Lourdes
in France.

Great and Little Traditions conjoin when she is worshiped as Our
Lady of Guadalupe in Mexico. Here the Virgin is manifested in many
different guises. There have been attempts to superimpose the figure
of a savior Christ on her long-lived hegemony, yet the Virgin, as
Guadalupe, has ever emerged victorious. It is she who integrates the
folk and mainstream cultures of Mexico. It is the Virgin of Guadalupe
who expresses the sociopolitical uniqueness of the entire Mexican
population. In the words of Eric Wolf, the Virgin of Guadalupe is a
"national symbol."[2]

## The Virgin of Guadalupe in Mexican Ethnohistory

The importance of the Virgin of Guadalupe derives, in part, from a long and close association between her and the Mexican people. In keeping with one of the major themes of Spanish expansionism in the sixteenth and seventeenth centuries, the military campaign that brought Mexico into the framework of the Spanish Empire was imbued with a proselytizing zeal. The conquistador, Cortes, states in his first report (1519) to the Spanish crown: "The captain reprimanded the princes for their religious and other practices, whereupon they requested that he provide them with precepts around which to organize their lives. The captain instructed them to the best of his ability in the Catholic faith, raised a wooden cross on top of a high house, and left them an image of Our Lady, the Virgin Mary" (my translation).[3]

This early orientation to Spanish religious ideas came to full florescence when the Virgin appeared on the morning of December 9, 1531, to a poor Indian named Juan Diego, who was on his way to receive religious instruction after he had been converted to Christianity. According to one of many accounts, while Juan Diego was crossing Tepeyac Hill, he heard heavenly music and a sweet voice calling his name. Soon he saw the Virgin, "radiant as the sun," her feet resting on the rocks, gleaming like precious jewels. She addressed him gently, calling him "my son," and said she wished him to tell the bishop that she wanted a church to be built on that spot—where the one for the Aztec goddess once stood—so that she might be near his people, to protect and love them.

Juan promised to obey her commands, and he managed to see the bishop after several frustrated attempts. The bishop listened to him incredulously and told him to return at a more convenient time. Juan returned sadly to the hill, where the Virgin awaited him. There he reported the result of his interview with the bishop and begged her to find a more worthy messenger; but she insisted that he had been selected as the one to represent her and told him to try again.

On the following day, Juan returned to see the bishop. He knelt at the bishop's feet with tears in his eyes, begging to be believed. The bishop was impressed that Juan's story was exactly the same as on the previous day. He sent him away more gently this time, telling him not to return without a token from the Virgin.

The next day, Juan stayed home because of an uncle's illness. The doctor said there was no hope; so Juan was sent to bring a priest who would administer the last rites. On his way to find a priest, Juan reached Tepeyac Hill. In his worry about his uncle, Juan had forgotten about the Virgin. He decided to take a roundabout path for fear he had incurred her displeasure, and in order to avoid a scolding. But the Virgin met him anyway. She said he must go to the place on the hill where he had first seen her and pick some roses, which were to be taken to the bishop. Juan obeyed and was astonished to find beautiful Castilian roses among the rocks where only cacti had grown before. The Virgin told him to hide the roses in his cape and take them to the bishop.

The attendants at the bishop's palace asked Juan what was in his cape. He tried to keep them from seeing the roses, but they refused to announce him unless he cooperated. When the servants saw the roses, they were as surprised as he, because the flowers seemed to have become a part of his cape. The servants reported this to the bishop, who immediately recognized it as a sign from the Virgin. Consequently, Juan was admitted into the bishop's presence. As he knelt and reached for the roses to hand to the bishop his cape fell to the ground. At that moment the image of the Virgin of Guadalupe appeared on the cape.

The news of this miracle spread rapidly. A chapel was built by the church authorities at the foot of the hill. Here the cape with the image of the Virgin was hung. People were converted by the thousands. Today the little chapel on Tepeyac Hill is a large domed basilica. Although the church is a beautiful national shrine, it is also a place for humble people who come to pray and give thanks for miracles performed on their behalf.

It is an accepted notion today that human groups adopt symbolic or ideological elements from another culture *less readily* than they do its material aspects. Why, then, was Guadalupe accepted so readily by the Indians? How did this figure, who was once identified with the religion of the conquerors, become a tutelary symbol for both the Indian and the Spanish populations? Answers to these questions are not difficult to find. On the one hand, the Spanish clergy and people immediately identified Guadalupe with the dark Virgin (also Guadalupe by name) who was patroness of west central Spain.[4] On the other hand, the Indian population accepted her as the miraculous incarnation of the Aztec earth and fertility goddess Tonantsi, Our Lady Mother, who, like Guadalupe, was associated with the moon. Also significant was the fact Guadalupe manifested herself at the very site where once a temple had housed the goddess Tonantsi. Her petite stature and dark complexion must have appealed to the Indians, who are similar in appearance.

Several attempts have been made to explain the Virgin's miraculous appearance on Tepeyac Hill.[5] Some interpretations are logico-rational. Others are purely theological. Yet on one point there is unanimity: according to the well-known Mexican playwright Rodolfo Usigli, from the moment of Guadalupe's miraculous appearance, "Mexico no longer belonged to Spain."[6] In short, the Mexican people had their own native patron saint.

Perhaps it is futile to decide whether a separate Mexican identity crystallized around the significant event of Guadalupe's appearance. Indeed, "Guadalupism," as the cult of the Virgin came to be called, may have served to reinforce separatist tendencies in the native-born population, which no longer regarded itself as Spanish. It is clear from the archives of the period that the adoration of Guadalupe had become so widespread and fervent that many priests urged the destruction of the shrine and cult. According to the priest/historian Bernardo Sahagun, shrine and cult were a satanic device to mask idolatry. The seventh-century cleric Jacinto de la Sierra concurred when he observed that it was the purpose of the wicked to worship the goddess and not the Most Holy Virgin, or both together.[7]

The skeptical attitude of many, and the open hostility of others, had little or no effect on the growing popularity of the Virgin. Once again the reasons are obvious. In 1544 there was a terrible epidemic in Mexico City in which thousands of people died. The Virgin's image was brought to the city and her presence was believed to have abated the pestilence. Again, in 1629 there was a flood, and her presence was believed to have caused the waters to subside.[8] The miracles she performed for families and individuals were many. Thus, in 1754, two centuries after her appearance, a Papal Bull recognized popular devotion to Guadalupe and declared her to be Patroness and Protectress of New Spain. Guadalupe's roles continued to multiply as her sphere of influence extended.

During the Spanish conquest of Mexico, and for a long time afterward, various images of the Virgin led the conquerors to victory in battles against the indigenous peoples. The Virgins received military honors and were given the rank of general because they led armies to victory. Therefore, it was quite appropriate for the patriot Father Miguel Hidalgo y Castilla to start the Revolution for Mexican Independence with the cry: "Long live the Virgin of Guadalupe and down with bad government."

During the eleven years of the Mexican Revolutionary Wars (1810–21) Guadalupe's image was carried on the banners of the insurgents, who began to refer to her as "La Conquistadora." General Manuel Felix Fernandez, who was active in the revolutionary wars against Spain, changed his name to Guadalupe Victoria. He was later one of the nation's presidents. Guadalupe's aid was also invoked in the war with the United States. Mexico lost the war, along with a large tract of her territory, but received an indemnity payment in return. The treaty that ended the war was signed in the city of Guadalupe Hidalgo, the home of Guadalupe's shrine. The Virgin also participated in the Civil War of 1911, which effectively curtailed the influence of the hereditary elite and made full citizens of peasants and the urban poor. Victory for the nationalist forces increased Guadalupe's influence and popularity.

Guadalupe's image began to appear everywhere—in churches, chapels, schools, and houses; on bridges; and even on liquor bottles. Her image was reproduced in paint, stone, metal, and glass. The basilica constructed at the foot of Tepeyac Hill in her honor is located about three miles from Mexico City's cathedral. It has come to be regarded as the most sacred shrine in Mexico and one of the holiest in Christendom. Because Guadalupe continued to lead nationalist troops to victory, it is no wonder that in 1945 she was crowned "Queen of Wisdom of the Americas." The religious services in this event lasted a week and were even more sumptuous than those which marked the four-hundredth anniversary of her appearance. Important religious representatives attended from all over the world.

## The Social and Political Correlates of Guadalupism

There can be no doubt of the strong political overtones in Guadalupe's rise to eminence. As soon as the Indian population began to flock to her shrine and accept the Catholic faith, both church and state in sixteenth-century Mexico secured Guadalupe a respected niche. High government officials and members of the Spanish elite continued in their devotion to the Virgin of Remedios, protectress of the early Spanish conquistadors, but Remedios lost ground to Guadalupe in a series of determined *political* confrontations. Guadalupe won the day when, as general of the Mexican Army of Independence, she and her followers conquered the loyalists led by the Virgin of Remedios. Indeed, sentiments had become so polarized that soldiers led by Guadalupe or by Remedios shot at the banners bearing the image of the "enemy" Virgin. The pope himself sanctioned Guadalupe's culturally accepted roles. One might argue that he was motivated by a desire to establish a degree of Latin American ecumenism through Guadalupe. But historical accounts suggest that there are other reasons for Guadalupe's salience. Her Spanish namesake had been associated with success and survival in the voyages of Columbus; sailors on board the Niña had made holy vows to honor Guadalupe's shrine back in Spain if their voyage were safe. Later an island in the newly discovered Americas was named after the Spanish Guadalupe.

The Virgin of Guadalupe has eclipsed all other male and female religious figures in Mexico. The Lord of Chalmas is a case in point. Shortly after Guadalupe's appearance to Juan Diego, members of the Augustinian order were honored by a self-revelation from the Señor of Chalmas; one of Mexico's four Christs, who are, today, always referred to as "saints." The Lord of Chalmas appeared at Ocuilcan, a village close to Mexico City, in a cave that was once the sanctuary of a bloodthirsty Indian god, Otzocteatl. In the beginning, the Christ of Chalmas had performed miracles and freed the country and surrounding villages and towns from the dangers of wild animals. He was also known for healing the sick. Yet today the Lord of Chalmas has no national cult.

The relative unimportance of the cult of the Lord of Chalmas has not deterred groups in the Mexican community who have attempted to supplant Guadalupe with male images and symbols. At the beginning of this century, a group of Mexican Catholics requested the Vatican's permission to proclaim the reign of the Sacred Heart of Jesus in Mexico. Permission was granted, though the coronation never took place on a yearly basis, as was originally intended. As one historian comments, "If this act of honoring the Sacred Heart had been confined to the religious sphere it would have been of slight importance to the government; [but] from the words and actions of the Catholics, it was obvious that the church meant to crown Christ not only symbolically, but actually to proclaim the temporal ascendancy of the Catholic religion in Mexico."[9] In short, the cult of the Sacred

Heart was interpreted as the beginning of a movement to supplant both the dark Virgin of Guadalupe and the Indian Christ of Chalmas with a thoroughly Europeanized figure.

In many respects, the superimposition of Spanish values upon native symbols has resulted in a synthesis of culture that is unparalleled. However, it is clear that this synthesis is not total. There is evidence of many cultural layers throughout Mexico; religious ideology and ritual, like all other institutions, are somewhat kaleidoscopic. There is, for example, a local patron or patroness for almost every village. Villagers maintain close relations with the pantheon of saints. Even the most trivial passions and amorous liaisons of the saints are known and freely discussed. In some parts of Mexico, the Virgin of Guadalupe is still addressed by her Indian name.[10] Thus, there are deviations from orthodox thought and practice in many spheres of Mexican religion. Yet Guadalupe is known to all. Throughout the nation she is beloved and honored, consulted, invoked, offered gifts, and called upon to perform miracles.

Any exploration into the meaning of Guadalupism must come to grips with anthropological theories that attempt to explain and predict the reaction of groups and individuals to alien ideas. Pagan practices, such as certain religious dances and the use of witchcraft, are still to be found in Mexico. On the other hand, orthodox Catholicism has replaced pagan practices in certain sectors of the population. Among other groups the Catholic religion has merely furnished elements that have been incorporated into a continuing paganism or have blended with pagan survivals. How then can we explain the centrality and long history of the cult of the Virgin, when the Aztec society of early Mexico offered its greatest sacrifices, and devoted its most brilliant feasts, to male gods? Further, because the Aztecs were a supremely religious people, with a high level of orthodoxy maintained by a hierarchy of priests, the indigenous beliefs must have been supported by strong sanctions.

To understand the reasons for this transition from male deities to the cult of the Virgin it is necessary to broaden our framework of analysis in its cultural and social dimensions. First of all, loyalty to the Catholic Virgin can be explained by new perceptions that crept into religious values in and around Tenochtitlan, the Aztec capital, at the time of the Spanish conquest. Briefly stated, the temple that had been built at the foot of Tepeyac Hill before the arrival of the Spaniards was tangible proof of new directions in religious expression. The Totonacs, one of the Indian groups grown weary of Aztec military depredations and human sacrifice, had begun to show great reverence to the mother goddess Tonantsi, who preferred the sacrifice of birds and small animals. It was they, and not the Aztecs, who built Tonantsi's temple. Further, the Aztecs themselves were by then tired of the need to satiate and mollify their bloodthirsty god of war, Huitzilopotchli, who had made them a conquering and prosperous people. Though the goddess Tonantsi did not displace the male deity, Huitzilopotchli, she did triumph over Coatlicue, the malevolent mother goddess of snakes and skulls. Coatlicue ceased to demand human blood after she had been supplanted as harbinger of death by Huitzilopotchli. In a symbolic sense, Guadalupe represents the Indian mother goddess in the third and most benevolent transformation.

## Guadalupe as Master Symbol

Guadalupe's rise to prominence illustrates how a clash of cultures may be minimized when new elements are communicable to and compatible with established traditions. The goddess Tonantsi had given Mexicans their cactus plant to provide them with its milk and *pulque,* a derived alcoholic drink that fires religious ecstasy. In early Mexico, *pulque* bolstered the courage of warriors going into battle. It also granted serenity to prisoners who were to be sacrificed to the gods. Intoxication could mean death and destruction, because those who allowed themselves to get drunk were slaughtered. However, even after the onslaught of Christianity, the loving Tonantsi continued to defend her children against the wrath of the Judeo-Christian God. According to legend, Tonantsi would not allow this foreign god to punish her children. Part of the folklore of Mexico expresses this protective function of the goddess: she challenged God, her son, to produce mother's milk (as she had done), to prove that his benevolence equaled his disciplinary harshness. It is God's role to punish; it is her role to nurture and intercede: "Not the milk of cows, not the milk of goats, but my own [human] milk," states the Aztec legend describing the encounter between Tonantsi and God. Tonantsi accepts the vows of the poorest people and answers their prayers. The Indians say she watches over midwives and mothers in childbirth. She cares for young children in heaven. In her guise as the Virgin of Guadalupe, the duties and accomplishments of the Indian goddess are broader in scope. In sum, as mother, protectress, and preserver of life, health, and happiness, the combined image of Guadalupe/Tonantsi transforms and binds together the diverse cultural streams of Mexican society at the level of their highest common, symbolic denominator. To borrow the words of the celebrated Mexican playwright, Rodolfo Usigli: "All social classes are Guadalupe worshipers —some by right of birth; others, in keeping with their religious beliefs; others, out of sentimentality or simply because they are revolutionary spirits" (my translation).[11] Guadalupe has become the master symbol of Mexico.


## The Virgin of Guadalupe
## in the Mexican Feminine Mystique

Analysts have often asked themselves whether symbolic systems are mere epiphenomena reflecting more fundamental social or psychological processes. In the Mexican case, there is a demonstrable convergence between psychic and social phenomena related to the religious symbolism associated with Guadalupe. The important question that needs to be asked is how Mexicans adapt to the strain for consistency in culture and society when religious and political institutions promote the same symbols, but infuse them with somewhat different meanings.

Guadalupism evokes strong and sometimes contradictory responses. Although most people acknowledge Guadalupe as a meaningful image in Mexican culture, some do not. For instance, the president of Mexico expelled an archbishop from the country because he had encouraged Catholics to celebrate the four-hundredth anniversary of the appearance of Guadalupe with great ostentation. These contradictory attitudes reflect many sociocultural facts. The Mexican population is heterogeneous. The nation has had a somewhat troubled history, yet once the wounds of the 1911 Civil War healed, Mexico knew a level of integration it had never experienced before. Increased industrialization benefited the elite. An agrarian reform safeguarded the investments of the poor. Mexico was proud of its hybrid cultural heritage. On the other hand, the revolution was markedly anticlerical, and its leaders have campaigned to erase many of the values that were formerly held dear. In other words, some sectors of the population invest the Guadalupe symbol with primary meanings;

other sectors view the symbol as hardly relevant to everyday concerns, although it may sometimes evoke strong emotional responses.

Because symbolic systems are mental constellations that establish pervasive and powerful motivations in individuals and groups, and because the Guadalupe symbol persists in the cognitive processes of the population, other important questions must be asked: for example, what are the processes that prompt people to cling to an ideal that is being eroded by a new social philosophy? If the power of the symbol begins to wane, it may be reinterpreted rather than discarded.

Most general accounts of Mexican culture suggest a high level of conformity between religious ideals and secular values, especially with regard to male and female roles. Mexican vital statistics show a birth rate of 4.4 percent (1971), one of the highest in the world. Roman Catholic condemnation of birth control devices is certainly an influential factor, but there is also evidence that *the role of "mother" is one of the most prized and sacred in the community*. Many social analysts insist on this element of Mexican culture: "A mother is seldom faced with the dilemma so publicized in the United States, of having to choose between her children and her paid job. . . . The granting of sick leave to the mother of a sick child is . . . a matter of the employer's duty to respect the sacredness of motherhood which the individual woman shares with the Virgin Mary and with the great mother goddesses of pre-Christian times."[12]

In his study of Mexican psychology, R. Diaz-Guerrero, a native son, finds that the mother figure remains infused with strong emotion for most people. When asked the question: "Is the mother for you the dearest person in existence?" more than 85 percent of his respondents (95 percent of the males, 86 percent of the females) answered in the affirmative.[13]

There is no doubt that the sacredness of mother and the ideal of feminine purity are deeply embedded in Mexican consciousness. Once again the community's ethnic roots and its social history offer an explanation. The symbol of the chaste Virgin Mother, which Guadalupe represents, has strong secular roots in Hispanic American culture. Indeed the attitude is part of a culture complex that links Hispanic America to Spain and the entire Mediterranean world. According to J. G. Peristiany, the cultural, social, and intellectual moorings of Mediterranean culture are intertwined in two themes: *honor* and *shame*. In the family and community, the division of labor assigns the role of defender to the male. The female is the repository of the family's honor. Peristiany vividly illustrates this Mediterranean social ideal in a highland village of Cyprus: "Woman's foremost duty to self and family is to safeguard herself against all critical allusions to her sexual modesty. In dress, looks, attitudes, speech, a woman, when men are present should be virginal as a maiden and matronly as a wife. If it were possible to combine the concepts of virginity and motherhood the ideal married woman would be a married mother—virginal in sensations and mind."[14]

The Spaniard Julio Caro Baroja draws attention to the darker side of this theme: "Since the honour or shame of the female sex was a matter of such concern to their families, the demonstration of personal supremacy in this constituted one of the most remarkable triumphs. In other words . . . Don Juan [the seducer] needs to be explained in sociological terms, and not in terms of psychology or psychopathology."[15]

In short, the ideal of female purity seems to have prompted a reactive pattern in the social behavior of males, and has polarized ideal behavior patterns for both sexes. Caro Baroja calls this reactive pattern the "morality of prestige."

In Mexico, indeed, in all Latin America, the ideal of masculinity was developed in a social atmosphere in which maleness was demonstrated by forceful, dynamic activities. From the sixteenth century, in the roles of conquerors, priests, and soldiers, the male population at large could force its will on subject peoples. At the time of the conquest the male/female ratio in the population was unbalanced. Men had come seeking gold and adventure; they had not come as settlers intent on establishing homestead and family. Yet there was great potential for wealth. There were also numerous available women among conquered Indian groups. The efficient aspects of "manliness" were therefore demonstrated in combativeness and sexual athleticism. In short, the Iberian/Spanish morality of prestige converged with the new ideal of dynamic forcefulness. It is also the morality of the soldier, because the ideal is attained through individual force. This pattern persists today. Among the eastern Mediterranean people, J. K. Campbell notes that the physical characteristics of masculinity are important. A man must be *varvatos*, that is, "well endowed with testicles" and the strength that is drawn from them.[16] In Mexico, to be respected, a man also needs to demonstrate that he has *bolas*. He has to be *macho*, that is, "all male."

Scholars who have devoted themselves to comparative studies of Mediterranean and Latin American cultures have noted an extremism in the machismo complex that is not totally derived from Spanish and

Mediterranean roots. Samuel Ramos, one of Mexico's leading intellectuals, theorizes that the exaggerated behaviors of the Mexican male are compensatory devices that attempt to conceal an inferiority complex. He suggests that the Mexican has found it necessary to struggle against a feeling of cultural inferiority vis-à-vis imposed European cultural forms, dating back to the Spanish colonial period. Hence the cult of the superman. Other analysts argue that, although the constraining aspects of Mexican culture are historically generated, they are also a result of patterns of social interaction. One thesis suggests that the origins of polarized roles in Mexican culture go back to the Latin family and "its highly status-oriented values originating in the Latin aristocracy, pretentious even with their means, and setting standards to which the vast majority are hopelessly inferior."[17] Thus, the foundations of the contemporary Mexican psyche must be sought in family life. This conclusion is not based solely on the proven assumption that the family in every culture is one of the prime agents of enculturation. It is also true that personality orientations are reinforced when the conditions of childhood correspond with personality traits of adults in the society. Diaz-Guerrero is brief and forceful in his appraisal of male and female roles: "The Mexican family is founded upon two fundamental propositions: the unquestioned and absolute supremacy of the father and the necessary and absolute self-sacrifice of the mother. These two fundamental propositions in the family derive from more general existential value orientations or, better, [from] generalized socio-cultural assumptions which imply an indubitable biological and natural superiority of the male."[18]

The psychological and social corollaries of culturally accepted gender distinctions are well documented.[19] The ethnographic accounts of family life in Mexico are filled with poignant scenes of female self-abnegation. In his well-known *Children of Sanchez*, Oscar Lewis's central character, Marta, declares that her children are her world, that she wants nothing of their father, that the children themselves dislike their father and do not even call him "papa."[20] The woman whom Marta most admires and who is her ideal of womanhood is her Aunt Guadalupe (the Virgin's namesake), a woman "who knew how to suffer." The poorest male seeks several wives and proves his manhood by giving them children, but the women with whom he is most at ease are submissive, unattractive, or older than he. Confident, aggressive, and attractive women are generally mistresses, not wives, so that a break in a romantic relationship need not damage a man's self-esteem. Wife beatings are common. Yet the woman who remains unmarried and childless is the butt of cruel jokes; she is considered neurotic (a *cotorra*, or "parrot") as a result of her failure to fulfill her biological destiny, rather than as a result of powerful social sanctions against the unmarried. The unmarried woman who is not preoccupied with protecting her virginity is a shame to family honor, a "bad girl" who is fair game to all. Nevertheless, the society provides all females with an alternative: they may choose to be pure, virgin, submissive, and honored by all as wife and mother.

In her pilot study on the birth of feminist consciousness in urban Mexico, the political scientist Evelyn Stevens offers a negative prognosis for change, despite the worldwide feminist movement. For, according to Stevens, Mexican women can "eat their cake and have it too."[21] Stated otherwise, despite the strains and stresses of her role, the Mexican woman reaps great rewards. Her moral superiority over the male is unquestioned. Like the Virgin of Guadalupe she is pure and triumphant.

The difficulty in determining the influence of Guadalupe worship on the Mexican, especially the female psyche, is somewhat complicated by the divergent, though not contradictory, explanations of the role of woman offered by scholars whose work has centered around the Guadalupe theme in Mexican culture. If the image of woman as crystallized in Guadalupe is one of purity, innocence, maternity, and devotion, how do we explain Guadalupe the defender, when the role of defender in Mexican family life is reserved for the male? Explanation is complicated by the fact that some theorists see mother worship as a projection into the metaphysical realm of the most positive relationship in the culture. Others insist that the importance of the divine mother is a compensation for weak female/maternal relationships. Lewis portrays the mother as nurturant and, like Wolf, points to the parallelism between her and the Virgin of Guadalupe. The people studied by John Bushnell in the village of San Juan Atzingo see God as a demanding, fear-inspiring figure who provides and also punishes —but the Virgin is a comforting, permissive figure who is the object of unashamed displays of affection. "*Mamacita Linda!* My beloved, darling mother!" worshipers cry as they kiss her image. However, according to Bushnell, it seems apparent that the Virgin of Guadalupe fulfills a definite and probably deeply felt need in the lives of many adults for a mother figure. The adult who places the Virgin in the mother role is attempting to recreate a satisfying relationship that was once experienced, but never fully renewed.[22]

Thus, Bushnell's psychodynamic theory presents the Virgin as the sublimation of a perceived need. Wolf, Carl Batt, and Lewis choose a sociocultural framework and see the ideal woman, the mirror image of Guadalupe, as the tender protective mother. Others use an ethnohistorical explanation and examine Mexico's Mediterranean heritage, which points to the influences of male/female segregation amidst class relationships. In this framework the ideal woman is virginal, chaste.[23] These different types of analysis seem to parallel the transformations we have described above, that is, the mother goddess as an early Coatlicue (evil mother) becomes Coatlicue/Tonantsi (good mother), and then Tonantsi/Guadalupe (chaste, protective mother).

The problem we have posed is not fully solved, however, for there are other contradictions in the data. Guadalupe worship is generally represented as universal throughout Mexico. Yet Bushnell records that worshipers of Guadalupe tend to be men rather than women. This fact requires crosscultural analysis for clarification.

## The Mother Goddess as a Crosscultural Phenomenon

In his archaeological and documentary study, *The Cult of the Mother Goddess*, Edwin James undertakes a painstaking review of the ancient world and demonstrates the genetic links among woman's biological destiny as genetrix, her cultural role as nurturer, and the psychosocial origins of mother worship among the Euro-Semitic people from Neolithic times onward. Early mother goddesses have both dark and benevolent facets. To some extent their modes of expression represent universal, psychological reactions to the Great Mother archetype.[24] However, James does not reflect on the absence of the figure of a Great Mother in many well-known, especially Western, contexts. He also overlooks Guadalupe's childlessness, which has been interpreted by other scholars as a symbol of the Virgin's "immediate" rather than "derivative" power.[25] There is a major weakness in James's argument. He examines the Judaic antecedents of the cult of the female, which was finally suppressed by Jehovah's prophets even after its reintroduction by powerful King Solomon. However, he does not fully explain how or why there are two divergent traditions in the Christian church, the one in which the Virgin is celebrated as the mother of the church (*Mater Ecclesia*), the other in which she is worshiped as the mother of God (madonna). Neither does he abstract a principle to explain the Virgin's power to perform miracles.

James's basic argument is that the mind of primitive man grasped only as much as his powers of observation of nature in her tangible aspects permitted. The male/female principle became increasingly polarized as man noted basic differences in the male/female generative potential and social roles. The problem James evades is one that is central to Erich Neumann's examination of the persistence and dominance of the mother figure in religious cults all over the world. According to Neumann, "The relating of all ideologies to human nature is one of the decisive intellectual gains of our time."[26] To him the mother goddess is the embodiment of the female principle, which is always alive and seeking expression in the psychic depths of man. In Neumann's view, the dynamic of man's psyche is the union of opposites, a fact that explains the importance of the male/female principle, as well as the ambivalence in symbols such as the divine and malevolent mother. Neumann also argues that the creation of symbols may be spontaneous and conscious or compensatory and subconscious. The factor that persists is the struggle for balance in the human psyche.

Other scholars have contributed to the debate. In his well-documented work *The Hebrew Goddess*, Raphael Patai also notes that goddesses are ubiquitous. Even among the monotheistic Hebrews, the One and Only God is eternal, omnipotent, omnipresent, and omniscient. This God, who is "just, good, compassionate, merciful and benevolent, is *male* principally as an artifact of Hebrew language structure. Since being pure spirit, He is without body, He possesses no physical attributes and hence no sexual traits."[27] Because in the Hebrew language every noun had either the masculine or the feminine gender, the divine creator became patriarchal, and guardians of religious orthodoxy vehemently and continually pruned religious ritual of all elements of a twin divine presence. "Hebrew monotheism," concludes Patai, "may have been unable to exorcise the tenacious goddess, and it is not at all improbable that, even if she slumbered for several centuries, she awoke and reclaimed some of her old dues in the figure of Mary."[28] In this view, the goddess persists or reemerges because she is the projection of everything a woman can be in order to sustain man.

As interesting and plausible as the above analyses are, an important question will be posed by those who insist that man's religion is a projective system patterned to his psychic needs and fears. The question will also be asked by those who, in turn, insist that religious systems are revealed truths that serve as guides to everyday life and ethics. The new question, briefly stated, is this: If the mother goddess, whether it be Guadalupe or another, is both nurturer and defender, benevolent and punitive, in what ways does she in essence differ from male gods, when even the Hebrew/Christian, patriarchal Jehovah indulges in such maternal behavior as protecting his children under his wings?[29]

There can be no doubt that Guadalupe's roles reflect social and cultural dimensions of Mexican life. Guadalupe is the great, revered mother, the most idealized figure in Mexican culture. In everyday secular life the mother image is more concentrated, more primary in its meanings: mother is pure and, above all, she is devoted to serving and defending her children against the authoritarian father. Whatever the strains, stresses, and conflicts of family life, mother symbolizes the defender and intercessor.

## Conclusion

Specialists in religion are quite aware that the study of the worship of mother images is a promising area for research. This is also an area that will receive increasing attention from those involved in the cross-cultural analysis of women's roles. There are, however, broader concerns to which this preliminary overview and the work of other scholars may contribute.

According to Diaz-Guerrero, of every two women in Mexico City, one is maladjusted or neurotic, whereas this is the case for only one of every three males. The important question to be asked at this point is: Do the neurotic tendencies Diaz-Guerrero mentions derive from the warping of women's aspirations for a less restricted life, or do they derive from the over-idealization of the Virgin Mother and its influence on the female psyche? Diaz-Guerrero sums up his analysis with the following remarks: "Respect—an increase in social prestige or status—can be accorded the Mexican women simply for their age, or because they are mothers, or simply because they are women; it can even be inferred from facts reported in this study that the improvement in status derived from earlier attitudes . . . can easily come into conflict with improvements in status derived from attitudes favoring equality."[30]

In the light of these remarks, a central issue rises to the fore and poses a broader and far more significant question: *What is the relation-*

*ship between sex role complementarity and equality in a social system?* This is a philosophical question that does not lend itself to superficial analysis. Still, it is instructive to note that mother goddesses are dominant figures in cultures that ideally polarize male/female roles. Secondly, as the data from many Roman Catholic countries and from the Hindu and Buddhist world indicate, mother goddess worship seems to stand in inverse relationship with high secular female status. Thus, in the West, the worship of the Virgin stands alongside the self-abnegation of women and the patriarchal, authoritarian attitudes of males. In the East, the *Code of Manu*, India's book of religious laws, suggests that a husband should be worshiped by his wife even though he be unfaithful or totally devoid of good qualities.

The lesson to be learned here points to the alienating forces that derive from a marked polarity of roles. As the data given here indicate, once sex-linked roles are polarized and woman is idealized in compensation for her actual position in the social scheme, the contradictions between the real and the ideal demand social and cultural dichotomies among the female population. The working mother in a quasi-feudal society can be self-actualized only if she can rely on servants, and the servant must neglect her own children. There are "good girls" because there are "bad girls."

Does not this analysis suggest that man's conception of the divine expresses his perception that God is both male and female in personality attributes—in short, androgynous? There is every indication in the data presented here that the secular counterpart of this perception strives for expression. In sum, the neurotic tendencies of both men and women in the studies cited may result from the social requirement that people, unlike the Great Mother, conform to gender distinctions that are linear and choose between nurturant tendencies and strong action orientation.

## Notes

1. Pope Pius XII called for a correct balance in Mariology and Marian devotion. Pope John XXIII sounded the same note. In 1951 the Holy Office issued a warning against Marian excesses (*New Catholic Encyclopedia*, 9:368).

2. Wolf, "The Virgin of Guadalupe," pp. 34–39.

3. Cortes, *Cartas de Relacion*, p. 11.

4. This was in the region of Estremadura, where her image was found by a shepherd on the banks of the river bearing her name. King Alfonso XI had

just won a victory over the Moors (A.D. 1326) near the spot where the statuette was found. For some reason, which is impossible to ascertain, the Spanish church subsequently forbade the carving of images of Guadalupe.

Other sources (for example, Aradi, *Shrines to Our Lady*) posit a longer relationship between the Spanish Guadalupe and her worshipers. According to the legend recorded by Aradi, the statuette was the one that had been given to Bishop Leander of Seville by Pope Gregory. Fearful of losing this great treasure in the Saracen wars (A.D. 711) the Spanish Knights, who had taken the statue when they fled to the mountains, buried it. After their death in battle, no one recalled its existence until it was rediscovered by the shepherd, Gil.

5. Braden quotes the great archbishop Sahagun: "It was a felicitous idea of the early missionaries to have our Lady of Guadalupe make her appearance on the identical site of ancient fame, already celebrated as the place of worship of the older female deity" (*Religious Aspects*, p. 47). Toor also draws attention to this fact (*Mexican Folkways*, p. 172).

Usigli favors the miraculous explanation, although he hints at the possibility of human intervention (*Corona de Luz*). The Vatican itself has taken pains to support the orthodox view, and copious evidence is filed in its library. Other scholars have minimized the conscious role of the Spanish clergy by suggesting that the Virgin's name, as told to Juan Diego, was Maria Coatlalopeuh, which meant "the one who has dominion over serpents." Because this word and Guadalupe are almost homophonous in the Spanish ear, the Virgin was mistakenly called Guadalupe.

6. Usigli, *Corona de Luz*, p. 117.
7. Also see Madsen, *The Virgin's Children*, pp. 28, 29.
8. Toor, *Mexican Folkways*, p. 175.
9. Quirk, *The Mexican Revolution*, pp. 131, 132.
10. Madsen, *The Virgin's Children*, pp. 28, 29.
11. Usigli, *Corona de Luz*, p. 1.
12. Stevens, "Marianismo," p. 99.
13. Diaz-Guerrero, *Psychology of the Mexican*, p. 13.
14. Peristiany, *Honour and Shame*, p. 182.
15. Caro Baroja, "Honour and Shame," p. 110.
16. Campbell, "Honour and the Devil," p. 146.
17. Batt, "Mexican Character," p. 200.
18. Diaz-Guerrero, *Psychology of the Mexican*, p. 3.
19. See Batt, "Mexican Character"; Diaz-Guerrero, *Psychology of the Mexican*; Stevens, "Marianismo"; and Wolf, "The Virgin of Guadalupe."
20. Lewis, *The Children of Sanchez*, p. 318.
21. Stevens, "Marianismo," p. 99.
22. Bushnell explains that in village families the mother is the source of food. She is the family nurse and the dependable center of the household, but in family relationships disturbed by sibling rivalries, and by the patriarchal status of the father and the taboo that precludes open display of

affection, the mother soon ceases to be a comforting haven of security available for every demand. In the kindly and beneficent Virgin of Guadalupe, Bushnell concludes, the Mexican finds the mother figure he craves ("La Virgen de Guadalupe," pp. 262, 263).

23. Interestingly, Wolf distinguishes a facet in Guadalupe worship that has a bearing on this aspect of family relationships. He sees the symbol as charged with the energy of rebellion against the father. The image of Guadalupe thus embodies the hope of a victorious outcome of the struggle between generations. Freudian theorizing on goddess worship is also suggestive here. According to Freudian analysts, goddess worship is the stage in the early development of the individual in which the mother is the powerful source of both deprivation and gratification. Once the child has come to terms with the sexual role of the mother vis-à-vis the father, he repudiates the mother by thinking of mother as pure and virginal; hence the virginity of the goddess image. ("The Virgin of Guadalupe," pp. 34–39).

24. James, *Mother Goddess*, p. 202.

25. See Quirk, *The Mexican Revolution*, p. 4. In orthodox Roman Catholicism the Virgin acts as intercessor with God the Father and God the Son.

26. Neumann, *The Great Mother*, p. 268.

27. Patai, *The Hebrew Goddess*, p. 21.

28. Ibid., pp. 203, 204.

29. See Pagels, "What Became of God the Mother?" pp. 293–303.

30. Diaz-Guerrero, *Psychology of the Mexican*, pp. 91, 92.


# Bibliography

Aradi, Zsolt. *Shrines to Our Lady Around the World*. New York: Farrar, Straus and Young, 1954.

Batt, Carl E. "Mexican Character: An Adlerian Interpretation." *Journal of Individual Psychology* 25 (1969): 183–201.

Braden, Charles. *Religious Aspects of the Conquest of Mexico*. Durham, N.C.: Duke University Press, 1930.

Bushnell, John. "La Virgen de Guadalupe as Surrogate Mother in San Juan Atzingo." *American Anthropologist* 60 (1958): 261–65.

Campbell, J. K. "Honour and the Devil." In *Honour and Shame: The Values of Mediterranean Society*, edited by J. G. Peristiany, pp. 171–190. Chicago: University of Chicago Press, 1966.

Caro Baroja, Julio. "Honour and Shame: A Historical Account of Several Conflicts." In *Honour and Shame: The Values of Mediterranean Society*, edited by J. G. Peristiany, pp. 79–130. Chicago: University of Chicago Press, 1966.

Cortes, Hernan. *Cartas de Relacion*. 2d ed. Mexico City: Editorial Porrua, 1963.

De la Maza, Francisco. *El Guadalupismo Mexicano*. Mexico City: Porrua y Obregon, 1953.

Diaz del Castillo, Bernal. *Historia Verdadera de la Conquista de la Nueva España*. Mexico: Editorial Porrua, 1964.

Diaz-Guerrero, R. *Psychology of the Mexican: Culture and Personality*. Austin: University of Texas Press, 1975.

James, E. O. *The Cult of the Mother Goddess*. London: Thames and Hudson, 1959.

Laurentin, Rene. *Queen of Heaven*. Translated by Gordon Smith. Dublin: Clonmore and Reynolds, 1956.

———. *The Question of Mary*. New York: Holt, Rinehart and Winston, 1965.

Lewis, Oscar. *The Children of Sanchez*. New York: Random House, 1961.

Madsen, William. *The Virgin's Children: Life in an Aztec Village Today*. Austin: University of Texas Press, 1960.

Neumann, Erich. *The Great Mother: An Analysis of the Archetype*. Princeton, N.J.: Princeton University Press, 1955.

*New Catholic Encyclopedia*. "Devotion to Blessed, Virgin Mary." Vol. 9, 1967.

Pagels, Elaine H. "What Became of God the Mother? Conflicting Images of God in Early Christianity." *Signs, Journal of Women in Culture and Society* 2, no. 2 (1976): 293–303.

Patai, Raphael. *The Hebrew Goddess*. New York: Ktav Publishing House, 1967.

Peristiany, J. G., ed. *Honour and Shame: The Values of Mediterranean Society*. Chicago: University of Chicago Press, 1966.

Pescatello, Ann. "The Female in Ibero America: An Essay on Research Bibliography and Research Directions." *Latin American Research Review* 7, no. 2 (1972): 125–41.

Quirk, Robert. *The Mexican Revolution and the Catholic Church, 1910–1929*. Bloomington: Indiana University Press, 1973.

Ramos, Samuel. *Profile of Man and Culture in Mexico*. Austin: University of Texas Press, 1962.

Stevens, Evelyn P. "Marianismo: The Other Face of Machismo in Latin America." In *Male and Female in Latin America*, edited by Ann Pescatello, pp. 90–100. Pittsburgh: University of Pittsburgh Press, 1973.

Toor, Frances. *A Treasury of Mexican Folkways: The Customs, Myths, Folklore, Traditions, Beliefs, Fiestas, Dances and Songs of the Mexican People*. New York: Crown Publishers, 1947.

Usigli, Rodolfo. *Corona de Luz: Pieza Anti-historica en Tres Actos*. New York: Appleton Century Crofts, 1967.

Wolf, Eric. "The Virgin of Guadalupe: A Mexican National Symbol." *Journal of American Folklore* 71 (1958): 34–39.

# 2

## The Tonantsi Cult
## of the Eastern Nahua
### by Alan R. Sandstrom

This paper is an examination of the beliefs and ritual behavior surrounding a female deity who plays a key role in the life and thought
of Nahua Indians inhabiting the southern Huasteca region in east
central Mexico.[1] These Nahuas are the remnants of the great Toltec
and Aztec civilizations that flourished far to the west on the great
central plateau dominating the mid-region of Mexico. Today they are
scattered over the remote and hilly region of the southern Huasteca,
often building their villages on the crumbling ruins of the civilization of their long-forgotten forebears. The census of 1970 found over
100,000 Nahuas in the southern Huasteca, most of whom follow a
traditional life-style far removed from that of the cities or towns.

The Huastecan Nahua live in the foothills of the Sierra Madre
Oriental, a region characterized by dense tropical forests. They maintain themselves through slash-and-burn horticulture based on the
machete and dibble stick. Relatively poor soil conditions coupled with
high annual rainfall lead the Nahua to rotate their fields every two or
three years. There is considerable labor involved in clearing new fields
preparatory to planting, and usually male members of a patrilineal
extended family share in the work. In general, the entire horticultural
cycle relies very little on Western farming methods or technology.[2]
The main crops grown include maize, beans, squash, and chilies.

All Nahua in the area speak Nahuatl as their native language. Villages vary greatly in the degree to which members can also speak
Spanish. Nahua religious beliefs are oriented around a series of
deities or spirit entities that have been partially syncretized with

hristian elements. Judging from statements made by informants ..nd the elaboration of rituals, one female deity is the most important member of the Nahua pantheon. This is the goddess Tonantsi, whose name can be translated from Nahuatl as "our sacred mother."[3] When the Nahua speak in Spanish they refer to Tonantsi as the Virgin of Guadalupe, for in their minds Tonantsi and the Virgin are the same.

The relationship between the Virgin of Guadalupe and Tonantsi has an interesting history. Guadalupe is the official patron of all Christian Mexico. The circumstances of her miraculous appearance in A.D. 1531 have been examined by many authors,[4] and her appeal to a wide range of people from the sophisticated urban dweller to the rural village farmer is well documented.[5] However, this official role of the Virgin of Guadalupe in modern Mexico should not obscure the fact that she derives from the pre-Christian concept of the goddess Tonantsi. The Virgin was dark-skinned and spoke Nahuatl when she appeared on the site of a temple devoted to the worship of Tonantsi. In a sense, Guadalupe is a "Christianized" version of Tonantsi. Thus, she represents a continuity of Indian belief within modern Mexico. It is not surprising, then, that Guadalupe and Tonantsi are combined in the thought of many modern Indian peoples.

The continuity of pre-Christian elements in the Guadalupe/Tonantsi complex presents a problem for the analysis of mother worship. Is it legitimate to view these deities as a unitary phenomenon? It seems highly unlikely that the Guadalupe of a Mexico City business executive is homologous with the goddess Tonantsi of a Nahua villager. The first difficulty for the anthropologist is to define carefully the phenomenon under scrutiny. This can be accomplished best through a series of local studies that focus on the meaning a particular deity or type of deity has for a community. There are two senses in which meaning must be established so that comparisons can be made either within a complex nation-state like Mexico or crossculturally. First, there is the meaning that people attach to the deity, such as the ideas or concepts associated with her. What is the semantic load carried by symbols of the deity? In what areas of life is she influential? The second sense of meaning is in the consequences for behavior of interaction with the deity. How do rituals and social events surrounding the deity reflect and serve to define her in people's lives and thoughts?

In this analysis of Tonantsi, I use a logico-deductive approach to address certain kinds of questions, while neglecting others. I propose a means of explaining behavior by predicting it. The predictions are based on certain assumptions that, although not subject to empirical verification themselves, lead to new and fruitful analyses of the Tonantsi cult. Verification and explanation are achieved in this method of analysis through accurate predictions; it is the potential for prediction—not the agreeableness of the assumptions—by which the method should be judged. By analyzing the meaning of Tonantsi, I try to isolate what it is that motivates her followers and thus underlies the rituals held on her behalf. I hope, by defining the relationship between Tonantsi and her followers, to lay the ground for a cross-cultural definition of mother deities and a uniform means of analyzing mother deity rituals.

Two observations about the Nahua Tonantsi ritual that occurred near the end of my fieldwork have prompted the interpretation presented here. First, despite preconceptions to the contrary, it became obvious that there is a wide variance in degree of religious devoutness among villagers. Some people are fervent believers, whereas others strongly profess agnostic or even atheistic convictions. Yet despite the claims of nonbelievers, many of them play important parts in village ritual life. The rituals must do something important for people, whatever their degree of religious belief.

The second observation is the inverse relationship I noted between the level of wealth or resources controlled by a household and its participation in ritual life. In other words, I found that the richest households frequently remain aloof from village rituals. On the other hand, somewhat poorer households are frequently active in them. There are exceptions, to be sure, but these are usually related to some special problem. For example, a rich family may allocate much of its wealth to curing rituals if one or more members have some chronic disease.

In any event, these two observations led me to the conclusion that rituals in general are seen by the villagers as essentially transactional in nature. Nonbelievers and less-well-endowed villagers engage in them in order to get something. Wealthier households, despite their greater resources, do not feel it advantageous to expend much wealth on ritual transactions. These data indicate that Nahua rituals can be viewed as part of the strategies used by villagers to maximize utility.

The fundamental assumption of the method I propose to follow in interpreting the Tonantsi cult is that ritual is a strategy employed to maximize something valued by the participants. Following the lead of formalist theorists,[6] who view social interaction as a kind of transaction by which individuals maximize their own utility, I view rituals directed toward Tonantsi as a kind of symbolic transaction carried out between villagers and the goddess. In this view, people are seen as decision makers who behave in order to elicit rewards. Rewards are defined simply as any desired end, including prestige, security, money, produce, freedom from disease, protection, and fertility. My assumption is that even with regard to ritual, people are not automatons who behave mindlessly because of tradition alone, or in response to some vague need for social solidarity. The full implications of ritual activity may not be completely apprehended by the participants, but each person has good reasons for his part in the transaction.

Two points need clarification. First, it is not necessary to assume that reward or utility is identical for each participant. The mix of desired ends varies from person to person, and so there probably is no totally uniform set of goals sought after by individuals or the "group." The second point is that my method need not assume that ritual participants are conscious of the transactional nature of their endeavor. If asked, they may or may not verbalize what they are doing. Although I do believe that people have conscious reasons for participating in ritual occasions, what is important for our purposes is not so much the state of consciousness of the people as how they behave. The Nahua behave as if they are engaging in ritualized transactions. This "behaving as if" is real and is the basis for the consistency of social patterns described here.

The assumption that ritual observance is a kind of transaction implies a certain view by the people in a culture of the nature of spirit entities. As I have already suggested, people are not passive victims of culture but are actively engaged in living it. There is no clear distinction between the ethnographer and the community observed, because the people themselves are engaged in the process of observation and interpretation.[7] That human beings feel an overriding need to explain their experiences and to live by general ideas of order seems indisputable.[8] Members of a culture share experiences and share to some extent the traditional means of making sense of them. They make common assumptions about the nature of reality and humanity's place in it. In short, they share a common metaphysic or world view, which acts to interpret reality and gives them a sense of order and the assurance that even anomalous occurrences are explainable in terms of ordinary experience.[9]

A world view is composed of a set of axioms that underlie the beliefs and practices which form a culture. These axioms are not

created anew with each generation but rather are seen as the fundamental truths that have been gleaned from thousands of years of
human experience. A world view is a statement, in reduced terms, of
the ongoing process by which generations of ancestors have succeeded in making sense out of life experiences. But because the historical and even daily experiences of each social group differ, owing
to factors of ecology, economy, political reality, technology, and so on,
the world view and cultural systems that each produces and sustains
will also differ. The main distinction between groups will be in how
the various cultural systems create a congruence between behavioral
patterns and perceived cosmic order.[10]

Humans have always peopled their worlds with a series of spirits,
gods, saints, and creatures that may fall outside *our* perceived realm
of ordinary experience. The heritage of any society inevitably includes reference to spiritual entities. These entities are not make-
believe or particularly fantastic to the members of the society; to them
spirits are simply another aspect of reality. Many people have daily
encounters with spirits, through prayer, offerings, or fearful avoid-
ances. I view many spirit entities or deities as devices for attributing
causation or for interpreting observations of the world. They constitute a kind of "theory" by which aspects of observed phenomena
are organized and highlighted, and by which thought is oriented.
Thus, the problem of diversity of observed phenomena is reduced,
members of a culture can use deities as a means of organizing their
view of reality, and experience is placed in a context of perceived
order.

I am speaking here not of the origin of religious belief but rather of
the continuous dynamics that generate and support it. The problems
of fertility, proper rainfall, and freedom from disease that permeate
Nahua religious concepts are fundamental ones for horticulturists.
Their pantheons of spiritual entities are not arbitrary, but oriented to
conceptualizing and expressing those elements of the universe that
underlie life itself. I do not mean to imply that religious behavior is
only an extension of pragmatic and empirical procedures into realms
where humans lack direct control. It is, instead, a highly complex
process whereby people specify the forces that underlie their exis-
ence. Once identified, these forces are conceived in such a way that
they can literally be *dealt* with. The existence of spiritual entities identified with important forces, such as germination, disease, and growth,
not only allows humans to conceptualize often highly abstract processes and phenomena but also provides a way for them to interact

with these forces. Belief in spiritual entities, then, is not an extension of scientific control but rather allows the extension of social transactions into the realm of the sacred.

The problem in dealing with spirit entities is how to carry out transactions with them. Clearly, direct exchange such as that carried on between friends or kinsmen or in other face-to-face situations is inappropriate when one of the parties is both nonhuman and not physically present. The exchange in these cases will be carried on symbolically in the form of religious rituals. Therefore, it becomes important in the analysis of ritual to be able to understand what it is that is being communicated symbolically. We need to know what the practitioners are offering and what it is they hope for in return. In short, we need to analyze the symbolic content of the ritual.

Following Clifford Geertz, I will define "symbol" as any object or act that serves as a vehicle for a conception.[11] For our purposes the most important aspect of ritual symbols is their instrumental value. We must view symbols as means to some end and then determine how they are employed in order to reach it. They are both a means of communicating and at the same time the thing communicated. A religious ritual is a complex symbolic act meant to establish contact with important nonhuman entities that exist in wider reality, and, through the ritual medium, to induce obligations in these entities relative to the welfare of individuals and the community. Through prescribed actions a communication link is established, and through offerings, whether these be music, libations, prayer, food, or sacrifice, a transactional link is forged. There is no guarantee that spiritual entities will reciprocate: the ritual may have been performed incorrectly; the offerings may be insufficient or the practitioners impure. The fact that people continue a ritual, however, is a strong indicator that it is still considered effective. More important, the practice of rituals is an affirmation that the people perceive order in the universe and that over the long run justice will prevail.[12] Ritual affirms a given world view to be a valid interpretation of human experience.

## Ritual and Reality

Before proceeding to the ritual itself, I will outline briefly a few of the general features of Nahua cosmology. Without some knowledge of how the villagers structure the universe, their ritual behavior may appear meaningless or irrational. The Nahuas divide the universe into four major regions. The first of these is on the surface of the earth and constitutes the locus of everyday activities. In Nahuatl, this realm is called *tlali*, which seems to carry the same connotation as the English word "earth." The second region corresponds to our concept of the heavens. Called *ilwihkaktli* in Nahuatl, this realm is where the stars are located and is the place where several local deities either originate or presently abide. The third region lies underneath the earth and is called *miktlan*, "place of the dead." This underworld realm is where all the souls of those who die from natural causes continue to live. It is connected to the surface through a series of doors that correspond to the numerous pre-Columbian ruins that dot the village. The fourth region is a watery realm called *apan* ("water place"); there go all the souls of those who die by drowning, by lightning, or by other violent means.

Both harmful and beneficial deities are associated with each of these regions. The heavens are the home of the high god Toteotsi, who has little or no interest in the affairs of men. Tlixiwantsi, a benign hearth deity associated with the heavenly realm, is located in the stones surrounding the main cooking fire in each house. In the underworld, Tlakatekolotl reigns supreme, although he is by no means an incarnation of evil like the Christian devil. The water realm is overseen by Apanchane, the lady of the water, who looks out for the village but who must be constantly propitiated. In sacred caves on earth live the masters of the seeds, who control the productivity of "their children," such as the important crops grown in the village. Tonantsi, the deity that controls general fertility and the seedmasters, also lives on earth, but she has no specific abode because "she is everywhere."

In addition to the four realms and the spirit entities that exist within them, there is a larger presence that exists more or less in the background of ritual behavior. This presence, felt not only at rituals but during everyday life as well, is the earth (*tlali*). The earth has the world of men on its surface, the world of souls beneath its surface, the world of water that exists between these two, and the world of stars above. The earth is a sentient being whose bones are rocks, blood is water, and flesh is the soil. It is literally and figuratively the ground of existence, the living entity that mediates among all elements in the universe to provide humans with a place and means to live and, thus, the possibility of life itself.

## *Tlakatelilis*: The Ritual

The ritual devoted to Tonantsi begins each year on December 20 and runs continuously until the night of December 24. This rite is called *Tlakatelilis* in Nahuatl and is often equated with Christmas (*Navidad*) by outsiders because of the coincidence of dates. However, *Tlakatelilis* means "causing birth" in Nahuatl, and even a superficial examination of the observance reveals it to be a fertility ritual. The purpose of *Tlakatelilis* is to confer benefits of fertility on villagers and their crops. There are numerous symbolic methods for accomplishing this purpose, including the playing of sacred music, the formation of processions to carry an image of Tonantsi to each house, the construction of altars, and the making of offerings. The particular ritual occasion described here took place in the village of Puyecaco, Ixhuatlan de Madero, during the month of December in 1973. This village is inhabited by 582 people and is representative of the hundreds of Nahua settlements of the southern Huasteca.[13]

Preparations for *Tlakatelilis* begin about ten days before the official start of the ceremony. During the preparations, men and boys gather nightly at the shrine, or *teopamitl* ("God's place"), and practice their dance steps. A guitarist and violinist provide the dance music and a leader begins each step and provides a model, which the others follow. This leader is selected because of his superior abilities in executing the complex movements of the dance.

On the morning of the first day, about twenty-five men sit outside the shrine folding colored strips of paper. The folded strips will be placed on a bamboo framework along with small mirrors, colorful bandanas, and ribbons. This frame fits on the head and is worn by the dancers during their performance. Inside the shrine, preparations are made to form a procession that will go to each house in the village. People crowd in the entrance while two ritual specialists called *tlamatiketl* ("people of knowledge") are busy making arrangements at the back of the building.

The shrine is a building typical of others in the village. It measures about four by five meters and has a thatched roof and walls made of mud-covered wood and bamboo poles. Inside, two crude, narrow tables against the wall opposite the entrance serve as an altar. Between the two altar tables is a large wooden cross set up on the floor. On the altar are many ritual objects, prominent among them a plaster statue of the Virgin of Guadalupe resting inside a blue wooden box.

Beside the box, on the altar itself, there is a plaster statue of Joseph and one of Mary.

There are four basic elements that make up the procession: the ritual specialists (here referred to as curers), two musicians, a group of about twelve young, unmarried girls ranging from five to fifteen years of age, and an old woman censer (*kopalmitotiketl* in Nahuatl and *copalera* in Spanish). In the shrine the curers attach a black cloth carrying strap (tumpline) to the blue box containing the statue of Guadalupe, as the musicians begin to play. The musical pieces played for this occasion or for any highly sacred ritual are called *xochisones* ("flower songs"), or, generically, *costumbre* music. They have a lilting, almost whining, quality to Western ears and are highly rhythmic and repetitive. There are many different melodic and rhythmic variations in this particular type of music, each of which is associated with a specific part of the *Tlakatelilis* celebration.[14]

As the music begins, the girls form into a tight group near the altar tables. The censer picks up a brazier heaped with smoking copal bark and begins a graceful, swaying dance in time to the music. During her dance, the old woman incenses the statues on the altar and the group of girls standing before it. The curers hand out burning yellow beeswax candles to the girls. One of the older girls accepts the blue box from a curer and, by passing the carrying strap across her fore-head, places it on her back. The other two statues are handed out to two girls as the musicians file out of the hut, continuing to play the sacred music. The old woman follows them carrying the brazier. She in turn is followed by the girls bearing the statues.

The procession heads for a group of compounds, containing the houses of a patrilineal extended family, that lie some distance behind the village schoolhouse. When the procession arrives at a house, chairs are brought out for the musicians; as the people in the procession pass through the entrance, they are showered with marigold petals by women of the house. Inside, a table has been decorated with a piece of highly embroidered cloth. The statues of Guadalupe, Mary, and Joseph are taken from the girls and placed on the table, along with the burning candles they carried. Strings of marigold blossoms called *xochikostli* (*rosario* in Spanish) are placed on the statues by the male head of the household as the brazier is replenished with hot coals from the firetable. The censer begins to dance to the music and incenses the altar and the people in attendance.

Next, offerings are brought out by members of the household, received by the curers, and placed underneath the small table. These frequently include about five liters of maize, a liter of beans, some soft drinks, and a small bottle of cane alcohol called *aguardiente*. A candle is lighted by a curer and placed near the offerings. Meanwhile, the girls are tightly grouped and swaying in time to the music, which drones outside. Then the curer begins to chant, and as the censer dances she incenses him and the altar. The women of the house now scatter marigold petals over the altar.

At this point one of the curers takes two unlighted candles and parades them to the lighted candle on the earth floor. Continuing to chant, he picks up four grains of maize and six of beans from the offerings and rubs them on the candles. A smoking incense brazier is placed on each side of him by onlookers as he lays down the seeds before the statue of Tonantsi (the Virgin of Guadalupe). The two candles held by the curer are placed next to the statue in the blue box. Then the offerings are given to two men, each of whom is carrying a large cloth bag. The maize is placed in one of these bags and the beans are emptied into the other. All the corn and part of the beans will be sold in the market in order to pay for the large communal offering held on the last day of the ceremony.

Then, at the direction of the curers, each member of the family approaches the altar and gives two short bows. Meanwhile, the head of the house places some money on the altar; this, after a few minutes, is handed to one of the men carrying the cloth bags. Then, when the family is finished paying obeisance, the drink offerings are passed around to all in attendance. Before actually drinking, however, each person sprinkles a few drops from each bottle on the earth.

The curer begins to chant again while squatting before the altar. Beneath him are all the empty bottles of cane alcohol and soft drinks. More copal bark is added to the brazier by the censer as the wife of the household head is given a fresh candle by the curer to burn later. Burning candles are given to each of the young girls and the three statues are passed once again to their "bearers." The musicians, who have been playing constantly, stand and lead the procession to the next house in the compound. This procedure, which lasts about twenty minutes, is followed at each house in the village.

At dusk, the house-to-house peregrination is halted so that Tonantsi may rest for the night. The procedure for switching from daytime activity to nighttime inactivity is relatively brief and not elaborate. The procession moves to a predetermined place, usually a neighboring compound, and stops before an arch that has been constructed at one end of a small clearing. At the opposite end of the clearing, under the eave of a house, a small table has been set out, covered with a heavily embroidered cloth.

The woman of the household showers the entire procession with marigold petals as it passes through the arch. The old woman incenses the little table, and while she continues to dance, the statues are unloaded by household members and placed on it. The candles are taken from the girls and placed around the edge of the little table. The musicians come forward, continuing to play ritual music, bow low before the altar, and switch to dance music as they rise. At this point, the ritually active period has ended and the dancing begins.

Food is prepared in each of the houses of the host compound and everyone in attendance eats. The dancers, all of whom are male, slowly gather in anticipation of a full night's performance. Each wears a colorful headdress and carries a small gourd rattle (*ayakachtli*) in the right hand and a "flower" made of wood and covered with aluminum foil in the left. The dancers form two parallel lines, perpendicular to the small table altar. They face the statues and the dance leader stands between the lines of men. The musicians sit near the altar table and face the dancers as they play. Music and dancing continue through the night, until full daylight, when the exhausted musicians and dancers give way to the daytime events of *Tlakatelilis*.

Early the next morning, the curers, censer, and little girls arrive. They carry out a ritual at the host house, just as previously described. There is no transition between the dance and ritual music as witnessed in the evenings. Suddenly the musicians begin to play ritual music and the dancers either retire to their houses or stand around to watch. The principals, led by the musicians, leave through the arch and proceed to another house.

After four days and nights of ritual performance and dancing, the tone of the proceedings changes. The curers, who are highly intoxicated and exhausted, carry out their functions with less coordination. The dancing censer incenses somewhat sleepily and the girls are obviously tired. On the morning of the third day people begin to set off small firecrackers during the ritual and procession as it moves from house to house. By the fourth day, these are exploded at varying intervals both night and day. The dancers continue to perform with enthusiasm but by the third night signs of wear begin to show. Finally, the musicians, some of whom play night and day, are in an extreme state of intoxication and exhaustion.

On the morning of the last day, the dancers continue until noon.

Preparations are made to decorate the large altar in the shrine. Outside, a large leaf- and flower-covered arch is constructed to the left of the open area in front of the building. Opposite this arch, a table is placed under a second arch some distance away. Inside, a similar arch is constructed both over the large altar and on the opposite wall. When the procession arrives, it stops at the first arch as two dancing censers incense both the arch and the people. The musicians enter playing ritual music while a woman sprinkles marigold petals over the people who pass under the arch. The statues are unloaded onto the table. Several women approach, place lighted candles on it, bow, and move away. The dancers each bow to the altar. Then each young girl places her candle on the table, bows to Tonantsi, and backs away. At the point when the last dancer bows, the musicians strike up dance music and the men line up and begin to dance. Upon finishing their bowing, the girls form into a tight group, and then sway in time to the music.

As the dancers perform, several men begin to make altar adornments for the large offerings to be held in the evening, which marks the culmination of the *Tlakatelilis* ceremony. There are four basic types of altar adornments. The first of these is called *se koyoli* (*coyol* in Spanish) and is made by splitting a 40–45 centimeter palm leaf and using one of the strips to tie one or two marigold blossoms to the base of the remaining strip. Two variations of the *se koyoli* constitute the second type of altar adornment. The first is made like a *se koyoli* except that it has five rows of flowers tied to the palm leaf. This is called a *makwili xochitl koyoli*, or a five-flower *coyol*. The second variation is made with seven rows of marigolds and is called *chikome xochitl koyoli* (seven-flower *coyol*). A third set of altar decorations is made by impaling several marigold blossoms on flexible strips of bark. These flower loops are called *xochikostli* in Nahuatl and *rosarios* in Spanish. Finally, wooden crosses about 20 centimeters high are made from sticks cut from a live tree and covered with marigold blossoms.

All altar adornments include the tropical marigold. Called *sempoal xochitl* (twenty-flower) by the villagers, this beautiful orange and yellow blossom is considered to be the "companion" of maize. Through association with maize, marigolds are linked to the processes in the universe that lead to life itself. It is hard to overestimate the importance of the marigold for the symbolic and ritual life of the village. This flower, which not coincidentally is grown in the fields, is considered to be consummately beautiful and ultimately worthy of decorating the most sacred of spots. So much does the symbol of the flower permeate Nahua life and thought that it is not unusual to see men carrying around bouquets as they walk throughout the village.

The men complete the task by making eight circular palm "wheels," decorated with marigold blossoms. These are called *sitlame* ("stars"). In the afternoon, one of the curers takes the completed adornments and begins to decorate the altar (*tlaichpamitl*) in the shrine. The musicians have ceased playing dance music and are now providing a background of ritual pieces. A curer places a lighted candle on the earth floor between the two tables that form the altar. Adornments are laid on either side of this candle. Next, the curers lay the palm decorations on the altar. Two men help a curer tie all eight "stars" on the arch over the altar. Bundles of palm decorations are tied to each cross, and yellow candles are slipped into the fiber that holds them. One of these crosses is taken to a nearby house and placed by the fire. Another is taken to a small cave, where a spring is located; the cross is tied to a tree that grows nearby. A third cross has been stood up on the floor display in the shrine, and the fourth is placed on the main altar.

Outside, the little table that holds the statues is decorated. In addition, one five-flower and one seven-flower *coyol* have been leaned against the statue of Tonantsi inside the box. The second five-flower *coyol* has been leaned against the statue of Mary, and the remaining seven-flower *coyol* is leaned against the image of Joseph.

In the evening, the curer begins the sacrifice of the chickens that will be cooked and offered to Tonantsi. Ritual music is played and the censer dances and incenses the area. Packed into a tight group, the young girls sway in unison to the music. The curer incenses and then picks up a live chicken. He holds it over the main altar and chants aloud in Nahuatl asking that Tonantsi witness the killing. Next, he breaks the chicken's neck and lays it on the floor. Then, after killing a second chicken, the curer pours a drop of soft drink on four sides of each bird. Next, he sprinkles a drop of cane alcohol over the display on the floor, in the brazier, and finally at the head and feet of each chicken. He then hands the bottle around to the onlookers, each of whom pours a drop to the earth before drinking. Next, the curer picks up the smoking brazier and incenses the dead chickens, the floor display, the main altar, the young girls, and finally all the onlookers.

As the dead chickens are removed by a woman, one curer takes out a thick wad of variously colored paper and begins to fold individual sheets. Outside, the musicians are playing and about eighteen men and boys are dancing for Tonantsi. A different pair of musicians continues to play ritual music inside, where the curers are about to cut paper figurines. On the altar and floor display there are many bottles of soft drinks and beer, each fitted with a little collar of four marigolds. The curers cut paper figurines for a cleansing designed to rid the ritual areas of potentially harmful spirits.[15] Soon the standard cleansing offerings are brought in: an egg, tobacco, cane alcohol, cornmeal, herbs, and candles. A curer gathers these into a bundle with the paper cutouts and uses it to rub all the people congregated both inside and outside the shrine. Then the bundle is carried over to the house in which the chickens are being cooked and used to cleanse the women in the house as well as the fireplace. Although the cooking is being done over large fires outside the house, firebrands are brought in and placed on the firetable for this cleansing. The curer then goes to a ruined stone pyramid in the center of the village and performs a standard cleansing procedure, using all the paper figurines.

Near midnight the censer begins to dance at the shrine. The curer reappears and begins the process of returning Tonantsi from a temporary altar outside to her rightful place on the inside altar. The five- and seven-flower *coyoles* are handed out by the curers to the girls, who have now gathered by the outside altar. Then lighted candles are given to everyone. The musicians outside strike up sacred music as candles are given to the dancers. Firecrackers are set off, the statues are handed out to the girls, and a curer stands in the shrine door wildly waving everyone on. All participants, each with a candle, follow the young girl who carries Tonantsi. The entire group walks around the shrine four times as the musicians continue to play. Many participants have sparklers as well as candles, and sounds of firecrackers add to the swirling disarray that circles the shrine.

After the fourth revolution, the girls lead everyone into the building, where a curer unloads the statues and puts them back on the altar. The girls place their burning candles all along the altar and each moves from right to left, bowing down its entire length. Each statue is adorned with *coyoles* and candles by various onlookers. Most people now follow the girls' lead and move along the altar bowing. Then, as the censer dances, both curers move up and down the altar chanting and incensing. During this phase of the ritual, a bottle of cane alcohol is passed around and enjoyed by most active participants.

As people file out of the shrine the cooked chickens and pots of steaming food are brought in. Dishes are filled with the hot food and placed on the table altar and on the floor display. Cups are filled with coffee or chocolate and placed by the dishes. The censer begins her swaying dance as the young girls form into a tight group. As they sway in time to the music one of them rings a small bell to call the spirits' attention to the offering. The curer picks up some candles, parades them along the altar, and begins to chant. Rockets are set off, and the dancers continue to perform outside the shrine as the curer places pairs of lighted cigarettes along the table and floor altars. A lighted white candle (used only on altars to the earth) is placed on the floor display.

One of the young girls shakes a rattle in time to the music as she and her companions continue to sway as a group. The curers pour about one-quarter of each bottle over the main altar, and then pass the remaining contents to the group of girls standing nearby. Next, the cups of coffee or chocolate are poured over the altar and floor display. Soaked pieces of bread are thrown under the altar onto the floor as pieces of cooked chicken are scattered over the display.

After offerings are scattered over the adornments, some cups and dishes are refilled with a small portion of each of the items of food and drink. All of these are incensed and then carried over to the house where the food was prepared and where the cross had been placed near the fire. The two candles lashed to the small cross are taken out and lighted nearby. A curer, now holding a brazier, chants and incenses the fire. As two cigarettes are lighted, he pours a bit of all the other offerings into the fire. Another set of offerings is prepared back in the shrine and carried by the curer to the spring that represents the home of Apanchane, the water spirit. A procedure similar to that described at the hearth is followed here. The offerings are spread on the rocks surrounding the spring and Apanchane is beseeched to accept them.

Once the curer arrives back in the shrine, the remaining offerings are consumed by the people still in attendance. The other curer proceeds to chant and incense the altar for several minutes. In about an hour, he will begin the short ritual sequence that is used to create ties of ritual kinship. However, this procedure occurs after any major ritual occasion and is not connected to the *Tlakatelilis* ceremony per se.

There is no ritual activity the next day. People go about their normal daily routine in apparent disregard of the previous five days of ceremonial observance. Several informants state that "no one works today," although people are carrying loads of wood they have cut, and smoke is rising from a few of the fields, indicating the burning of brush. The door of the shrine is closed; only a lone candle burns on the earth floor, bearing witness to the previous day's activity.

## *Tlakatelilis*: The Meaning

Tonantsi is clearly the central figure in the *Tlakatelilis* ritual. The peregrination from house to house is meant to bring her blessing to each family in the village. At night, the costumed dancers perform in order to keep her company or entertain her while she rests from the activities of the day. The final massive offering is directed specifically at her person to elicit her favor on the entire village. Her importance to the villagers of Puyecaco is indicated by the fact that the shrine in which she normally resides is reserved specifically for her. Only *Yankwik Xiwitl* (New Year's) is celebrated in the same building. Even this ritual is partially aimed at Tonantsi.

The key to understanding why Tonantsi enjoys such an important place in Nahua life can be found through examination of the concepts symbolized by the two altar adornments *makwili xochitl* (five-flower) and *chikome xochitl* (seven-flower). One of each adornment was leaned against the image of Tonantsi during the culminating day of *Tlakatelilis*. The five- and seven-flower *coyoles* are associated with maize, the basic crop of the Nahua, but they signify more than this. According to informants, the seven-flower symbol also signifies maleness (*macho*) or the male sexual principle. The five-flower design, on the other hand, signifies femaleness (*hembra*) or the female sexual principle. Tonantsi carries the abstraction somewhat further. She is more than maleness and femaleness, she is the result of interaction between the two—a mother. She is, in short, a symbolic representation of the principle of fertility.

One sense of the meaning of Tonantsi, then, is her association in the minds of the Nahua with the complex processes of fertility. But Tonantsi is symbolic of fertility in its broadest sense. She is equally associated with germination, productivity, fecundity, fruitfulness, growth, birth, conception, motherhood, well-being, food, generosity, and the unity of siblings because of common motherhood. She is what Victor Turner calls a polysemic or multivocal symbol, in that she stands for many things.[16] She is also a "summarizing" symbol because she operates "to compound and synthesize a complex system of ideas, to 'summarize' them under a unitary form."[17] However, all the meanings attached to her by the Nahua are understood to emanate from the productive unity of the male and female principles. Thus, her symbolic form organizes diverse but related phenomena observed and experienced by the Nahua, forming a link between processes in nature and the satisfaction of desires.

It is the linking of observable natural processes to the Tonantsi symbol that allows participants with diverse attitudes and conceptions to support the *Tlakatelilis* ceremony. Some villagers say they believe in the literal existence of Tonantsi as she is represented by the statue. Others claim that Tonantsi has no independent anthropomorphic existence but that she represents an observable process in nature. The vast majority, however, fall somewhere between these extremes. They rely on the thinking of the curers and the activities expressed during rituals to define their belief structure. All villagers, however, are fully aware of the basic tenets of the traditional system of religious beliefs. No matter how this traditional system is perceived, all appear to believe that life would not be possible outside the workings of nature and society symbolized by Tonantsi and other members of the Nahua pantheon. Dedicated atheists or agnostics of course may participate in the *Tlakatelilis* ceremony for a variety of reasons, including the desire to win social acceptance, to enjoy the color and activity, or as an excuse to drink. However, the ritual itself is action that has meaning to most villagers in relation to the reality of Nahua experience.

The second sense of the meaning attached to Tonantsi, defined by the behavior surrounding her, can be determined by examining the ritual itself. *Tlakatelilis* is a complex and lengthy ceremony, but not incomprehensible if the association between Tonantsi and fertility is kept clearly in mind. Once this association is understood, much of the ritual activity becomes clearer. The ceremony celebrates not the birth of a god, as in the Christian holiday at Christmas, but the fact of birth itself. Tonantsi is fertility in the sense of potential for birth. Hence a group of young, unmarried virgins follow the image around to each house. The ritual is designed to bring fertility to the household, not only for the crops but for the people and particularly the young girls. In a sense, the young girls are "potential fertility" personified. This theme is brought into each household through the auspices of the ritual.

Accompanying the image of Tonantsi is a statue of Joseph, whom the Indians consider to be her son, and another statue of Mary, who is the son's wife. These statues represent the work spirit (*ekihte*) and his wife. They flank Tonantsi because it is believed that work is the intermediary between human desires and successful fertility. This is particularly the case with the growing of crops. Work is almost a physical entity that is applied to the untamed jungle to create a field. Only through a substantial investment of labor can the field be made to bloom with life-sustaining maize, beans, and other products.

Throughout the ritual we see symbolic acts that serve to communicate ideas or states of being. The censer is continually sacralizing the objects in the ceremony. While walking, the young girls carry lighted candles to signify their status as part of the procession. The musicians play the various ritual pieces to represent different parts of the ritual as it is performed at each house. Marigold petals are sprinkled over members of the procession as they enter the houses to symbolize further the sacred nature of the event. The curer rubs the grains of maize and beans on the candles while he chants, asking Tonantsi to bless the seeds of the household with her power of life. The candles are saved to be burned at the large offering so that the interests of each household are represented there. Each member of the household pays obeisance to Tonantsi through bowing, and the curer terminates the ritual by asking her to accept the offerings.

The procedure for stopping for the night involves entering into an area defined by an arch at one end and the table for the statues at the other. The arch in this context is said to be a door leading to a kind of temporary shrine. On the morning of the last day of the ceremony, we see the arch being used in this way again. The procession moves to the area in front of the shrine, preparatory to the large offering to be held that night. Arches set off the area that once again will hold Tonantsi for several hours until the inside altar is prepared. The shrine itself is adorned with two arches, one over the door, the other over the altar on the opposite wall. Thus, arches are used to signify a ritually set-off area.

According to informants, altar decoration is designed to make a "beautiful place" at which to give offerings to Tonantsi. The stars are placed on the arch representing the heavens. An array is placed on the floor so that offerings can also be made to the earth. One decorated cross is placed by the fire, which is associated with the celestial realm. Other crosses are placed in spots symbolizing the other regions: by the spring (water), on the altar (earth's surface), and under the altar (earth or underworld). The seven-flower *coyol* (masculine principle) has been leaned against the image of the spirit of work and the five-flower *coyol* (female principle) against his wife.

After sacralizing the chickens in the incense, the curer kills them and further signifies their sacred status by placing drops of cane alcohol on all four sides of them. After the cleansing, the curer directs the procedures for replacing Tonantsi on her altar. This is not done directly, but only after everyone has circled the shrine four times. The exact reason for this circling is not entirely clear. Possibly it symbolizes the four-day peregrination just undergone by Tonantsi. Also, the number four has some sacred connotation in its own right, and the act of circling the building could be a form of sacralization.

The *Tlakatelilis* ceremony terminates on the last day with offerings to Tonantsi, Tlaltetata (father earth), Tlixiwantsi (fire), and Apanchane (water). The offerings are made by first sacralizing the food in copal smoke, then setting it on the altar, and finally spreading it over the altar decorations. As is the case with all offerings in the village, the people who are present ultimately consume almost all the food. It is believed that the spiritual entities eat the essence of what is offered to them, leaving only a tasteless shell.

The rituals that make up the *Tlakatelilis* ceremony can be divided into two basic clusters. On the one hand, there are those actions that serve to establish and maintain contact with the relevant spirit entities. This group I shall label the communicator cluster. Communicator actions may be further divided into two groups. First are the acts that serve to create a proper atmosphere or setting for the ritual. The proper setting for *Tlakatelilis* includes decorated altars with arches constructed over them. Candles are lighted and incense is burned to separate ritually significant areas. The mood is conditioned by music, dancing, and the continuous consumption of cane alcohol. Second are the acts that serve actually to convey offerings or information to the proper spirit entities. When the curer chants throughout the ritual he is beseeching the spirits to accept what is offered. He rubs participants with bundles, sacrificial birds, and candles so that disease-bearing spirits will leave the body and receive the offerings. By pouring food on altars and casting offerings into the fire and water the curer ensures that proper spirits receive their share.

The second major ritual act found in *Tlakatelilis* is the offering itself. There is some overlap between the communicator and offering clusters, because some of the means used to set the environment are considered to be kinds of offerings. For example, music and dancing are both a necessary component of the setting of certain rituals and are considered to be "beautiful gifts" to the spirit entities. However, for analytical purposes, the distinction between communicator and offering clusters is both valid and useful. Any ritual in the village of Puyecaco, no matter how small, contains within it some kind of offering. In fact, offerings are the reason for holding rituals. The communicator cluster is important only as an instrument for conveying offerings to spirit entities.

The central place of offerings in religious rituals establishes the primary strategy employed by the Nahua in soliciting rewards from spirit entities. By convincing spirit entities to accept the gifts, villagers induce obligations among them, thus increasing the probability that rewards will be forthcoming in return. Ritual offerings are a kind of investment of time and wealth in exchange for increased odds that the spirits will fulfill their end of the bargain. As previously mentioned, there is no way to force Tonantsi to comply with the transaction because, for one thing, she symbolizes processes and elements in the universe that are more powerful and pervasive than humans. The idea conveyed is that of humbly offering gifts in order to oblige more powerful exchange partners.

Ritual exchange is basically an unequal transaction from an economic point of view. The villagers trade food, drink, time, and effort in return for fertility, children, success, and even life itself. Rituals are used to convey valued items to spirit entities as a way of obligating them to take an active interest in human welfare. But without the intervention of spirits, there would be neither life nor rituals. In a sense, the debt owed to Tonantsi can never be paid by trading valued items through ritual means. This basic imbalance in the material realm is compensated for in the social realm.

If the transactions were materially equivalent (i.e., if the Nahua merely got an equivalent return on their ritual investments), then the spirits would be accorded status similar to customers in the market. Because the ritual transaction of *Tlakatelilis* is seen to be unequal, Tonantsi is accorded deference, awe, and respect as part of the payment, in anticipation for her services to the villagers. Ritual, then, involves not only an exchange of material items, but an exchange of social values as well. The great power of Tonantsi means that these social values can have sufficient magnitude to produce a profound psychological impact on believers.

If ritual is a form of transaction distinguished only by its specialized procedures, it follows that the amount of wealth invested in it will be commensurate with the reward that is sought. Maximum utility for each household in Puyecaco is a mix of valued ends including produce, manufactured items of consumption, health, protection, and children. Not everyone values the same things in the same way, and thus maximum utility for various households will be composed of different mixes of ends. Wealthier households have generally, attained a higher level of utility through technological and social means. Consequently, they are less likely to rely on ritual strategies than poorer households. However, not all valued ends are so easily maximized. Some households will have problems with crop productivity or with any of a number of contingent factors over which control is less certain. It is in these areas of uncertainty that ritual strategies come to be relied upon. The degree to which a household allocates its resources to the *Tlakatelilis* ceremony will depend, then, on the degree to which its members wish to improve their mix of the specific type of valued ends made possible by Tonantsi.

Each household allocates different amounts of its total resources to support ritual activity. The exact amount employed by a specific household can be difficult to measure because rituals entail a variety of costs. Besides money, produce, and other rather easily measured variables, there is considerable time and even skill that must be invested. A man's time spent on a ritual must be measured against what he could have produced had he been engaged in some other activity. However, from the point of view of the Nahua, allocating resources to rituals is not simply a drain on the household; it is instead an additional means of increasing utility. There are two basic types of goals people try to achieve through the ritual: personal and community. Personal goals are those which will benefit individuals or the members of a single household. The first three days of the *Tlakatelilis* ceremony, with rituals performed at each house, are meant to achieve personal goals. It is important to note, however, that the ritual means of achieving personal benefit are composed of conventional, socially shared symbols. Community goals are achieved through rituals designed to bring benefit to the whole village. The food offered during *Tlakatelilis* exemplifies a community goal. Individual goals are closely tied to community goals because production units in Puyecaco village are composed of a whole range of households that may fall outside residence and kinship groups.

The villagers participate in *Tlakatelilis*, then, with specific purposes in mind. These purposes are concrete, conscious, and not oriented toward creating some vague solidarity or affirmation of abstract principles. However, the people do not expend the time, effort, and other resources on *Tlakatelilis* with the idea of an immediate and equivalent return. The Nahua expect returns from their rituals, but they recognize that rewards do not come directly from deities or spirit entities. Rewards will be expressed in the workings of the natural environment, the elements and processes symbolized by Tonantsi.

The view of the *Tlakatelilis* ceremony presented here has the advantage of enabling the anthropologist to explain why certain people choose to support the ritual actively. It has the additional advantage of allowing the observer to predict ritual participation, should factors enter to change the equilibrium reached between individual actors and the realization of their wants. For example, we can predict that people experiencing difficulties in crop production or childbearing will allocate more resources for the Tonantsi ritual—more than other people, and more than they themselves would offer in a better year. In addition, should village yields decline, owing to soil depletion or other factors, we can predict an overall increase in resource allocations to the *Tlakatelilis* ceremony. Much as the economist can foretell how people will allocate their resources under given market conditions, the anthropologist should be able to predict the extent to which villagers will allocate their resources to ritual transactions.

The approach outlined here has the added advantage of illuminating factors that motivate people who participate in rituals. By recognizing that people everywhere are in a position of having to make strategic allocations of their always limited resources, the anthropologist can gain a greater awareness of the symbolic dynamics that go into holding a ritual. Returning to *Tlakatelilis*, we can now see that the altar or display is above all a seat of transaction. It is here that offerings of food, drink, tobacco, time, and effort are exchanged for the expected cooperation of spirit entities. Communicator action clusters like chanting, rubbing ritual participants, and spreading food offerings on the altar are means of actually carrying out the exchange process. Villagers state that altars such as those set up for *Tlakatelilis* are places of beauty for the spirit entities. This is undoubtedly the immediate and conscious reason for constructing them. However, I believe that the symbolism expressed in altar construction is deeper and can be related also to the transactional nature of rituals. In order to show this, we must first look at Nahua beliefs surrounding the construction and maintenance of a field.

The field is more than just a place where men go to scratch out a living day after day.[18] It is instead a personal creation and a source of considerable pride. Fields are spaces of order and logic cut out of the tangled tropical forest; they are man's imprint on a wild and sometimes dangerous natural environment. Each cultivated plant is watched for insect damage, mounds are formed to protect roots, and weeds are carefully cut away. A well-kept field is an accomplishment that brings prestige to its owner. It is a completely masculine creation, and to a large degree the reputation of a particular man or boy rests on the quality of his fields. The field is more than land: it is land that has been brought into the Nahua social and cultural sphere.

The transformation of land into a field is accomplished through human effort. There is no expectation that spirit entities or good fate will somehow provide for the village. Thus, "work" (*ekihte*) as a concept takes on an almost sacred aspect. It will be recalled that Tonantsi is accompanied on her rounds of the village by images representing "work" and his wife.

Viewed in the context presented here, the field serves as a locus or seat of exchange for the villagers. On the one hand, it is where work is invested to produce sustenance and the necessary productive surplus. On the other, it is where all the symbolized elements and processes central to rituals of increase fulfill their obligations to the community. Thus, the field becomes the locus where those important religious elements—the earth, sun, water, seeds, work, and fertility— interact to generate and sustain Nahua existence. In essence, the altar is where villagers obligate spirit entities and the field is where these same spirit entities satisfy the villagers' expectations of them.

The altar, then, is an analogue to the field. In fact, this is exactly what it is meant to symbolize. Altars are always composed of three basic levels: sky, earth's surface, and earth as an entity. These are signified respectively by the arch, the table surface, and the display on the floor. It is significant that the primary adornment found on top of altar tables is the *se koyoli* palm with marigold blossoms. *Coyol* adornments may signify many things, but the main semantic load they carry is that of growing maize. Marigolds are the *compañeros* of maize, and the green palm leaf is not unlike the maize plant. The central place of maize in village life undoubtedly accounts for its inclusion as part of the altar, but there is also the possibility that, by extension, the *coyol* adornments symbolize all crops.

Offerings of cooked and otherwise processed agricultural products are presented on the table top to the various spirit entities. Floor offerings are directed to the earth, both to enlist its cooperation and so that it will not become annoyed at being "scratched" during planting times. Raw agricultural produce is received during harvest time from the surface of the field, which is the symbolic equivalent of the table top. Just like the altar table, a field lies between the sky realm above and the earthly realm below. Ritual process in the village of Puyecaco, then, is a continuous flow of obligation-inducing offerings that are, for the most part, consistently returned by spirit entities.

At the outset I stated that I believe Tonantsi to be a mother deity. She embodies elements that would seem essential in any definition of a mother deity: her femaleness; her direct association with fertility and reproductivity; the fact that she is viewed by most villagers as an actual mother who takes a direct interest in human affairs; her approachability by ritual means on questions of fecundity; and her unification of experientially heterogenous phenomena through common symbolic association. Only crosscultural comparisons of female deities will allow a more complete and detailed definition of the phenomenon of mother deities.

The method outlined here can help us avoid simplistic formulations. For example, the fact that a deity is female alone does not qualify her as a mother deity. She must also be seen to have additional attributes and certain consequences for the behavior of her followers. This method takes into account multiple factors that influence the strategies of mother worshipers. For example, the ecological, technological, political, and social variables are important in understanding the options open to people and the kinds of experiences they will undergo in pursuing their goals. In addition, by focusing on the motivation of worshipers we can predict behavior, determine symbolic meanings, and gain insights into how rituals change. If technological or economic changes lead people to alter their mode of production, causing symbols to lose relevance, or if ritual innovations, such as a revitalization movement, offer better ways of accomplishing ritual ends, we can assume that people will modify their ritual strategies accordingly.

But it is important that we look at mother deities from the point of view of the two kinds of meaning outlined previously. Mother deities must be seen as part of the dynamic process by which people make sense out of their experiences and through which they act on their own behalf. This process is logically connected to the means by which people strive to meet their own requirements through technological skills and economic allocation of their social and material resources. By understanding the meaning that mother deities hold for people and by examining the situations and experiences from which such meaning derives we will be in a position to delineate the process that continuously generates and supports beliefs and practices surrounding mother deities.

## Notes

1. The ethnographic data that forms the basis of this paper was gathered during two field trips to Mexico covering a total of over fourteen months. The first trip lasted two months in the summer of 1970, and the second extended over twelve months in 1972–73. Research was carried out with the help of the Latin American Studies Program of Indiana University and the Instituto de Antropologiá in Jalapa, Veracruz, Mexico.

2. For a general description of indigenous Mexican communities see Sandstrom, "Realm of the Sacred"; Provost, "Culture and Anti-Culture"; and Redfield and Tax, "Mesoamerican Indian Society."

3. Sometimes written Tonantzin in other dialects of Nahuatl.

4. See the article by Campbell in this collection. Also see Wolf, "The Virgin of Guadalupe."

5. For theoretical treatments of similar problems see Madsen, *The Virgin's Children*; Wolf, "The Virgin of Guadalupe"; Marriott, *Little Communities*; Singer, *Great Tradition of Hinduism*; Redfield, *The Primitive World* and *The Little Community*.

6. See Schneider, *Economic Man*.

7. As Murphy states it, "Everyman is an anthropologist or sociologist of sorts, equipped with certain bodies of knowledge about established customs, fixed expectations regarding persons and situations and an operating notion of what his society is like" (*Social Life*, p. 6).

8. Geertz, "Religion as a Cultural System," p. 13.

9. Ibid., p. 15.

10. See ibid.

11. Ibid., p. 5.

12. Geertz, *The Interpretation of Cultures*, pp. 90, 108.

13. See Sandstrom, "Realm of the Sacred."

14. For a commercially available recording of the music played during this ritual see Sandstrom and Provost's "Music of the Modern Aztecs."

15. For a complete description of cleansing procedures see Sandstrom, "Realm of the Sacred."

16. Turner, *The Forest of Symbols*, p. 50.

17. Ortner, "On Key Symbols," p. 1340.

18. Sandstrom, "Religion in a Nahua Community."

# Bibliography

Geertz, Clifford. *The Interpretation of Cultures*. New York: Basic Books, 1973.
————. "Religion as a Cultural System." In *Anthropological Approaches to the Study of Religion*, edited by M. Banton, pp. 1–46. London: Tavistock Publications, 1966.
Madsen, William. *The Virgin's Children: Life in an Aztec Village Today*. Austin: University of Texas Press, 1960.
Marriott, McKim. "Little Communities in an Indigenous Civilization." In *Anthropology of Folk Religion*, edited by Charles Leslie, pp. 169–218. New York: Random House, Vintage, 1958.
Murphy, Robert. *The Dialectics of Social Life*. New York: Basic Books, 1971.
Ortner, Sherry B. "On Key Symbols." *American Anthropologist* 75 (1973): 1338–46.
Provost, Paul J. "Culture and Anti-Culture among the Eastern Nahua of Northern Veracruz, Mexico." Ph.D. dissertation, Indiana University, 1975.
Redfield, Robert. *The Little Community: Peasant Society and Culture*. Chicago: University of Chicago Press, 1960.
————. *The Primitive World and Its Transformations*. Ithaca, N.Y.: Cornell University Press, 1953.
————, and Tax, Sol. "General Characteristics of Present-Day Mesoamerican Indian Society." In *Heritage of Conquest*, edited by Sol Tax, pp. 31–39. New York: Cooper Square, 1968.
Sandstrom, Alan R. "Ecology, Economy and the Realm of the Sacred: An Interpretation of Ritual in a Nahua Community of the Southern Huasteca, Mexico." Ph.D. dissertation, Indiana University, 1975.
————. "Economy, Ecology, and Religion in a Nahua Community: Some Preliminary Considerations." MS. Instituto de Antropologia, Jalapa, Veracruz, 1970.
————, and Provost, Paul J. "Sacred Guitar and Violin Music of the Modern Aztecs." Ethnic Folkways Records, FE 4358.
Schneider, Harold K. *Economic Man*. New York: Free Press, 1974.
Singer, Milton. "The Great Tradition of Hinduism in the City of Madras." In *Anthropology of Folk Religion*, edited by Charles Leslie, pp. 105–66. New York: Random House, Vintage, 1958.
Turner, Victor. *The Forest of Symbols*. Ithaca, N.Y.: Cornell University Press, 1967.
Wolf, Eric. "The Virgin of Guadalupe: A Mexican National Symbol." In *Reader in Comparative Religion*, edited by William Lessa and Evon Vogt, pp. 226–30. New York: Harper and Row, 1958.

# TWO

The European
Madonna Complex

# 3

## In Quest of the Black Virgin:
## She Is Black Because She Is Black
### by Leonard W. Moss and
### Stephen C. Cappannari

In 1944 the senior author (Leonard Moss) wandered into a church in the south Italian town of Lucera. In a niche adjacent to the altar his gaze fell upon a representation of the Virgin Mary. He stood transfixed as he realized the face and hands of the statue were black. He asked the priest, "Father, why is the Madonna black?" The good father's response was, "My son, she is black because she is black." Though this answer might have satisfied the priest's parishioners, it served to tantalize the young soldier. He went off in quest of black madonnas and still searches for the answer some thirty years later.[1]

Is it possible that the Virgin Mary was indeed black? If by "black" one means negroid, it is doubtful at best. According to New Testament sources, Mary was of the line of Aaron, thus a Semite.[2] Perhaps, like contemporary eastern Mediterranean types, she was dark of visage. Early Christian sources noted the passage in the Song of Songs: "I am black but comely, O ye daughters of Jerusalem, As the tents of Kedar, As the curtains of Solomon. Look not upon me that I am swarthy, That the sun hath tanned me."[3] Mrs. Jameson remarks: "Because some of the Greek pictures and carved images have become black through extreme age, it was argued by certain devout writers that the Virgin herself must have been of very dark complexion; and in favor of this idea, they quoted from the canticles, 'I am Black, but comely . . .' But others say her complexion became black only through her sojourn in Egypt. At all events, though the blackness of these antique images was supposed to enhance their sanctity, it has never been imitated in the fine arts. . . ."4

An examination of the literature will reveal a plethora of interpretations regarding the Song of Songs. There have been many theological controversies waged on the passages of this book. Both Jewish rabbinical synods and Christian scholars have attached a mystical interpretation, treating the Song as an allegory of God and his people (Christ and his church).

> *Song of Songs*
>
> Male voice:    Your lips are like a scarlet thread and your mouth is lovely.
>
>                       Your cheeks are like halves of pomegranate. [4:3]
>
> Male voice:    You are stately like a palm tree
> and your breasts are like its clusters.
> I say I will climb the palm tree and
> lay hold of its branches.
> Oh may your breasts be like clusters of the vine
> and the scent of your mouth like apples. [7:7]
>
> Female voice:    I am my beloved's and my beloved is mine.
> Come my beloved, let us go forth into the fields.
> . . . let us go early to the vineyards and
> see whether the vines have budded . . . the grape
> blossoms have opened . . . the pomegranates in
> bloom. . . .
> There I shall give you my love. [7:10]

What a relationship! It is on the basis of this mystical view that the Song has been included in the Jewish Passover liturgy and in the various versions of the Holy Scriptures.

In the third century, one of the church fathers, Origen, described the Song as a nuptial poem sung at the marriage of Solomon and the daughter of an Egyptian pharoah. Ample evidence has been amassed to discard this hypothesis. More recent interpretations hold that the story is a collection of rustic folksongs used in wedding festivities in the northern Holy Land. Certainly, the erotic passages seem to bear evidence for this argument.

The authorship of the Song is commonly credited to Solomon. However, serious objection to this claim has been raised by many students of the Bible. The style and language of the passages are those of an age much more recent than the time of Solomon, who died circa 931 B.C. Evidence of Greek cultural diffusion is present in the Hebrew text. It is likely that the Song, incorporating older elements, was compiled in written form some six hundred years after the time of Solomon.

Hebrew scholars describe the story as one concerning the trials of a Shulamite maiden who was in love with a shepherd. Her brothers, disapproving of the union, put her to work tending the vineyards, where she was blackened by the sun. Courtiers of Solomon chanced to pass the vineyards and were impressed by the rare beauty of the Shulamite. They attempted to persuade her to accompany them to Solomon's court. After her refusal, they led her away as a captive. Solomon tried to win her love and sang of her beauty. But the maiden remained true to her shepherd lover.[5]

*Nigra sum sed formosa*, which means "I am black but beautiful," may go a long way in fighting racism, but it tells us little about the color of the Virgin Mary.

By 1952 I (Leonard Moss) had collected nearly one hundred samples of black madonnas in various parts of the world. Many swarthy Byzantine madonnas are to be found in Eastern Orthodox churches. I drew this collection to the attention of a colleague, Stephen C. Cappannari, and together we began to ponder the mysteries of the blackness. After some months of cogitation we assembled what seemed to be a reasonable hypothesis and wrote a paper for oral presentation to the American Association for the Advancement of Science (December 28, 1952, St. Louis). Apparently our discussion touched the raw nerves of some rather religious members of the audience, for every priest and nun walked out. Other reactions were less hostile, and we were urged to submit a somewhat lengthier version of our thesis for publication.[6] Upon its publication, a picture of a black madonna graced the cover of the *Scientific Monthly*.

We were confused by the hostile reaction of the religious members of our original audience. The confusion was clarified immediately after publication: the chaplain of the Newman Club at Wayne State University gave a sermon in which he fulminated against the campus atheists who would defile the name of the Blessed Virgin. Let us examine the central argument of our original thesis.

Our analysis of the black representations of the Virgin Mary led us to create a three-fold classification of types. First, there are the dark brown or black madonnas with physiognomy and skin pigmentation matching that of the indigenous population. In this class we include such madonnas as Nuestra Señora de Guadalupe in Mexico City,[7] the Virgin of Costa Rica, and the various negroid madonnas found in

Africa. Though it is unlikely that the Roman Catholic church has ever given official approbation to these madonnas, they are tolerated probably as one way of bringing the religion closer to the local populations. The anthropological concept of anthropomorphism contains the truism that man creates representations of gods in his own image.

Second, there are various art forms that have turned black as a result of certain physical factors. The change in color may have been brought about by (1) deterioration of lead-based pigments (some of these madonnas have been repainted in lighter flesh tones only to turn dark again); (2) accumulated smoke from the use of votive candles in areas adjacent to the statues or paintings; (3) smoke damage from a fire in the church; (4) oxidation of the silver used in the construction of the image; or (5) other physical factors such as the accumulation of grime over the ages.

Third comes our residual category for which there is no ready explanation. These madonnas are black and are renowned as miracle workers.[8] It is this class of European madonnas that is investigated here. The hypothesis that there has been an attempt to anthropomorphize the Virgin is not tenable, because the natives of these regions are Caucasoid. The various physical explanations cited in our second group do not seem applicable to this category; with the various madonnas under question we find (1) that there is no evidence for physical deterioration of the pigment (no smoke damage, no oxidization, and so on), or (2) that where there is evidence of such physical change, the madonna has been repainted *black*. Such madonnas are to be found in diverse locations within Europe: France, Germany, Italy, Poland, Spain, and Switzerland. Most of them appear to have been made black originally.

It is difficult to rule out artistic license. Perhaps, in a burst of creativity, the artist simply chose to represent the Virgin in a black medium. It is impossible to reason from the artifact to the thoughts that lingered in the mind of the creator. It is, however, highly unlikely that the church would grant the artist the right to depict the madonna in any way that whim and caprice might ordain. Unless we have other evidence to suggest liberties taken by the artist, we must rule against this explanation for our third category.

Within this category, we felt it necessary to eliminate two representations of the Virgin from further consideration in the development of a hypothesis. One case is that of Our Lady of Altötting (*Schwarzen Mutter-Gottes*), the most effective miracle-working image in Bavaria. Local legend holds that the Black Mother of God was preserved from smoke damage despite the ravaging of the church by flame in the year A.D. 907. The face, hands, and feet of this statue allegedly turned black "with age" at a later date. This explanation is deficient in that it fails to explain why the rest of the statue did not undergo similar deterioration. Moreover, according to the art historian George Lechler, who was familiar with the icon, the art form is that of the seventeenth century. He believed it to be a copy of an earlier form.[9] The statue is highly revered and is surrounded with many *ex voti* (gifts) attesting to the graces given.

Case two is the madonna at Czestochowa, Poland. The Virgin of Jasna Gora (*Matka Boska*) was declared "Queen of Poland" by King John Casimir in A.D. 1656. According to legend this most famous of Polish madonnas is attributed to Saint Luke, who painted a portrait of the Virgin on the cedar wood table at which she had taken her meals. However, the figure is distinctly thirteenth- to fourteenth-century Byzantine in form, and the skin pigmentation is characteristic of this stylized portraiture. According to the art historian Ernst Scheyer, who studied this madonna at the behest of the Polish government, the present image was restored in the nineteenth century and painted somewhat darker than previously.[10]

How the image came to Czestochowa is debatable. One legend maintains that Saint Helen, mother of Constantine, brought the painting from Jerusalem to Constantinople. Local legend describes the miraculous appearance of the portrait borne on the wings of angels. For those who would rather explore the alternative possibility of human agents of diffusion, it may be noted parenthetically that a non-divine queen of Poland circa A.D. 1515 was Bona Sforza of Bari, Italy. Bari was and remains the major seaport linking Italy with the Levant. This area abounds with black madonnas, some of which are Byzantine in origin.

Also debatable is the origin of the scars on the face of this portrait. One legend holds that they were inflicted by a Swedish saber when the Queen of Peace was carried in battle by Polish troops. Another explanation maintains that the picture was slashed in a moment of rage by a Hussite invader.

Strange to relate, a much darker portrait of the Virgin of Jasna Gora is to be found in the Hospice of the Great St. Bernard Pass in Switzerland. When this product of the Polish artist Kosmoski was installed in 1956 an estimated 1,500,000 pilgrims came to the shrine in Poland and

960 masses were celebrated. Even in Doylestown, Pennsylvania, a shrine of Our Lady of Czestochowa is maintained by the Pauline Fathers. There she is depicted in lighter flesh tones.

Having discarded the Altötting and Czestochowa madonnas from our residual category, we were faced with some thirty images which were black miracle workers and for which we had no explanation. Having plotted these on a map of Europe, we noted that all of our madonnas are to be found in regions once occupied by the legions of imperial Rome. Let us note some of the history and legends associated with these images.

The statue of Our Lady of Montserrat, Spain, was supposedly carved by Saint Luke in Jerusalem; hence the name la Jerosolimitana. Legend holds that it was brought to Barcelona by none other than Saint Peter. The holy image was removed from Barcelona during the Moorish invasion of Catalonia in A.D. 718. It was rediscovered in A.D. 880 hidden in a cave near Montserrat. Earliest archival notations indicate that the image has been black at least since A.D. 718.

Our Lady of the Hermits at Einsiedeln, Switzerland, exhibits a history that may be traced as far back as A.D. 835. Saint Meinrad built a chapel to the Virgin that year. Local tradition, however, alleges that the statue was brought there by Crusaders returning from the Middle East. The statue does not appear to be Byzantine in origin, nor does it give evidence of being a ninth-century German or Helvetian art form.

The Black Virgin at Chartres, France, dates back to the fourth century. Early Christian travelers to that area found an altar presumably made by the Druids upon which was seated a woman holding the figure of a child within her arms. This pagan image was black in color. The cathedral, founded in the fourth century, was dedicated to the Virgin and Child. Although the present statue of the Notre Dame du Pilier at Chartres is depicted as black, it is of more recent origin (sixteenth century). Equally famous is the Black Virgin of Le Puy. According to one authority, Emile Saillens, a favorite name given to girls in this region of France is Mélanie. After the original publication of our paper we became acquainted with the little-known work by Saillens on the black madonnas of France. Unfortunately, his volume went to press just in time for the publishing house to be destroyed in a U.S. bombardment during World War II. A limited number of copies of this scholarly work were preserved.[11]

The sanctuary of the Madonna Nera of Tindari, Sicily, occupies the site of a fifteenth-century church built on the ruins of a temple to Cybele that was mentioned in the writings of Strabo and Pliny. (Re-

1. Our Lady of the Hermits, Einsiedeln, Switzerland.
*(Photograph by Leonard W. Moss)*

2. Madonna of the Hermits in full regalia.
*(Photograph by Leonard W. Moss)*

cent excavations have unearthed portions of the earlier Greek complex of temples.) Greek influence in Tindari dates to the founding of the city by the elder Dionysius in 395 B.C.; the colony was established by Peloponnesian exiles driven from their homeland by Spartans. The black Virgin at Tindari is one of the two most revered Sicilian images of the madonna.

Enna, in central Sicily, was known as Castrogiovanni until 1926. (In still earlier times it was given the Arabic appellation Kasr-Yanni.) It was the ancient Castrum Ennae (Fortress Ennae). Founded circa 664 B.C. by the Syracusans, the town was considered a choice prize by the many invaders of Sicily. The mountain upon which the town is situated was the principal seat of worship for Ceres in Roman times and Demeter during the earlier Hellenistic period. A temple to two goddesses, Ceres and Proserpina, built at the summit of the mountain, was the object of pagan pilgrimages before the introduction of Christianity to the central hinterland in the eleventh century. The present church, Madonna della Visitazione, built by Queen Elenora in 1307, incorporates in its south wall a pillar of the old temple of Ceres. The present statue of the madonna adorning the church is of mid-nineteenth-century origin. The image of the Virgin here is not black.

Ancient Enna was sacred to both Ceres and her daughter Proserpina. It was at the shores of the Lake of Enna that the abduction of Ceres' daughter by Pluto took place. According to the earlier Greek mythology, Persephone (Proserpina) was called Savior, having gone through death and resurrection. It is at Enna in Sicily that one finds the most interesting adaptation of pagan symbolism by the Roman Catholic church: until the mid-nineteenth century, the images of Ceres and Proserpina were used in the church as the Virgin and Infant Jesus, despite the fact that *Proserpina was female!*[12] A papal order by Pius IX removed the pagan statues to an adjacent museum that is, somehow, never open to public viewing.

W. A. Paton says this about the ritual connected with the Enna madonna:

> On the day of the fete of the "Madonna of All the Graces"
> her worshippers place before her statue large sheaves of grain and
> bunches of wild flowers, and form processions in her honor,
> composed of men in long white tunics, who carry flowers in their
> hands, make offerings of grain and other products of the soil before
> the altar in the churches. . . . it seems most reasonable to believe
> that many of the old pagan rites have been preserved in their

essential forms in the Christian ceremonies of today. . . . it is safe
to assume that Christian priests have added little to that ritual [of
Demeter], have taken little from it, and today religious ceremonies
practised by the farming communities of Sicily are essentially the
same as they were twenty-five centuries ago, with the exception
that Christian saints have usurped the honors and dignities
of pagan deities.[13]

The history of the region of Apulia in southeastern Italy shows
frequent and prolonged culture contact with the various groups that
have occupied the Mediterranean in general and south Italy in particular. On this basis we looked for indications of diffusion. Legend
maintains that around 975 B.C., Diomedes, king of Etolia (a section of
ancient Greece), landed at Rodi and journeyed to the temple of the
goddess Minerva at Lucera. There he remained, established a kingdom, married the daughter of the king of Daunia, and built a temple
to Ceres (goddess of grain). Diomedes also built temples to Calcas
(also known as Calcante—god of prophecy) and Podalirius (god of
medicine) at Castel Drione, site of the present-day San Severo.[14]

This region of southeast Italy was occupied by two indigenous
Italic tribes, the Pencezi and Messapi. To the north were the Sanniti.
According to local legend, this area was first visited by the Phoeni-
cians as early as the tenth century B.C. Phoenician temples to Ma or
Ammar were utilized by the Greeks, who rededicated these same
temples to the Cretan goddess Rhea or Cybele. Cybele, the mother
goddess, gives birth to Demeter, the Greek goddess of grain, fertility,
and earth. It is pertinent to our thesis that there are actually two
Demeters: one is the sorrowful Eleusinian mother; the second and
more powerful is Demeter Melaina, or the Black Demeter, associated
with the fertility of black earth.

The Greeks built temples to Demeter in and around the area of
Foggia. Lucera existed as a city-state independent of Rome until 400
B.C.; then it allied itself with Rome; and later (319 B.C.) it became a
colony of the republic. It was during this period that the cult of
the Egyptian goddess Isis was introduced into the area by seagoing
natives of Puglia. Isis is of the earth and is likewise depicted as black.

Parenthetically, we should note the death-resurrection theme associated with Isis-Horus-Osiris. Jung observed that this Egyptian triad
is an anticipation of the Christian Virgin-Jesus complex.[15] Herodotus
suggested the connection between the Egyptian goddess Isis and
the Greek Demeter Melaina. Although the Romans never explicitly

acknowledged the connection, it seems evident that Ceres is an adaptation of Demeter. At this point it should be stressed that the Roman Ceres is likewise depicted as black and, through Proserpina, is associated with death and resurrection.

It is said that Saint Peter on his way to Rome in A.D. 42 installed Basso as bishop of Lucera. Saint Basso reputedly built a church to the Virgin Mary on the precise spot occupied by the Roman temple to Ceres. The church was dedicated to the Madonna della Spiga (literally, sheaf of wheat, and later, ear of corn). Historic evidence is not clear about whether the church can be traced to Basso or the more recent Saint Padro (208–50). After the fall of Rome the region of Apulia was subject to many powers that invaded and occupied the south. Frederick II invited the Moslems to his royal court at Lucera in 1225 and built a mosque for them on the site of the Madonna della Spiga shrine. After the death of Frederick II and the defeat of his bastard son Manfred, the succeeding Anjou dynasty forced the Moslems out of Lucera and rebuilt the mosque into the present-day cathedral of San Francesco. The statue of the Virgin was reinstalled in 1300.

Santa Maria, patron of Lucera, is credited with the liberation of the city from the Moslems by Charles II. A second major miracle attributed to this representation of the Virgin is the end of an epidemic of cholera on July 13, 1837. The statue was reported to have miraculously moved its eyes on that date and for two consecutive days thereafter, bringing an end to the epidemic that had ravaged the city. If veneration (*dulia*) and adoration (*hyperdulia*) are accorded saints and the Virgin Mary, then the only word for the degree of reverence given to this image is that of worship (*latria*). The madonna is worshiped for her power rather than for the grace normally associated with the Virgin. The statue of Santa Maria is showered with wheat, corn, and other sacrificial offerings on feast days, particularly on those which coincide with the planting and harvesting seasons. The Virgin is accorded powers relating to fertility: human, animal, and vegetal.

Elsewhere in southern Italy one finds other examples of black madonnas. The present-day church of Santa Maria di Siponto occupies the site of the ancient city of Sipontom. This city was abandoned because of threatening floods in A.D. 1256. The inhabitants moved to Manfredonia, three kilometers to the east. Records indicate that the present church was constructed prior to A.D. 1117. Before its reconstruction by Julius III in 1508, there are indications that the Moslems had used the building as a mosque. The lower level of this church contains the tomb of Aemilius Tullius (A.D. 593) and the miracle-working madonna. Renowned for powers of fertility, this icon is said to be Byzantine in origin.[16]

Farther to the west, near the site of the ancient Abellinum, is Monte Vergine. At the summit of this mountain was the temple to Ceres in which the high priest Atys held sway as the Sibylline oracle. The mountain was known as *l'orto di Virgilio* ("Garden of Virgilius"); Virgilius was a great necromancer and compounder of herbal drugs. Christianity was late in coming to this stronghold of pagan belief. In A.D. 1119, William of Vercelli dedicated the mountain to the Virgin Mary and founded a Benedictine abbey on the site of the temple to Ceres. Swinburne, the English author and traveler, acknowledged the tribulations involved in establishing Christianity in this part of southwest Italy:

> The missionaries sent among them to preach the faith of Christ found no means of conversion so easy and efficacious as those of admitting some of the names and ceremonies of the old church into the ritual of the new one. By thus adopting many tenets and forms of Paganism, they reconciled their proselytes to the idea of exchanging Jupiter for Jehovah, and their *laris* [tutelary deities] and *penates* [household deities] for saints and guardian angels. To this expedient of priestcraft must be ascribed many strange devotions and local superstitions, still prevalent in Roman Catholic countries, which ought not be confounded by the adversaries of that church with its real doctrine. All the truly learned and sensible persons of that communion reject, abhor and lament such depravations; and, were it possible to reason rude minds out of hereditary prejudices, would since have abolished them.[17]

La Madonna di Constantinopoli is enshrined in a church that contains four standing columns of *porta santa* marble that were part of the original temple to Ceres. This portrait of the Virgin is in two parts. The bust, carved of brown wood, is the work of Montano d'Arezzo and was completed about A.D. 1340. The head was brought from Constantinople by Catherine, wife of Philip d'Anjou, the titular emperor of that city. Legend holds that this painted head was the work of Saint Luke in Antioch.[18] Swinburne takes issue with the legendary origin of the head: "This image is of gigantic or heroic proportion, and passes for the work of St. Luke the Evangelist, though the very size is an argument against its being a portrait from the life, had we even the slightest reason to believe he ever handled the pencil. There are in Italy and elsewhere some dozens of black, ugly Madonnas, which all pass for the work of his hands, and as such are revered."[19]

Other black madonna statues and paintings attributed to Saint Luke are found in Bari, Custonaci, Loreto, Messina, and Rome in Italy; Brno, Czechoslovakia; and Tenos, Greece. Swinburne explains that there was a painter in Constantinople called "Holy Luke" because of his piety and exemplary life, devoted to painting representations of the Virgin in the manner of the Byzantine style. His work was later attributed to Saint Luke, because no one knew of another saint or painter by that name. Swinburne casts doubt on the idea that Saint Luke was ever an artist.

Catholic sources, for the most part, have denied the possible connection between the black madonnas and earlier earth goddesses. Nevertheless, Saint Augustine noted that the Virgin Mary represents the earth and that Jesus is of the earth born. Archbishop Hamilton in his Scot's Cathechism (1552) stated, "[these statues] darkened into something not far from idolatry . . . when . . . one image of the Virgin [generally a black or ugly one] was regarded as more powerful for the help of suppliants. . . . "

At this point our hypothesis begins to emerge: the black madonnas are Christian borrowings from earlier pagan art forms that depicted Ceres, Demeter Melaina, Diana, Isis, Cybele, Artemis, or Rhea as black, the color characteristic of goddesses of the earth's fertility. Along this line, in 1335, a prior at the Chalis Monastery in France, Guillaume de Deguilleville, noted that Mary represents the earth, which is the body and darkness. Hence, Mary, being of the earth, can rightfully act as celestial attorney for all earthly sinners.[20]

Authorities on medieval art forms have demonstrated the influence of classical mythology on the paintings of the Middle Ages. It is entirely possible that some medieval painters borrowed from classical themes, dropped the original forms, and related them to the Virgin Mary.[21] However, in our quest we are concerned with some images that seemingly predate this period of the Middle Ages. We are probably dealing with more direct forms of culture borrowing, possibly owing to direct culture contact.

We will reiterate that all the black madonnas are *powerful* images; they are miracle workers (although not all miracle-working images are black). They are implored for intercession in the various problems of fertility. Pilgrimages covering hundreds of kilometers are made to these specific shrines. The degree of adorational fervor far exceeds

3. Diana of Ephesus is an outstanding example of an earth mother deity, portrayed here with multiple breasts.
*(Photograph by Leonard W. Moss)*

that attached to other representations of the Virgin. For example, until the last decade, when the practice was explicitly forbidden by church authorities, pilgrims journeying to the shrine at Mount Vergine would climb the steps of the church on their knees, licking each step with their tongues. We are, thus, equating the blackness of the images with their power. The attitude of the pilgrim approaches not reverence but worship (*latria*).

Students of mythology have long noted that "black" could be regarded as a quality of the earth. Jungian and other schools of psychology have equated black with the fertility of the earth, the power of death, and a fear of darkness.[22] Although we do not claim that any such necessary and inherent relationships would obtain in all cultures, this association clearly holds true for the European cultures involved in our thesis.

Prolonged close culture contact between groups in a relatively restricted geographical area invariably results in an exchange of culture elements. Over long periods of time, continuing contacts between two diverse cultures will bring forth a fusion of elements in a new pattern that is a melding of both forms (syncretism). This mode of culture change is called diffusion, that is, achieved cultural transmission.[23]

Cultural change is a dynamic process by definition. Acculturation involves an ongoing transmission of cultural elements, not all of which are readily verbalized or transmitted. The physical or outward form of the element is more easily transmissible than the symbolic or representational meanings. For instance, the borrowing group may adopt the form and adapt the group's own meanings to it. Reinterpretation of borrowed elements occurs in all realms of culture, including religion. Adherents of a faith believe that borrowed (syncretized) culture elements are part of the original belief system.

Anthropology is replete with examples of syncretism and reinterpretation in the general process of acculturation. The development of Hinduism is a classic case of syncretism. Equally illustrative and analogous to our topic is the almost endless and intricate modification of the various Egyptian deities in the early dynastic periods. For example, when the capital of Egypt was moved to the city of Thebes, Amon, the local sun god, merged with Ra, the national sun god, to become Amon-Ra.[24]

The cultural changes in any society are always influenced by its preexisting customs and institutions. This is not to say that displacements never occur, or that innovations never obliterate older patterns of behavior. For the most part, however, man is not easily detached from the patterned customs and beliefs he has fashioned for himself. The adoption of new beliefs is facilitated when they can be equated in some fashion with older, more compatible experiences.

For thousands of years, diverse cultures have coexisted in the Mediterranean basin. Prolonged contact through trade, invasions, occupations, and colonizations led to a melding of innumerable cultural elements. Religious ideas were constantly interchanged and reinterpreted. It is fruitless to attempt to seek origins in such a mélange.

In his analysis of the black madonnas of France, Saillens noted:

> The worship of Mother Earth has been universal. She is the night from which arise all living things and into which they vanish. Hence the innumerable black goddesses. . . .
>
> Another, whose power was challenged by St. Paul, was Artemis of Ephesus. Six hundred years before . . . an image of this Artemis had landed at Marseilles with some tin importers from Phocea. The Ephesian Artemis was the patroness and oracle of those particular Greeks. Before embarking on their distant venture, they had consulted her. She had not only approved them but sent with them a replica of her image, with a priestess, Aristarke, to serve the new image. Therefore, the Black Artemis accompanied the Greeks in Gaul wherever they drove their caravans or founded colonies.
>
> In Roman Gaul, Isis came to be worshipped in a few places and Cybele practically everywhere.
>
> The Church at first banned all images, but she had to submit to popular wishes and traditions.
>
> When Christian images were at last allowed, some very ancient images, sometimes uncouth, were miraculously discovered in unfrequented spots (woods, caves, etc.) where the pagan peasantry had hidden them. The clergy blessed these images under Christian names and often built temples for them just where they had been found. According to the local legends, the images refused to stay put in the parish church. In fact, the clergy regarded them with suspicion. Pilgrimages began, distinct from regular worship at the orthodox church. The most famous of these images were black.
>
> Now, if the French Black Madonnas were former Cybeles, we ought to find them scattered more or less evenly all over France, since Cybele was worshipped by all Gaul. But such is not the case. Their distribution points to a Greek origin. They are found along the "tin portage" Boulogne-Marseilles, in Gallo-Greek

emporia and on mining sites. It appears therefore that Christianity easily uprooted Cybele, hardly older than Gaul itself, while the Black Artemis, implanted six hundred years earlier, held its ground and kept sprouting.

Our Black Madonnas have always been the subject of exceptionally deep devotion. On several occasions, they have played their part in French history. For instance, in 1429, the year of decision when Joan of Arc, against her father's wishes, rode to Chinon and spoke to the King, her mother, Isabelle, walked from Lorraine to Le Puy, to pray to the *Vierge Noire*. Le Puy stood on one of the routes of the tin trade.[25]

Evidence similar to that amassed by Saillens does not appear to be readily available for the Italian madonnas. Indeed, we doubt that a clear line of borrowing could be readily established in the case of Roman or early Christian Italy. Roman hostility to foreign religions was a consistent element even during the Republic. In 205–204 B.C., the *Magna Mater* ("Great Mother") of Pessinus was brought to Rome from Africa. Following the Sibylline ordinance, it was believed that this statue would force Hannibal to leave Italy. The black stone representing the goddess was solemnly received by Scipio and the noblest women of the state and deposited in the Temple of Victory. It may be that the Roman officials were unaware at the time of the orgiastic worship of the mutilated priests, but they soon came to know it, and a *senatus consultum* (order of the senate) forbade any Roman citizen to take part in it. But the example of wild emotion had been given.[26]

The Romans carefully distinguished between the official religion of the state and the living religions of man. In his discussion of an Italian religious folk feast, Tentori notes:

> From the repression of the Bacchanals to the persecution of the Christians, the Roman state consistently adhered to a policy of rejecting all religious innovations, which it regarded as sociocultural phenomena potentially capable of undermining its own established structures. Christianity appeared as *the* religion of man par excellence. Where Roman paganism projected its power and protective services beyond the individual to the benefit of the *familia*, the *gens*, and the *res publica*, the new religion of Christ offered its scheme of salvation to *every* man, proposing the vision of the *Civitas Dei* as the final and supreme goal.[27]

Expanding trade relations of the Roman Republic and the later territorial expansion of the empire brought in its wake a corresponding increase of new religious ideas. Tentori furthers his discussion by noting:

> In 139 B.C. the Jews and the Chaldeans were expelled from Rome. The Egyptian mystery cults were banned in the last decades of the republic. Augustus reconfirmed these measures, and he was seconded by Agrippa. Tiberius subjected the same cults to a violent persecution, which was subsequently extended to the Jews. Claudius later banished the Jews and quelled the tumults inspired by a certain Cresto, which is the earliest evidence we have of the presence of Christians at Rome.[28]

Though scholars continue to debate the reasons for the Fall of Rome, it is clear that imperial overexpansion was one major factor. The political problems of the third century gave rise to administrative restructuring of the late empire. As the borders of the empire became more far flung, political, ethnic, and social uncertainty became a way of life. The old order, particularly the official religion of the state and the rise of the emperor cults, was constantly being challenged by new ideas. A power vacuum was created on the mainland of Europe when the capital was transferred to Constantinople. In this chaotic period, Christianity openly challenged the established order.

Religious innovations from the East proved popular with many strata of the Roman population. Mithraism had a great impact on certain segments, particularly the Roman army. Whole legions adopted this faith as their official religion. Mithraism, in a real sense, was a self-defeating movement—only males could be converted. During the period of Nero, Judaism proved to be fashionable for ladies of the upper class. Some few males were recruited to the Mosaic faith. Flavius Clemens, cousin of the emperor Vespasian, was condemned for drifting into atheism. (Jewish ways were regarded as atheism, because the Jews worshiped an unnamed and unseen god.) His wife, Flavia Domitilla, niece of the emperor Domitian, was sent into exile because of her conversion. Though its popularity waxed and waned among women, Judaism made little impact on Roman men. The ritual of circumcision appeared to be too taxing a tribute to pay to Jehovah. Christianity imposed no such burden; through Christ, male converts could be circumcised in their hearts.

Christianity, with its promise of eternal life and personal salvation, was a formidable opponent to the existing religions, official or foreign.

The early missionary bishops were apparently good applied anthropologists. The letters of Saint Paul attest to his ability to be all things to all men. Long before there was a discipline of anthropology, these proselytizers realized that new ideas are more readily accepted if they can be made more compatible with the existing culture. Whyte noted:

> In the year 601 A.D., Pope Gregory I (Gregory the Great) wrote as follows to his priests . . . who were attempting to convert the heathen Britons—and were not making much progress:
> "We must refrain from destroying the temples of the idols. It is necessary only to destroy the idols, and to sprinkle holy water in these same temples, to build ourselves altars and place holy relics therein. If the construction of these temples is solid, good, and useful, they will pass from the cult of demons to the service of the true God; because it will come to pass that the nation, seeing the continued existence of its old places of devotion, will be disposed, by a sort of habit, to go there to adore the true God.
> "It is said that the men of this nation are accustomed to sacrificing oxen. It is necessary that this custom be converted into a Christian rite. On the day of the dedication of the temples thus changed into churches, and similarly for the festivals of the saints, whose relics will be placed there, you should allow them, as in the past, to build structures of foliage around these same churches. They shall bring to the churches their animals, and kill them, no longer as offerings to the devil, but for Christian banquets in name and honor of God, to whom, after satiating themselves, they will give thanks. Only thus, by preserving for men some of the worldly joys, will you lead them more easily to relish the joys of the spirit."[29]

Christianity thus became dominant over the existing faiths of the empire. It is in this light that we offer our hypothesis that the black madonnas exemplify a reinterpretation of pagan customs, that they have functioned as aids in the preservation of continuity in the transition from pagan beliefs to Roman Catholicism.

As Tentori notes, the dualism and conflict between the official religion and the living religions of the people continues to the present day.[30] Perhaps it is as Levi worded it: *Christ Stopped at Eboli*.[31] The institutional church never penetrated the hinterland. There, paganism remains the way of life.

## Notes

1. The senior author dedicates this essay to the memory of Stephen C. Cappannari. His death, in 1974, ended our twenty-two year relationship as friends, colleagues, and coresearchers. I am forever indebted to him for inducting me into the discipline of anthropology. I wish to acknowledge the many helpful ideas exchanged in our correspondence with Emile Saillens, whose work on the black madonnas of France was nearly a casualty of World War II. Finally, my thanks to Alfred Vagts for his many contributions in our quest of the black madonna. One of his recent findings must be shared with the reader. This statement was gleaned from Arnold Kunzli's biographical profile of Karl Marx and casts a whole new dimension for exploration:

> Karl Marx [wrote] to his wife, Jenny, [from] Manchester, in 1856, where he was visiting with Engels: "Bad as your portrait is, it serves me to the best purposes, and now I understand how even the 'black Madonnas', the most offensive of the portraits of the divine mother, could find indestructible veneration, and even more venerators than did the good portraits. At any rate, none of these black Madonna images has ever been more kissed, more ogled at and more adored than your photograph, even though it is not black, is sour and by no means reflects your dear, sweet, kissable, *dolce* face." [Vagts, Personal communication, 1975]

2. Luke 1:5, 36.
3. *Holy Scriptures*, p. 2.
4. Jameson, *Legends of the Madonna*, p. 63.
5. Lehrman, Introduction, pp. x–xiii, 1–32.
6. Moss and Cappannari, "The Black Madonna," pp. 319–24.
7. Wolf, "The Virgin of Guadalupe," pp. 34–39.
8. This category represents approximately 35% of our original sample.
9. Lechler, Personal communication, 1952.
10. Scheyer, Personal communication, 1952.
11. Saillens, *Nos vierges*.
12. Sladen, *Sicily*, pp. 315–24.
13. Paton, *Picturesque Sicily*, pp. 250–53.
14. Corrado, *Lucera*, pp. 1–38.
15. Jung, *Psychology and Religion*, p. 85.
16. Hare, *Cities*, p. 286.
17. Swinburne, *Travels*, p. 121.
18. Ayscough, *Saints and Places*, p. 348.
19. Swinburne, *Travels*, p. 123.
20. Jung, *Psychology and Religion*, p. 126.
21. Panofsky and Saxl, *Metropolitan Museum Studies*, pp. 228–80.
22. Jung and Karenyi, *Science of Mythology*, passim.

23. Herskovits, *Man and His Works*, p. 523.
24. Frankfort, *Ancient Man*, pp. 31–121.
25. Saillens, "Letters from the Mailbag," p. 4.
26. Vagts, Personal communication, 1975.
27. Tentori, "An Italian Religious Feast."
28. Ibid., n. 35.
29. Whyte, "Values in Action," p. 2.
30. Tentori, "An Italian Religious Feast."
31. Levi, *Christo si e fermato ad Eboli*.

# Bibliography

Ayscough, J. *Saints and Places*. New York: Benziger, 1912.
Corrado, G. *Lucera, sella storia della patria*. Lucera: Tipografic Scepi, 1937.
Frankfort, H., ed. *The Intellectual Adventures of Ancient Man*. Chicago: University of Chicago Press, 1946.
Hare, A. J. C. *Cities of Southern Italy and Sicily*. New York: Routledge, 1905.
Herskovits, Melville J. *Man and His Works*. New York: Alfred A. Knopf, 1948.
Holy Bible. Luke. Revised Standard Version. New York: Nelson and Son, 1953.
Holy Scriptures. Song of Songs. Philadelphia: Jewish Publication Society, 1954.
Jameson, Mrs. *Legends of the Madonna*. New York: Houghton Mifflin, 1890.
Jung, Carl G. *Psychology and Religion*. New Haven: Yale University Press, 1938.
_____, and Karenyi, K. *Essays on a Science of Mythology*. New York: Pantheon Books, 1949.
Lechler, George. Personal communication, 1952.
Lehrman, S. M. Introduction and Foreward to *The Five Megilloth*, edited by A. Cohen. Hinhead, Surrey: Soncino, 1946.
Levi, Carlo. *Christo si e fermato ad Eboli*. Torino: G. Einaudi, 1947.
_____. *Christ Stopped at Eboli*. New York: Farrar, Strauss, 1963.
Moss, Leonard W., and Cappannari, Stephen C. "The Black Madonna: An Example of Culture Borrowing." *Scientific Monthly* 73 (1953): 319–24.
Panofsky, E., and Saxl, F. *Metropolitan Museum Studies*, no. 4. New York: Metropolitan Museum, 1953.
Paton, W. A. *Picturesque Sicily*. New York: Harper, 1897.
Saillens, Emile. In "Letters from the Mailbag." Paris: New York Herald Tribune, 1958, p. 4.
_____. *Nos vierges noires leurs origines*. Paris: Les Editions Universelles, 1945.
Scheyer, Ernst. Personal communication, 1952.
Sladen, D. *Sicily*. New York: Dutton, 1907.

Swinburne, Henry. *Travels in the Two Sicilies*. Vol. 1. London: Emsley, 1783.

Tentori, Tullio. "An Italian Religious Feast: The *Fujenti* Rites of the Madonna dell'Arco, Naples." In this volume.

Vagts, Alfred. Personal communication, 1969.

———. Personal communication, 1975.

Whyte, William F. "Values in Action." *Human Organization* 17 (1958): 1.

Wolf, Eric. "The Virgin of Guadalupe: A Mexican National Symbol." *Journal of American Folklore* 71 (1958): 34–39.

# 4

## The Cult of Brigid:
## A Study of Pagan-Christian
## Syncretism in Ireland
### by Donál Ó Cathasaigh

Recent inquiries into the authenticity of certain saints by the Roman Catholic church emanate from modern anthropological and historical studies. Local saints, especially those reputed to have lived in the transitional period, when pre-Christian to Christian assimilation was most active, have lost their honored places in the "Calendar of the Saints."[1] The church has not actively attempted to discredit her former patrons and patronesses; she has simply instructed the faithful that many of the "old school" fail to satisfy the rigorous requisites for canonization and no longer qualify for the attendant rights and privileges of sainthood. The Catholic world greeted the news of de-sanctification with apathy, possibly because the majority of the "elder saints" had already lost currency, whereas more-favored elder saints would retain devotees in spite of Vatican judgments. They were saints by consensus.

Irish venerables of the fifth and sixth centuries were among those scrutinized by Roman authorities, though investigations of Brigid and Patrick, the fifth-century patrons of Ireland, have not led to an official disqualification. In spite of inferences by prominent Celticists—Myles Dillon, Nora Chadwick, and Proinsias MacCana—that the Christian Brigid is the personification of a Celtic goddess,[2] and research by the historian T. F. O'Rahilly that yields, not one, but two Saint Patricks,[3]

This essay was originally written for this volume but has since been published in the *Mankind Quarterly* 19 (June 1979): 311–28.

the church has retained both Brigid and Patrick as "Calendar" saints. They continue to be commemorated on February 1 and March 17 in Ireland and internationally. They are specially revered in rites at Irish holy wells, on mountain heights, and among ancient ruins.

Brigid and Patrick survive partly because of a long-standing significance and partly because a matriarchal symbol and a druid saint cannot readily be dismissed. Patrick's "Confessio," a document that admits of a humble cleric persecuted for his beliefs, contrasts starkly with the spell-casting, druidic figure of Muirchú's seventh-century *Life*.[4] O'Rahilly's "Two Patricks" resolves the confusing chronology of Patricius by disclosing that there was also a Palladius who had antedated him as bishop. But Joseph Duffy's defense of Patrick's spirituality, which minimizes the historical arguments, reiterates the saint's legitimacy.[5] Patrick is for the moment secure.

About Brigid there has been scant evidence.[6] Still, certain questions need to be asked about her origins, her functions in early Irish society, and existing traditions and lore that testify to her eminence in the Celtic scheme. In what sense is Brigid a Christian saint? To what extent is she the personification of a Celtic deity? A consideration of mythological sources and histories and lives of the saints and an examination of surviving Brigidine festivals and lore suggest a pagan-Christian syncretism.

## The Celtic Goddess

Early Irish society was an amalgam of the indigenous non-Indo-Europeans, builders of the megalithic tombs, and the Celts, who came from the Continent in successive waves from the fifth to the first centuries B.C. Next to nothing is known about the earliest inhabitants. About the Celts, scholars have synthesized a body of evidence from the accounts of ancient historians, the archaeological and linguistic data collected principally in Gaul and Britain, and the pseudo-historical Irish manuscripts of the later eleventh century and after.[7]

The earliest Celtic migrations to Ireland are dated approximately 500 B.C.; and for the half millennium preceding the birth of Christ, they are traced both from Europe directly into Ireland and from Europe across Britain. What is certain is that, by the second century B.C., an advanced continental culture (La Tène) had reached the

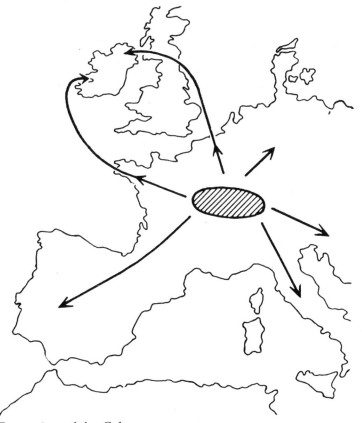

4. Expansion of the Celts, ca. 400 B.C.

island, and that, by the first century, the Belgae had closed ranks and the Goidels (Gaels) had swept in from the Continent. By the advent of Christianity, sometime prior to A.D. 431,[8] political maneuvering continued, but there was a coalescence of the various Celtic migrations and the emergence of a dominant Goidelic strain.

Meanwhile, Roman occupation of Gaul and Britain had gone forward, and as a result, the character of Celticism had been dramatically altered in both areas. The cultural link with Ireland had been fractured, and the hybrid Gallo-Roman civilization that replaced it had shed much of its Gaulish "barbarism." The principal custodianship for the Celtic heritage passed then to those on the edges of the Roman world—to the insular Celts of Ireland.

When Christianity was introduced in the fifth century A.D., the country already had well-defined political divisions, a stratified feudal system, and a vernacular that unified the entire population. It was bound, too, by common religious beliefs and practices and by a druidic order charged with ritual and divination. Though the precise nature of Celtic rubrics has been lost to us, the religion appears to have fused elements of polytheism, pantheism, and primitive magic. Indeed, the artifactual findings and mythological scraps hint that the Celts commemorated a loose confederation of impersonal "overgods," topographical (nature) deities, and "divine magicians."[9]

Identifications of more than four hundred gods and goddesses (three hundred of which occur in the literature only once) have been turned up by scholars over the years. The overgods, like Lugh (Samíldanách—"the many skilled"), were the more prominent and had a universal significance throughout the Celtic world.[10] When, in the accounts of his military campaigns, Julius Caesar described a Gaulish pantheon with Mercury supreme, it is clear that his reference was to the god Lugh. There are two inscriptions from Spain and Switzerland and a wide distribution of derived place names—Lyon and Laon in France, Leiden in Holland, and Leignitz in Silesia—that attest to Lugh's presence among the Celts on the Continent. He is the Lleu of the Welsh tale "Math vab Mathonwy" and the stammering deliverer of Irish divinities who originates overseas. Lughnasa, the major harvest festival, certainly celebrated him.

There are other deities approaching Lugh in importance, among them the triadic goddess called Brigid. Caesar singles out this "Gaulish Minerva," mother goddess and patroness of the arts, as primary among the distaff pantheon. And, though his parallels may be more descriptive than literal, it is surely the Celtic Brigid who bears the closest resemblance to his Minerva. Brigid's name suggests "the exalted one" and is cognate with that of the Brigantes, a far-ranging tribe of Britain and the Continent. Besides a sanctuary to Minerva in Britain, there are four Gallo-Roman inscriptions; and the rivers Brent (in England), Braint (in Wales), and Brigid (in Ireland) testify to the prestige of the goddess throughout the Celtic world.

When Cormac MacCuileannáin, the bishop and king of Cashel, compiled his *Glossary* at the end of the ninth century, he provided the following entry on Brigid: " . . . she was a goddess whom poets worshipped, for very great and very noble was her superintendence, therefore call they her goddess of poets by this name, whose sisters were Brigit, woman of smithwork, and Brigit, woman of healing,

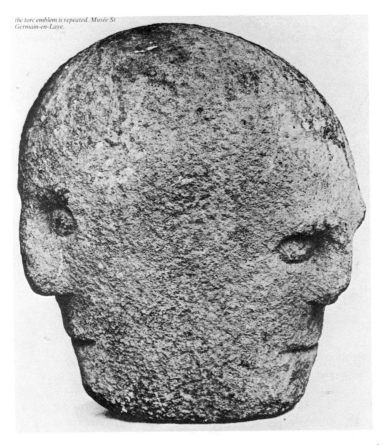

the torc emblem is repeated. Musée St Germain-en-Laye.

5. The tricephalic stone head from Corleck, county Cavan, provides a Brigidine type. *(Photograph by Donál Ó Cathasaigh)*

namely, goddesses—from whose names Brigit was with all Irishmen called a goddess."[11] The Celts regularly formulated paradigmatic triads, and the representation of a Brigidine trinity comes as no surprise. What is particularly noteworthy here is that the attributed functions of poet, physician, and artisan were critical to the cultural survival of a primitive society. In fact, Brigid's station was such that, if we understand Cormac's *Glossary* rightly, her name came to be synonymous with the word "goddess."

Robert Graves, in *The White Goddess*, considers a succession of tales

6. Italianate interpretation of Saint Brigid.

that simultaneously identify the Triple Goddess Brigid as the mother of the Dagda (the "Good God" and "Great Father"), as the Dagda's mate, and as his three daughters bearing the same name.[12] Later it is said that three of the Dagda's descendants—Brian, Iuchar, and Iuchurba—married the three princesses who together owned Ireland —Éire, Fodhla, and Banbha. (Éire is the Irish name for Ireland; Fodhla and Banbha are metaphoric substitutes for Éire in the early poetry.) This identification might be irrelevant if T. F. O'Rahilly, interpreting a gloss on a ninth-century text, had not introduced the notion that the three *gods*, called Brian, Iuch(i)r, and Úar, were also sons of the *banfhili* (woman poet) Brigid.[13] Still, the contradictions that complicate the problem of positive identification tend to reinforce both the preeminence and the triune nature of the goddess.

It is difficult to resist etymological speculations that connect Brigid to the goddess Danu of the *Tuatha Dé Danann* in the Irish Mythological Cycle.[14] It is a credential that would further establish her as the matriarchal Celtic deity. But Brigid's several blood associations with the All-Father Dagda—as his mother, his bed partner, and his daughter(s)—and her connections with symbolic riverine waters (life fluids) are additional manifestations of maternity. Moreover, if Imbolc, the spring rite celebrating the lactation of ewes, was her festival and if she functioned as "household protector," as the scholarship strongly implies, the cult of a mother goddess can be confirmed and collaborated from the syncretism of the pagan-Christian traditions.

The position of female deities in Celtic religion has been underestimated and obscured. Most goddesses seem to have been topographical—that is, they have connections with land formations (Anu —"The Paps of Anu"), lakes or rivers (Boann—the Boyne), and sacred wells (Brigid—Bridewell)—and seem to have served as guardian and fertility genuses. Oblations and sacrifices would have been offered at their sanctuaries. However, the druidic rubrics, preserved as they were in oral formulas, have long been forgotten, and Irish monastics, as the later redactors of the myths, had little reason to commit pagan beliefs to manuscript.

The monks recast the mythology as history, translated the gods to heroes, and rejected whatever was inimical to Christian teaching. What is perhaps more important is that these celibate scribes were often antifeminist reformers with a strong ascetic bias. They were probably responsible for editing out the creation myth and expurgating the texts of sexual allusions.[15] The female deities would have suffered at their hands.

Certain of the Celtic goddesses retained their vigor and were metamorphosed into Christian saints during the transitional period. For example, the Caillech Bhérri, a tutelary deity associated with the Kerry peninsula, was transformed from an ancient divinity to an aged nun. Fragments of a disjointed eleventh-century poem, titled "The Nun of Beare," illustrate the dilemma of melding such conflicting personalities. And Saint Brigid, the Catholic patroness of Ireland, shows incredible likenesses to the Celtic goddess from whom she takes her name. But is the saint simply a euhemerization of the goddess or is she a historical personage of fifth-century Ireland? A study of the histories and hagiographies should resolve this mystery.

## The Abbess Saint

The biographical-historical references to Saint Brigid are numerous, though none is dated earlier than the seventh century. In that period, Broccan is credited with a Latin hymn celebrating her life and deeds, and Cogitosus, a member of the Brigidine community at Kildare, wrote a prose *Life*.[16] But Brigid was Cogitosus's patroness, and it was important that he transmit "a few of the many things handed down by the great and most wise."[17] Not only would Brigid's sanctity and miracles redound to the spiritual reputation of the Kildare community, they would establish its institutional primacy over the province of Leinster. There is no question that, after the seventh century, Kildare had achieved such prominence.

*Cill-dara* ("Church of the Oak") became a thriving monastic center, if not "a great metropolitan city," as Cogitosus claimed. It had jurisdiction over a sizable region (*paruchia*), though it is improbable that its domain stretched "from sea to sea." There were, in his time, two segregated communities—one male and presided over by a bishop, the other female and headed by an abbess—that shared a partitioned timber chapel. This mixed arrangement with a double line of succession was very likely the first of its kind in Ireland. In a century and a half, Brigid's settlement had expanded from a modest oratory to a monastic village complete with a scriptorium, a "studio" for metal arts, and a mill. It was located five miles from the village of Knockaulin, a former pagan sanctuary.

What Cogitosus provides in his *Life of Brigid* is a pseudo-saga, a catalogue of marvels and miracles attributed to the saint. He would

have his epic heroine to rival Deirdre or a Medb in the secular literature and his saint to rival Patrick.[18] According to Cogitosus and
later dependent biographers, Brigid was daughter to a slave woman
of Dubhthach (tenth in descent from Felimidh, the second-century
lawgiver-king of Ireland). Because Dubhthach's wife became jealous
of the bondsmaid, the king was pressed to sell his slave, and he sold
her to a druid. Brigid, the daughter of the king, was thus born into
the household of a druid, but as a slave. Her birth was attended by
celestial wonders.

In later years she returned to her father's house to perform domestic duties, but Dubhthach's wife insisted that the daughter be sold
into bondage. When he realized that Brigid's generosity was deplet-
ing his resources, Dubhthach finally submitted and brought her to
the king of North Leinster. The girl, a radiant beauty, was sought
after by suitors, but she rejected them because she had dedicated
herself to the contemplative life. Sometime later, with seven other
virgins, she consecrated herself to Christ and eventually returned
to her father's lands in Kildare, where she founded the monastic
community.

Cogitosus logs a number of "miracles of plenty" associated with
the saint. She dispenses butter, which is immediately replenished;
she performs triple milkings, changes water to ale and stone to salt.
She offers hospitality to the poor and comfort and healing to the
infirm. To Cogitosus she is Brigid the All-giving. Geraldus Cambren-
sis reports, in 1186, that there was at Kildare an inviolable sanctuary
with a perpetual ashless fire tended by twenty nuns (of whom Brigid
was one).[19] Keating lists fifteen holy women named Brigid, the most
eminent of whom is "Bridget, the daughter of Dubhthaig."[20] He con-
firms a genealogy for the saint. And Whitley Stokes, writing his pref-
ace to a translation of *Three Middle Irish Homilies*, sums up Brigid's life:
"Brigit was born at sunrise neither within nor without a house, was
bathed in milk, her breath revives the dead, a house in which she
is staying flames up to heaven, cow-dung blazes before her, oil is
poured on her head; she is fed from the milk of a white red-eared
cow; a fiery pillar rises over her head; sun rays support her wet cloak;
she remains a virgin; and she was one of the two mothers of Christ
the Anointed."[21]

The abbess-saint had responsibility for tradition-bearing (poetry),
healing, and metalwork. The sanctuary at Kildare retained the eternal
flame of a Brigid-Minerva cloister and was watched over by a score
of chaste nuns resembling vestal virgins. The name *Cill-dara* strongly

suggests the substitution of a Christian oratory for a druidic site, a suggestion underscored by the geographical proximity of monastic settlement and pagan sanctuary. But, beyond these striking similarities, the goddess and saint share more than a name: they share an important maternal significance.

Like the Nun of Beare, this tutelary goddess of the province of Leinster has been transformed into a tutelary saint of Leinster, and the mother of gods is referred to as "the second Mother of Christ," "the Mary of the Gael," and "the Mother of the High King of Heaven." There are frequent allusions to fertility and lactation; and Imbolc, the spring rite, has been appropriated as the feast day of the Christian Brigid. Moreover, pagan imagery associated with sexuality—enlarged breasts and exaggerated pudenda—has been sublimated so that the saint now corresponds more closely to the Virgin Mother of Christ.

The medieval hagiographers not only reiterate the extravagant miracles attributed to Brigid by Broccan, Cogitosus, and other early biographers of the saint, they add apocrypha derived from saga, scriptural, and classical sources. Brigid, like Deirdre, is reportedly thrown from a cart and cuts her head on a stone; and, like Christ, she multiplies foodstuffs for distribution to the hungry and cures the lepers and the lame.[22] Her remains, once interred at Kildare, are said to rest with those of the other major Irish saints, Patrick and Columcille, in a common grave near the village of Downpatrick.[23]

Today Brigid is the patroness of Ireland, but devotion to her extends throughout the Celtic world: in Scotland she is well known as Saint Bride, and in Wales she is Saint Ffraid. In England there are upwards of nineteen pre-Reformation dedications to her, most of them in the west country.[24] Her feast day, February 1, is specially observed in Ireland, Wales, Australia, and New Zealand.[25] Interestingly, the Christian Brigidine tradition has flourished among people of Celtic stock and in areas where the Celts and their descendants have settled in numbers.

Though it is difficult to discount the testimony of early historians and hagiographers, the evidence that they present is unconvincing. Historicity demands inquiry beyond hearsay and speculation. In Broccan's metrical life and Cogitosus's *Life*, there are no ascertainable facts or chronologies. Both writers are spiritual devotees of the saint, and Cogitosus has the added motivation of establishing territorial jurisdiction for his monastery. Brigid is, in fact, associated with *two* sites in Leinster—Faughart in county Louth, where she is reputed to have been born and reared, and Kildare, where she is said to have

7. Ireland: province and county.

established a house of learning. But Faughart, as a place of pilgrimage (a stream and holy well), conjures cult rituals that are clearly un-Christian and outside Cogitosus's references; Brigid's early association with the nunnery at Kildare has remained unsubstantiated.[26]

The genealogies that link the saint with the chieftain Dubhthach cannot be credited any more than other early Irish genealogies that harken back to mythological heroes and kings. The disinterment of the ninth century is explicable in light of Danish invasions, and reburial in a common grave with Patrick and Columcille implies a kind of sanctity by association, but it contradicts Irish social and religious customs. What this accumulation of biographical data serves to illustrate is a complicated conversion from myth and saga to pseudo-historical tradition. In effect, it shows how the Celtic religion was modified over time and space and how Christian monastics, unable to dispell the shadow of a vigorous matriarchal deity, grafted her name and functions onto a saint who became mother and exemplar to the Irish.

It is altogether likely that there were Christian Brigids in fifth-century Ireland. Keating mentions no less than fifteen "religious women" of that name. It is, of course, possible that one or another of these women founded the community at Kildare. Certainly there is adequate proof that such an institution existed, that there were groups of pious Christian women, and that one group resided at Kildare. Still, the evidence indicates that the Brigid that has come down to us as a saint is the symbol of Celtic continuity and the euhemerization of an ancient goddess. An examination of the surviving Brigidine festivals and lore will further that judgment.

## The Festivals and the Lore

In *The Festival of Lughnasa*, Maire MacNeill catalogues pilgrimages, assemblies, rites, and lore associated with Lugh, the dominant Celtic god; but MacNeill's study is more than a compendium of folk practices and folk beliefs.[27] It posits the strong influence of pre-Christian traditions on Christian customs and offers a model for inquiry into the influences of pagan rituals on current devotional exercises.

Because Brigid has been afforded a primacy in the Irish tradition, there are numerous folk customs and beliefs, deriving from antiquity, that attend her person and her feast. Ó Súilleabháin lists some of these:

> Young boys (Brídeoga: "Biddies") went from door to door carry-
> ing a churndash dressed as a woman and asked for some gift.
> Rushes or straw were left outside the house on the Eve of the Feast,
> and at nightfall a young girl went out, brought the bundle to
> the door, and knocked, asking in the name of Brigid to be admitted.
> When this was done, crosses (of various designs and materials,
> according to different districts) were woven or otherwise made, to
> the accompaniment of a traditional prayer. A meal was then taken,
> and the crosses were placed both in the inner side of the thatched
> roof and in the outhouses to invoke protection for the family
> and livestock. . . . A girdle (crios) was also woven of straw or
> rushes that evening, and both the members of the family and the
> cows passed through it for protection against illness. A cloth,
> known as brat Bhríde (Brigid's cloak) was left in the open that night
> and was then preserved for the healing powers it was said to have
> acquired. Another ancient custom was the throwing of a sheaf
> of oats or a cake of bread against the doorstep that evening to
> "drive away hunger" and to ensure a supply of food for the family
> during the year.[28]

Though the Brigidine folk customs appear somewhat complicated, they provide another level of interpretation of the role of the goddess-saint.

Until recently the cult of Brigid survived reasonably well intact in Ireland, though there were regional variations in the customs de-scribed by Ó Súilleabháin. The Biddies certainly replaced female sur-rogates of the saint, exemplary virgins of the townlands who often bore her name. The churndash, besides its obvious symbolic con-nection with milking, served as the foundation for an effigy of Brigid that was carried in procession to welcoming households. Rushes that were brought in by the young girl (again, a Brigid) were usually spread beneath the festive table as a mat. There was an elaborate ritualistic entrance: the girl seeking admittance knocked three times, each time repeating, "Go down on your knees, do homage, and let Blessed Bridget enter the house." When this had been said for the third time, those inside responded, "Oh, come in, you are a hundred times welcome."[29] An appropriate prayer of thanksgiving for health and safety to family and kine was afterward recited by the parents.

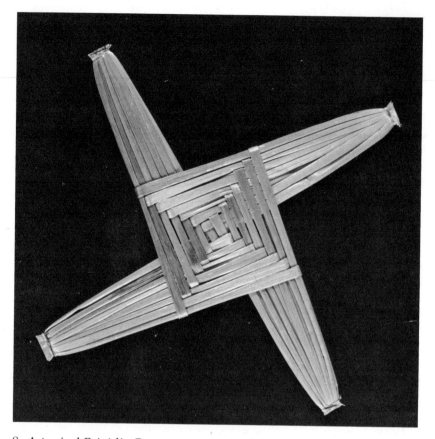

8. A typical Brigid's Cross, woven near Saughart, county Louth.
*(Photograph by Donál Ó Cathasaigh)*

In some areas the rushes were then gathered up and woven into crosses, girdles, and ties and spancels for cattle and sheep. The crosses might be blessed with holy water before being ceremoniously set in the thatch of the cottage or byre. Remnants of the rushes were afterward collected and made into a tick mattress for the saint, whereas the rushtips furnished lighting. It was believed that the artifacts protected the inhabitants and their animals from natural calamities—particularly fire, storm, and lightning. Mattress, girdle, and the special piece of cloth called a *brat Bhríde* were believed to have exceptional curative powers, especially with respect to illnesses of childbirth and in countering barrenness.

9. Brigid's Cross with Italianate image of the saint superimposed.
*(Photograph by Donál Ó Cathasaigh)*

The sheaf of oats or the cake of bread that was thrown against the door vanquished hunger, but a second cake was often placed outside the window as an oblation to the saint or to provision a needy traveler. An abundance of fresh butter and milk also graced the ceremonial table (*brídeóg*). So Brigid's functions in the folk tradition complement those of the antecedent goddess. The spring rite, signaling, as it does, rebirth in nature and new growth in the fields, certainly cannot be as recent as Christianity. Fertility and guardianship of the land were, after all, the domain of the Gaulish Brigid.

If the Celtic universe is directed by mysterious energies and the preservation of harmony in nature is man's first concern, there must be associated spells, charms, and formulas. And, in the cyclical order, there must be oblations to restore fertility to the fields and promote sympathetic magic. It is inevitable that, in the course of centuries, religious symbolism will be dissipated; still, in the rituals associated with Brigid, there are vestiges of an ancient maternal deity who provides abundance and who heals and protects.

In addition to the folk customs and beliefs noted by Ó Súilleabháin, there are pilgrimages to holy wells, sacred streams, and ancient ruins to commemorate the saint. The most impressive pilgrimage is that which leads to a shrine in the townland of Faughart in the northeast corner of county Louth, where the cult of Brigid flourishes to the present day. It is there that Brigid is thought to have been born and there that she is said to have consecrated her virginity to Christ, founded a convent, and erected a chapel.

In fact, there is at Faughart an ancient church ruin identified in the *Ordnance Survey Letters* (A.D. 1836), the correspondence of the British land surveys, as "Tea-pull Aird also [as] Tea-pull Brighde na hAirde Móire." There, too, is Brigid's stone, probably the stanchion for one of the Irish high crosses. But the Hill of Faughart has earlier prominence; in the vicinity there are megalithic tombs, souterrains (underground passages), raths (forts), and antiquarian artifacts. The place even takes its name from associations with the great heroes of the ancient saga literature.[30] It would seem that, as the old order passed, a Christian community came to replace it, raised a cross, and constructed a chapel of the new order. Colgan, writing in 1647, remarked that, although a monastery of canons once resided at Faughart, the place had been a parish church for nearly six centuries.[31]

Brigid is, of course, the patroness and heroine of Faughart. Material tokens of miraculous cures and mementos of favors received—bits of cloth, bandages, eyeglasses, and rosary beads—adorn bushes around an outdoor shrine, and an elaborate web of legend substantiates the local "activities" of the saint. Over the years references to prominent area families have crept into the reportage. The most popular account, however, concerns Brigid's flight from a determined suitor, during which she is said to have knelt near the bank of the stream and plucked out her eye to avoid being recognized. So credited is the incident that a curious collection of large stones situated near the stream mark every movement of the saint. The "headstone," "hoof-mark stone," "knee stone," "waist stone," and "eye stone" remain focal points of the pilgrimage and provide the faithful with tangible evidence of the event.

The pilgrimages, which are undertaken twice yearly, on the first Sunday in February and the first Sunday in July, attract thousands of devotees. Since the turn of the century the severity of the asceticism surrounding the pilgrimage—rigorous fasts, penitential exercises, and extended vigils—has been modified dramatically; still, there is more than a suggestion of the past. The prescribed ablutions in the stream and the prayer circuits round large stones and the ubiquity of antiquarian monuments hint at elaborate pre-Christian rituals. The shrine at Faughart conjures an ambience of magic and druidism, and its topography insists on the continuity of Celticism.

Though the modern pilgrimage has been documented as far back as the first half of the seventeenth century, it was "discouraged" by British authorities during the latter half of the nineteenth century. But the Irish language tradition survived in Faughart and private devotionalism continued. In 1903 a bone fragment reputed to have been taken from the skull of Saint Brigid was brought from Lisbon, Portugal, and enshrined at the parish church of Faughart. At about this time there was also a revival of interest in the pilgrimage, and former devotees were called upon to reconstruct the order of the rubrics. In July 1934 a new shrine, complete with a replica of the Lourdes grotto, Calvary figures, and canopied altar, was erected.

The exercises of the revised pilgrimage call for special invocations, the recitation of the rosary, a sermon to suit the occasion, a litany, and benediction of the Blessed Sacrament. Celticism has apparently given way to Romanism at last. Still, there is a private rite that leads hundreds of the faithful to the stream and the big stones. Many pray their way around the stones and hang tokens on bushes. After a millennium and a half the cult memory of stones and stream survives.

## Conclusion

When the seventh-century lives of Brigid were written, the cult of a Celtic Brigid had not yet run its course. Attributes of the tutelary goddess of Leinster were therefore appropriated by the earliest biographers and grafted onto Leinster's tutelary saint. The goddess of poetry, healing, and the metal arts thus became the Christian patroness of learning, healing, and domestic arts. Because the celibate monks could not transfer the strong sexual/maternal qualities of the Celtic Brigid to her Christian counterpart, they virginized her, identified her with the Mother of Christ, and hailed her as "Protectress of Ireland."

Still, sexual/maternal aspects derived from the Celtic goddess have carried over. The spring rite (Imbolc), Saint Brigid's feast, is associated with lactation, and attendant folk beliefs continue to stress abundance of milk and milk products. Moreover, the pilgrimage, suggestive of a druidic ritual, celebrates a stream (symbolic of amniotic fluids) once sacred to a pre-Christian community.

Surely the scribes, in tampering with the mythology, have altered the character of the mother goddess; but they have also preserved, in the Christian tradition surrounding the saint, the only extant composite of a Celtic matriarch. Undoubtedly there were fifth-century Brigids who entered the contemplative life and were associated with the settlements at Faughart and Kildare, but the overwhelming evidence is that the Brigid of the "Roman Calendar" is essentially Celtic. Though there has been a syncretism of the pagan and Christian personalities, the mother goddess of the Celts survives and, what is more, she still eludes the Vatican "saint hunters."

## Notes

1. "The Calendar" is the official listing of saints in the Roman Catholic church and authenticates those currently recognized.

2. Dillon and Chadwick state that Brigid "appears to have been Christianized as St. Brigit" (*The Celtic Realms*, p. 144). Chadwick argues that "St. Brigid herself, if she ever existed, appears to have taken over the functions of a Celtic goddess of the same name and comparable attributes" (*The Celts*, p. 181). And MacCana notes that "no clear distinction can be made between the goddess and the saint" (*Celtic Mythology*, p. 35).

3. O'Rahilly, *The Two Patricks*.

4. See Hughes, "Early Christian Ireland," p. 79.

5. Duffy, *Patrick in His Own Words*.

6. The late Father F. O'Briain had begun an extensive study of Brigid. His notes are in the archives of the Franciscan House of Studies, Killiney, county Dublin, Ireland.

7. MacCana reflects that the rewriting of tradition continued through the twelfth-century pseudo-history *Leabhar Gabhála Éireann* [Book of conquests of Ireland]. Fragments of the MS are dated late eleventh century.

8. Though A.D. 431 is the traditional date for the Christianizing of Ireland, historians are agreed that missionaries had made converts sometime earlier.

9. See VanHamel, "Aspects of Celtic Mythology," pp. 207–48.

10. MacCana, *Celtic Mythology*, pp. 27–29.

11. Quoted in Hyde, *Literary History of Ireland*, p. 53.

12. Graves, *The White Goddess*, pp. 101, 102.

13. O'Rahilly devotes several pages to interpretations of the phrase *tri dee Danann* and introduces the gloss (*Early Irish History*, pp. 314–16).

14. The *Tuatha Dé Danann* combined the various groups of pre-Goidelic deities, and the name appears to mean "People of the Goddess Danu."

15. Bowen, "Great-Bladdered Médb," pp. 31–34.

16. The metrical life in the *Book of Hymns* (eleventh-century MS) is ascribed to Saint Broccan or Brogan Cloen who lived in the early seventh century (Hyde, *Literary History of Ireland*, p. 163). Cogitosus's version of the *Life* appears in Colgan's *Trias Thaumaturga*.

17. Quoted in Hughes, *Early Christian Ireland*, p. 227.

18. Bowen, "Great-Bladdered Médb," pp. 30, 31.

19. McNeill, *The Celtic Churches*, p. 80.

20. Keating, *General History of Ireland*, p. 389.

21. Quoted in Hyde, *Literary History of Ireland*, p. 161 n.

22. Coulson, *The Saints*, p. 145.

23. Ibid.

24. Thurston and Attwater, *Lives of the Saints*, p. 229.

25. Ibid.

26. Ibid., p. 226.

27. MacNeill, *The Festival of Lughnasa*.

28. Walsh, *The Four Masters*, p. 62.

29. Danaher, *The Year in Ireland*, p. 20.

30. MacIomhair, "County Louth," pp. 120, 121.

31. Quoted in ibid., p. 255.


# Bibliography

Bowen, Charles. "Great-Bladdered Médb: Mythology and Invention in the *Táin Bó Cualnge*." *Éire-Ireland* 10 (1975): 14–34.

Chadwick, Nora. *The Celts*. Harmondsworth, England: Penguin Books, 1974.

Cogitosus. *The Life of Brigid*. In Colgan's *Trias Thaumaturga*. Louvain, 1647.

Coulson, John, ed. *The Saints: A Concise Biographical Dictionary*. New York: Guild Press, 1958.

Danaher, Kevin. *The Year in Ireland*. Cork: Mercier Press, 1972.

Dillon, Myles, and Chadwick, Nora. *The Celtic Realms*. New York: New American Library, 1967.

Duffy, Joseph. *Patrick in His Own Words*. Dublin: Veritas Publishers, 1972.

Graves, Robert. *The White Goddess*. New York: Farrar, Straus and Giroux, 1970.

Hughes, Kathleen. *Early Christian Ireland: Introduction to the Sources*.

Cambridge: Cambridge University Press, 1972.

———. "The Golden Age of Early Christian Ireland." In *The Course of Irish History*, edited by T. W. Moody and F. X. Martin, pp. 76–90. Cork: Mercier Press, 1967.

Hyde, Douglas. *A Literary History of Ireland*. London: Ernest Benn, 1967.

Keating, Jeoffry. *General History of Ireland*. Translated by Desmond O'Connor. Dublin: James Duffy and Sons, n.d.

MacCana, Proinsias. *Celtic Mythology*. London: Hamlyn, 1970.

MacIomhair, Diarmuid. "Townland Survey of County Louth." *County Louth Archaeological Journal* 16 (1966–68): 111–24, 254–63.

McNeill, John T. *The Celtic Churches: A History, A.D. 200 to 1200*. Chicago: University of Chicago Press, 1974.

MacNeill, Móire. *The Festival of Lughnasa*. London: Oxford University Press, 1962.

O'Briain, F. "Saga Themes in Irish Hagiography." In *Feilscrihbinn Torna: Essays and Studies Presented to Professor Tadgh Ua Donnehadah*. Cork, 1947.

O'Rahilly, T. F. *Early Irish History and Mythology*. Dublin: Dublin Institute for Advanced Studies, 1964 .

———. *The Two Patricks*. Dublin: Dublin Institute for Advanced Studies, 1957.

Thurston, S. J., and Attwater, Donald, eds. *Butler's Lives of the Saints*. New York: P. J. Kennedy and Sons, 1956.

VanHamel, A. G. "Aspects of Celtic Mythology." *Proceedings of the British Academy* 20 (1934): 207–48.

Walsh, Paul. *The Four Masters and Their Work*. Dublin: At the Sign of the Three Candles, 1944.

# 5

# An Italian Religious Feast:
# The *Fujenti* Rites of the
# Madonna dell'Arco, Naples
## by Tullio Tentori
## Translated from the Italian by
## Jerome Reichman and
## Mariangela Reichman

Once a year the Sanctuary of the Madonna of the Arch, which is located in the village of Santa Anastasia in the Province of Naples, becomes the setting in which the cult of the *fujenti* reaches its climax. This event, circumscribed in time and place, lends itself to different interpretations according to the bias of those who observe it. From the nonscientific point of view, it seems an abnormal or at least a peculiar phenomenon today, one that some regard as a curiosity, others abhor, and still others feel in tune with their own way of expressing faith. The ethnographer and the historian believe it is an event worth recording and photographing for the light it sheds on ancient or archaic cultural traits, especially those still surviving in the most backward areas of southern Italy. To the student of folklore it is a popular religious feast, an example of those ancient traditions that should at least be preserved in documentary form precisely because they are destined to perish in the inexorable leveling process of modern technological life.

This article was previously published in *Cultures* 3 (1976): 117–40. The editor would like to thank UNESCO Press for permission to reprint it in this volume. Slight alterations have been made to bring the article up to date.

To the anthropologist, moreover, this feast is not an isolated fact so much as a situation to be evaluated and understood as follows: (1) in the perspective of the social and cultural structures and milieu that sustained it in the past and continue to do so in the present; (2) in relation to the processes of acculturation and transformation—past and present, whether unrecognized or the source of conflict—that characterize the society of which the cult is an expression; (3) in terms of the rapport—on the ideological, political, religious, social, and cultural levels—between the society that practices the cult and the larger society of which it is a part; and (4) in the framework of the coexistence—sometimes based on compromise, sometimes the result of tensions—between the state religion (the official, institutionalized version) and the religion of the people (or the living version).

As an anthropologist and director of the Museum of Folk Arts and Folklore (a national institute located in Rome), I had the opportunity to study the rite of the *fujenti* in 1972. That year a number of journalists pressed me to witness the feast because of the conflict that had been brewing between the church and authorities of Naples and the worshipers concerned. In fact, the bishops of Campania, in a public and official writ of censure, had admonished the faithful to keep the forthcoming ceremony within the bounds of dignity and propriety and to avoid instances of fanaticism and irreverence wholly alien to the spirit of the Catholic religion and to the modern way of life. This antecedent, about which I shall have more to say later on, focused the attention of the press and public opinion on the case of the *fujenti*, and their role in a local feast dear to certain subordinate classes was thus thrust from its placid, traditional setting into the limelight of national interest and curiosity.

As it turned out, I found the feast of the *fujenti* an extremely fertile source of anthropological observation. Among other things, it allowed me to look beyond the temporal and spatial limits of a given situation to the broader horizon of the processes of transformation, crisis, and development that characterize present-day Italian culture and society.

## The Cult

The *fujenti* are zealous devotees of the Madonna of the Arch whose sanctuary is at Santa Anastasia, a small village on the slopes of Mount

Vesuvius not far from Naples. This is a very depressed area in which the Alfasud automobile plant was built in 1969. It has led to the creation of a center of industrial development in a zone normally characterized by an agricultural economy and high rate of unemployment, and its workers and employees are drawn from the Naples area as well as from the local residents. The development of this zone is still in progress, and other industries have sprung up alongside the Alfasud plant.

The Madonna of the Arch is believed to possess the power to heal every sort of ailment, physical as well as mental. Presumably, she can also resolve any and all problems concerning family, social, and individual life.

The extent of this faith in the madonna's prompt and prodigious powers is demonstrated by the proportions of the feast dedicated to her (in terms of both quantitative participation and collective zeal); by the kind of prayers and supplications her devotees address to her; and, above all, by the votive offerings they shower upon her "for favors granted." Most of these votive offerings consist of small wood paintings by anonymous, popular artists who specialize in such work. They portray the devotee's situation—his drama, dangers, and mortal perils—and the happy resolution of that same situation thanks to the miraculous intervention of the madonna. In cases of illness or infirmity, the votive offerings may be pieces of sculpture, mainly in wax, that reproduce the affected part of the body that was healed. They may also consist of the medical aids and devices, such as crutches and orthopedic supports, that the donor required until the sudden disappearance of his physical handicap.

These countless votive offerings line the walls of the sanctuary and those of the various quarters in which the faithful are received, and they fill several storerooms as well.[1] The subjects they depict cover the whole range of human misfortunes and vicissitudes, as well as calamities that befall entire communities: a fall from a horse, a tree, or a wagon; accidents involving various means of transport; a shipwreck; a holdup staged by bandits; knifings and other scenes of vengeful violence—not to mention earthquakes, plagues, and wars. In those depicting illnesses, cases of lung disease with expectoration of blood constantly recur.[2]

The *fujenti*, that is to say, the devotees of the Madonna of the Arch, make their pilgrimage to the sanctuary on the first Monday after Easter. On this occasion, they come running or skipping from their home villages in a sort of "uniform" that consists of a white shirt and

10. A family on a pilgrimage to the Madonna dell'Arco. The children are carrying a drawing of an accident that took place. The madonna is being thanked for her part in curing the victims of this accident. *(Photograph by Lello Mazzacane)*

trousers and a blue sash worn around the waist and across the back. They are supposed to go barefoot, though today they wear white stockings that are removed before entering the sanctuary.[3]

For centuries the *fujenti* have been organized in associations headed by a president and a vice-president. Today these associations are called Catholic Workers' Unions or, more simply, unions. There are 310 of them in the diocese of Naples alone, and the total membership amounts to 30,000 persons.[4] The rule is that these associations should be governed by charters subject to the approval of the rector of the sanctuary, who should also ratify the nomination of the presidents.

Associations are also to be found in towns or villages far removed from the specific region in which the cult is rooted (the Mount Vesuvius area and Naples).[5] The cult probably originated on the slopes of Mount Somma and then spread rapidly to broad zones in the Naples district. Its diffusion was facilitated by exchange through migrations as well as by the favorable cultural humus, that is to say, a destitute and abandoned population readily inclined to invoke magic and the supernatural against the exploitation and domination to which other men subjected them.

Today various associations have their own social centers, where members gather to organize the feast, to enjoy recreational activities (card games, billiards, pinball machines, and the like), and to hold meetings that serve to foster group solidarity and the eventual exchange of favors. Social and ceremonial objects (such as charters, files, funds, banners, sacred images, and various cult objects) are kept at these centers, and, when technically feasible, it is here that they prepare the altars, trophies, and floats (except those that are extremely large) that the devotees customarily bear on their shoulders in the procession on the Monday after Easter.

Contact between the sanctuary and the unions is maintained through the bulletin published by the Dominican friars who exercise religious jurisdiction and also through "inspectors" or coadjutors— volunteers and laymen—who report to the rector.[6] From time to time various events are held to solidify the bonds between the associations and the sanctuary and to strengthen the faith of the members.[7]

In the period just before Easter, the *fujenti* collect funds by begging for alms in a loud and blustering fashion. Those assigned this task don their characteristic "uniforms" and proceed from street to street and from house to house, skipping, dancing, and shouting as they press their demands for money donations. When these are refused, they insist with effrontery, not merely out of fanaticism but also to fulfill the penitential duty implicit in the role of those who beg "for reasons of faith."

The funds thus collected are changed into bank notes of large denominations (five thousand and ten thousand lire each), which are pinned ostentatiously to the association's banners on the day of the pilgrimage. The money is a tangible sign of support for and participation in the feast and, therefore, of the association's own prestige.

The funds collected, minus organizational expenses, are in theory turned over to the sanctuary to defray maintenance and operating costs and to broaden the scope of its religious activities. In reality, it seems that only part of the revenue is given to the Dominican friars who preside over the church. According to a statement by the rector of the sanctuary in the weekly magazine *Panorama*,[8] total donations in recent years amounted to nearly one-half billion lire, whereas the church allegedly received only a few million.[9]

## "The Feast on Monday" in Albis: Notes on the Ritual of 1972

As noted, the rite of the *fujenti* takes place on the Monday after Easter. At dawn, or even during the night if there is a considerable distance to be covered, the pilgrims gather in front of their home churches and await the blessing of the parish priest. If the hour is very early, they forgo the blessing and merely kiss the door of the church.[10]

The devotees form a group under the orders of a president or "commander" or one of his representatives. They carry with them the objects and paraphernalia that will be used to render homage to the madonna: paintings, statues, votive offerings, tall wax candles (sometimes weighing 30–40 kilograms), trophies, and elaborately adorned canopies. Many of these objects are particularly bulky and heavy, and several devotees bear them on their shoulders by turns.

The standard-bearer precedes the group, and the leader frequently shifts his position as he keeps order in the ranks and animates the participants. The formation itself, which is called "a company" (in military idiom) or "a squadron" (in naval parlance), is made up of a varying number of men and women of all ages. In general, the men tend to predominate, there are few children, and the total number of participants ranges from about thirty to one hundred.[11]

The members of each company proceed in double file. Some of them wield rods with which they are allowed to keep the crowd of onlookers from blocking the passage of the column; this is why the devotees of the Madonna of the Arch who take part in the ritual are known as *vattienti* (*battenti*, "beaters") as well as *fujenti* (*fuggenti*, "those who flee"). It is said that the *vattienti* once dealt blows to themselves rather than to the crowd, as a sign of penitence, but this is no longer the case.

The companies halt before altars and shrines along the route of the pilgrimage, and these interruptions serve to regulate the flow of those arriving at the sanctuary. This is necessary because each formation enters the church by itself and must therefore await its proper turn.

The halting and waiting increase the eagerness of the pilgrims to reach their goal: impatient and excited, they perspire, shout, sing, dance, and pray. Their invocations grow louder and more passionate, and the bands play with greater fervor.

At the door of the church, just before entering, each company reforms its ranks, and, with dancing steps, all move forward and then backward three times in a row. Then the members of the group throw themselves onto their knees and in this position cross the threshold of the church. In former times they would lick the floor with their tongues as they crawled to the main altar, a custom that has long been forbidden. But even today there are fanatics who perform this act of devotion despite the prohibition of both church and lay authorities and surveillance of the police.

Once inside the sanctuary, the participants' excitement grows so intense that even the commander of the company can no longer keep them under control. Advancing between two banisters that keep back the crowd of spectators, they cry aloud, mingling prayers, supplications, and groans in a great din. The *fujenti* seem to be in a trance, to be "different" from their usual selves. Not all of them manage to proceed on their knees; some stand up and run, others fling themselves abruptly to the ground and the impact of their bodies on the marble floor resounds like a series of slaps.

A few faint dead away and still others are seized by convulsive fits. The *fujenti* thus stricken are immediately removed to a first aid tent, where, as a rule, they promptly recover. Soon they get up from their cots, leave the tent, and mingle with the festive crowd.

The rest of the *fujenti* continue to the altar, where they remain on their knees, each in his turn. This is the moment in which the devotee's direct rapport with the madonna is given its most intense expression in the form of aggressive and insistent supplications that reflect all the suffering and frustrations of the poor. It is claimed that even threats are addressed to the madonna, though personally I did not hear any.

Besides praying, imploring, shouting, and weeping, the devotees present the Virgin with wax candles, votive offerings, fresh or imitation flowers, and other gifts. In 1972, according to a rough estimate, the candles heaped before the altar weighed about 2,000 kilograms. Bulky and heavy gifts are deposited before entering the church. Outstanding among those of 1972 were a small altar offered by a workers' union from Nola (it was shaped like a boat and weighed 150 kilograms); a destroyer and four torpedo boats, each more than 1 meter in length, built of burnt match sticks; and a religious mosaic made of five-, ten-, and twenty-lire coins, 5 meters long and 3 meters wide, which was offered by a company from Marignanella.

The *fujenti* are not allowed to remain for long in front of the sacred image, because they must make way for the pilgrims in the succeeding companies who await their turns. At a command from the leader, the kneeling devotees rise immediately and head for the sacristy that gives onto the porch and alms room where one exits from the church. There is no sign of resistance and no delay; on the contrary, all respect the rules of a ritual that has a decidedly martial air.[12]

When they leave the church proper, the pilgrims remain in the alms room for a while and then gather under the porch and in the gardens. Here they regain their composure and their strength. Many are assisted by relatives who dry their perspiration, help them to put on fresh clothes, and serve them food and drink. Then they all disperse to the streets and squares of Santa Anastasia, where the usual village festival is in full swing, with its street vendors' stalls, taverns, decorations, illuminations, music, and swirling crowds.

In 1972 twenty-five thousand *fujenti* took part in the rite, of whom about one thousand required treatment in the first aid station.[13] About two hundred thousand pilgrims in all attended the festivities.

In that year the *fujenti* began to arrive at about six o'clock in the morning, when dawn was breaking. It is worth noting that the first pilgrims to arrive enjoyed the special privilege of gathering the perspiration or tears of the Madonna: that is to say, the moisture formed on the wall behind the sacred effigy. Several devotees told me that if one touched the wall and then one's head with the same hand it would cure headache. According to the rector of the sanctuary, whom I interviewed, the faithful perform this act of magic on any ailing part of their body in the hopes of effecting a cure.

11. A family travels to the Madonna dell'Arco in the back of a three-wheeled truck. *(Photograph by Lello Mazzacane)*

In 1972 the companies succeeded one another without interruption until evening. Then the little village of Santa Anastasia, its streets lit up by strings of colored lights and filled with noisy, euphoric crowds, became the scene of a festive celebration that lasted late into the night.

Often the pilgrims continue their revelry after returning to their home villages, where some even find the strength to compete for prizes and to perform folk dances. At Giugliano, Nola, Pomigliano d'Arco, and other towns dances are held every evening of the week following Easter.

According to the musicologist Roberto De Simone, these dances express themes of violent aggressiveness with strong sexual overtones. Most of them are performed by men only, but there are some in which both sexes take part and others for women only. In one dance figure, for example, a woman is stationed in the center of a group of men who seem to feign an assault upon her. Normally, the rhythm is provided by tambourines and castanets played by the dancers themselves. De Simone adds that these airs, and especially the instruments employed, evoke the music that accompanied the ancient cults of Cybele.

Besides the traditional forms of games and amusements held after the ritual, more modern pastimes have recently been introduced. These grow ever more prominent, and they add a strident note to the festivities.[14]

## Origins of the Cult of the Madonna of the Arch

In attempting to shed light on the origins of this cult, we must begin by observing that it consists of two basic components. One is the worship of the holy image of the madonna, and the other is the manifestation codified in the ritual of the *fujenti*. Because these are superimposed upon one another without being fused into an integrated whole, each must be examined separately.

On the subject of the first component, our primary sources are the data and other information supplied by historians and hagiographers, as well as by the oral tradition. Where the second is concerned, analogies with earlier cults provide a basis for reconstructive hypotheses.

Historians seeking to trace the origins of this particular form of Marian worship have pushed their research as far back as the second half of the fifteenth century. The first historical source—a manuscript by Father Arcangelo Dominici, dated 1608—states that in the place where the sanctuary is situated at present there was a country shrine, in the shade of a lime tree, that contained a painting of the Virgin, who was called the "Madonna of the Arch."[15] Father Dominici describes the image of Mary as follows: ". . . she tenderly embraces her

Most Holy Son with her left hand, and he grasps an apple with his right hand."

A fair was held near the shrine on the Monday after Easter, and it was on this day, in the year A.D. 1450, that the miracle occurred.[16] During a game of pall-mall,[17] one of the players failed to score because the ball got caught in the lime tree. In a fit of rage, the man grabbed the ball, uttered a string of oaths, and hurled it against the holy image, which began to bleed. Awed by the miracle, the crowd would have lynched the sacrilegious player (perhaps a peasant from Nola) if the count of Sarno had not chanced by at that very moment. The count, whose official titles were Great Avenger of the Kingdom and Commander of the Company to Repress the Bandits, saved the wretched fellow from the fury of the mob. Asserting his authority, nonetheless, the count himself held a summary trial as a result of which the man was sentenced to death by hanging. He was then hanged from the branches of the lime tree that shaded the holy shrine, and the tree withered.

A further series of miracles ensued, which moved the people to build a small chapel in the place of the shrine. In her new abode, the madonna continued to work wonders and, according to Father Arcangelo Dominici, the chapel was soon filled with painted votive offerings rendered in thanksgiving for favors granted.

The small chapel decayed with the passage of time, but no one seemed to care. Then the madonna herself besought its restoration by appearing in a dream to a pious noblewoman, Eleonora of Santa Anastasia, the widow of Marcantonio of Sarno. This lady accordingly undertook to reinforce the walls of the little church; and a few years later another Neopolitan noble, Scipione de Rubeis Capece Secondito, was prompted by thanksgiving for a favor granted by the madonna to further strengthen the building, which he also embellished. This work was carried out toward the middle of the sixteenth century.

In 1590 a new wonder occurred that rekindled the ardor of the faithful. The protagonist was an ugly and evil woman, about forty years old, named Aurelia del Prete, who was said to be "the enemy of everything good and of every form of human and Christian consolation."[18] A few years earlier this woman had injured her foot while hewing wood and vowed to offer the Madonna of the Arch two wax feet if she recovered. When the wound healed, the woman duly purchased the two wax feet at Naples; but they fell from her hand and broke, and Aurelia began to curse and trample upon them in anger.

Subsequently, on the Monday after Easter 1589, Aurelia del Prete went to the feast of the madonna with her husband, who was fulfilling a vow. She also intended to sell a piglet at the fair. But she lost the animal and spent hours searching for it before she found it again near the image of the Virgin, together with her husband. Enraged, she began to curse and, seizing her husband's votive offering, cast it to the ground and trampled upon it. The next year, during Lent, illness struck Aurelia's lower limbs (a "dry gangrene"), and during the night between Easter Sunday and Monday 1590, her feet suddenly fell from her legs. Aurelia's family put the feet in a basket only to find that they could not remove them afterward. This induced them secretly to bury both the basket and the feet. But word leaked out; the authorities had the feet unearthed, and these were displayed on the main altar for a while and then in another prominent position in the church.

The new miracle revived the fervent worship of the Madonna of the Arch, and the little church was soon unable to hold the ever-growing number of the faithful and their votive offerings. Thus, on May 1, 1593, the bishop of Nola laid the cornerstone of the building that constitutes the present sanctuary. The inscription on the stone mentioned "the blasphemer, Aurelia, whose feet were chastized on the twentieth day of April in the year 1590."

The cult continued to flourish from 1600 to the present day. Father Arcangelo Dominici's manuscript and the pamphlets by the Dominican friars all contain long lists of miracles.[19] The beneficiaries are mainly peasants, fishermen, and sailors, though some members of the upper class are also mentioned.

The "history" of the origins of this cult is unusual, and it contrasts with the customary forms of the Marian legends describing the miraculous apparitions of the Virgin. In these she is often depicted as grieving over the evils of the world, yet always benignly provident, protective, and consoling; and her first miracle is normally some extraordinary deed that heals and regenerates life. Instead, the story of the Madonna of the Arch evokes an atmosphere of violence and provocation, and in a sense it is also ambivalent. Man scorns, the Celestial Mary inflicts punishment. The blasphemous ballplayer strikes the holy image: he is hanged and the lime tree withers. The ungrateful and ill-tempered woman tramples on the votive offering: her detached feet remain intact in the church, exposing her punishment to public view.

The avenging role ascribed to the madonna is definitely uncharacteristic. It does not harmonize with the idea of the Heavenly Mother, gentle and patient, who gathers the afflicted to her bosom.[20]

How can this role be explained? The simplest and most plausible hypothesis is that deep-rooted pre-Christian traditions were still alive in the territory around Naples in the fifteenth century and that they to some extent estranged the people from the Catholic religion. Perhaps some shock involving penitence and punishment was needed to renew the fear of God in them and to reestablish religious observances that had been neglected or abandoned.

The cult of the *fujenti*, whose origins I shall shortly discuss, could substantiate such a hypothesis. For the moment, however, two aspects of the legend must be stressed if we wish to interpret the cult of the Madonna of the Arch in terms of the cultural context from which it sprang: the game of pall-mall and the miracles performed by the madonna.

*The game of pall-mall*. Pall-mall,[21] which was played in the area until recent times, must have been very old and much relished by the local inhabitants. On this point we may cite a ban dating from A.D. 1600 that the Spanish viceroy, Carlo di Tappia, had inscribed in marble at the church of the Madonna of the Arch located at Miano (not far from Santa Anastasia): "By virtue of the present ban we order that, from this day hence, no person of any station or condition whatsoever shall attempt to play pall-mall in front of the Church of Our Lady of the Arch."[22] From this it may be inferred that a century and a half after the wondrous event at Santa Anastasia the game known as pall-mall was still played on church squares and that this custom was considered unseemly, if not sacrilegious, by clerical and lay authorities alike. We may therefore hazard a guess that, back in 1450 a deep-rooted custom—pleasing and superstitiously ritualized, perhaps, but at the same time viewed with distaste by a certain social class that was averse to any genuinely popular manifestation—became the basis of a "story" that was manipulated so as to rouse the people and restore Christian faith.

*The miracles of the Madonna of the Arch*. Among the miracles listed by a series of publications on the cult of the Madonna of the Arch, mention is made—from the seventeenth century on—of persons who were miraculously freed from the devil's influence and from "spells." The madonna, it is said, "frees human bodies from evil spirits"; "she is the terror of demons."[23] The example given is that of a man "possessed by an evil spirit" and "tormented by those infernal monsters," who returned to his senses thanks to the "compassionate Mother's" intervention. Again, there are the cases of a woman who vomited a crooked nail and of a fifteen-year-old boy who expectorated a black stone (both are diabolic signs). In the same vein, we are told of "obsessed" women who were forcibly dragged before the holy image and who thereafter recovered their sanity. Even some of the wood paintings used as votive offerings portray exorcism and possessed persons.[24]

That the cult of the Madonna of the Arch is permeated with magic certainly constitutes no unique or isolated phenomenon in the Catholic religion as it is popularly practiced. The outcasts, the downtrodden, the exploited who cannot free themselves from the yoke other men inflict upon them put their trust in the supernatural—a blend of magic and religion—discovering in that world a reassuring and gratifying form of escape. Their "trust" is an act of liberation that, by means of active and participatory dynamism, strips their resignation (the pivot on which historically determined Catholicism turns) of its implicitly devitalizing consequences.

What deserves instead to be underscored in the present case is that the exorcising elements of the cult concern forms of hysteria manifested by possessed persons or by those cast under a spell. And the representation of hysteria is precisely the dominant feature of the rite of the *fujenti*.

As stated earlier, the rite of the *fujenti* is the second component of the cult of the Madonna of the Arch. Yet despite the fact that this folk ritual so obviously characterizes the cult of the madonna, no mention is made of it in our historical sources, including both Father Dominici's manuscript and the propagandistic pamphlets composed in the sixteenth century by the Dominican friars (members of the very order that administers the Sanctuary of the Madonna of the Arch and that participates in the ceremony of the *fujenti* to the extent at least of appropriating the material fruits of their quest for alms). This silence is intentional, a convenient and easy way of rejecting noninstitutionalized forms of religion and nonofficial forms of culture that differ from those sanctioned by the current stereotypes.

Father Raimondo Sorrentino, writing in 1930, is the only author to speak of the rite, and he gives it a mere fleeting reference in a rather disparaging and indifferent tone. "On the Monday after Easter," he notes in the appendix to his book, "groups of men dressed in white with coloured bands around their waist and across their backs come running, barefooted and in double file, from their distant villages or from Naples to the Sanctuary. The purpose, *so they claim*, is to perform *some sort* of traditional act of devotion to Mary."[25]

Given the lack of sources, the following hypotheses concerning the rite of the *fujenti* may be advanced: (1) it arose at the same time as the cult of the madonna; (2) it arose in a period subsequent to that in which the cult originated; (3) it arose in a period prior to that in which the cult originated.

Hypotheses 1 and 2 appear unconvincing. The ritual seems to be performed by people whose basic personality structure could not have been formed in a single generation or even several generations.[26] If the rite was a sudden and improvised behavioral invention, one would surely find some trace of it in the literature, despite the disparaging indifference with which the historiographers regard popular culture. Proof of this is the fact that the sources do mention that the chapel and later the church were filled with votive offerings.

Hypothesis 3 has more merit, even if it is grounded on circumstantial evidence. Bearing in mind the historical period in which the cult of the Virgin Mary originated, the legends surrounding its foundation, and the type of society in which it was manifested, this hypothesis may be formulated in the following general terms; we are dealing with the phenomenon of a contamination or superimposition of two cults, one pagan and the other Christian. This may have resulted from a spontaneous syncretism effected by the people themselves. Alternatively, it may have been a consequence of psychological manipulations carried out or fostered by ecclesiastical authorities who undertook to promote the Catholic cult of Mary and who opposed the residual elements of pagan culture still surviving in the countryside around Somma, on the slopes of Mount Vesuvius, and along the coast as far as Naples and Pozzuoli.

In this perspective, the following considerations deserve attention: the founding of the sanctuary may be seen as part of the affirmation and expansion of the Marian cult that was promoted by the Council of Trent (1545–63). With regard to the Madonna of the Arch, indeed, the year 1590 marks the turning point from the legendary stage to the laying of the cornerstone of the church by the bishop of Nola. Efforts to introduce the cult of the Virgin Mary in the Mount Vesuvius area might have met with a hostile or indifferent reception. It should be recalled that the shrine dedicated to Mary was built on the ruins of a Roman aqueduct or of some other ancient structure. Moreover, the function of certain underground structures known to exist in the area even today cannot be explained by their local owners (the last traces of these are about to be destroyed by bulldozers at work on new building sites). The hostility or resistance of the populace to the Marian cult is also suggested by the very legends surrounding its origins. Instead of rewarding her devotees, the Madonna of the Arch punished the faithless and the blasphemers, and it is the authorities rather than the people who are the instruments of this punishment. The

King's Great Avenger hangs the first blasphemer, a poor peasant, and the "authorities" order Aurelia del Prete's feet to be dug up and displayed in the church as proof of her sacrilege and castigation. This seems to indicate that the dominant culture conditioned the religious transformation of the people by manipulating traditional beliefs as a function of the institutionalized cult.

The zone in which the sanctuary of the Madonna of the Arch was built was the least accessible of all the districts in the Mount Vesuvius area. It is one of those isolated and difficult-to-reach zones that tend to be among the most conservative, as ethnological studies on the dissemination of cultural traits have shown.[27]

The peasants in the Mount Vesuvius area, who probably descended from Roman slaves, were not bound to landlords except by a tie of economic dependence. It is known that esoteric cults of the Great Mother, which originated in the Orient, spread among the Roman servant classes.

Centers of the cult of the Great Mother may be found in various parts of southern Italy.[28] With particular regard to cults originating in the Orient, we know that in Roman times there was a temple of Isis at Pompei and a temple of Serapis at Pozzuoli (both of which are less than twenty kilometers from Santa Anastasia in a direct line). In these places, Christianity may not have proved an easy task. Bartolo Longo, who at the end of the last century founded the Sanctuary of the Madonna of Pompei (a cult that fiercely rivaled that of the Madonna of the Arch), proclaimed the triumph of the Virgin Mary in a land that was "the abode of the pagan dead."

The Great Mother is a beneficent consoler: *Mater dei salutaris*. And in the Villa of Mysteries at Pompei there is a fresco portraying the worshipers of Isis in certain poses that evoke the exaltation of the *fujenti*.

Attis, the son of the Great Mother, Cybele, was called "the good shepherd" like Christ, and he would die and be reborn in harmony with nature's own rhythms. His mystery, like the mystery of Easter, was celebrated in the spring. The feast of the Madonna of the Arch must likewise be regarded fundamentally as a spring initiation rite characterized by a show of astounding vitality (the running, the dancing, the fits of hysteria). In this connection, one must remember that the term *fujenti* (*fuggenti*, "those who flee") indicates a dynamic emotional state, whereas the term *vattiente* (*battente*) derives from the word *vattiare*, which means "to baptize, to initiate."

The flight and running are dynamic acts associated in ancient Mediterranean culture with the state of being possessed (as, for example, the possession of Io by Hera). Only by reaching a set goal could the liberating catharsis be obtained.[29] This type of possession catharsis, represented symbolically (and on the level of unconscious reproduction) in the ceremony of the *fujenti*, may be reflected in the madonna's deliverance of possessed persons and of those cast under a spell.

These considerations may be marshaled to support either of two theses. One is that the similarities between the old and the new creeds in terms of ritual traits and goals created some confusion in the minds of simple, unsophisticated worshipers, a thesis that suggests a spontaneous syncretism on the part of the people. The other is that an ideological campaign was undertaken to graft the cult of the Virgin Mary onto a deep-rooted pre-Christian religious tradition that was congenital to the people. What matters in either case is that the institutional church, in dealing with the ritualizations of the Madonna of the Arch and their complex cultural implications, finds itself in a compromised position from which it cannot easily escape today.

## Church Attitudes toward the Rite of the *Fujenti*

That the institutionalized church adopted a tolerant attitude toward the rite of the *fujenti* is shown by the fact that for centuries—with the tacit support of the ecclesiastical authorities—the sanctuary flourished and grew precisely because of the fervid religious aura (with its concomitant stimulus to tourism) conferred upon this holy place by the ceremony on the Monday after Easter. The sanctuary was enlarged, the votive offerings were suitably housed, and needed restorations were carried out. A modern, fully equipped hotel was built, and it provides bar and restaurant facilities. Historical studies of the cult were fostered, and an information bulletin began to be published.

As previously observed, the Dominican friars who administer the sanctuary appropriate part of the alms collected by the *fujenti*, and this demonstrates their full involvement in, and coresponsibility for, at least the "temporal" side of the religious manifestation. To be sure, Father Raimondo Sorrentino took a dim view of the rite of the *fujenti* in the book he published in 1930. But this was not a defense of religious orthodoxy so much as a statement of his own prejudice against a "different" form of culture belonging to some subspecies of the human race that expressed itself in a "weird," "unpleasing," and "unseemly" manner.[30] On the whole, then, we may affirm that, up to the Ecumenical Council known as Vatican II (1962–65), the church accepted the feast of the *fujenti* (and utilized it at the local level).

The Vatican II Council marked a decisive turning point in the history of the church. Among other things, it laid down clear guidelines for a return to the authentic contents of an evangelic message that had been sullied by the contamination of temporal power, by the age-old accretions of cultural superstructures, and by spurious cultural superimpositions that lie between magic and religion.

In the spirit of this council, the church began to subject the Catholic creed to a process of purification. It took a stand against dubious or fictitious saints, it opposed religious rites that betrayed a pagan character, it made the Word comprehensible by eliminating the barrier of Latin from the liturgy, and it invited the faithful to share collectively in the eucharistic celebration. To fully comprehend the later course of ecclesiastical action, moreover, it must be seen that the spirit of the council harbored two very distinct guiding principles capable of producing two separate and nonparallel currents of ideas and endeavors. One of these was concerned with accepted practice, a conservative attempt to safeguard the institutionalized ecclesiastical system from dangerous contaminations and compromises ever more apparent and deplorable in the present context of rapid sociocultural evolution. The second was concerned with the vital prophetic message, the Christian's attempt to recover his own evangelic identity through a quest for man's liberation irrespective of his particular set of beliefs.

After the council, in 1966, the church began to examine the "case" of the *fujenti*. The result was "a set of rules for the *fujenti*" that appeared in the January/March issue of the bulletin published by the sanctuary. The six categoric and rather laconic injunctions that emanated imply a highly critical opinion of certain aspects of the feast. The first concerns women: "Women are hereby forbidden to take part in the companies or squadrons formed by men. It is fitting that they proceed in separate groups, in a dignified manner, without running, and that they be decently dressed. Let them exercise self-control to avoid the ridiculous fainting spells to which their highly emotional natures may incline them." Clearly, this discrimination between the sexes with its specific reference to the behavior of the women (which, in succeeding rules, is repeated and extended to all the pilgrims) and to their hysterical fits (there is no parallel censure of the men, who are no less subject to them) is less a function of ecclesiastical ideology than of male chauvinism based on prejudices that still circumscribe the position of women in society.

Briefly summarized, the other rules seek to enforce standards of dignified behavior and to ensure an orderly approach to the church. They also require pilgrims to attend mass before departing for the sanctuary, and they forbid the holding of contests and the awarding of prizes in connection with the pilgrimage.

But these rules were not obeyed, and in 1971 the bishops of Campania felt obliged to address a message to those who make the pilgrimage to the Madonna of the Arch. In a low-keyed statement couched in the paternalistic language of an informal sermon, the bishops justify their intervention in terms of "their responsibility for the purity of the faith and of the divine worship and for the straight and narrow path of the people of God." The *fujenti* are "beloved brethren" whose "simplicity," "sacrifices," and "enthusiasm" are admirable. The bishops' strictures are cautiously phrased "recommendations" not to dance, not to carry the image of the madonna when soliciting alms, and to behave with "dignity," "propriety," and "discipline." They are also concerned with the pilgrims' associations:

> We are gratified by the knowledge that every day, after work, you amuse yourselves at your meeting places in the presence of the image of the madonna, which is always illuminated and surrounded by flowers. The gathering of brothers beneath the smiling and indulgent gaze of the Virgin is soothing to your physical and spiritual forces, and it tends to strengthen the bonds of Christian love among you. Allow us to say, however, that such recreation (card playing and the like) should be governed by the laws of God. Avoid anger, oaths, scurrilous language, and do not allow gambling to jeopardize your family life and peace in any way. The fruits of your labour should be spent to sustain your families and to educate your children. The family is sacred. God curses anyone who endangers the welfare of the family.

The tone of the statement is conciliatory and at times even flattering, and recourse is made to the same language and stereotypes that the traditionalist church has habitually used in addressing the masses (e.g., "the smiling and indulgent gaze of the Madonna"; "the Virgin herself would suffer and weep"; "the Lord wanted the Marian Sanctuaries to arise in the world as places of joyous encounter between men and God under the charming eyes of Mary, the Mother"; "God curses . . ."). But this betrays not so much the need to make themselves understood by humble and simple people as the prudence and discomfort of those who know they cannot abruptly impede popular forms of religious expression that, for centuries, were accepted, fostered, and exploited to strengthen the power of the church.

The January/March 1972 issue of the *Bollettino* of the Sanctuary of the Madonna of the Arch contains "a set of rules for the success of the pilgrimages" in accordance with the spirit underlying the bishop's own "recommendations." This time, however, no mention is made of the dances, the begging, the unseemly behavior, or the women. The categorical prohibitions of 1966 are not repeated, and the various measures proposed merely tend to ensure the proper organization and satisfactory outcome of the religious manifestations. Yet it was precisely in this climate of moderate ecclesiastical intervention that the case of the *fujenti* was turned into a public issue with scandalous overtones in the press.

General elections in Italy had been scheduled for May 1972, right after Easter. In the course of preelectoral skirmishing between the parties, the conservative Neapolitan press reported that the archbishop of Naples, Cardinal Corrado Ursi, had vetoed the holding of the feast of the *fujenti* on the Monday after Easter.[31] To single out the archbishop in person as being responsible for a collective attempt by the bishops of Campania to repress the profane aspects of the feast in honor of the Madonna of the Arch was a political expedient (in point of fact, the bishops had merely "deplored" these aspects without prohibiting them). It sought to exploit both the ideological leanings ascribed to the archbishop and the dominant cultural attitude in the Naples area, where the monarchic structure of society is viewed with favor. Specifically, Cardinal Ursi is considered a "liberal" by the conservative wing of the Christian Democrat party, which receives a majority of the votes in the Campania region, and by that part of the clergy which supports these right-wing elements.[32] If the cardinal had been considered personally responsible for some revolt by the *fujenti* against his veto, or if the *fujenti* had publicly and flagrantly disobeyed his orders, conservative propaganda would have made political capital out of his resulting loss of face.

As matters turned out, the 1972 edition of the feast of the Madonna of the Arch, which I attended, was held as usual, with all the customary proceedings. Then, in 1973, the bishops of Campania issued a paper entitled "The Popular Cult and the Ecclesiastical Community," in which the problem is examined in general terms, with no specific

12. Devotees eating after the pilgrimage to the Madonna dell'Arco. *(Photograph by Lello Mazzacane)*

references to any particular rites and feasts. The authors of this paper recognize that popular religious feasts are "a means of breaking the daily routine" and that they constitute "pauses that free the participants from the pressures of need and neuroses." But they nonetheless deem it necessary to prevent these feasts "from becoming nothing more than an expression of resurgent paganism." To this end, the bishops lay down a set of "practical rules" for the observance of folk-cult practices with the avowed aim of purifying these same practices and of conferring upon them "a convincing aura of pastoral and liturgical propriety." Finally, they affirm the principle that "religious feasts fall under the exclusive jurisdiction of the ecclesiastical authorities" who are to control their administrative, financial, and organizational aspects through the parish priests.

This is not the place to discuss this paper in depth, nor are we in a position to analyze theological propositions. In a religious perspective, however, this attempt to convert a popular ritual into something pure and aseptic by filtering out its worldly and profane elements strikes one as a contradictory reductive operation, to say the least, one that in effect would transform an "existential mode" of religious expression into a functional "instrument" of the system.

On the psychological and cultural planes, moreover, the authoritarian presumption implicit in the attempt to prefabricate a "model," to administer it, and to impose it upon the people would seem to reveal grave errors of judgment. In the specific case at hand, it would amount to depriving the people—destitute and instrumentalized as they are—of a moment of creative and liberating "magic" in their approach to God. Above all, it would heighten the conflict, which is always with us in the background, between the culture of the dominant and that of the subordinate classes.

In keeping with the strictures of the bishops of Campania, the *Bollettino* of the Sanctuary of the Madonna of the Arch (January/March issue, 1973) contains a new list of unconditional norms and prohibitions. Seven in number, these reiterate the rules of 1966, including the warning to female pilgrims, who are required to dress and behave with dignity and who are forbidden to join the ranks of the men or to allow themselves to faint.

## Official Religion versus Living Religion

What has so far been said about the attitudes of the institutional church toward the cult of the *fujenti* must be viewed, historically and anthropologically, in a broader and more complete cultural and religious context that transcends the limitations of a documentary record. Here the point to be made is that the theoretical and empirical patterns characteristic of the relation between church and folk cult in the case of the *fujenti* are themselves but a further instance of the specific form of antithesis between the state religion and the religion of the people that characterizes the unbroken religious history of Italy.

This theme of the dualism—ever alive and present—between two heterogeneous forms of religion was treated in a concise historical essay published in 1947 by Raffaele Pettazzoni.[33] Pettazzoni's study starts from the year 186 B.C., in which the Roman state put a bloody end to the esoteric religious movement of the Bacchanals. The Bacchanals[34] formed religious, not political, sects. Yet they were viewed in a political light by a Roman state that was suffering the dire consequences of the long Second Punic War, a state that was governed by the conservative party of Cato, who opposed every innovation. The Bacchanalia constituted a "mystery," an occult and unfathomable world that seemed a fount of dark threats to the codified structure of the Roman political and religious system. Its mystery and "immorality" were interwoven in a questionable existential context that was "different" from that of Rome, so solid, legalitarian, and taken for granted. It was an ideal drama, Pettazzoni declares, a conflict between *the* religious world espoused by the state and *a* religious world espoused by man.

From the repression of the Bacchanals to the persecution of the Christians, the Roman state consistently adhered to a policy of rejecting all religious innovations, which it regarded as sociocultural phenomena potentially capable of undermining its own established structures.[35] Christianity appeared as *the* religion of man par excellence. Where Roman paganism projected its power and protective services beyond the individual to the benefit of the *familia*, the *gens*, and the *res publica*, the new religion of Christ offered its scheme of salvation to *every* man, proposing the vision of the *Civitas Dei* as the final and supreme goal.

Yet, after the persecutions and as a result of historical processes reaching from Constantine to Theodosius, it was precisely to Christianity that the Roman state assigned the task of resolving the age-old problem of the religious unification of the empire. It was the most widespread religion in all the provinces (by virtue of the fact that it was a religion of the people); but the spirit animating it was also the most alien to the state religion and the least compatible with paganism, whether Roman or that of the mysteries. In the end, when Christianity itself became a state religion, both the pagan gods and the Roman Empire perished together.

The elimination of paganism and the advent of religious unification did not mark the end of the conflict arising from the dualism between state religion and religion of the people. On the contrary, as Pettazzoni observes in his historical study, it reemerged in the Middle Ages "in the only way compatible with Christian exclusiveness, that is to say, under the common banner of Christianity itself." This is the perspective in which we must view the struggles between the Holy Roman Empire and the church and those between the emperor, who wanted religious supremacy, and the pope, who wanted political supremacy.

This dualism, according to Pettazzoni, did not end even with the constitution of the civil state and its separation from the church. This is because the "secular" sphere that the state wishes to govern contains something sacred within it, whereas the realm of the sacred belonging to the church encroaches upon parts of the secular sphere that the church refuses to yield.

Though Pettazzoni coherently applies his thesis to the various stages of Italian history, it suffices for our purposes to underscore his clear identification, in the context of Roman history, of the conflict between state religion and "other" religions (foreign cults and mysteries), which he termed "of man" by virtue of their emphasis on the individual and their contraposition to the official religion. In other words, the dualism between the two forms of religion is quite sharply configured in this historical context. Moreover, Pettazzoni shows that when Christianity became "absolute," owing to its exclusivist nature, the religious dualism within its bosom continued to operate either in the form of a conflict between the state (which has an undeniable religious character) and the church (whose religious values harbor conspicuous political implications) or in the form of reciprocal interference in the political and religious contents that determine the makeup of both organisms.

Although we recognize the signs of religious dualism in the compromises and interaction between the temporal and spiritual powers (between that which Christianity has become as a historical construction and that which it ought to be as an evangelic stage of human existence), we think that, in the Christian context, the dualistic tension between state religion and religion of the people has a dimension and a significance that is directly analogous to what Pettazzoni identified in the historical context of Rome. On one side stands the church as institution: a complex theological, ideological, territorial, administrative, and financial structure that in the course of its historical development ends by becoming a state. On the other side we find the living religion of man: the Christian religion of the people, imbued with misery and suffering, wavering between faith and magic, projected toward a "celestial" world, a liberator of man the slave. This last is a religion that may sprout from the thrilling improvisation of a saint (the Franciscan movement was originally a folk religion, for example), from collective participation in what is experienced as a miracle, from legends and traditions, or from an ancient and archaic cultural matrix. Whatever its origins, it takes root among the people, eluding the grip of orthodoxy and overflowing ecclesiastical and canonical boundary lines. It renders the secular holy and it makes sacred things profane, because humble and simple men need to see and "to touch" in order to believe and take heart.

These "two" religions have coexisted under the "common banner" of Christianity throughout the entire span of its history, that is to say, from the point where the church became a "structure" up to the present time. A historical analysis of this interaction would prove highly rewarding and would place our enquiry and its documentary material at the service of a sociological and anthropological study of religious phenomenology in Italy. But this subject cannot be dealt with here, and the following considerations will therefore have to suffice. So-called popular forms of religion are *the* religion of the subordinate class (even though members of the dominant class may participate in them). The motives that impel members of the dominant class to take part in folk cults are wholly antithetical to those governing the participation of the poor, though they fit in with the "traditionalist" religious schemes of the precouncil church. The poor and the exploited place their trust in the supernatural to liberate themselves from human conditioning, from exploitation, from want; whereas the "haves"—the middle and upper classes, as the case may be—seek contact with God to gratify and reassure themselves with regard to their present positions. Religious phenomena have, therefore, a cultural dimension and, more fundamentally still, a social dimension. The aim of the institutional church to "modify" the folk cults by purifying them of spurious secular and pagan accretions seems to be vitiated by an uncritical optimism, to say the least, when it presumes that such modification can be achieved through "rules," "papers," and "writs of censure." Behind the cult there lies a human condition that is what truly requires modification. The liberation of man, which is so often invoked today, will not be brought about either by an illusory ideological exploit or by a project that can be codified in precepts. It is instead a political, social, cultural, and religious "commitment" of which human society as a whole must be persuaded.

## Notes

1. For a description of the painted votive offerings in the sanctuary, see Toschi and Penna, *Le tavolette*.

2. Tuberculosis of the lungs is a social malady that primarily strikes the undernourished and those who live in unwholesome environmental conditions.

3. Making the pilgrimage barefoot was forbidden by the church authorities. With rare exceptions, this seems to be the only "rule" the *fujenti* obey.

4. According to a statement in the *Bollettino del Santuario*, p. 3.

5. Some of these towns lie as far as thirty-five kilometers from Santa Anastasia.

6. The rector told me that these included a night watchman, a railway employee, the owner of a shoe store, and a lawyer.

7. A conference of the presidents of the unions was held at the sanctuary in March 1974, with the Supervisory Council of the Neapolitan Curia in attendance. On May 1, 1974, four hundred members made a pilgrimage to the Cathedral of Naples.

8. *Panorama*, no. 312.

9. Sums of 300,000 lire (in 5,000- and 10,000-lire notes) were attached to several banners witnessed by the author in 1972. There were also dollar bills and other foreign currency that had been donated by emigrants.

10. So states Father Raimondo Sorrentino in *Storia della miraculosa immagine*. This book more or less follows several seventeenth-century pamphlets published by the Dominican friars to propagate the miracles worked by the Madonna of the Arch.

11. Every company must report the number of its components to the Dominican friar who supervises the entry of the groups into the sanctuary. On the basis of these declarations, yearly statistics are compiled on the number of *fujenti* taking part in the rite.

12. For example, commands such as "attention" and "at ease" are issued. Before they kneel in front of the altar, the men execute a military salute by raising the hand to the forehead.

13. As previously noted, these statistics are compiled by the Dominican friars on the basis of the figures reported for each of the "companies." Attendance in 1973 was at about the same level; there was a slight decline in 1974, when it rained. In April 1977 there were 21,351 *fujenti* organized in 238 groups. Ninety-four of these groups were permanent associations established in and around Naples. This same year 525 persons needed first aid after being overcome by emotion during the festival. Most devotees marched (without cars) to the sanctuary, and 80 groups used no shoes.

14. Modern amusements include popular music concerts, sometimes with name artists, and prizes for the best painting (of nonreligious subjects as well), for the best singer, and even for the most elegantly dressed child. The bishops of Campania and the administrators of the sanctuary, who issue the "rules" governing the feast, have taken a dim view of these nonreligious events and the tendency to use funds collected for the Madonna of the Arch and the sanctuary to meet the expense.

15. Cantone in *Storia di pomigliano d'arco* affirms that this denomination stemmed from the fact that the shrine had been built on the remains of an arch of the Roman aqueduct that carried water from Serino to Nola.

16. This is the date given by Father Dominici, but other historians disagree. In the pamphlets written by the Dominican friars to propagate the miracles of the madonna, the year is given as 1500 (Rosella, *Il sacro Campidoglio*; Ayrola, *L'Arco celeste*; Montorio, *Lo zodiaco di Maria*). Pellet (*Naples contemporaine*) [Paris, 1894]) speaks of 1517.

17. *Palla a maglio,* or pall-mall: a rudimentary form of golf in which the players strike a wooden ball with a mallet about a meter in length.

18. Sorrentino, *Storia della miraculosa immagine,* p. 40.

19. See n. 16.

20. The cult of the Madonna of Pompei, which was established near Santa Anastasia toward the middle of the last century, is based on this more traditional stereotype. The new cult seriously rivaled that of the Madonna of the Arch, and in this competition it has been victorious.

21. See n. 17.

22. De Boucard, *Usi e costumi di Napoli,* p. 924.

23. Rosella, *Il sacro Campidoglio.*

24. Toschi and Penna, *Le tavolette.*

25. Sorrentino, *Storia della miraculosa immagine,* pp. 192–93; italics mine.

26. Basic personality is that part of the personality that is acquired through child-rearing methods and educational processes and contents. Though these tools differ from society to society, their number is usually limited in each case and they tend to be similar in nature. As a result, each society produces one or several types of basic personality. This limitation on the variations of basic personality is greater in traditional societies that are not highly stratified. Here changes in basic personality occur very slowly and only in the course of many generations.

27. Compare the methodology expounded in the works of Schmidt, Cooper, and Sapir.

28. For a study of this cult see James, *Mother Goddess.*

29. De Martino, *La terra del rimorso.*

30. Here is how Father Sorrentino phrased it: "The spectacle is weird, unpleasing, and hardly religious." He expressed the hope that "it will become possible to eliminate unseemly and censurable forms of worship" (*Storia della miraculosa immagine*).

31. The news item appeared in the daily papers *Roma* and *Il Mattino,* as well as in various magazines.

32. We are dealing with a cultural context that prefers power to be concentrated in the hands of a single person. In ascribing the bishops' unpopular intervention to Cardinal Ursi, the aim was to discredit the decision and the authority on which it rested in the eyes of the people. Compare the interview in the weekly magazine *Panorama,* no. 389.

33. Pettazzoni, "Una storia religiosa d'Italia," pp. 69–76. A French translation entitled "Religion de l'état et religion de l'homme" appeared in *La Revue de Culture Européene,* pp. 45–55.

34. The Bacchanals were devotees of a Bacchic (or Dionysiac) religion of an esoteric character. Membership in the community, which was initially reserved to women and later opened up to men, was gained by initiation after long and laborious proceedings. The ceremonies were held at night in the woods by the banks of the Tiber, beneath the slopes of the Aventine hill. The historical sources—the *Senatus Consultum* of 186 and Tito Livio (bk. 39)—record that the choral singing of psalms, the music of timpani and cymbals,

and sinister howling were to be heard in the vicinity. Lighted torches moving in the darkness were also seen (they were borne by women who ran along the river bank).

35. In 139 B.C., the Jews and the Chaldeans were expelled from Rome. The Egyptian mystery cults were banned in the last decades of the republic. Augustus reconfirmed these measures, and he was seconded by Agrippa. Tiberius subjected the same cults to a violent persecution, which was subsequently extended to the Jews. Claudius later banished the Jews and quelled the tumults inspired by a certain Cresto, which is the earliest evidence we have of the presence of Christians at Rome.

## Bibliography

Ayrola, Father L. *L'Arco celeste* [The celestial arch]. 1688.
*Bolletino del Santuario della Madonna dell'Arco* 81, no. 1 (Jan./Feb. 1974).
Cantone, A. *Storia di pomigliano d'arco*. 1923.
De Bouchard. *Usi e costumi di Napoli* [The uses and customs of Naples]. Milan, 1970.
De Martino, Ernesto. *La terra del rimorso* [The land of remorse]. Milan, 1960.
James, E. O. *The Cult of the Mother Goddess*. London: Thames and Hudson, 1959.
Montorio, Father P. *Lo zodiaco di Maria* [The zodiac of Mary]. 1715.
*Panorama*, no. 312 (Apr. 13, 1972), no. 389 (Oct. 4, 1973).
Pettazzoni, Raffaele. "Idea di una storia religiosa d'Italia" [The idea of a religious history of Italy]. *La rassegna d'Italia* (Milan) 2, nos. 6, 7, 8 (1947): 69–76.
———. "Religion de l'état et religion de l'homme." *La Revue de Culture Européene* (Paris) 3, no. 5 (1953): 45–55.
Rosella, Father Pietro. *Il sacro Campidoglio* [The holy capitol]. Naples, 1653.
Sorrentino, Raimondo M. *Storia della miracolosa immagine di Maria SS. dell'Arco e del suo Santuario*. Pompei: Francesco Sicignano, 1931.
Toschi, Paolo, and Penna, Renato. *Le tavolette votive della Madonna dell'Arco* [Wood paintings as votive offerings to the Madonna of the Arch]. Cava dei Tipreni, Italy: Di Mauro, 1971.

# 6

## The Worship of Mother Earth
## in Russian Culture
### by Joanna Hubbs

Boris Pilnyak, in an early postrevolutionary story of Russian rural life, draws together the complex of emotions linked to the notion of the earth as mother among the peasantry:

> Mother Earth, like love and sex, is a mystery; for her own
> secret purposes she divided mankind into male and female; she
> lures men irresistibly; the peasants kiss the earth like sons, carry
> her with them as an amulet, talk softly to her, cast spells in her
> name to charm love and hatred, sun and day. The peasants swear
> by Mother Earth as they do by love and death. Spells are woven
> over her, and in the night a naked widow who has known all things
> is harnessed to a plow, and the plow is guided by two naked
> virgins who have the earth and the world before them. It is for a
> woman to take the part of Mother Earth. But Mother Earth herself
> is fields, forests, swamps, coppices, hills, distances, years,
> nights, days, blizzards, storms, calm. . . . You can either curse
> Mother Earth or love her.[1]

Earth appears here as maternal life force and beguiling siren, but also as witch and destroyer who holds men in her grasp and lures them to their deaths. Russian literature of the nineteenth and twentieth centuries resonates with similar evocations of her power. As Mother Russia, she is sometimes cursed as a devouring sow. More often she is represented as a mystical and maternal source of life and strength defining the limits of human experience.[2] The historian of religion George Fedotov sees the urge toward communion with a maternal force, present throughout art and folklore, as the basis of Russian religiosity: "At every step in studying Russian popular religion," he writes, "one meets the constant longing for a great divine female power. . . . Is it too daring to hypothesize, on the basis of this religious propensity, the scattered elements of the cult of the Great Goddess who once reigned upon the immense Russian plains?"[3]

My purpose here is to suggest how in religion, folk custom and lore, literature, and social structure, the centricity of the worship of the feminine, though aboriginal, is challenged, modified, but never eliminated. I explore only a few of the cultural implications of this fact in the concluding pages of this essay, which deal with Soviet society. What I present here, then, is a brief and highly compact synopsis of an approach to a complex phenomenon, bringing to it as much evidence to support my thesis as space permits.

## Prehistoric Traces of the Cult of a Great Goddess in Russia

Despite Fedotov's caution, archaeological excavations revealing a profusion of female figurines from the Paleolithic and Neolithic eras indicate that Russia was in fact not only a cradleland but also a diffusionary area for the cult of a maternal goddess, symbol of nature as mother, whose seasonal cycle is assimilated to human and animal life.[4] Recently, a U.S. and a Soviet scholar have suggested the dominant position of a Great Goddess in a Neolithic culture dated from around 5000 B.C. and centered in the Ukraine and Moldavia.[5] The excavation of the agrarian civilization of Tripolye has disclosed a number of well-preserved house-shaped shrines. Inside, female figurines are grouped around altars and hearths.[6] At the lowest levels, dating from the sixth millennium, the goddess still assumes her Paleolithic form as deity of hunters and gatherers, as their mistress of animals. She is represented in zoomorphic shape. Sometimes she appears as a mother bear, or with a serpent's head, nursing a tiny snake. Often she is a bird whose back is filled with clay eggs. To stress her transformational nature, she is shown not only as snake and egg, but also as frog and butterfly.

The early embodiments of the goddess indicate the farming community's hunting origins and its ignorance or perhaps denigration of the masculine role in reproduction. The fact that the transformational element is accorded importance suggests that the goddess was seen as creating her offspring parthenogenetically, through her own magic. The notion of self-insemination is further expressed in other

Tripolye artifacts related to early agricultural rites, which reflect the goddess's function as rain giver. Ruler over both earth and sky, she was thought to moisten the very soil out of which she would create life.[7]

Only in the later Neolithic period at Tripolye is man's role as inseminator emphasized, a recognition perhaps related to the advent of stock breeding, which emerged as an offshoot of woman-dominated hoe agriculture. Stock breeding pointed toward effective control over the reproductive processes of nature. As man and livestock appeared to aid in the labor of the fields, so the figure of the goddess is now modified to reflect her dependency upon masculine fertilization. She is represented as a pregnant goddess accompanied by a male son and consort, the dying and reviving vegetation god. By the fourth millennium, the presence of this couple parallels Near Eastern development.[8] At this point a break in the cult seems to occur and the goddess as central symbol of a maternal universe is challenged by her masculine consort. He will, over the ensuing millennia, increasingly attempt to free himself from her sphere, assuming her powerful role, while at the same time derogating the importance of feminine functions and affirming the all creative aspect of masculine fertilization.

## The Coming of Patriarchy

Modifications in the cult of the goddess seem to coincide with a bifurcation into farming and pastoral societies. This division brings the beginning of a patriarchy linked with the nomadic herders of the Eurasian steppes (later to be known as Indo-Europeans). Incursions into the Near East, the Mediterranean, and Western Europe resulted in the patriarchalization of agricultural civilizations. Tripolye was savagely destroyed, but its legacy persisted in the substratum to nourish further cultural development in Russia, as in the Balkans. More frequently, however, the invading patriarchs accommodated their divinities to those of the indigenous goddess-worshiping cultures. Though they brought with them a social and religious organization asserting masculine functions, the Indo-European invaders did not immediately denigrate the importance of a Great Goddess. The arrogation of her powers was piecemeal. Male divinities representing sun, rain, and wind began to impose their potency upon an earth presented in more and more passive terms, as the maternal soil in need of the fecundating sky to create life. The practice of cremation marks a symbolic revolt against the clutches of Mother Earth by "freeing" the body to ascend to the sky, rather than to descend underground into her realm.

In the area of the Black Sea, the cult of a Great Goddess identified with a matriarchal population of the first millennium appears to have been assimilated by Greek and Scythian intruders.[9] The sixth-century Greek historian and traveler Herodotus suggests that the story of an encounter by Herakles with a cave-dwelling half-serpent goddess and his union with her reflected a myth of Scythian origin.[10] Herodotus's distinction between nomadic and agricultural Scythian tribes may indeed refer to a distinction between native and invading tribes, and his account of the Scythian conquest of the man-hating Amazons and subsequent marriage with them suggests an accommodation between the patriarchal invaders and indigenous matriarchal tribes. Of course, this is speculative. But when we turn to Herodotus's description of the Scythian pantheon, we find a Great Goddess surrounded by sky gods. The double-tiered nature of the pantheon indicates a fusion between two sets of divinities. The top triad is dominated by a Great Goddess identified by Herodotus with the Greek Hestia, goddess of the hearth. She is accompanied by the goddess Earth, who is in turn associated with a husband called "Father" (Papeus). Whereas this group is predominantly feminine, the divinities of the second group are preeminently male, as though reversing the top order. Three gods—whom Herodotus associates with Apollo, Herakles, and Ares—flank the single, but "Celestial," Aphrodite. The function of these male gods seems to imply attempts to deny chthonian dependency: Ares, the war god, linked with the falling of meteorites, is represented in the form of a sword stuck into a mound and presides over a cremation cult; Apollo appears as the inseminating sun god; and Herakles is, in fact, the heroic slayer of feminine elements, serpent strangler and tamer of the Amazons. Yet despite the marked growth in the representation of male power, the worship of a Great Goddess was, from the testimony of cult objects discovered by archaeologists, central to the initiation of Scythian warriors. Moreover, the masculine priesthood claimed to derive its power—and its feminine attire—from Aphrodite.[11]

The anomaly of a central goddess in the patriarchal Scythian society, a society that regarded women as chattel, may be traceable not only to the influence of the farming population's rites but to the Scythian religion itself. Shamanic elements reflect memories of the omnipotent Paleolithic and Neolithic cave mother and mistress of animals. Though Mircea Eliade and others who have studied sha-

13. Goddess with animals in nineteenth-century Russian embroidery.

manism have related it to herding and hunting cultures, the Soviet anthropologist L. Shternberg has suggested its connection with
underworld cults concerned with fertility over which the feminine
presides.[12] Furthermore, shamanic initiatory ceremonies offer a vivid
image of the central empowering function of the feminine in the
future shaman's acquisition of magical powers. Often the figures represent a mistress of animals, and the pattern of descent prior to ascent
in a number of rites enacted by the shamanic candidate refers us not
only to puberty rituals but also to the pattern of death and rebirth of
the seasonal god.

## Feminine Divinities of the Slavs

The results of the process of patriarchalization of farming communities by waves of nomadic invaders are apparent as we move from
the Scythians and their successors to the religion of the Slavs who
coalesced into the Russian state by the ninth century A.D. At first
sight, the Slavic pantheon seems bereft of feminine influence. Only
one goddess appears and she is considered to be a divinity of secondary importance—a goddess for women. The male deities of the invader and warrior ruling classes, the Nordic Varangians, are now
empowered with the fertility functions that the Great Goddess of
Tripolye once held. But on closer examination we find that the status
of these gods is invariably traceable to feminine powers. For example,
the smith god Svarog is accompanied in Slavic mythology by a group
of maidens called *vily*, to whom offerings are made in caves and at
springs. These maidens are capable of transformation into animals, as
is Svarog himself. The reference to empowerment by female spirits is

elaborated in a myth that tells of an original unity of man with the maidens. They had taught him to plow, raise abundant harvests, and bury the dead. But because of his sins, disharmony was created and man was separated from his original mothers. When they disappeared from the earth in anger, they retained their protective qualities but also acquired evil ones by becoming mistresses of death who lured men to their realms. In fact, Russian scholars agree on the aboriginal worship of female spirits associated with water and forests among the Slavs and trace the names of male divinities to invading populations.[13]

The central role of a feminine deity worshiped by a peasant aboriginal population is further suggested in the motifs of Russian prerevolutionary folk art. In wood carvings, embroidery, house decorations, and jewelry appears a goddess resembling one represented on Scythian artifacts. She is flanked by animals and accompanied by horsemen. The assertion of her central role in the natural order suggests a conflict between peasant and ruler. For it is not the peasant who pays homage to the goddess but mounted warriors, nomads who had controlled peasant society for millennia. The peasants appear to have denied that their rulers governed the earth or had even established the dominant social order. In the art of peasant craftsmen and women, these proud and powerful lords are obliged to pay reverence to the feminine force of life, either in the form of a goddess or, in schematization, as the tree of life.[14] This feminine and omnipotent presence may thus have represented the Mother Moist Earth (*Mat' Syra Zemlia*) so frequently invoked in folksong and lore.

In the official ninth-century pantheon reflecting the imposition of dominant male gods by Nordic invaders, the goddess Mokosh (whose name implies moisture) is relegated to secondary importance —presiding over women, childbirth, and animals.[15] In these functions, however, clear elements of the former omnipotence of a Great Goddess are still apparent. Her association with moisture may refer back to a prehistoric origin as the self-fertilizing rain goddess whose presence we saw at Tripolye and whose continuing image is reflected in the Mother Moist Earth of folklore.

The cult of ancestors central to clan (*rod*) existence, which was assimilated by the Slavs to the agricultural cycle, is dominated by feminine divinities linked with Mokosh that are called *rozhanitsy*.[16] These are goddesses of fate as well as childbirth, and they are accompanied by a male deity called Rod, who may embody symbolically the collective souls of the dead ancestors in the maternal earth. Thus, Rod may be linked to the notion of a dying and reviving vegeta-

14. Northern Russian embroidery motif, portraying the goddess surrounded by warriors and sun disks.

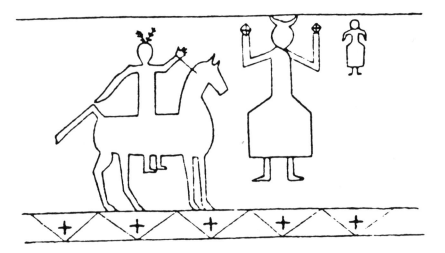

15. The goddess-and-horseman motif in Russian embroidery.

16. The goddess flanked by horsemen in Russian embroidery.

tion god. The rights to land and power were invested in the Varangian princes, who, through connection with the *rod* or clan and its linkage with the ancestors, were the first rulers of the Russian state. In this manner, though officially derogated, the presence of a maternal goddess of creation and death insinuated itself into the rites of the rulers and reflected their need for accommodation with the beliefs of the native population in order to assume power over them.

## The Feminine in Russian Orthodoxy, Folklore, and Family Structure

With the introduction of Christianity by princess Olga and her grandson Vladimir, ruler of Kiev in the tenth century, the mother goddess/ dying god duality is reasserted in the form of Mary and Jesus; the distant father god, Jehovah, is generally invoked through the Mother and her Son. The affinity of the Mediterranean fertility elements in Christianity with the Slavic maternal cult results in the Russian Orthodox stress upon the sacredness of nature. Mary is perceived as a transformational vessel that transmutes spirit into matter. She is linked with the goddesses of birth, clan, and fate, the *rozhanitsy*, as birth giver. The depiction of her son as the "Humiliated Christ" stresses the fertility-related doctrine of humility in Orthodoxy, in which echoes can be heard of the dying and reviving vegetation god. In fact, the church focuses upon the Resurrection. At Easter, Christ is greeted with words uttered for the revival of the Egyptian fertility god Osiris: "Christ (Osiris) is risen!"

The Byzantine builders of the first Russian church in Kiev, Saint

Sophia, are said to have painted above the altar an immense image of a woman with hands raised, in order to suggest to the pagan Slavs the association of the Christian feminine deities, Mary and Sophia, with the pagan Great Mother whose image with uplifted arms adorned folk art.[17] Princes and rulers in turn were identified with the Humiliated Christ rather than the proud and distant Jehovah. They were obliged morally to lay down their lives in the defense of the motherland. Thus, in medieval religious verses from the *Book of the Dove*, the tsar is described as one who preeminently "believes in the Mother of god" and whose function it is to "defend the House of the Mother of God."[18]

The dual Christian-pagan system of belief in the first Russian state at Kiev had its roots, I would suggest, in respective matriarchal and patriarchal orientations: the peasants' connection with the maternal earth as "fatherless children of Mother Earth" counterpointed by the ruling elite's identification with a masculine sky god, Christ, whose image incorporated agrarian sacrificial elements. For though the prince and his followers ruled, their administration was conditioned by the acceptance of the earth as a source of power—a source from which the legendary *bogatyrs* or knights were said to draw their strength. Mother Earth was still conceived of as the mother of Russian principalities, and cities were referred to as mothers: "Mother Kiev," "Mother Moscow," or "Mother Vladimir." In the *Book of the Dove* the tsar's stewardship extends over a feminine domain: "Which city is the mother of all cities? . . . which river . . . the mother of all rivers? . . . which beast . . . the mother of all beasts?" asks the writer.[19] Clearly, the ruler was seen to perform his role as Christ and defender in the sphere of the maternal.

We need only turn to Russian folklore to find ample corroboration. Here the image of the all-inclusive feminine is that of the witch Baba Yaga, associated with the hearth, who, with her mortar and pestle, performs her dual functions of fertilization and destruction without a consort. Through her initiatory hut the youths must pass on their quests; she will help or hinder their progress toward the conquest of the princess who will, through matrilineality, give one of them right to rule. She is Vasilisa the Fair, or Wise, in her positive aspect, and her wisdom provides the youth with the resources for his quest—a quest in which she herself can be the prize.

The evidence for this transition from matriarchal to patriarchal structure can be extended to include a study of the Russian family. Evel Gasparini presents the provocative thesis that the original Slavic family was not patriarchal and, more interestingly, that the Slavs were not Indo-Europeans, as most scholars have maintained.[20] Like those few who had suggested a matriarchal basis in Russian culture before him, Gasparini points to certain matrilocal and matrilineal mores of the tribes described in twelfth-century documents.[21] Not only does he argue that land ownership was at one time feminine, associated with the woman-dominated hoe agriculture, but he shows that the great family or *zadruga* still retains traces of matriarchal clanship, traces resistant enough to survive the imposition of patriarchal structures. In effect, Gasparini lends support to my thesis that the Slavs were originally a matriarchal grouping of tribes, repeatedly conquered by Indo-European invaders who imposed a patriarchal social structure and introduced both plow and cattle into a woman-dominated hoe agriculture. The assimilation of woman with cattle and property is reflected in the custom of bride capture and bride price, but wedding rituals bear witness to echoes of endogamy or fear of patrilocal marriage. More generally, the stress in prerevolutionary Russia upon beating the woman into submission, making of her both slave and martyr, and denigrating her importance reflects, by the obsessive vigil over obedience, the overwhelming power that she evoked. Woman is associated with the earth, which also is "struck" by man with plow and harrow. And yet woman's power cannot be destroyed! In an old legend, Mother Earth is said to complain to God about the pain inflicted by man's labors. God answers, "Do not cry, for in the end you will eat them all."[22]

## Images of Mother Earth among the Russian Intelligentsia

As mother, seducer, dreaded witch of death and puberty rites, woman and earth represent all the forces that threaten to engulf the masculine and must therefore be chained, like the peasant population, for the nurture of the ruling elite. But like Dostoevsky's priestess of Mother Earth in *The Possessed*, upon whose crippled body the devils of patriarchal society feed, woman, associated with the maternity and creativity of the earth, is nonetheless regarded as the vehicle for man's salvation, his moral and spiritual rebirth. Both woman and peasant refer to that maternity and are thus victims of a patriarchal order that fears them, controls them, and exploits them: at the base of the prerevolutionary culture is the village, which revolves around feminine fertility rites and feeds its rulers. It is the feminine and enserfed nation (*narod*) upon which the masculine and autocratic fatherland (*otechestvo*) depends and which it must control. But that act of control and submission is rooted in the mythological structure I have been describing, that of the Mother Goddess and her son and consort, the dying god—a structure that infuses the whole culture and imposes itself on the entire course of Russian history. It is implicit in the emergence of the seventeenth-century concept of "Holy Russia" in opposition to the self-assertive consort tsar, who assumes too rapidly the figure of Jehovah, while abandoning that of the sacrificed son. It finds obsessive expression in the writings of the Russian *intelligentsia*, the tortured "passion suffering" children of the unhappy marriage of Mother Russia and Father Tsar, who take up the mantle of the dying god cast aside by the treacherous husband.

Russia—the earth, mother, and mistress—is vividly celebrated in poetry and prose by nineteenth-century intellectuals whose sense of alienation from the peasantry and the earth evokes a guilt, expiated only by sacrifice of self through some form of union with the maternally conceived masses. The conflict between patriarch-tsar and motherland assumes in the psyches of the intelligentsia—individuals often nursed by peasant women but torn away from them to be schooled in the Western rationalist tradition—the guise of a struggle between emotion and intellect, self-assertion and self-abnegation. Above all, there emerges the idea of a woman, or some ineffable feminine force, who would lead the anguished intellectuals to salvation, an idea that obsessed the literary imagination before and after the Revolution.[23] The twentieth-century Russian writer Evgenii Zamiatin, in a futuristic novel *We*, describes the blissful maternal aspect of a mysterious feminine entity within the context of her permanently revolutionary nature, an endless chain of death and rebirth: "All the universe was one unembraceable woman and we were in her very womb; we were as yet unborn—we were joyously ripening."[24] Boris Pasternak sends his wandering Dr. Zhivago in quest of a woman savior. He perishes after union with her in the snow-covered countryside, whereas she, in a Pietà-like scene, makes the sign of the cross over his dead body.[25] For if this savior can lead to salvation, it is on the road to Calvary that she is encountered demanding self-sacrifice and death. The Soviet poet Alexander Blok experiences her sinister powers, her chthonian thirst for sacrifice. In his poem "The Intellect Cannot Measure the Divine," the self-assertive individual finds himself overcome by her demands: here she assumes the form of "the Venus of Russia."

Not for the first time she visited the world
But for the first time there thronged her way
Different warriors, champions of a new mold . . .
*And strange was the gleam in the depths of her eyes*.[26]

Not long before his death, Blok wrote of his "darling Russia": "She devoured me anyway, that impure, snuffling, Motherland, Russia; like a pig her young."[27]

## Echoes of the Worship of a Mother Goddess in Soviet Russia

Although we have observed the persistence of the mythological image of a divine feminine and maternal presence among certain post-revolutionary writers, does the Soviet regime (having denied Mary, the Mother of God) provide new outlets for expression of maternal power? On the surface it appears that woman has been "purged" from the ruling pantheon. One could in fact argue that despite the Bolshevik party's avowed aims and active policies of liberating women from patriarchal bondage, the process of patriarchalization itself has been intensified. In spite of their considerable activity before, during, and after the Revolution, no women stand enshrined among the "Fathers"—Marx, Engels, and Lenin. Nor have women acceded to leadership since Lenin's death.[28]

The new Soviet woman is created in man's image to meet masculine needs for control over nature. Freed from the authority of husband and father, represented as comrade to her male partner, she is defined as a worker for the state and is subordinated to the authority of masculine rule. Her fecundity, the ancient source of her power, is harnessed to serve that state and subjected to its regulation. Freedom of abortion, for example, the most tangible and yet symbolic way in which women can control their relationships to male authority, was suspended prior to World War II and for years afterward, in order to furnish workers and soldiers for the motherland.[29] If a woman's "labor" yielded an abundant crop of children, she was rewarded much as especially productive workers (*stakhanovites*) were singled out for glorification as patriots. But motherhood, *unless* useful for the state, was represented as a secondary aspect of the woman worker's duties.[30] In a well-known socialist realist novel of the 1920s, a mother abandons her child by placing it in a children's home to be raised by the state, so that, having performed her function as birth giver, she can donate her energies and her independence from family ties to fighting and working for the Party.[31]

We can see in the relationship of the Soviet regime to women, and analogously to the Russian land, much the same pattern of control as characterized past millennia of Russian history. Implicit in the understanding of Marxist thought by Russian intellectuals of the nineteenth and twentieth centuries are earlier patriarchal justifications for control. A Russian emigré scholar's summary of Marxist theory illuminates the manner in which Christ-haunted and guilt-ridden intellectuals interpret its conclusions: the universe, he explains, is the result of a dialectical process within matter itself. Man is an integral part of this material cosmos and as an individual ceases to exist after death. His life, however, has a purpose, for he must liberate the earth "from the sin of exploitation." Each can find fulfillment in this service. However, "the final value belongs to the collectivity; it alone is confident of immortality."[32] We find here an acknowledgment of man as child of earth (matter) and at the same time a justification for the Christlike function of liberating the earth and thereby finding salvation in a man-created collectivity.

Not only do Christian notions find expression in this interpretation of Marxist views, but we hear echoes of the older sources of a maternally conceived earth and an analogous mother-oriented collectivity. Nonetheless, Marxism in its Bolshevik form makes it incumbent upon an ideologically committed vanguard and its leader to perform the task of enlightening the masses and leading them toward a vision of a new collectivity made possible only "from above" and effectuated, as in the manner of the first Russian rulers, the Varangian princes, militaristically: workers, like soldiers, march to orders and programs of production handed down from above. And yet the source of the power of the rulers ("an integral part of the material cosmos") is, as among the Varangian princes, conceived of as rooted in earth—in the masses linked with maternal powers. We find in the conclusion of Stalin's own *History of the Bolshevik Party* the stern reminder of maternal origins and sources. The Bolsheviks, he writes, resemble the Greek hero Anteus and Russian knights (*bogatyrs*), in that they derive their immense strength and power from the mother. The Party, he continues, is tied to the mother, embodied in the masses who gave it birth, who nourished and brought it up. As long as it remains attached to its mother, it will remain invincible.[33] But the Party must nonetheless keep a firm control over her powers.

I would argue that the intense nationalism of the Soviet citizen, which in the nineteenth century had been evoked as an aspect of "the Russian Soul" in its gravitational pull toward the maternal soil, assumes the central place of the Mother of God and refers to the worship of earth even more directly than in the Christian representation. A Western journalist described a recent conversation with a Soviet scientist who tried to express to the American his love for the motherland by calling it "umbilical." It is, he said, like that of a child who blindly returns his mother's love.[34] More specific still in its linkage of mother to earth is the story told by an older Soviet citizen about a sage "who advised Russians to take the good Russian earth and put it in their mouths, to eat it and take its nourishment directly because the soil was the source of Russian character and culture."[35] The astonishing popularity in the 1960s of a poem by a four-year-old child, a poem that became a popular song throughout the Soviet Union, reflects that longing for the maternal:

Let there always be a sky
Let there always be a sun
Let there always be Mama
Let there always be me.[36]

The continued worship of Mother Earth through ancient rituals has not, however, been entirely displaced into abstract or emotional manifestations. The expression of feminine power, which has survived millennia despite repression by rulers, has always, as we have seen, insinuated itself into the center of national life from underground sources. The resistance to the ideology of the rulers finds concrete manifestation in the continued practice of pagan rites by a portion of the Russian population—peasant women.[37] Proving exceedingly difficult to liberate, older peasant women were finally abandoned by the regime.[38] Ignored, derided by the rulers as old hags, clinging obstinately to church and icon, they were represented, in effect, as the dreaded paradigms of the feminine—witches. As modern "priestesses" of the cult of earth, worshiped now in a Christian context, peasant women continue to perform the ancient seasonal rituals and dominate, at christenings and burials, the rites of passage in the villages.[39] In a postwar ethnographic study of the village of Viriatino from prerevolutionary times to the 1950s, Soviet researchers admit to the continued presence of pagan as well as Christian rites. For example, the festival of the Koliada, performed around Christmas, focuses on the death and rebirth of a seasonal god, associated with the sun and linked closely with feminine power.[40] During the festival a group of mummers, made up principally of single women dressed in costumes to assume the form of an entire family, go from house to house, singing, dancing, and demanding offerings.[41] They foretell the coming harvest, as well as who will marry in the coming year.

Furthermore, village women still retain the protective qualities of the chthonian Mother Goddess. In fact, the practice of women performing magical rites to protect animals and human beings from evil spirits by circling the yards of their houses could still be observed long after the Revolution.[42] There also remained the planting ritual, in which the whole family gathered around the icon and recited the Virgin's Prayer.[43] One Soviet ethnographer suggests that the very fact of stripping away much of the church hierarchy creates a relapse to pagan custom.[44] That is not to say that the church has been abandoned by the portion of the female population that the government characterizes as old and illiterate: services are heavily attended by *babas* ("women" and "old women").

The *baba*, with her dominant role in the maintenance of religious rites in which pagan elements commingle with Christian beliefs, is, as she has been in the past, assimilated to the suffering maternal earth. Contemporary intellectuals and writers continue, as before, to nurture a martyred and Christlike relationship to the motherland. The "Thaw" marking the end of Stalinism produced novels, poems, and short stories in which again the peasantry was idealized as the maternal source of goodness and virtue. In a number of literary works the Russian stove, traditionally the seat of the *baba*, has become the embodiment of the motherland.[45] Poets continue, whether in dissident or "officially approved" verse, to celebrate Russia in the image of the feminine and equally oppressed church, which can take the very form of its chief worshiper, the *baba*: "Across Russia our dear churches stand. . . . They sigh, moan, groan / And cry like old women. . . . "[46] Or again, after the poet has described his descent into the underworld where oppressed Russia, like the ignored *babas*, has been banished, he continues: "You, Russia, wash / Your tears and pus / With my blood. . . . In the place of Russia / I'll remain in hell."[47]

Over the past fifty years, in the popular arts as well as in literature, the relationship of son to Mother Earth has been brilliantly evoked in the productions of the Soviet cinema. Two masterpieces of the early postrevolutionary period, Dovzhenko's *Earth* (1930) and Pudovkin's adaptation of Gorki's *Mother* (1920), present haunting images on the theme of the sacrifice of the son to release the energies of the mother, as revolutionary force or as soil. Glagolin's film *The Return to Earth* (1922) forcefully identifies communist teachings with Christ's message. The sacrifice of the soldier son for the motherland is the theme of the postwar *Liberated Earth*, directed by Medvedkin (1946). And in Chukhrais's *Ballad of a Soldier* (1959) we see the childlike hero returning on his leave, not to bride but to mother. From Leningrad to Berlin, looming tall over the collective graves of soldiers who died in the course of the Great Patriotic War, immense statues of women crown the sacrifice of their sons.

Has the Soviet regime succeeded in eradicating the Great Mother Goddess from its pantheon? In Solzhenitsyn's short story "Matryona's House," his hero returns from labor camp to the home of a poor, abused, and ignored peasant woman. She is not only the good mother but is associated with Christ in her selflessness:

> We had lived side by side with her and never understood
> that she was the righteous one . . . *without whom,* as the proverb
> says, *no village can stand.*
> *Nor any city.*
> *Nor our whole land.*[48]

# Notes

1. Pilnyak, *Mother Earth*, p. 51.
2. See Cherniavsky, *Tsar and People*, p. 214. A nineteenth-century thinker, Rozanov, expresses vividly the sense of containment when he writes: "I am like a child in his mother's womb, but one who does not wish to be born; it is warm enough in here" (quoted in Poggioli, *Rozanov*, p. 36). The twentieth-century poet Biely voices an almost despairing demand for escape from an all-consuming motherland: "Vanish, vanish in space, Russia, my Russia" (*Stikhotvoreniia*, p. 137).
3. Fedotov, *The Russian Religious Mind*, p. 362.
4. See James, *Mother Goddess*, p. 258. For studies of prerevolutionary archaeologists that touch on the cult of the Great Goddess in south Russia, see Minns, *Scythians and Greeks*; and Rostovtzeff, *Iranians and Greeks*. Mongait (*Archaeology in the USSR*) gives an overview in which mention is made of the proliferation of female figurines at Paleolithic sites.
5. See Gimbutas, *Gods and Goddesses*; and Rybakov, "Cosmogony and Mythology." Gimbutas refers to the Tripolye culture by the name of Cucutemi, after Moldavian sites; Rybakov uses the Russian name of Tripolye, after a site close to the city of Kiev.
6. The houselike shape of the shrines is interesting; in some instances female figurines are shown grinding corn or seated around the hearth, suggesting the notion of house as identified with woman. It has been argued that the dwellings of the Paleolithic period—caves and pits—were regarded as openings in the womb of the earth in which the children of the Earth Mother found shelter. (See Levy, *The Gate of Horn*, p. 3.)
7. Rybakov, "Cosmogony and Mythology."
8. See Gimbutas, *Gods and Goddesses*.
9. See Rostovtzeff, *Iranians and Greeks*.
10. Herodotus, *The Histories*. The half-woman half-serpent goddess appears in Russian folklore and art as a *sirin* (siren) and seems to be linked to female water spirits called *vily*, *bereginy*, and *rusalki*. See n. 13 below.
11. Dumezil, "Les 'Énarées' scythiques," pp. 249–55.
12. Eliade, *Shamanism*, p. 78; Shternberg, "Shamanism and Religious Election," pp. 61–84.
13. For example, the sky god Stribog, associated with the weather, is traced to the Indo-European father god, the Vedic Dyaus, who in his capacity as rainmaker became pregnant, that is, became feminine. "Could Stribog have been a feminine deity originally?" asks Vernadsky (*Kievan Russia*, p. 52). The god Stribog is associated with a consort, the only feminine Slavic deity, Mokosh, whose name implies moisture (Toporov, "Fragment slavianskoi mifologii," pp. 16, 17). Given this linkage of Stribog and Mokosh, there appears to be in the very name of the goddess a hint of original parthenogenesis. Certainly, even though she is deemed a minor divinity by most scholars, she is nonetheless regarded as the most ancient of the Slavic

pantheon, appearing later as *Mat' Syra Zemlia* ("Mother Moist Earth") in Russian folklore and preserving the notion of self-fertilization—earth and moisture—in her descriptive name. In fact, the earliest observers of the customs of the pagan Slavs (among whom the sixth-century A.D. Byzantine historian Procopius gives the most vivid account) noted the worship of trees and of feminine spirits of lake and river shore called *bereginy*, to whom the *vily* were later assimilated. The *bereginy*, associated with the union of earth and water, were linked with the sacred tree of the Slavs, the birch (Rybakov, "Drevnie elementy," pp. 104, 105). Also see Rybakov, "Cosmogony and Mythology," in which he argues that the Great Goddess of the Tripolye culture was closely connected with rain. The identification of the birch tree with a goddess was stressed in prerevolutionary folk rituals connected with the seasonal cycle, in which the birch was dressed in women's clothing or decorated with ribbons.

14. Netting, "Russian Peasant Art," p. 65.

15. On the Nordic sources of Slavic mythology see Chadwick, *Russian History*.

16. Komarovich, "Kult roda," pp. 85–97. *Rod*, from *rodit'*, means to give birth. On the linkage of the clan with the seasonal cycle see also Smirnov, "Drevnie-Russkii dukhovnik," pp. 261–83.

17. Rybakov, "Cosmogony and Mythology," p. 105.

18. Alexander, *Russian Folklore*, p. 345.

19. Ibid.

20. Gasparini, *Il matriarcato slavo*.

21. See Kovalevsky, *Modern Customs*; Elnett, *Family Life in Russia*; and Seifert, *Die Weltrevolutionäre*. Here I take "matriarchal" to mean matrilocal and/or matrilineal. Clearly, the religious focus upon a mother goddess suggests echoes of a mother-centered society.

22. Smirnov, "Drevne-Russkii dukhovnik."

23. Billington, *The Icon and the Axe*, p. 557.

24. Zamiatin, *We*, p. 224.

25. Billington, *The Icon and the Axe*, p. 558.

26. Blok, "The Intellect Cannot Measure the Divine," in *The Twelve*, p. 7.

27. Cited in Besançon, *Le Tsarévich immolé*, p. 237; translation mine. The psychological ambivalence associated with the power of the maternal archetype is explored more fully than in Besançon's Freudian context in Neumann's *The Great Mother*.

28. On the role and numbers of women in government from the period after the Revolution to the present see Mandel, *Soviet Women*.

29. Ibid., p. 75. In December of 1979 the first feminist journal was published and circulated within the dissident "underground." Called *Zhenshchina i Rossiia* (Woman and Russia), it contained a number of articles denouncing the patriarchal structure of the Soviet state and protesting the material conditions of women, particularly in connection with abortions and maternity care, but also in connection with the problems of a patriarchally

structured family that operates de facto as a matristic one. (See in particular Malakhovskaia: "La famille maternelle," pp. 13–15.) The French women's movement was the first to receive and translate a copy smuggled out of the Soviet Union, and there has as yet been no English translation of the text. The journal *Hebdo des femmes en mouvements* devoted an entire issue to the reproduction of the first issue of *Zhenshchina i Rossiia*. The editors and several of the contributors were promptly exiled to the West because, in the words of the editor T. Mamonova, with whom I spoke recently, the government saw a feminist movement as particularly threatening to its authority. Among the contributors were a number of writers who invoked the cult of the Mother of God as the rallying point for the Russian feminist movement. That group has now begun another journal called *Maria*. (For interviews with the exiled Russian feminists see Morgan, "The First Feminist Exiles," p. 49.)

30. Gasiorowska, *Women in Soviet Fiction*.

31. Gladkov, *Cement*. The same attitudes that made the prerevolutionary peasant woman a workhorse appear also in Soviet life. For example, the Soviet woman is expected to have a job and still deal with all household chores, which Soviet men deem "unmanly" work. Clearly, the reality behind ideological pronouncements is one of control rather than freedom for a woman's development. Although Soviet women have had access to jobs that Western women have only in the past decade been "permitted" to perform, one senses behind this liberalism not so much the notion of equality of the sexes as the older view of woman as beast of burden. Women do not earn as much as men. See Mandel, *Soviet Women*, p. 107.

32. Zernov, *The Russians*, p. 159.

33. Stalin, *Histoire du parti communiste*, p. 429, cited in Besançon, *Le tsarévich immolé*, p. 43.

34. Smith, *The Russians*, pp. 304–6.

35. Ibid., p. 430.

36. Todd, "Recent Soviet Literature," p. 44.

37. As of 1969 the peasantry constituted 43% of the Russian population. See Mandel, *Soviet Women*, p. 73. It should also be noted that while the urban woman works, she likes to leave her children with her *babushka* (diminutive of "grandmother," a word used to designate older women), who is generally of peasant origin. The care of the female relative is much preferred to that of the child-care centers. But this preference also means that the child may have access to the ancient lore and ritual that the *babushka* may pass on to it. Smith reports hearing the comment that each generation would produce new *babushkas* (*The Russians*, p. 434).

38. Gasiorowska, *Women in Soviet Fiction*, p. 33.

39. Dunn, "The Importance of Religion," p. 355. Dunn does not suggest that peasant women are associated with the cult of Mother Earth. She simply points to the continuation of pagan rites by peasant women under the Soviet regime.

40. Vernadsky, *Origins of Russia*, p. 111.

41. Benet, *The Village of Viriatino*, p. 285.
42. Dunn, "The Importance of Religion," p. 355.
43. Ibid., p. 354.
44. Ibid., p. 370.
45. Zekulin, "The Countryside in Soviet Literature," p. 392.
46. Vladimirov, *Grani*, p. 23, cited in Todd, "Recent Soviet Literature," p. 48.
47. Ibid., p. 49.
48. Solzhenitsyn, "Matryona's House," pp. 90, 91; italics mine.

# Bibliography

Alexander, Alex E. *Russian Folklore*. Belmont, Mass.: Nordland, 1975.
Benet, Sala, ed. and trans. *The Village of Viriatino*. Garden City, N.Y.: Doubleday, 1970.
Besançon, Alain. *Le Tsarévich immolé*. Paris: Plon, 1967.
Biely, Andrey. *Stikhotvoreniia*. Moscow: Z. I. Gzhebin, 1923.
Billington, James. *The Icon and the Axe*. New York: Alfred A. Knopf, 1970.
Blok, Alexander. *The Twelve and Other Poems*. Translated by J. Stallworthy and Peter France. London: Eyre and Spottiswoode Press, 1970.
Chadwick, Nora K. *The Beginning of Russian History*. Cambridge: Cambridge University Press, 1946.
Cherniavsky, Michael. *Tsar and People*. New York: Random House, 1969.
Dumezil, Georges. "Les 'Énarées' scythiques et la grossesse de Narte Hamyc." *Latomus: Revue d'Études Latines* 5 (1946): 249–55.
Dunn, Ethel. "The Importance of Religion in the Soviet Rural Community." In *The Soviet Rural Community*, edited by J. R. Millar, pp. 346–75. Urbana: University of Illinois Press, 1971.
Eliade, Mircea. *Shamanism*. Princeton, N.J.: Princeton University Press, 1964.
Elnett, Elaine. *Historic Origins and Social Development of Family Life in Russia*. New York: Columbia University Press, 1926.
Fedotov, George. *The Russian Religious Mind*. Vol. 1. New York: Harper and Row, 1960.
Gasiorowska, Xenia. *Women in Soviet Fiction*. Madison: University of Wisconsin Press, 1968.
Gasparini, Evel. *Il matriarcato slavo: antropologia culturale dei protoslavi*. Florence: Sansoni Publishing, 1973.
Gimbutas, Marija. *The Gods and Goddesses of Old Europe*. Berkeley: University of California Press, 1974.
Gladkov, Fedor V. *Cement*. Translated by A. S. Arthur and C. Ashleigh. New York: International Publishers, 1960.
Herodotus. *The Histories*. Translated by A. de Selincourt. London: Penguin Books, 1963.

James, E. O. *The Cult of the Mother Goddess*. New York: Praeger Publishers, 1959.

Komarovich, V. "Kult roda i zemli v kniazheskoi srede XI–XIIIvv." *Trudy otdela drevnerusskoi literatury (Akademia Nauk SSSR)* 16 (1960): 84–104.

Kovalevsky, Maxime. *Modern Customs and Ancient Laws of Russia*. New York: Burt Franklin Press, 1926.

Levy, Gertrude Rachel. *The Gate of Horn*. New York: Faber and Faber, 1946.

Malakhovskaia, N. "La famille maternelle." *Hebdo des femmes en mouvements* 10 (1980): 13–15.

Mandel, William M. *Soviet Women*. Garden City, N.Y.: Doubleday, 1975.

Minns, Ellis H. *Scythians and Greeks*. Cambridge: Cambridge University Press, 1913.

Mongait, A. L. *Archaeology in the USSR*. Gloucester, Mass.: Peter Smith Press, 1970.

Morgan, Robin. "The First Feminist Exiles." *Ms.* 10 (November 1980): 49–56.

Netting, Anthony. "Images and Ideas in Russian Peasant Art." *Slavic Review* (Mar. 1976): 48–68.

Neumann, Erich. *The Great Mother: An Analysis of the Archetype*. Princeton, N.J.: Princeton University Press, 1963.

Pilnyak, Boris. *Mother Earth and Other Stories*. Translated by Vera T. Reck and Michael Green. Garden City, N.Y.: Doubleday, 1968.

Poggioli, Renato. *Rozanov*. New York: Hillary House, 1962.

Rostovtzeff, Mikhail I. *Iranians and Greeks in South Russia*. Oxford: Oxford University Press, Clarendon Press, 1922.

Rybakov, B. A. "Cosmogony and Mythology of the Agriculturalists of the Eneolithic." *Soviet Anthropology and Archaeology* 4, no. 2 (1965–66): 16–35, no. 3 (1965–66): 33–52.

———. "Drevnie elementy v russkom narodnom tvorchestve." *Sovetskaya etnografiia* 1 (1948): 90–106.

Seifert, Leo. *Die Weltrevolutionäre, von Bogumil, über Hus, zu Lenin*. Vienna: B. Amalthea-Verlag, 1931.

Shternberg, L. "Shamanism and Religious Election." In *Introduction to Soviet Ethnography*, edited by Stephen P. Dunn and Ethel Dunn, pp. 61–85. Berkeley, Calif.: Highgate Road Social Science Research Station, 1974.

Smirnov, S. "Drevnie-Russkii dukhovnik." *Chteniia obshchestva istorii i drevnostei Moskovskogo Universiteta*, (Apr.–June 1914), pp. 255–83.

Smith, Hedrick. *The Russians*. New York: Quadrangle, 1976.

Solzhenitsyn, Alexander. "Matryona's House." In *Half Way to the Moon*, edited by Patricia Blake and Max Hayward, pp. 13–53. Garden City, N.Y.: Doubleday, 1965.

Todd, A. C. "Spiritual Elements in Recent Soviet Literature." In *Religion and the Soviet State: A Dilemma of Power*, edited by Max Hayward and William Fletcher, pp. 37–55. New York: Praeger Publishers, 1969.

Toporov, V. I. "Fragment slavianskoi mifologii." *Institut slaviano-vedeniia (Akademiia Nauk SSSR)* 30 (1961): 14–32.

Vernadsky, George. *Kievan Russia*. New Haven: Yale University Press, 1973.
———. *Origins of Russia*. Oxford: Oxford University Press, 1959.
Zamiatin, Evgenii I. *We*. In *An Anthology of Russian Literature in the Soviet Period from Gorki to Pasternak*, edited by Bernard G. Guerney, pp. 163–353. New York: Random House, 1960.
Zekulin, Gleb. "The Contemporary Countryside in Soviet Literature: A Search for New Values." In *The Soviet Rural Community*, edited by James R. Millar, pp. 376–404. Urbana: University of Illinois Press, 1971.
Zernov, Nicolas. *The Russians and Their Church*. London: Society for Promoting Christian Knowledge Press, 1968.

# 7

## Postindustrial Marian Pilgrimage
### by Victor Turner and Edith Turner

Marian pilgrimages and images have had a dramatic resurgence in the nineteenth and early twentieth centuries.

In the Middle Ages, Mary as Theotokos, holding or even nursing her Divine Son, received much iconic representation. Marian devotion formed part of a vast system of beliefs and rituals. Early in the nineteenth century, though, the emphasis began to shift to Mary herself, as an autonomous figure who takes initiatives on behalf of mankind, often intervening in the midst of the economic and political crises characteristic of industrialized mass society.

As we have pointed out elsewhere,[1] the cultus of the Virgin Mary— and, a fortiori, Marian pilgrimage—depended on the doctrine of the communion of saints, expressed in the second clause of the ninth article in the received text of the Apostles' Creed. The Catholic interpretation of this doctrine, as we have seen, posits a spiritual solidarity linking "the faithful on earth, the souls in purgatory, and the saints in heaven in the organic unity of the same mystical body under Christ its head, and in a constant interchange of supernatural offices."[2] This view differs radically from the Protestant interpretation of the same clause of the creed by emphasizing the continuing, active relationship between the living and the dead. True, in 1519 Luther argued that

This essay was originally published as chap. 6 in *Image and Pilgrimage in Christian Culture*, by Victor Turner and Edith Turner (New York: Columbia University Press, 1978). The editor wishes to thank the authors and Columbia University Press for permission to reprint it here.

"the communion of saints" (and not the papacy) constituted the church. Later writers, however, have taken the phrase to mean an aggregate of persons having a community of faith and ties of Christian sympathy, but in no way organized or interdependent as members of the same visible body. Rejecting the doctrine of purgatory, and asserting that intercession by the saints would detract from Christ's mediatorship, the Protestant view tends to limit the communion of saints to the living and does not look favorably on the possibility of supernatural intervention by deceased saints. For the average Catholic, on the other hand, theological grounds do exist for admitting that possibility. In Catholic teaching, the good dead, but not the damned, may and do (as official reports of numerous devotions attest) communicate with the living, through apparitions, visions, dreams, and the like, and intercede with God to work miracles on behalf of the living. They do not communicate through mediums or diviners, as in animism or modern spiritualism, however, because they are not thought, officially at least, to haunt the fringes of the world of the living, the "middle earth," or to be semimaterial entities. The "good dead" are either saints in heaven or on their way to being saints through the fiery cleansing of purgatory. One's known and named ancestors are not capable of inhabiting shrines or ancestral tablets. For Catholics, prayer by the living to the saints in heaven, to intercede on their behalf with God, is also a mode of communication between members of the Church Militant and the Church Triumphant. Anyone who has lived in a society with a strong ancestral cult, as in tribal Africa, or China before the revolution, will find nothing unusual about this way of thinking. It is easy to comprehend "that corporate circulation of spiritual blessings through members of the same family, that domesticity and saintly citizenship which lie at the core of the Catholic communion of saints."[3] There is one important difference: whereas membership in an ancestral cult is "ascribed"—that is, dependent on ties of real or fictitious kinship (usually, lineal kinship)—membership in the communion of saints is "acquired," or "achieved," by faith, works, and submission to ecclesiastical rule. Nevertheless, the familial, domestic metaphor is highly appropriate to the Catholic concept of the communion of saints, and terms such as father, son, mother, daughter, brother, sister, spouse, are freely applied within that corporate body to created persons both living and dead, as well as to the uncreated Persons, the Father and Son of the Trinity. The Holy Spirit, moreover, personalizes the circulation of communitas through the entire corporate body.

The invisibility and intangibility of the spiritual and supernatural order obviously create problems regarding communication between incarnate and discarnate members of the church. How does one know, how can one feel sure, that one's prayer has been heard by God or a saint? And how does one know where a preternatural event has originated? These problems always arise when one posits the possibility of interaction between a visible and an invisible domain. If people pray for some benefit or for deliverance from calamity, and the desired consequences ensue, the earlier prayer is readily regarded as cause and the later good fortune as effect. But the "favors," as they are often called, are not sufficient proof that direct supernatural communication or intervention has occurred. There is still plenty of room for a natural explanation. Pilgrimages often begin when a considerable number of people are satisfied that a "sign" of supernatural intervention in human affairs has indeed been given at a particular place in a particular way. The sign must clearly be of a supernatural sort, whether it be an apparition witnessed by several people at once (as at Knock in Ireland or Fátima in Portugal) or a miraculous cure. Catholics have always held that the supernatural is not a theoretically derived conception, but a positive fact, which can be known only as a result of initiatives taken by beings or powers from beyond the sensory "veil." It is manifested through revelation, miracles, prophecies, and apparitions. The Catholic church considers itself a living body, perpetuated from biblical times on, through postscriptural and post-apostolic history; because the generative biblical era was full of revelations and miracles, the possibility remains that similar phenomena may occur today. Indeed, a mark of the true church is that it is electrically charged, so to speak, with the potential of miracle. Miracles did not cease at the death of the last apostle. The doctrine of the communion of saints posits that Jesus, who became man and had a human soul, his mother Mary, the apostles, and all the saints, whether canonized or not, are still, in some sense and at certain time, quasi-materially "present," and can manifest themselves to men and women like ourselves and mediate in various ways between the spiritual and material orders. The scenes of such manifestations are thought to be gaps in the curtain, tears in the veil, separating the two orders. If, for example, Our Lady appeared in the grotto of Massabielle near Lourdes, the popular assumption is that petitions offered there stand a better chance of being heard and answered than at home. It is not merely that making the long journey of pilgrimage is deemed more worthy than leading a decent life in one's village; more important, the place of revelation continues to "vibrate" with supernatural efficacy. This is not just magical thinking, for it refers to the theological doctrine, ethical in nature, that salvation, or "justification" (the passage from a state of sin to one of sanctifying grace or "justice"), is linked to the communion of saints, the reciprocal action of soul on soul in a corporate circulation of blessings—a view clearly opposed to the Protestant notion of justification through faith alone, which is essentially individualistic. Catholic thought supposes that there is actual merit to be had from interaction with one's "even-Christians," in the mode of good will.

We mention these elementary theological conceptions because they have for centuries been the stock-in-trade of the persons who go on Christian pilgrimages. When these ideas decline or are abolished, the pilgrimages tend to decline also, as they did in the seventeenth and eighteenth centuries in Catholic Europe. If one does not hold the doctrine of the communion of saints in the Catholic sense, one can no longer believe that one's spiritual and material welfare may be promoted in a particular place by the intercession of a saint—no longer thought of as one's brother or sister in a family spanning the ages.

The cults of regional and local pilgrimage saints have been steadily on the decline for almost a century in Europe. This deemphasis of pilgrimage saints may be partly due, as William A. Christian, Jr., has suggested, to a major change in the relationship between a traditional image of a saint and a specific territory, a sociogeographical region.[4] Saints' shrines mark "critical points in the ecosystem—contact points with other worlds." In the past, they also "marked off boundaries between village and village . . . cultivated and uncultivated land." Some of these shrines, as the result of various circumstances, came to be regarded as holier than others, their saints as more efficacious intercessors than others; in this way regional devotions were born, drawing pilgrims from a wide catchment area containing many parishes. William Christian argues that mobility and the mass media have broken down boundaries, that industrialization has led to the migration of labor and the reallocation of resources in the rural areas; non-Catholic schemes for living have had wide circulation, and the rise in the standard of living has made people loath to undergo such hardships as pilgrimage journeys, while natural means are at hand to procure benefits previously thought to be beyond the power and means of peasants and urban workers. Forces in the Catholic church itself, such as the Catholic Action movement (which involves the laity in the planning and management of church affairs and in proselytizing) and the major reforms promulgated by the Second Vatican Council, have contributed to bringing localized Catholic communities into regular contact with other worlds, ideas, life-styles.

One result of all this has been to undermine the influence of saints' images as *genii loci*, territorial demideities bound up ceremonially with the seasonal reproductive cycle, through feasts celebrated at critical points in the agricultural year. There are, of course, many exceptions to William Christian's generalization. The major saints—for example, Saint James in Spain, Saint Patrick in Ireland, and Saint Anne in French Canada—whose status as dominant symbols of religious nationalism were firmly fixed earlier, have not suffered so much from the attritional processes accompanying industrialism. The year 1971, in which July 25, the day of Saint James, fell on a Sunday, became a holy year for all Spain; more than three million pilgrims passed through the ancient cathedral shrine of Santiago de Compostela that year, and on the patronal feast day, members of the national cabinet participated in daylong activities, centering on the cathedral, to culminate the special holy-year program. As for Saint Patrick in Ireland, let us supplement what we have elsewhere said about the Purgatory,[5] by citing the *Connaught Telegraph* of August 3, 1972, with reference to the other major Patrician pilgrimage, the hard climb to the summit of the Reek, as the mountain Croagh Patrick is sometimes called, where the saint is believed to have fasted and meditated for forty days before beginning his definitive mission to convert Ireland.

> Prayers for peace throughout all Ireland were offered at Masses on the summit of Croagh Patrick on Sunday when about 40,000 people—many in their bare feet—made the annual national pilgrimage. Dry shale, after the recent fine weather, squally showers that fell from dawn, and a slippery descent, made the pilgrimage this year particularly hazardous on the three-and-a-half mile climb of the 2,510 ft. mountain. . . . There were 15 accident victims, and six cases were detained at the Co. Mayo Hospital, Castlebar. All were carried down on stretchers by the Knights of Malta.

May we say, parenthetically, that meteorological hazards are no new thing on Croagh Patrick. The *Chronicon Scotorum* recorded, at the year 1106, that Na Longain, bishop of Ardpatrick, was struck by lightning and killed; and, at 1113, the "Four Masters" note that a thunderbolt fell on the Reek on the eve of Saint Patrick's festival and killed thirty of those "engaged on the summit in fasting and prayer."[6]

But Christian is right about what he calls the "deemphasis" of local saints' shrines, especially minor pilgrimage shrines. This is certainly happening in Mexico, where we have seen the images of village and barrio patron saints frequently consigned to the sacristy, even to the lumber room. The mobility of mass society, with the permanent loss of many young people to the urban areas, undermines the efficacy and coherence of localized norms and value-systems. These factors have not influenced Marian devotion in the same way, however. The nineteenth century and the first half of the twentieth have constituted what has been called, in Catholic circles, the Age of Mary (though the Second Vatican Council, which tended to deemphasize Mariology, possibly for ecumenical reasons, has had the effect of discouraging excessive Marian zeal in very recent years). Some of the most popular Marian pilgrimages originated in this period. All of them began with a vision in which Mary delivered an important message. Unlike the messages characteristic of the medieval "shepherds' cycle" discussed elsewhere,[7] in which the Virgin instructed the individual visionary to found a shrine to her, the message of the modern visions is a general call to all humankind to repent and be saved. A considerable populist literature, often chiliastic in tone, has developed in connection with apparitional pilgrimages. The Virgin's message is identified with lower-middle-class interests, and both big business and international socialism are condemned as major causes of humankind's sins, the sins we are called upon to repent. Whereas medieval Marian pilgrimages are seldom known to have begun as the immediate consequence of a vision (the foundation narratives have a mythical quality and seem to have arisen long after the pilgrimages were operant), the postindustrial pilgrimages clearly owe their origin to particular visionary or apparitional experiences.

In *The Sun Her Mantle*, an influential study of the postindustrial pilgrimage phenomenon, John Beevers cites two texts as prophetically interconnected and centrally related. The first of these texts is a verse from the Apocalypse: "And now, in heaven, a great portent appeared; a woman that wore the sun for her mantle, with the moon under her feet, and a crown of stars above her head." The second is a statement by Pope Pius XII, from his *Evangeli Praecones* (1951): "The human race is today involved in a supreme crisis, which will end in its salvation by Christ, or in its dire destruction."[8] Beevers links the modern appearances of the Virgin (often cloaked in the imagery of the apocalyptic vision), with the "supreme crisis" referred to by Pius XII. "From 1830 to 1933, the Blessed Virgin . . . appeared at nine places in Europe: at five in France, one in Ireland, one in Portugal and two in Belgium. At two of these places, she appeared only once. At the others she made several appearances. At all but one, she spoke, sometimes many sentences. . . . On our response to her messages

17. The sick awaiting benediction at the major Marian shrine
in Ireland, Our Lady of Knock. *(Photograph by Victor Turner)*

may depend our temporal and eternal future."[9] This tendency to
regard Mary as a sibyl is often depreciated by theologians, who insist
that nothing can be added to the deposit of faith, the body of revealed
truths and principles of conduct given by Christ to the apostles, to be
preserved by them and their successors. Visions cannot add to, or
even embellish, the deposit of faith; if genuine, and not spurious or of
diabolic origin, they can only enhance devotion to, and perhaps understanding of, the truths there contained. The church obviously has
a strong interest in strengthening and periodically revivifying faith in
its basic doctrines and tenets. As abstractions, these have scant attractive power, except for intellectuals. But if these concepts are associated with a vision in all its social circumstances—for instance, the
appearance of the Queen of Heaven to a poor peasant girl—the im-
poverished masses, the damned of the earth but blessed of heaven,
can easily identify with such a figure. Theological abstractions are

18. The mass at the gable of the apparition at Knock.
*(Photograph by Victor Turner)*

fleshed out with historical circumstances through a clearly perceived imagery, and eventually through a pilgrimage process involving the faithful in a reenactment of the generating vision. The problem of the church is to assess whether the circumstances of the vision can form an appropriate symbol-vehicle for doctrines valid for all human generations, everywhere and always. Where there is too great a disparity —bordering on the grotesque, ridiculous, or improbable—between the alleged vision and the deposit of faith, the church, working through its corporate scrutinizing mechanisms, rejects the vision as not of God, and nips the devotion in the bud. (Nevertheless, some alleged miracles, such as the Host's reputedly turning to blood at Joaseiro in Brazil, have given rise to pilgrimage devotions by popular fiat, despite ecclesiastical censure.)

It is possible that the Catholic church has been motivated to support (or, at any rate, not to oppose) such visions, because they give emotional expression to doctrines under fire from scientific and ratio-nal criticism. Marian doctrines, by patristic and subsequent tradition, hinge on the notion of Mary as the new Eve, redeeming mankind from the original sin of the first Eve. The new Eve entails a first Eve; Mary and Eve are structurally interconnected. Modern evolutionary theories, however, have claimed the prestige of science, in an age of mounting technological achievement, to argue against the notion that a special creative act of God brought humanity's first parents, Adam and Eve, onto the terrestrial scene. Lamarck and Etienne Geoffroy Saint-Hilaire had proposed evolutionary theories before Darwin—Lamarck in 1809, in fact. The miracle of Lourdes preceded the publi-cation of *The Origin of Species* (1859) by one year, but the evolutionist issues had been raised at least half a century before that. The church must have recognized that if, in the view of the masses, Mary truly lived, then Adam and the first Eve would have lived, too, and man would be seen as more than just a nodal point on the wavering line of biotic evolution, indeed, as the "express image and likeness of God," qualitatively distinct from the animal kingdom. If theological argu-ment could not prevail among the faithful, against the evolutionists, then popular movements, rooted in and stimulated by corporeal vi-sions, and associated with a plethora of miraculous cures, could con-vince the people that biblical times were not dead, that they continued through the church. An urgent, though sometimes muted, polemical tone pervades the arguments supporting devotions founded on cor-poreal visions, a tone deriving from the conflict between expanding, humanist atheism and major religion, the latter magnificently orga-nized and philosophically entrenched, fighting for its life in a cultural equivalent of Darwin's "survival of the fittest"—in a contest between cultural "pseudo-species," to use Erik Erikson's controversial term.

Yet the redoubtable conservative Cardinal Alfredo Ottaviani, re-garded as an archfoe by the proponents of Catholic reform, wrote an article in the Vatican newspaper *Osservatore Romano*, in 1951, caution-ing Catholics about accepting visions too credulously. "Even the most accredited visions cannot furnish us with new elements of life or doctrine, but only with new motives for fervor. True religion abides essentially, not only in the conscience, but in the love of God and the consequent love of our neighbor." "New motives for fervor" indeed proliferated in Marian visions, miracles, and devotions. Though "feu-dal and idyllic relations," in the words of the *Communist Manifesto* (1848), were ending, and with them many of the regional and district saints' devotions, a generalized, universal mother, "heart of the heart-less world," the Mother of God, was available to the dispossessed, uprooted masses of Catholic Europe; according to immemorial pilgrimage tradition, she had many times manifested herself to the poor and despised. France of the post-Napoleonic era might well be thought of as a peculiarly appropriate soil for the seeds of Marian devotion. Exhaustion and depression at the failure of the emperor's campaigns; the growth of industrialism and bureaucracy; the emergence of a proletariat, lumpen proletariat, and petite bourgeoisie, in distinctive forms; the overt failure of rationalism and the Goddess of Reason, all provided auspicious conditions for mass receptivity to allegations of the ingress of supernatural power into a flawed natural scene. Collective salvation was longed for, by whatever means, traditional or unconventional.

Foremost among the Marian pilgrimages in France that arose from apparitions occurring in the post-Napoleonic era are (in chronological order, according to the date of their generative apparitions) the following: *La Sallette* (on September 19, 1846, two children, Mélanie Mathieu Calvat and Maximin Giraud, had a vision of the Virgin); *Lourdes* (the Virgin appeared to Bernadette Soubirous eighteen times between February 11 and July 16, 1858); *Pontmain*, in Mayenne (on January 17, 1871, the Virgin predicted the speedy end of the Franco-Prussian War);[10] *Pellevoisin*, in the department of Indre (February 13 to December 8, 1876, the Virgin appeared to a maidservant, Estelle Faguette, and told her, among other things, that she could no longer restrain her son, and that "France will suffer much"—which later commentators have taken to apply to the two world wars).

Beevers cites a fifth major set of Marian apparitions occurring in France in this period; that is, the series of visions experienced by Saint Catherine Labouré. Those visions generated the widespread cultus of the Miraculous Medal. Although Saint Catherine Labouré's visions occurred between July 1830 and September 1831, and therefore antedated the others in our list, we do not include them there, because, unlike the pilgrimage devotions, the cultus of the Miraculous Medal—which has come to be associated with a number of organizations, such as the Archconfraternity of the Holy and Immaculate Heart of Mary, the Association of Children of Mary, and the Legion of Mary, as well as the Association of the Miraculous Medal itself—has no prime locus, but is diffused throughout the Catholic world. Unlike the visionaries of the pilgrimage devotions, moreover, Catherine Labouré was a religious, a Daughter of Charity (like other French visionaries, though, she was of rustic origin and just barely literate). Some medieval pilgrimages (for example, that to Aylesford in Kent, which originated in a vision of the Virgin Mary experienced by a Carmelite prior, Saint Simon Stock) owed their beginning to the dream or vision of a religious, but even in the Middle Ages, the laity, particularly the poor, played a fundamental role in determining where, when, and how pilgrimages would develop. This tendency continued, both in modern Europe and in the colonial areas. We have elsewhere noted the role of Indians in the genesis of the Mexican pilgrimage devotions of Guadalupe, Ocotlán, and Los Remedios; there were many more.[11] In other Latin American countries the same trend prevailed. The regular connection between Mary, the laity, the poor, and the colonized, in the rapid development of pilgrimages from visions and apparitions of the corporeal type, and from related miracles, points to the hidden, nonhierarchical domain of the church, with its stress on the power of the weak, on communitas and liminal phenomena, on the rare and unprecedented, as against the regular, ordained, and normative.

In the post-Tridentine period, the visions (sometimes imaginative or intellectual rather than corporeal) of religious have often given rise to generalized devotions, rather than pilgrimages. The cultus of the Sacred Heart of Jesus (which was revitalized by the Visitation nuns following the revelations of Margaret Mary Alocoque, a member of the order, in the latter part of the seventeenth century) and the early nineteenth-century Miraculous Medal devotion, mentioned earlier, are two important examples. Nearly every parish has a devotion of this kind (or did have, before Vatican II), often formalized in a sodality or fraternity. Such devotions attempt to purify, and render more virtuous, life in a familiar, structured place, rather than to seek initiatory renovation through a journey to a far shrine—one where the Mother of God is believed to have appeared to a humble lay person, short-circuiting all the customary ecclesiastical connections. We have argued that the dominant symbols of the church are multivocal, deriving their cognitive meaning from generalized, universalized theology and ethics, and their orectic or emotional-volitional charge from their particular, local geography and history. The generalized devotion, sponsored by religious orders and, ultimately, by the secular hierarchy of the structured church, lays initial stress on the normative pole, though it builds up meaning at the orectic pole through proselytization by the local sodalities. The pilgrimage devotion, generated by particular lay persons in specific localities, strikes a sympathetic chord throughout the church, not only among members of the same class as the visionary but among those of a higher class as well, because Catholic ideology values the lowly and the weak. Here the ever-present drive to semantic polarization expresses itself in the accretion of normative meaning to the deeply localized symbol-vehicle.

## La Salette

About the same time that Catherine Labouré experienced her visions of the Virgin, two children were born in the little town of Corps (then having 1,300 inhabitants), thirty miles south of Grenoble. These were the visionaries of La Salette, today an important pilgrimage center in France.[12] They were a girl, Mélanie Mathieu Calvat (born November 7, 1831), and a boy, Maximin Giraud (born August 7, 1835). Her father worked in a lumberyard and was desperately poor; Maximin's was a wheelwright and a drunkard, whose second wife, Maximin's step-mother, behaved to the child like the wicked prototypes in fairy tales, denying him food and love. Maximin lived by his wits, was illiterate, had no religious education to speak of, and could do little in life but take cattle to pasture. Maximin and Mélanie had known one another for only two days, when, on September 19, 1846, they joined forces to drive two small herds of cows up the mountain pastures to a stream near Corps, about five thousand feet above sea level. After lunching on rye bread and sour local cheese, the two cowherds fell asleep by the so-called Little Spring for an hour, an unusual circumstance. When they woke, they found that their eight cows were missing. They crossed the stream and eventually found the herd, but they had left their food satchels at the Little Spring. Returning to fetch them, the children saw a dazzling globe of light revolving over the stones surrounding the spring. They crossed themselves and prayed, for fear that they had encountered the devil. Then the globe began to swirl and appeared to boil, growing in size until it was about five feet in diameter. Slowly it opened. Within its shifting splendor of fiery color, Mélanie and Maximin could see the seated figure of a woman, with elbows on knees and face in hands. The children thought of attacking her with their cattle sticks. But the Lady then stood, removed her hands from her face, folded her arms across her breast, and in a low, musical voice told them to advance and hear the news she had to give. Her dress and ornament, as the children later described it, contained many traditional motifs of Christian iconography. On a chain around her neck she wore a crucifix, with a hammer represented on its left arm and a pair of pincers on the right (well known as Instruments of the Passion). She seemed also to wear a crown, from whose base, encircled with roses, sprang shafts of light. Her whole figure seemed transparent, composed of crystalline light, ringed in an almost blinding light, with a softer outer aureole that almost encompassed the children. An important detail, affecting the symbolism and interpretation of the vision ever since,[13] is that the Lady wept throughout the encounter. (It has often been noted that September 19, 1846, was an Ember Day, a special day of penitence in the Catholic calendar, and, before Pius X's reform of the Roman breviary, was also the eve of the Feast of the Seven Sorrows of the Virgin Mary.)

Though Mélanie and Maximin continued for years to elaborate on their first account in many matters of detail, that early account concerned the Lady's warning that, unless the people repented their prevailing religious apathy, she could no longer prevent the "heavy and powerful arm" of her Son from falling on the world. She then predicted that the potato crop would go on rotting until Christmas, that pests would devour the wheat, that the nuts would be grub-ridden, the grapes would rot, and the little children under seven would die of the palsy. Mélanie, who almost always spoke in the local patois, did not understand the term *pommes de terre*, which the Lady had at first used for "potatoes" (the cowherds thought that all *pommes* grew on trees). But when the Lady began to speak of the harvest, she apparently switched into fluent patois and continued in it till the end of her message.

She asked the children if they said their prayers well. When they replied, "Hardly at all," she urged them to say an Our Father and a Hail Mary every night and morning. She then stated that only a few elderly women went to mass any more, and that if others attended, when they had nothing else to do, they went only to jeer at religion. "And in Lent," she continued, "they go to the butchers as if they were dogs [instead of fasting]."

She then asked the children if they had ever seen spoilt wheat. When they said they had not, she reminded Maximin that a man in the nearby hamlet of Coin had once shown him and his father some ears of wheat that crumbled into dust when they were rubbed on the back of his hands; on the way home, Maximin's father had given him a bit of bread and said, "Here, my child, you can still eat bread this year, but if things go on like this, we don't know who will eat it next year."

"Right you are, Madame," Maximin replied. "I didn't remember it at first, but I do now."

Finally, the Lady said in French, "Well, my children, spread my message among all my people." She then moved past Mélanie, across the stream and up the side of the valley, "as though she hung above the ground and someone were pushing her," Maximin later said. At the top of the slope, she rose into the air, hung there for about half a minute, looked very sadly toward the southeast, in the direction of Italy, then seemed to "melt" into a globe of light like the one in which she had come; and the globe soon faded into "the light of common day."

The message seems simple enough: repent, pray, and attend mass. But the prophecy of potato and wheat blights and infant deaths excited attention. The usual sequence of events followed the children's return to Corps. Family and friends, and later the parish priest, heard the tale; they were skeptical, at first, then became convinced. Finally, the aged bishop of Grenoble, Philibert de Bruillard, set up two commissions, one of cathedral canons, the other of professors of the Grand Séminaire, to take testimony and gather evidence. They reported to him in mid-December 1846 that they were quite favorably impressed by the children's testimony, and their "simplicity and unshakable artlessness," but they nevertheless concluded that "there are certain things which arouse some caution about the truth of the Lady's words."

Later, in the summer of 1847, the bishop appointed two members of the faculty of the Grand Séminaire—Canon Rousselot, professor of theology, and Canon Orcel, the superior—to make a thorough investigation of the whole affair. Not only did these men interview the children separately and thoroughly, they also collected evidence from the local peasants that there were many extraordinary cures as a result of either the intercession of Our Lady of La Salette (the name of the mountain from which the Little Spring ran) or the use of water from the spring. The people also alleged that, since the apparition, the spring had flowed there uninterruptedly, though it was formerly dried up for most of the year.

By mid-October the bishop had established another commission of sixteen members, presided over by himself, to consider the canons' report and question the children further, first separately and then together. Twenty cases of healing were considered, and objections to the truth of the story were raised and probed. In the final session, on December 13, 1847, the majority of the commission approved the validity of the apparition. Yet the bishop then thought it "not prudent" to allow his clergy to accompany the faithful on the ever-growing pilgrimages to the mountain. He also authorized Canon Rousselot to publish on the happening at La Salette, reporting on the commission's findings. But four years passed before the bishop, in an episcopal letter of November 16, 1851, informed the six hundred or so churches of the diocese of Grenoble that "the apparition of the Blessed Virgin to two shepherds, on September 19, 1848, on a mountain in the Alps in the parish of La Salette, bears in itself all the marks of truth, and that the faithful are justified in believing without question in its truth." He then authorized the cult of Our Lady of La Salette. He sent a copy of the letter to the Sacred Congregation of Rites at Rome; the prefect of the congregation, with characteristic caution, spoke of "the praise-worthy thoroughness" of the years of investigation, and declared that "all was in order." Thus the devotion had received both diocesan and provincial approval.

Almost at once, in the secular world, the storm broke. In the post-Voltairian age, all phenomena proclaimed to be of preternatural origin immediately came under sharp critical scrutiny. It was to be expected, therefore, that scientists, skeptics, and freethinkers would question the La Salette apparition and the alleged miracles of healing at the new pilgrimage center. But the most serious opposition to the devotion came from within the church itself. First, there was the "incident of Ars" in 1850, involving Jean Baptiste Marie Vianney, the celebrated Curé d'Ars, a living legend for his holiness and for his ability to "discern souls" in confession. This nineteenth-century exemplar of Catholic sanctity (he himself became a goal of pilgrimage in his life-time, attracting more than a hundred thousand pilgrims to the undis-tinguished village of which he was parish priest, and was finally canonized by the church in 1925) declared that Maximin, the reputed boy visionary, had told him that "he had not seen the Blessed Virgin." The bishop of Grenoble, then on the point of authorizing the cult, tried to get the curé to modify his statement, but the curé replied:

> I had great faith in Our Lady of La Salette: I blessed and distrib-uted many medals and pictures representing the happening; and I gave away fragments of the stone on which the Blessed Virgin sat and always had one of these fragments on me. I even put one in a reliquary. I think, Monseigneur, that few of the priests in your diocese have done as much for La Salette as I have. When the lad told me that he had not seen the Blessed Virgin, I was tired for a couple of days. But after all, Monseigneur, the wound is not so serious, and if La Salette is the work of God it will not be destroyed by men.[14]

Men, and churchmen at that, did make a major attempt to destroy the devotion, however. The principal detractors were the Abbé Cartellier, curé of the St. Joseph parish in Grenoble; and the Abbé Déléon, curé of Villeurbanne, a parish quite close to Lyons but in the diocese of Grenoble. No love was lost between Déléon and the elderly bishop, who, at the end of January 1852, laid an interdict on Déléon, forbidding him to perform his priestly functions, on the ground that his private sex life gave scandal. In August of that year, Déléon published, under the pseudonym Donnadieu, a book entitled *La Salette —Fallavaux* [La Salette—valley of lies]. At the end of the year, the bishop announced his resignation, because he was very old and ailing. When the pope invited him to name his successor, he chose the Abbé Ginoulhiac, then vicar-general of Aix. Déléon now produced a sequel: *La Salette—Fallavaux, Part II*. When the new bishop was installed in May 1853, he tried to make peace in the diocese by offering to remove the interdict on Déléon, provided that the maverick priest would turn out the women he was living with, withdraw his books on La Salette, and write a personal letter of apology to the retired bishop. Déléon accepted these conditions, and the ban was removed. Nevertheless, it was not long before he returned to his onslaught on La Salette with a new book, *La Salette devant le Pape* (1854), backing up Cartellier. Déléon alleged, among other matters, that the new bishop of Grenoble had been offered the see on the sole condition that he support his predecessor's position on La Salette. (This allegation was strongly denied by both bishops, and by other high ecclesiastics, including a cardinal archbishop.) Déléon's main accusation, however, was that the Lady seen by the children was, in reality, a certain Mlle Constance de La Merlière, a wealthy and charitable middle-aged woman who lived at St. Marcellin, between Valence and Grenoble. According to Déléon, she had set off by coach, in September 1846, on a pilgrimage to the shrine of Notre-Dame du Laus in the department of Hautes-Alpes,[15] and had carried with her, in a hatbox, just such garments as the children had seen on the Lady of their vision. Déléon claimed that Mlle de La Merlière had left the coach clad in these garments, met the children, started to speak to them in French, and changed to the local patois when she saw that they did not understand her. After their conversation, she had seen a low cloud approach, walked toward it, and then hurried away under its cover. Later, some sisters at the convent of Le Laus had allegedly seen her dressed in the same attire. There had been no apparition, Déléon charged; rather, a harmless hoax by an eccentric and pious woman had escalated into a major new Marian cultus. Déléon's narrative was most circumstantial, full of names and dates. Unfortunately, inquiry disclosed that the abbé himself had resorted to fraud! Witnesses came forward to testify that on September 19, 1846, Mlle de La Merlière was at St. Marcellin, seventy-five miles from La Salette. And many other details in Déléon's account did not tally with documented facts: for example, he had stated that Mlle de La Merlière's coachman was named Fortin; but the owner of the coach service between Valence and Grenoble declared that Fortin did not enter his service until 1849, three years after he was said to have driven Mlle de La Merlière to Le Laus. This lady, moreover, was short and fat, neither luminous nor transparent, like the Lady in the alleged vision.

These arguments and counterarguments give a notion of the rhetoric and polemical style of mid-nineteenth-century controversies over apparitions and miracles and their role in the inception of pilgrimage devotions. It is tempting to analyze the Salette controversy, from the point of view of political anthropology, as a "social drama" or an "extended case history."[16] Historians have unearthed enough salient data to make this possible. Evidently, factions existed among the clergy of the Grenoble diocese, and they mobilized external support from higher officials of the church. As so often happens, however, people "voted with their feet," quite literally, whatever the clergy said or did, and the pilgrimage established itself, with the usual array of "cures" and spiritual and material "favors," and the rapid creation of pilgrim ways and facilities.

In 1851, before the detractors Cartellier and Déléon published their books, Pope Pius IX had officially declared that the faithful might accept the veracity of the apparition at La Salette. He took this step after having received letters in which Mélanie and Maximin recorded the "secrets" of La Salette—words the Lady had allegedly spoken to each individually, without the other's having heard what was said. The pope had promised the children not to reveal the details, for they had made a similar promise to the Lady. Later, he told the superior of the Missionaries of Our Lady of La Salette, an order founded at the shrine: "So you want to know the secrets of La Salette? Well, here they are: unless you repent, you will all perish."

What is interesting about La Salette is that it seemed to set the apocalyptic tone for the latter-day Marian pilgrimages. The notion of a "secret" communication is found again in the Fátima and Garabandal cultuses. The overt message contains a call to repentance— and sometimes a threat, if the people do not respond. The threat is either of local calamities (such as the potato and wheat blights foretold at La Salette) or of a widespread disaster. At Pellevoisin, for example, in the archdiocese of Bourges, the Virgin is said to have appeared to the housemaid Estelle Faguette, and told her sadly: "As for France, what have I not done for her? She still refuses to pay heed. Very well, I can no longer restrain my Son. France will suffer much."[17] The theme of penance is prominent, too, in the message Our Lady of Lourdes gave to Bernadette, and in that of Fátima, where three children, cousins aged ten, nine, and seven, were shown a vision of Hell, after which the Virgin told them: "You have just seen Hell, wherein are cast the souls of poor sinners. To save them, the Lord wishes to establish in the world devotion to my Immaculate Heart. If people do as I tell you, many souls will be saved, and there will be peace. The War [First World War] will end. But if people do not stop offending the Lord, another worse than this will start during the next pontificate."

As we noted earlier, a considerable populist literature has developed from apocalyptic Marianism. Seldom dealt with by theologians or intellectuals, this literature is highly influential among segments of the Catholic laity all over the world. The "messages" of La Salette, Pontmain, Beauraing, and other places of pilgrimage recognized by the Vatican are not the worst with regard to prophecies and admonitions. The messages accompanying the alleged visions at Garabandal in Spain, the grotto of Ulzio in Italy (near the French border), Palmar de Troya in Spain (near Seville), and many other places in France, Portugal, Venezuela, and elsewhere, are colorful and violent to an extreme, accompanied by quite ferocious denunciations of the Aggiornamento and other recent developments in the Catholic church. These "messages," particularly marked since the Second World War, are reminiscent of the doomsday writings of Jehovah's Witnesses and other millenarian movements; they are published and discussed weekly in such periodicals and reviews as *Michael* (formerly *Vers Demain*) in Rougement, Quebec, Canada, and *Maria Messajera* in Spain (Zaragoza).

These frenetic outpourings are totally different in quality from the Marian message of Lourdes. Though it also stressed penance, the Virgin's message at Lourdes had a simple, down-to-earth tone, like that of the Virgin of Guadalupe. But a fundamental difference derives from the nature of the visionaries. Neither Maximin Giraud nor Mélanie Calvat was a prepossessing individual—though, from the theological viewpoint, this need not be a stumbling-block, given the truths uttered by Balaam's ass! The spirit moveth where it listeth, whatever the quality of its vessel or instrument. Many who knew Maximin shared the opinion of Abbé Félix Dupanloup, who questioned the boy in 1848 (when Maximin was thirteen years old): "I have seen many children during my life, but I have seen few, if indeed any, who have made such an unpleasing impression on me. . . . The way he fidgets is really extraordinary. His character is peculiar. It has a kind of uncouth flippancy, a violent instability and something insufferably queer about it. . . . I had the greatest difficulty in preventing very serious suspicions from mastering me." Of Mélanie, the abbé said: "The girl seemed just as unpleasant in her own way. But she gives a better impression than the boy. According to what people say, the eighteen months she has spent with the nuns at Corps have improved her a little. Nevertheless, she seemed to me peevish and sulky, and silent because of her stupidity."[18]

Dupanloup, who later became famous as bishop of Orléans, eventually joined the camp of those who believed that precisely because the children were so displeasing their testimony had to be taken seriously—that is, because their description of the Lady and her words differed so sharply from their habitual outlook, they could not have invented it. The adult careers of Mélanie and Maximin were not particularly edifying either. When it seemed likely that La Salette was going to attain international prominence as a pilgrimage center, the visionaries were taken in charge by the church authorities, and received some support from the bishop of Grenoble and, later, from the pope. They were given a rather severe education at the convent of Corps, under the eagle eye of the Sisters of Providence. There they learned to read and write fluently in French, a skill that Mélanie was to put to embarrassing use. Maximin rebelled against convent restrictions more than once: his trip to the Curé d'Ars, for example, was made without permission. After a longish career as a drifter, he did a six-month spell as a papal guard. But, being fond of more than a glass or two of wine, he became involved with a wine merchant and "hustler," who persuaded him to join in selling, at high prices, an herb-flavored liqueur called Salettine, with his name on the label. When people were scandalized at this attempt to cash in on his holy vision, he replied: "I only did it to earn my living by the sweat of my brow."[19] Unfortunately, he was duped by his partner, who soon disappeared, leaving Maximin with a heap of debts—a tribute to his naiveté if not his innocence. On his deathbed, in 1875, Maximin called on God to be his judge that he had never lied about the apparition of La Salette, and he took several sips of water from the "miraculous spring" in order to swallow the Host during his last communion.

Mélanie provides an even more striking and hardly less interesting contrast to Bernadette Soubirous, as we shall see. Though both were shepherdesses, speaking the local patois, and both entered religious orders after making known that they had seen a vision of, and received a message from, a beautiful lady who appeared and disappeared in a miraculous fashion, the resemblance there ends. After making a series of attempts to be admitted to religious orders, Mélanie was finally permitted to take the Carmelite habit in a convent at Darlington in England. Before that, it appears, her head was turned by the adulation the people accorded her. She had become the center of a cult at Corenc, just outside Grenoble, where she had gone as a postulant after leaving the convent school at Corps. She used to tell tales of her life as a cowherd to a throng of admiring postulants and novices. One tale related how she had led packs and herds of wild animals through the woods in religious processions, chanting God's praises, the cross being carried by a wolf. The bishop of Grenoble visited the convent, rebuked her for her conceits and fantasies, and refused to let her make her profession as a nun. She then had a wild three weeks in the convent of the Daughters of Charity at Vienne, where she "refused to eat for nearly forty-eight hours, screaming until a crowd gathered outside the convent, and [she] tried to bite the Reverend Mother."[20] She obviously disrelished the style of the Sisters, who "before anything," according to their Rule, "strive for uniformity with the other Sisters and conceal everything which is in any way singular and peculiar to themselves." We will not detail the complex events that finally led to her profession as an English Carmelite, but this was only the beginning of Mélanie's career as a sibyl and prophetess. As an English Carmelite, she no longer considered herself under the canonical jurisdiction of the bishop of Grenoble, and she delivered herself of a stream of apocalyptic writings. The earliest of these, in the form of letters to the curé of her old parish, Corps, set the tone for later Catholic apocalyptic literature far more emphatically than the children's original account of the message of Our Lady of La Salette. Her utterances now became definitely anticlerical. She alleges that the Virgin told her: "Today and every day I am crucified by those who know Me, by many priests. They imagine they see, but it is not by my light, but by the light of the devil. Formerly, priests and nuns were the pillars of my Church, but today the pillars have fallen. Calamities are going to rain upon the world and then cries and groans will rise up to Me, but for a time I shall be as if dead."[21]

Mélanie later became homesick for France. She did not stay with any religious order for very long. For a time she was with the Sisters of Our Lady of Compassion at Marseilles. From 1867 to 1884, she lived quietly in Castellammare in Italy with her friend Sister Marie, teaching French for board and lodging, and receiving occasional sums of money from the then thriving Missionaries of Our Lady of Salette.

But she had a book brewing, and in 1879 she brought out *L'Apparition de la très sainte Vierge sur la montagne de la Salette*, bearing the imprimatur of Monseigneur Zola, bishop of Lecce (in southern Italy). In this book, Mélanie professed to deliver the full text of the "secret" given her by the Virgin. It was full of apocalyptic material. She claimed that the Blessed Virgin had commanded her to found a new order, the Order of the Mother of God; both men and women were to belong to it, and would be known as the "Apostles of the Last Days."[22] She further declared that in six or seven years, Saint Michael, the warrior archangel, would succeed the archangel Gabriel in the government of the world. Mélanie did not initiate this genre, which derives from well-known biblical prototypes (particularly the Books of Daniel and Revelation) and the powerful millenarian tradition of the Middle Ages, but she gave it a strong impetus among the struggling lower-middle-class Catholics of southern Europe and the New World, people of almost pathological respectability, crushed between big business and the organized working class. Her end was sad. Beevers, who believes in the authenticity of Mélanie's and Maximin's first vision, writes:

> There is almost unbearable pathos in the picture of the ageing woman, clothed in black, with a heavy, almost sullen face, wandering about France and Italy, her mind filled with bloody images of universal carnage, of falling mountains, gulfs of fire, and the evil splendour of anti-Christ and his legions riding in triumph across the world. Her life was almost without friends and one darkened by the conviction that spies and enemies surrounded her; materially it was one of penury and spiritually, one shot through with delusions. Old and defeated she returned to die (December 15, 1904) in the southern Italy she loved, to the hot little town of Altamura, decaying in the sun, far from the cool mountain meadow where, nearly sixty years before, her fresh young eyes had been dazzled by the radiant glory of the Mother of God.[23]

## Lourdes

Of the visionaries whose revelations have generated pilgrimages and have been approved by the church, only a few have been canonized.[24] Bernadette Soubirous is possibly the best known of these; her visions stand at the beginning of more than a century of pilgrimage to the grotto of Massabielle. Because Bernadette's visions and their religious, social, and symbolic consequences have been widely dealt with in the modern media, we shall be brief,[25] merely pointing up some decisive contrasts between La Salette and Lourdes, and between Mélanie and Bernadette. At Lourdes, she whom Bernadette called the Lady spoke only eleven times in the course of eighteen apparitions (between February 11 and July 16, 1858). All of her statements were single sentences; several were requests to Bernadette to undertake some simple action before a crowd, as for instance: "Go drink at the spring and wash yourself in it"; "Go eat that plant which you will find there"; "Go kiss the ground as penance for sinners." Such penitential exercises and personal humiliations are often regarded in the Judeo-Christian tradition as tests of faith and marks of saintly election. Bernadette was hard put to it to find the "spring" that the Lady had mentioned. She had to dig in the muddy sand of the grotto to open up the spring, and thus started the celebrated source of the miraculous "Lourdes water," which later developed into a flow of 32,000 gallons a day. Some of the water is piped into baths housed in a separate building where the pilgrims bathe; and many cures are attributed to its efficacy. Bernadette's washing and drinking provided the model for subsequent pilgrim behavior.

Other messages from Our Lady of Lourdes called for universal penance. Bernadette, like other Marian visionaries before her (Juan Diego, for example, who spoke with the Virgin of Guadalupe), was commanded "to tell the priests to have a chapel built here," for the Lady wished people "to come here in procession"—which they have done, of course, to the number of many millions. In her final message, theological in character, the Lady declared: "I am the Immaculate Conception." The date was only three years after Pius IX had proclaimed the dogma of the Immaculate Conception, the dogma that Mary was, in the first instant of her conception, preserved from the stain of original sin; that she was, in theological language, conceived immaculate. For the masses, the apparition seemed to confirm the dogma, by giving it a concrete embodiment, although, according to Catholic thought, this was not needed, because the proclamation by the pope *ex cathedra* is believed to be "perfect in its own order." Many critics of Pius IX's actions have hinted that these apparitions of the Immaculate Conception, which pointedly upheld his dogma, came at a suspiciously convenient moment. For the pope had it in mind, some time in the future, to proclaim another dogma, that of papal infallibility. The apparitions of Lourdes seemed to prove his case. Whatever the cause, Bernadette did announce the Lady's declaration

19. The grotto of the apparition at Massabielle near Lourdes.
*(Photograph by Victor Turner)*

on March 25, the Feast of the Annunciation, one of the three most ancient Marian feasts of the universal church.

The events and symbols connected with the Lourdes apparitions, whether influenced by clerical prompting or not, have a highly orthodox flavor, as contrasted with the heterodox, apocalyptic messages to Mélanie. Lourdes is not divinatory. The apparitions of Lourdes simply reinforce traditional doctrines; they add nothing to the "deposit of faith," though amateur Catholic exegesis delights in finding portents in apparitions, as we have seen. Some clerical exegetes have found a symmetry in the events comparable to that in a Lévi-Straussian analysis of myth—perhaps it is to be expected that a French Mary would work in a French fashion! For example, one commentator, Joseph Deery, finds "a harmonious arrangement in the eighteen apparitions."[26] In the first and second, as in the seventeenth and eighteenth, no words were spoken; "a silent establishment of contact was balanced by a silent breaking-off of contact." In the third apparition, the Lady spoke her first words; in the sixteenth, or third-last, her final words. In between were twelve apparitions (distributed equally over two weeks), manifesting her wishes: prayer (February 19–23); penance (the general demand, on February 24, was followed by specific instructions for exercises of penance, February 25–March 1); a chapel and pilgrimages, whereby her desire for prayer and penance might be fully realized (March 2–4). Thus we have three silent, twelve spoken, and three more silent apparitional communications, the numerical factors being the sacred numbers three (representing the Trinity) and four (the four Evangelists, the four Last Things—Death, Judgment, Heaven, and Hell—and the like). Deery also notes that the messages concerning prayer and penance were conveyed, appropriately, in the Lenten season. Further, Thursday was an important day in the series: "It was on a Thursday that Our Lady first revealed herself, that she requested Bernadette to return for a fortnight, that the miraculous spring was discovered in the course of the ninth apparition, that the fortnight ended, and that proclamation of her name was made."[27] Deery points out that Thursday, the day of the Last Supper, has been traditionally designated by the church for honoring the sacrament of the Eucharist, and states that Lourdes has become the world's greatest center of devotion to the Eucharist. Many of the miracles at Lourdes are reported to have occurred during the short service called the Benediction of the Blessed Sacrament, in which a bishop or priest blesses the long line of the sick, most of them in wheelchairs, by making the sign of the cross above them with the consecrated Host displayed in a monstrance.

The orthodox character of the Lourdes apparitions and their interpretation, as contrasted with Mélanie's fearful message, was matched by the paradigmatic sanctity, in Catholic terms, of Bernadette herself. Not that she was docile and serene, but she had a charisma of goodness, a singular human warmth, in no way denying her earthy peasant frankness, or even occasional roughness of tongue.

Once Bernadette was taken to a dress shop and was asked to describe the kind of dress material the Lady of her vision wore. The dressmaker showed her a fine piece of Lyonnaise silk. Bernadette replied: "Nothing like it."

"But, Mam'selle, this is the whitest and silkiest fabric in the city."

"That only shows," retorted Bernadette, "that the Blessed Virgin did not have her dress made by you!"[28]

Bernadette did not enter St. Gildas, the motherhouse of the Sisters of Charity and Christian Instruction of Nevers, until six years had passed after her final vision. There, despite intense homesickness and serious illness, she remained until her death, on April 16, 1879, in her thirty-sixth year, the twelfth year of her religious profession.

20. The benediction of the sick in the Lourdes precinct.
*(Photograph by Victor Turner)*

There are numerous stories of her phlegmatic, indeed heroic, endurance of suffering. She did not lose her sense of humor—another quality distinguishing her from Mélanie. Two years before her death, when she was suffering from a severe tubercular condition in her right knee, she said to another nun: "Pray for me when I am dead, because people will say, that 'little saint' doesn't need prayers, and I shall be left grilling in Purgatory."

Like Mélanie, Bernadette was entrusted with a secret; but, unlike Mélanie, she never divulged it, not even to the pope. Bernadette was asked by the bishop's commission: "Would you tell your secrets to the pope?"

21. The great nightly torchlight procession at Lourdes.
*(Photograph by Victor Turner)*

She replied: "The Blessed Virgin told me to tell no one. The pope is someone."

"Yes. But the pope has the authority of Jesus Christ."

"The pope has authority on earth," answered Bernadette. "The Blessed Virgin is in heaven." She refused to discuss the matter further and never raised it again herself.

The quality of her life as well as her visions led eventually to Bernadette's canonization on December 8, 1933, the Feast of the Nativity of the Blessed Virgin Mary. Lourdes, unlike La Salette, has become an authentic, international devotion within the Catholic church. Immense crowds take part in the rituals of the grotto and in the processions at the sanctuary. They speak all the languages of Europe, and many of Asia and Africa. The number of pilgrims continues to climb steadily. In 1950 nearly 1,600,000 persons visited the shrine. In 1958, the centenary of the apparitions, more than 5,000,000 came. In 1970 there were 3,100,000. In 1972, the year of our visit, 3,500,000 attended. The literature produced at the shrine is without apocalyptic overtones. *Lourdes: Journal de la Grotte*, the weekly paper, confines itself, quite unpretentiously, to information about different parties of pilgrims (gypsies, Australians from Melbourne, Limburg Hollanders, Barcelonans, to take a random count from two issues); historical articles on the shrine; an occasional sermon; and practical information about the shrine, the town of Lourdes, and the surrounding districts.

In Lourdes there is a sense of living communitas, whether in the great singing processions by torchlight or in the agreeable little cafés of the back streets, where tourists and pilgrims gaily sip their wine and coffee. Something of Bernadette has tinctured the entire social milieu—a cheerful simplicity, a great depth of communion.

# Notes

1. See Turner and Turner, *Image and Pilgrimage*, chap. 4.
2. Sollier, "Communion of Saints," p. 171.
3. Ibid., p. 174.
4. Christian, *Person and God*, pp. 48, 181, 182.
5. Turner and Turner, *Image and Pilgrimage*, chap. 3.
6. Quoted from D'Alton, *The Archdiocese of Tuam*, p. 321.
7. Turner and Turner, *Image and Pilgrimage*, pp. 41–42.
8. Beevers, *The Sun Her Mantle*, p. 5.
9. Ibid., pp. 9, 10.

10. Laurentin and Durand have compiled a collection of 111 documents (selected from more than a thousand) relating to the apparition and sanctuary of Pontmain, entitled *Pontmain: Histoire Authentique, Documents.*

11. See Turner and Turner, *Image and Pilgrimage,* chap. 2.

12. Our account of La Salette is based on the admirable summary by Beevers of the copious La Salette literature (*The Sun Her Mantle,* pp. 23–109).

13. See, for example, Bloy's "Celle qui pleure."

14. Beevers, *The Sun Her Mantle,* p. 62.

15. The shrine of Notre-Dame du Laus was founded on the site where, according to *The Catholic Encyclopedia* (1909, s.v. "Gap, Diocese of"), the Blessed Virgin appeared "an incalculable number of times," over a period of fifty-four years (1664–1718), to a shepherdess, the venerable Benoîte Rencurel. Interestingly, the pilgrimage is a late instance of the "shepherds' cycle" type, rather than a forerunner of the modern "visionary" pilgrimage. Gillett (*Famous Shrines,* 1:161–68), drawing on the shrine's literature and Northcote's *Celebrated Sanctuaries,* notes that Benoîte spoke not only with the Virgin but also with Saint Maurice, who showed her a healing spring; and that she once saw the Lady with a child. Though her conversations took place in the mountain pastures, she was told to instruct the people to rebuild and enlarge a ruined wayside chapel in the hamlet of Le Laus. Pilgrims each fetched a stone from a nearby quarry to do this. Despite initial opposition from the Embrun diocesan chapter, the pilgrimage throve. Oil from the lamp on the Virgin's shrine allegedly cures the sick.

16. See Turner, *Dramas, Fields, and Metaphors,* chap. 1.

17. See Banron, *Notice sur Notre-Dame*; and Gillett, *Famous Shrines,* pp. 288–339.

18. Quoted from Beevers, *The Sun Her Mantle,* pp. 50, 51.

19. Ibid., p. 97.

20. Ibid., pp. 84, 85.

21. Ibid., p. 87.

22. Ibid.

23. Ibid., pp. 94, 95. However, Mélanie still has her clerical defenders. As recently as 1973, Hyacinthe Guilhot published *La Vraie Mélanie de La Salette,* citing R. P. André Triclot that Mélanie "certainly practised the virtues perfectly" and especially lived the "eighth beatitude: that of the persecuted—probably the most difficult" (p. 17).

24. Benoîte Rencurel, for example, of Le Laus fame, was declared venerable by Pope Pius IX only in 1871.

25. There is an immense literature on Lourdes, both polemical and devotional. One of the fullest accounts of the apparitions and subsequent events is Estrade, *Les Apparitions de Lourdes.*

26. Deery, *Our Lady of Lourdes,* pp. 41, 42.

27. Ibid., p. 42.

28. Gillett, *Famous Shrines,* p. 204.

# Bibliography

Banron, P. *Notice sur Notre-Dame de Pellevoisin*. Lyons, France: St. Eucher, 1938.

Beevers, John. *The Sun Her Mantle*. Dublin: Browne and Nolan, 1953.

Bloy, Léon. "Celle qui pleure (Notre-Dame de la Salette)." In *Oeuvres*, edited by Jacques Petit, pp. 111–259. 1907. Reprint. Paris: Mercure de France, 1970.

Christian, William A., Jr. *Person and God in a Spanish Valley*. New York: Seminar Press, 1972.

D'Alton, Edward. *History of the Archdiocese of Taum*. Vol. 2. Dublin: Phoenix, 1928.

Deery, Joseph. *Our Lady of Lourdes*. Dublin: Browne and Nolan, 1958.

Estrade, Jean-Baptiste. *Les Apparitions de Lourdes*. Tours: Maison Mame, 1899.

Gillett, H. M. *Famous Shrines of Our Lady*. Vol. 1. London: Samuel Walker, 1949.

Laurentin, René, and Durand, A. *Pontmain: histoire authentique, documents*. Paris: Lethellieux, 1970.

Northcote, J. Spencer. *Celebrated Sanctuaries of the Madonna*. London: Longmans Green, 1868.

Sollier, J. F. "Communion of Saints." In *The Catholic Encyclopedia*, edited by C. Herbermann et al. New York: Appleton, 1911.

Turner, Victor. *Dramas, Fields, and Metaphors*. New York: Cornell University Press, 1974.

———, and Turner, Edith. *Image and Pilgrimage in Christian Culture*. New York: Columbia University Press, 1978.

# THREE

## The Great Goddess
## in South Asia

# 8

## The Goddess Kannagi:
## A Dominant Symbol of South Indian
## Tamil Society
### by Jacob Pandian

When the myth of the goddess Kannagi arose about two thousand years ago in ancient Tamil society, it reflected social, political, and religious structures of Tamil culture.[1] Despite structural changes that occurred in the following centuries the significance of the goddess remained the same; the religious theme of chastity symbolized by the goddess Kannagi has continued to be an important conceptual category for the Tamil people. Modern Tamil society is not politically autonomous and is structurally different from what it was about two thousand years ago, yet the symbol of the goddess plays a significant role in the maintenance of Tamil cultural identity. It is also important in the efforts of various sociopolitical movements that seek national autonomy or statehood for the Tamils.

The Tamils number about forty million today. If language is used as a criterion for cultural boundedness, Tamil culture is not confined solely within the geographical limits of the south Indian province known today as Tamil Nadu. Tamil communities are located in different parts of India, and Tamil speakers constitute a large section of the populations of Sri Lanka (Ceylon) and Malaysia. Although the principles of modern Tamil social organization resemble those of the

This essay was originally prepared for this volume. A similar article has been published by the author as "The Goddess of Chastity and the Politics of Ethnicity in the Tamil Society of South Asia," *Contributions to Asian Studies* 10 (1977): 52–63.

22. Image of the goddess Kannagi, symbol of ethnic unity among the Tamil people of south India.
*(Photograph by Jacob Pandian)*

"Hindu social order," with its hierarchically ranked caste groups, a distinctive Tamil culture has persisted with a literary tradition for over two thousand years.

The image of the goddess Kannagi looms large in the consciousness of modern Tamils. She is identified as the Goddess of Chastity (*pathini-theivam*) and as the Queen of Chastity (*karpuk-arasi*). Kannagi represents Tamil notions of female chastity and spirituality. She also serves as a metaphor to conceptualize the Tamil heritage of justice and the ideals of Tamil linguistic and cultural purity. In rare cases, Kannagi is worshiped as a manifestation of the mother goddess and as the Goddess of Faithful Wives; but she is primarily a deity who has great social relevance because her attributes reflect cherished Tamil social ideals. Often her image is used consciously in the secular arenas of ethnicity and politics.

No specialized rituals are associated with the worship of Kannagi; nor is there a viable cult or sectarian movement that focuses on her personality in Tamil Nadu. Ramanujan notes that Kannagi is "the eidos or archetype, worshipped as the Goddess of Faithful Wives in Tamil Nadu and Ceylon."[2] The Tamils, in general, believe that several temples once were dedicated to Kannagi. They refer to some of these as the Kannagi temples of ancient times. In rare cases where she is identified as the presiding deity of a temple, her attributes are more like those of other mother goddesses who are propitiated for protection against epidemics and other disasters. It is conceivable that the myth of Kannagi had its origin in the context of a disaster of great magnitude, but then acquired symbolic significance by linking fate, chastity, and justice in the ancient Tamil literary tradition.

The objective of this article is to discuss how the religious/conceptual category of chastity in Kannagi's life acquired political and ethnic significance and to suggest that Kannagi serves as a dominant symbol or semantic model for conceptualizing familial, ethnic, and political experiences in Tamil society.[3] Such a model is not a mere reflection of the social order but rather a symbol that mediates between sociopolitical realities and Tamil conceptions of personal, group, and national identity.[4]

Ancient Tamil territory was divided into three kingdoms, Chola Nadu, Pandiya Nadu, and Chera Nadu, which flourished in southern India from the third century B.C. to the third century A.D. The myth of the goddess Kannagi originated during this time. These kingdoms gradually declined, most of their territory falling under the political jurisdiction of non-Tamil Pallava kings in the north. In the ninth century A.D. a temporary revival of Tamil political autonomy saw one of the Tamil kingdoms holding political hegemony over most of southern India and Ceylon, a control to be replaced between the fourteenth and early seventeenth centuries by the rule of non-Tamil Telugu kings. During the seventeenth century frequent warfare among the Tamil, Telugu, and Muslim kings of southern India occurred, largely as a result of the political intervention by Dutch, French, and British trading companies that were stationed in Tamil territory. In the eighteenth century, the British became de facto rulers of this territory, and after the departure of the British in the twentieth century, the province of Tamil Nadu was formed as one of the "linguistic states" of India. Several political associations have emerged during the past fifty years with the goal of attaining a separate national status for Tamil Nadu.

Most of what we know about ancient Tamil social organization and religion is inferred from Tamil literary tradition before the third century A.D. The "Epic of the Ankle Bracelet" (*Silapathikaram*), which narrates the story of Kannagi's life and deification, was authored by a prince named Ilango Adigal during this period.[5] The epic gives a detailed description of the social and religious customs of the Tamils; and from it, and a few other writings of this period, we are able to derive the life-style and cognitive categories of the Tamil people.

The ancient Tamils had three overlapping systems of social classification: ecological, occupational, and class variables combined to establish social categories. The "caste" system, operating on principles of hierarchy, occupational specialization, and ritual separation, evolved between the third and ninth centuries A.D. After the third century A.D. a Brahmanical priesthood provided legitimacy for the system through the authority of Sanskrit literary sources. Thus, after the third century A.D., Tamil social organization resembled the all-India Hindu social order.[6] The main cleavage in Tamil society has been between Brahman and non-Brahman caste groups, with the latter identified as an "alien" social category by many leaders of Tamil cultural revivalism in the twentieth century.

In ancient times, worship of deified culture heroes was common, but the worship of the god Muruga and the mother goddesses was widespread throughout Tamil territory. The question whether mother goddess worship is an Aryan or non-Aryan trait has gained considerable scholarly attention. One of the recent statements addressed to this issue is by Stephen Tyler, who writes: "Associated with fertility and disease, the cult of the mother goddess represents one of the most ancient and persistent expressions of Indian religion. Since

other goddesses are practically non-existent in the earlier Aryan religious works, it almost certainly is a cult of non-Aryan religion."[7]

Louis Dumont raises the question whether it is correct to view
the widespread worship of *amman* as mother goddess worship.[8] He
argues that because the Tamils use the same term (*ammal*) for both
mother and all females (including children), it is not correct to interpret *amman* worship as mother goddess worship. He holds that it is
appropriate to label female deities only with reference to the diseases
they represent and that their functions must be studied in relation to
those of other deities in order to discover the relational structure of
Hinduism on an all-India basis. Dumont's interpretation stems from
the fact that he does not consider it necessary to understand what the
gods and goddesses mean to the believers themselves, only to make
sense of the data in a logical manner. The Tamils use the same term
(*ammal*) to refer to mother and all females not because they conceive
of every female as their mother, but because of the cultural theme that
females are sacred. *Amman* is the mother goddess not because she is
the mother of a group of people or of a village; female spirituality has
both benevolent and malevolent aspects, and the mother goddess
represents both these aspects as protector and punisher.

A central religious theme that has persisted unchanged for over
two thousand years is the conception of female chastity. Undoubtedly,
this conception and that of the mother goddess have similar roots,
but the principle of chastity was elaborated by ancient Tamils as a
category of sacred power, and the various attributes of this sacred
power were discussed in great detail with reference to the social implications of being a chaste virgin, wife, mother, and widow. Women
in general were seen as capable of having sacred power, but this
power was believed to be possessed only by those who were chaste.
In other words, chastity was given an ontological status, and its
attributes were enunciated with reference to chaste women.

George Hart demonstrates how the now-widespread female chas-
tity/spirituality complex had its origin in south India, probably in
Tamil society.[9] From a comparative analysis of Tamil and Vedic literature, Hart shows that chastity was not a religious category for the
Indo-European speakers who entered India. He notes that the Hindu
scriptures of a later date make references to such a category, adding
that this was because the indigenous south Indian concept was borrowed by Indo-European speakers. G. Morris Carstairs provides a
psychoanalytic interpretation of the concept of the sacred power of
women,[10] and Tyler offers an interpretation showing how the Indian

family household generates the conception of malevolent and benevolent attributes of womanhood and relates such a conception to
mother goddess worship.[11]

## Genesis of the Myth of Kannagi

As indicated earlier, the Tamil "Epic of the Ankle Bracelet" (*Silapathikaram*) narrates the life and times of the goddess Kannagi.[12] The author, Ilango Adigal, focused on Kannagi as a metaphor by means of
which he could conceptualize the political and ethnic experiences
of the Tamil people and demonstrate the validity of the religious-
conceptual category of chastity.[13] The reality of Tamil justice and
ethnicity was portrayed through Kannagi's experiences as a chaste
woman. From the epic we understand that in spite of the occupational, religious, and political differentiation within Tamil society,
notions of fate, love, chastity, morality, omens, justice, and divinity
were the same for all Tamils; Ilango Adigal organized these themes
around Kannagi's experiences in the three kingdoms.[14]

Kannagi was the daughter of a prosperous merchant living in the
Chola kingdom. She was trained in all the genteel arts and married a
successful merchant named Kovalan. Their marriage was happy until
Kovalan encountered a dancer of great charm and wit in the person of
Madavi. The dancer's beauty and art attracted Kovalan to the extent
that he took up residence with her, forgetting his chaste wife, Kannagi. This liaison between Kovalan and Madavi did not last long,
however. At an annual Tamil ceremony, Kovalan sang a song which
indicated to Madavi that he was thinking about another woman. In
order to tease him, Madavi in turn composed a poem referring to
another man. Kovalan, suspecting that Madavi was unfaithful toward
him, severed his ties with her.

Kovalan returned to his wife a broken man. He had lost all his
wealth in his relationship with Madavi and was depressed at his
bleak prospects. But Kannagi consoled him and gave him her diamond embedded ankle bracelets. Because Kovalan might sell the
ankle bracelets to start a new business, he decided to undertake a
journey to Madurai, the capital city of the Pandiya kingdom.

On reaching Madurai, Kovalan concluded that it would be better
for Kannagi, who had come with him, to find temporary residence
somewhere in the city. Kavunthi Adigal, a Jain woman ascetic who
had accompanied them, suggested that Kannagi could stay with a

herder woman named Mathari. When the couple arrived at Mathari's house in the city, Kannagi cooked an elaborate meal that was fated to be Kovalan's last. After resting briefly, Kovalan proceeded to the bazaar alone with one of Kannagi's ankle bracelets.

In the bazaar, Kovalan saw the chief goldsmith of the Pandiya king and, hoping that he could sell the ankle bracelet to the queen, asked the goldsmith to estimate its price. The goldsmith, however, had recently stolen an ankle bracelet belonging to the queen; as Kovalan asked him to evaluate Kannagi's ankle bracelet, the thief contemplated a scheme to implicate Kovalan. Because the ankle bracelet produced by Kovalan resembled the queen's, the goldsmith believed that he could convince the king that Kovalan was the thief and ask for his execution, thus covering up his own guilt. While Kovalan waited trustingly, the goldsmith proceeded to the king. The king, eager to please the queen by giving her the ankle bracelet, accepted the word of the goldsmith without verification and bade his soldiers recover the ankle bracelet and execute Kovalan. The goldsmith took the soldiers to his house, where Kovalan was waiting; although the soldiers doubted whether a person of Kovalan's countenance could have committed such a crime, the goldsmith succeeded in goading one of them to accomplish the king's command to behead him.

Kannagi, anxiously waiting for Kovalan's return at Mathari's house, soon heard that he had been executed. In uncontrollable grief and anger she ran to the site where Kovalan's corpse lay. At the sound of her wailing the corpse appeared to come alive and proclaim the injustice done, whereupon Kannagi proceeded to the king's palace to declare her husband's innocence and challenge the king's authority. The king, courteous during his audience with her, reasoned that it was his duty to render justice by killing a thief. Kannagi protested that her husband was innocent, claiming that the ankle bracelet which Kovalan had had in his possession was one of the two belonging to her, and she mentioned that they contained diamonds. As the queen's ankle bracelets contained pearls, the king commanded his soldier to bring the ankle bracelet recovered from Kovalan. Kannagi dashed the ankle bracelet to the floor, dislodging a piece of diamond, which struck the king's mouth. The king, who could not bear the idea that he had rendered injustice and in the process had himself become a thief and murderer, fell from his throne in despair and died. The queen, seeing the death of her husband, also died of despair.

Outside the palace, Kannagi tore her right breast with her hand and to avenge the wrongful execution of her husband cursed the city of Madurai where the calamity had occurred. Fire broke out wherever the drops of her blood fell and the city was engulfed in flames. For fourteen days, Kannagi wandered toward the Chera kingdom and was seen being transported to the skies in a chariot.

The deification of Kannagi as the Goddess of Chastity was ordered by the Chera king, who was told of Kannagi's transcendence and of her experiences in the Pandiya kingdom. Deciding to dedicate a temple in her honor, the king undertook the long journey across the north of India to the Himalayan mountains to secure the proper stone to build her idol. After the successful completion and dedication of the temple, Kannagi was proclaimed the Tamil Goddess of Chastity.

## The Religious Category of Chastity

The ancient Tamils conceived of chastity as an entity in itself that had sacred or mystical attributes when associated with women who were considered spiritual because they were chaste. Thus, the equation of female spirituality with chastity constituted a religious conceptual category. Through Kannagi's life and experiences, the religious category of chastity was validated for the Tamil people. The relationship of female spirituality and chastity was fully manifested in the life of Kannagi; she was the embodiment of Tamil virtues and the essence of chaste womanhood. But her experiences also demonstrated the validity of chastity in the context of Tamil justice and ethnicity: being a chaste woman, she had the power to render justice, and such justice was conceptualized as an attribute of Tamil ethnicity. Her image accordingly became a metaphor to explain justice and ethnicity in association with chastity. This association can be schematically presented as follows:

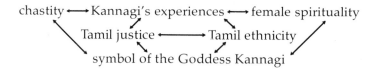

In the experiential domain of political and legal authority, Kannagi drew upon her spirituality, the source of which was chastity, declared the innocence of her husband, and caused the burning of a city. The justice she sought to materialize was an idealized conception of the Tamils. Her challenge to the erring Pandiya king—whether it was proper for him to remain a king when he had made the grievous mistake of ordering the death of an innocent man—was a repudiation of political authority that had lost its moral and legal base. Her personal quest for justice thus became identified with a Tamil quest.

Kannagi demonstrated by her life that the Tamils were ethnically one. Despite the existence of different religious orientations and occupational specializations, the vehicles of conceptualizing justice and ethnicity were the same everywhere among the Tamils. Kannagi was a Hindu belonging to the merchant community, but her companion and guide en route to Madurai was a Jain ascetic, and in Madurai she lived with a member of the herder community. Her experiences occurred in all three kingdoms, uniting them experientially into a single cultural whole, conveying the sense of common heritage and peoplehood.

The association of chastity and female spirituality occurs in modern Tamil society today as it did in the past, and the religious category of chastity remains an integral component part of the Tamil world view. Ideally, the stability and moral sanctity of the family household are enhanced through the presence of a chaste woman. She is the light of the household and performs the ritual of waving the fire in front of the deities of the household, invoking them for protection.[15]

It is the image of Kannagi, however, that enables the religious category of chastity to have ethnic and political referents and thus expands it into a larger semantic model for the Tamil people as a whole.

## The Dominant Symbol of Kannagi

Certain mythological and symbolic representations, such as Kannagi, the goddess of chastity, serve as dominant symbols that evoke deep sentiments in their believers. As these symbols have multiple referents and meanings, their use often blurs the distinctions between different conceptual domains. The dominant symbol of Kannagi incorporates several themes associated with different domains of cultural experience, such as politics and ethnicity, and serves to mediate between conceptions of identity and sociopolitical realities; it is also used in different sociopolitical contexts. Because the symbol incorporates several themes associated with the spirituality of Tamil womanhood and chastity, it evokes deep emotions in the believers.

A full understanding of the structure, meaning, and referents of a dominant symbol can be gained only by examining the symbol's historical evolution, along with its use in different social contexts. The component elements of the symbol may draw on one another's referential empirical reality, and the believers may selectively use the components relevant to their social or personal needs. However, the totality of the symbol's meaning is evident to the believers even when the entire symbol is not operationalized.[16]

Tamil cultural revivalism began during the nineteenth century with the publication of various ancient Tamil texts, including the "Epic of the Ankle Bracelet" (which was buried in private libraries for centuries). Although, as P. Spratt correctly notes, conflicts "between those who prefer Sanskrit and those who favour Tamil texts for certain religious purposes go back for centuries,"[17] the mass production of Tamil literature resulted in a wide recognition that there once existed a Tamil civilization that evolved independently of the northern Sanskritic civilization. The view also emerged that Sanskritic tradition and a Brahmanical priesthood, along with the social classification system called "caste," were alien to the Tamils.[18]

During the twentieth century, when educational and occupational changes altered the social consciousness of a number of non-Brahmans, a political conflict emerged between the upholders of the Sanskritic tradition (the Brahmans) and the non-Brahmans. By linking Brahmans with northern Hindi speakers, several non-Brahman leaders identified themselves as the protectors of Tamil culture, sought political autonomy for the Tamils, and in that process defied the federal government of India. A number of sociopolitical movements with an ideology defending Tamil culture and language emerged, such as the Dravidian Association and the Dravidian Advancement Association. These were identified as the Dravidian Movement, a form of Tamil cultural revivalism.[19]

The most fundamental principle involved in the symbol of Kannagi is that it enables believers to associate chastity with politics and ethnicity. Through Kannagi's life and experiences, the Tamil religious theme of relating chastity and female spirituality has become a meaningful concept for organizing political and ethnic experiences. The goddess represents female chastity and spirituality, but functions as a dominant symbol to orient the Tamils to their heritage of justice and to sustain linguistic and cultural purity.

Tamil cultural revivalists perceive a correspondence between the threat to Tamil language and the chastity of womanhood. It is significant that the Tamil term for rape means "the destroying of chastity."[20] A raped woman is devoid of any sacred power. The revivalist ideology indicates that Tamil culture and language were "violated" by the Brahmans and that it is necessary to redeem their chastity. The duty of the Tamils, according to this ideology, is to punish the violators, just as it is the duty of every male to punish the destroyers of female chastity.

To have a chaste language and culture is to share in the spirituality of chastity. For just as Kannagi sought justice and claimed ultimate victory, the Tamils as a whole can seek justice and be victorious in their conflict with Brahmans and Hindi speakers. Today in Tamil society resistance continues against (1) the use of the Hindi language (which is the national language of India), (2) the use of Sanskritic religious texts in temple ceremonies (with Brahman priests officiating), and (3) the worship of divinities identified as Aryan. In the 1960s, when Hindi was introduced among the Tamils as a language to be taught in schools and used in government work, self-immolations occurred in protest. Hindi was seen as corrupting Tamil culture and debasing Tamil womanhood.

During the past fifty years, revivalist leaders have been attempting to eliminate Sanskrit words and derivatives in the Tamil language. There has also been an attempt to eliminate from Tamil culture such Sanskritic elements as the custom of using Brahmans as officiating priests in temples and in the performance of rites of passage. A large number of publications sponsored by the revivalists extol the chastity of ancient and medieval princesses, poetesses, and other prominent women, and the authors write in a language they identify as "chaste Tamil."

Any reference to chastity has at once several meanings: it can be the chastity of one's own mother, wife, or sister, or that of Tamil womanhood, but it can also be the chastity of language and culture; defending the chastity of language and culture is tantamount to defending the chastity of one's own mother, wife, or sister, or that of Tamil womanhood in general. Implicit or explicit references to the qualities of Kannagi represent not only the spirituality of Tamil womanhood but also the qualities of Tamil language and culture. These representations are essentially explanations of why and how the women and the language and culture ought to be safeguarded.[21]

## Conclusion

Needless to say, the goddess Kannagi is not a symbol of identity in the sense that the Tamils consider themselves the descendents (spiritually or biologically) of Kannagi or regard themselves as followers of a sectarian movement with Kannagi as its prophetess. Instead, the symbol of Kannagi provides the Tamils with a meaningful theory of familial, ethnic, and political experiences, relating these different experiential domains to the concept of chastity. A Tamil speaker's awareness of his distinctive linguistic and cultural heritage is linked with his awareness of the symbol of Kannagi.

As there are a number of different caste and religious groups within Tamil society, much variation exists in their beliefs concerning Kannagi. This, however, does not mean that there are different legends about her. Whereas some worship her as a manifestation of the mother goddess and invoke her name in times of duress, others look upon her as a legendary character with no religious significance. To recognize the sacredness of women who are chaste is to celebrate the sanctity of one's linguistic and cultural heritage, which is chaste. In this sense the symbol of the goddess assures personal and cultural integrity. The violation of one's language and culture is a moral act similar to the destruction of female chastity. Just as one does not conceive of oneself as the offspring of an unchaste woman, one does not conceive of one's linguistic and cultural heritage as unchaste.

Language serves as an important boundary mechanism in India. Ethnicity, however, "is frequently related more to the symbol of a separate language than to its actual use by all members of a group."[22] It is possible to conclude that the presence of the symbol of Kannagi has to a considerable extent enabled the Tamils to remain culturally and linguistically distinct. Tamil is the least Sanskritized of the Dravidian languages. A historical continuity of themes that can be identified as Tamil spans more than two thousand years. During the early stages of the conflict between Brahmans and non-Brahmans, the unity of all the Dravidian-speaking groups, such as the Tamils, Kannadigas, Telugus, and Malayalees, was emphasized, and an attempt was made to form a Dravidian country composed of all Dravidian speakers. It is significant that the Tamils stood steadfast in their opposition to Hindi. It was only among the Tamils that an ethnically oriented political party became powerful, with the extensive support of the masses.

## Notes

1. This study is based on fourteen months of fieldwork and library research

conducted in Tamil Nadu, India, during 1970 and 1971. Investigation of the
historical continuity of Tamil themes was undertaken as part of a study
of Tamil revivalism. A section of the data presented here was gathered
through participant observation in a Tamil village and discussions with some
of the leaders of Tamil revivalism.

This is a modified version of a paper titled "Kannagi: An Emblematic
Goddess of Tamil Society," presented at the Seventy-fourth Annual Meeting
of the American Anthropological Association in 1975.

2. Ramanujan, "A Tamil Epic," p. 105.

3. The concept of "dominant symbol" is used fruitfully in Turner's analysis
of the relationship between ritual symbols and social dynamics ("Ndembu
Ritual," *The Ritual Process*, and "African Ritual"). The concept is used in this
paper to indicate that the symbol of Kannagi relates the cultural experiences
of different domains, incorporating several themes.

4. The function of chastity symbolism in the Tamil society of Sri Lanka is
not analyzed in this paper, because my concern is to show how the symbol of
the goddess is used in the context of cultural revivalism in Tamil society that
is geographically located within the national boundaries of India.

5. Scholars disagree about the period and authorship of the "Epic of the
Ankle Bracelet." Most place the epic in the first or second century A.D. and
consider Ilango Adigal to be the author, but Ramanujan holds that it was a
work of the fifth century A.D. ("A Tamil Epic," p. 104).

6. See Tyler, *India*, pp. 105–8.

7. Ibid., p. 100.

8. Dumont, "A Structural Definition," p. 191.

9. Hart, "Women and the Sacred," pp. 230–50.

10. Carstairs, *The Twice-Born*.

11. Tyler, *India*.

12. The "Epic of the Ankle Bracelet" has been interpreted as a poetic
expression of the workings of Karma, with the ankle bracelet as a symbol of
fate (see Ramanujan, "A Tamil Epic"). But such an interpretation fails to
show why the author of the epic used the religious category of chastity
to convey the historical experiences of the Tamils. The author of
the epic conceived of the bracelet as a symbol of chastity and not as a symbol
of fate: it was the custom of chaste women to wear ankle bracelets.

13. Jesudasan and Jesudasan point out that Ilango Adigal cultivated "the
cult of the worship of chaste women . . . as an independent cult of Tamilnad"
("Tamil Literature," p. 94).

14. Nayagam notes that Ilango Adigal "synthesized in this epic a description of the triple monarchy of the Tamils, their historical greatness, their
principal cities, the lives of the people of the five regions, and their
characteristic music and song and dance" (*Tamil Culture*, p. 86).

15. The customs that prevail in the Tamil household today are a continuation of what has existed for over two thousand years. Hart observes,
"Chastity was conceived of as a tangible quality in the woman who possessed

it, producing domestic peace and light" ("Women and the Sacred," p. 237).

16. The underlying theoretical assumption of this essay is that "culture operates as a system of shared symbols" (Geertz, *Interpretation of Cultures*) and that anthropological investigation entails a discussion of how "people create order" (Tyler, Introduction).

17. Spratt, *DMK in Power*, p. 10.

18. Twentieth-century scholars view Hindu civilization as a system that evolved in the context of the interaction between indigenous Dravidian cultures and alien Indo-Aryan cultures between 1000 and 500 B.C. The basic elements of the civilization are generally interpreted as having existed in the Dravidian cultures (Tyler, *India*). Thus, a Brahmanical priesthood is not alien. However, Sanskrit, which was spoken by the priesthood of Indo-Aryan cultures, became the dominant language of metaphysical discourses in the whole of northern India and in some parts of southern India; and with princely patronage, a distinctive orientation that is called the "Sanskritic tradition" evolved with the Brahmanical priesthood as its custodians. Such a tradition became established in Tamil culture also, and as Sanskritic scholars dominated the religious and literary tradition of the Tamils, the erroneous view that Tamil culture and language derived from a hypothetical Sanskritic civilization was projected (Spratt, *DMK in Power*, pp. 10–13).

19. The Dravidian Movement has been identified variously as an "anti-Brahman movement," "Tamil separatist movement," "anti-Hindi movement," and "Tamil revitalization movement." Most leaders of the movement genuinely believe that Tamil culture and language are facing destruction through the domination either of Brahmans or of northern Hindi speakers. (See Devanandan, *Resurgent Hinduism* and *The Dravida Kazhagam*; Hardgrave, *The Dravidian Movement*; Irschick, *Conflict in South Asia*; and Spratt, *DMK in Power*.)

20. Hart shows how the "vocabularies of Sanskrit and Tamil show different conceptions of the role of chastity." To the Indo-Aryans the word for rape meant "enjoying a woman by force" ("Women and the Sacred," pp. 243, 244).

21. The author discussed Tamil concepts with sixty-nine school students of both sexes between the ages of twelve and eighteen in a village school during 1970 and 1971. In such discussions the concept of chastity was mentioned by all, with a few relating it directly to the goddess Kannagi and the purity of Tamil culture.

22. De Vos, "Ethnic Pluralism," p. 15.

# Bibliography

Carstairs, G. Morris. *The Twice-Born: A Study of a Community of High Caste Hindus*. 1957. Bloomington: Indiana University Press, 1967.

Devanandan, Paul D. *The Dravida Kazhagam: A Revolt against Brahmanism*.

Bangalore: Christian Institute for the Study of Religion and Society, 1960.

———. *Resurgent Hinduism: Review of Modern Movements*. Bangalore: Christian Institute for the Study of Religion and Society, 1959.

De Vos, George. "Ethnic Pluralism: Conflict and Accommodation." In *Ethnic Identity: Cultural Continuity and Change*, edited by George De Vos and L. Romanucci-Ross, pp. 5–41. Palo Alto, Calif.: Mayfield Publishing Co., 1975.

Dumont, Louis. "A Structural Definition of a Folk Deity of Tamil Nad." In *Reader in Comparative Religion: An Anthropological Approach*, edited by William A. Lessa and Evon Z. Vogt, pp. 189–95. New York: Harper and Row, 1972.

Geertz, Clifford. *The Interpretation of Cultures*. New York: Basic Books, 1973.

Hardgrave, Robert L. *The Dravidian Movement*. Bombay: Popular Prakashan, 1965.

Hart, George L. "Women and the Sacred in Ancient Tamilnad." *Journal of Asian Studies* 32, no. 2 (1973): 233–50.

Irschick, Eugene F. *Politics and Social Conflict in South Asia: The Non-Brahmin Movement and Tamil Separation, 1916–1929*. Berkeley: University of California Press, 1969.

Jesudasan, C., and Jesudasan, H. "A History of Tamil Literature." In *Tamil Culture and Civilization*, edited by Xavier S. Thani Nayagam. Bombay: Asia Publishing House, 1970.

Nayagam, Xavier S. Thani, ed. *Tamil Culture and Civilization*. Bombay: Asia Publishing House, 1970.

Ramanujan, A. K. "A Tamil Epic: Cilappatikāram, 'The Lay of the Anklet.'" In *Lectures in Indian Civilization*, edited by Joseph W. Elder, pp. 104–6. Dubuque, Iowa: Kendall/Hunt Publishing Co., 1972.

Sastri, Nilakanta K. *Development of Religion in South India*. Bombay: Orient Longmans, 1963.

Spratt, P. *DMK in Power*. Bombay: Nachiketa Publications, 1970.

Turner, Victor. *The Ritual Process: Structure and Anti-Structure*. Chicago: Aldine Publishing House, 1969.

———. "Symbols in African Ritual." *Science* 179 (1973): 1100–1105.

———. "Symbols in Ndembu Ritual." In *Closed Systems and Open Minds*, edited by Max Gluckman, pp. 20–51. London: Manchester University Press, 1964.

Tyler, Stephen A. *India: An Anthropological Perspective*. Pacific Palisades, Calif.: Goodyear Publishing Co., 1973.

———. Introduction to *Cognitive Anthropology*, edited by Stephen Tyler, pp. 1–23. New York: Holt, Rinehart and Winston, 1969.

Willis, R. G. "The Head and the Lions: Lévi-Strauss and Beyond." In *Reader in Comparative Religion: An Anthropological Approach*, edited by William A. Lessa and Evon Z. Vogt, pp. 313–22. New York: Harper and Row, 1972.

# 9

## The Village Mother in Bengal
### by Ralph W. Nicholas

Mother herself is a person to be worshiped in Hindu Bengal. In this, however, she is no different from the father: the honor, respect, and devotion worshipfully offered to the father are the prototypes of what one's mother should receive. Mother and father together are said to be the givers of a person's birth, body, food, knowledge, deliverance from fear, and liberation. The joint responsibility of parents for their children is but one of the many ways of stating the complementarity of the sexes that is emphasized in Hindu cultures. In this cultural scheme, the mother, as a wife, is always dependent upon her husband and is second, after him, to receive the veneration of her children. A similar relationship of complementarity with subordination often seems to prevail among Hindu divinities. The male gods are commonly depicted with their wives seated properly at their left hands. In this manner the beneficent goddess Lakshmi often accompanies Narayana, the chaste and long-suffering Sita accompanies Rama, and the beautiful daughter of the mountain, Parvati, accompanies Shiva. However, to accept a view of the feminine half of the Hindu pantheon as simply a collection of "consorts" of the gods would be to miss something fundamental about Indian religion as well as to pass silently over a critical part of what Hindu cultures say about women.

There is a large body of Hindu myths relating the autonomous, often powerful actions of goddesses (*devī*). One of the most commonly used Sanskrit words for "power," Shakti (*śākti*), is also a name for a goddess, designating either an individual or a class of power-wielding feminine divinities. The most ancient Indian myths contain references to goddesses, but they seem to be of lesser importance than the gods and are not separately worshiped. It is not in ancient texts, the Vedas,

Brahmanas, Upanishadas, or Epics, that we find the myths of powerful, independent goddesses, but rather in the Puranas and later literature, beginning about the sixth century A.D. From that time onward
there is a continuous tradition, extending throughout India and up to
the present, of the worship of goddesses, including the discovery of
new ones and the composition of new myths about them. Such goddesses are often named after their fathers or husbands by changing the gender of the name from masculine to feminine. However,
even in early Puranas goddesses are sometimes identified as Ambika
("mother" or "good woman"), as well as Chandi ("angry") or Durga
("fortress" or "formidable"), for whom there are no equivalent male
deities. Overtly maternal images—succor, nurturance, intercession,
deliverance—are by no means always at the forefront in myths and
rituals addressed to Indian goddesses. Underlying all such deities,
there is the widely held Hindu concept that the male (*puruṣa*) is by
himself incomplete and inert, and must be conjoined with an active,
feminine "nature" (*prakṛti*) in order to act in the world. Like Shakti or
"power," the term Prakṛti (which is often used to mean all that is
signified by "nature" in English) may be used to designate a goddess
or class of goddesses. The complementary interaction of masculine
and feminine in Hindu thought is well summarized in the expression,
"Shiva without Shakti is a corpse" (*śiva śaktihīna śava*).

The cultures of the Christian West, with their single transcendent masculine divinity, whom "no man hath seen . . . at any time"
(John 1:18), finds its antithesis in the exuberant polytheistic iconolatry
of Hinduism. Judaism, Christianity, and Islam have all done battle
against religious systems with large pantheons, female deities, demi-
gods, and demons. Some angels, the Blessed Virgin, a panoply of
saints, and Satan and his hosts remain as minor pockets of polytheism in the Semitic religions. Islam claimed a share of India, mainly
through the preaching of an inward religion and a pantheistic god.
But the largest part of the South Asian population has continued over
millennia to work out religious meanings through a set of understandings embodied in a very large, complexly interconnected array
of myths, deities, and modes of worship. Additions are often made to
the set, but deletions are rare. To call these understandings "Hinduism" is mainly a convenience to outsiders; and indigenous Indian religion contains numerous "isms" of its own, although these tendencies
lack the exclusivity of Western sectarianism.

For centuries, Western scholars (as well as those persons for whom
some aspect of Hinduism seems to offer religious meaning missing

from our own tradition) have sought to make sense of Indian religion. The contribution of anthropologists to this effort consists mainly in trying to make intelligible the Indian religion of ordinary life, describing and explaining the deities, rituals, and myths of people in the villages, towns, and regions accessible to personal investigation. We have been able to demonstrate that various linguistic groups and castes often show proclivities for one or another group of deities, a particular set of myths, and specific patterns of worship. However, it would be too optimistic to think that a breakdown of India by language and caste will provide *the key* to Hindu diversity. The line of analysis I pursue here might suggest such a pattern in regional religious orientations. But permutations of what I have seen in Bengal are found in the other linguistic areas of India and among other castes, involving somewhat varying groups of deities, myths, and manners of worship.

Bengal is the region around the mouths of the Ganges; its core is the 50,000-square-mile delta formed by the Ganges and Brahmaputra. The predominant language of the region is Bengali, the easternmost of the Indo-European languages. The larger part of the area is included in Bangladesh, where about 90 percent of the population is Muslim. (Why Bengalis should turn from Hinduism to Islam is a fascinating problem in cultural history that I cannot discuss here.) The remainder of the region constitutes the Indian state of West Bengal, in which Hindus predominate. Bengali Hindus are characterized throughout the South Asian subcontinent by several distinguishing features: in religion, it is their peculiar attachment to mother goddesses (despite the fact that a detailed examination of religious preferences in West Bengal would probably show the male god Krishna to be the popular favorite). Calcutta, the capital of the state and the metropolis of eastern India, is a pilgrimage place of the goddess Kali.

The eastern part of Midnapur District, in West Bengal, is a part of the lower Ganges delta. In this area there is a cluster of eight villages, known collectively as Kelomal, which were inhabited by about 3,700 people of 21 different castes in 1968–69.[1] These villages are all of comparatively recent origin, having been settled during the last two hundred years. Previously, the area was too low-lying and deeply flooded during the monsoon season to permit continuous habitation. The affairs of landed estates and of several small kingdoms in the locality brought a nucleus of high castes, Kayasthas (traditionally scribes) and Brahmans (traditionally priests and teachers), into the center of this village cluster. However, the majority of the inhabitants belong to the somewhat anomalous caste that is now called Mahishya (Māhiṣya).[2]

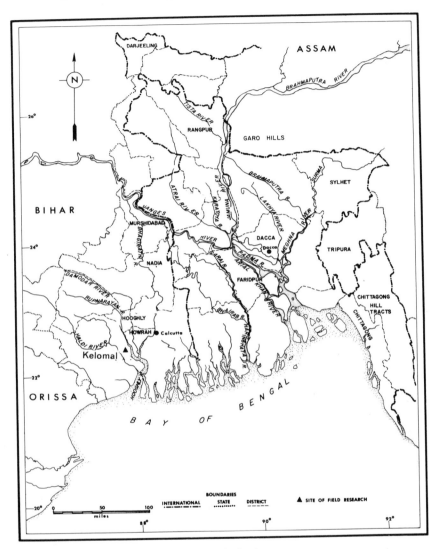

23. Bengal, West Bengal, and Bangladesh.

This caste is a minority of the population at the center of Kelomal, but it preponderates increasingly with distance from the high caste houses and constitutes the whole of the population of the most pe- ripheral village. I refer to the Mahishyas as "somewhat anomalous" because, although they appear close to the ideal type of a yeoman

peasantry, preferring to pursue the respectable occupation of agriculture, they are not counted among the nine "true Shudra" castes of
Hindu Bengal. Excluded from this group, they do not receive the
services of high-ranking Brahmans. Their ceremonies are performed
by a separate Brahman caste generally known as Brahmans Created
by the Pronouncement of the Sage Vyasa (Vyāsokta). They prefer to
designate themselves as the Original Vedic Brahmans of Gaura (i.e.,
Bengal) (Gaurādya Vaidika Brāhmaṇa). This emphasis on autochthonous origins is probably appropriate for the priests of the Mahishyas,
who appear to be descended from the earliest inhabitants of the
lower Ganges delta. (The higher-ranking Brahmans, in contrast, are
believed to have immigrated from north India.) The issue of who
is indigenous and who is immigrant, if the history were known,
would turn into a question of "more" and "less" indigenous, of earlier or later immigration. But in the historical and cultural perception
of people in Kelomal, the Mahishyas appear as the autochthons—
often referred to by themselves and by high people as simply "the
Bengalis."

Until the recent abolition of zamindari tenure,[3] the land was under
the control of the high castes and it was Kayastha zamindars who
exercised the predominant social and political authority over the locality. Yet at the same time the villages, as unified social entities, were
regarded as belonging to the Mahishyas. Though landed control over
the area by Kayasthas has recently changed, the old system has not
been totally erased. Kayasthas still appear as the petty chiefs of Kelomal and symbolically enact their kingly roles in certain ways. However, the man who is "master" (*kartā*), or "supervisor" (*āmin*) of each
village is a Mahishya. Corresponding to this cultural distinction between the petty "kingdom" (*zamindāri, parganā, rājya*) and the "country" (*deśa*) or "village" (*grāma*) is a distinction between two goddesses,
each of whom is addressed and venerated as a "mother" by Bengali
Hindus.

Durga the formidable, slayer of the Buffalo Demon (Mahiṣāsura),
identified with Parvati, daughter of Himalaya and wife of Shiva, is
foremost among the divine mothers of the Kayasthas. Her worship is
held with great pomp and splendor each autumn in permanent pavil-
ions (*maṇḍapa*) maintained in the houses of the principal Kayastha
and high-ranking Brahman families of Kelomal. I cannot say much
about Durga here; her personality, worship, and mythology are very
complex. However, a few of her characteristics are important in understanding what follows. The central image of the goddess is made
afresh each year; she does not dwell permanently in the houses where

24. The goddess Durga receiving worship from a Brahman priest in the house of a high caste family. With Durga are her daughters, Lakshmi (*left*), goddess of prosperity, and Sarasvati (*right*), goddess of learning. The face of the Buffalo Demon, who is about to die, is visible behind the back of the priest.
(*Photograph by Ralph W. Nicholas*)

she is worshiped but, rather, visits annually as a daughter coming from her husband's house, bringing her four children with her. She is invariably represented as of benign countenance, with a golden complexion that symbolizes the red principle of action (*rajaḥ guṇa*) shining faintly through the pure white of the principle of truth (*sattva guṇa*).

At the same time, she is always shown trampling the corpse of the dying Buffalo Demon as she spears him with one of the weapons she carries in her ten hands. She is always very beautiful, with long almond eyes and a triangular face, full, high breasts, a slender, graceful waist, and appealingly rounded hips. In short, she is as sexually desirable to a man as only a greatly idealized woman could be—and, as his mother, she is sexually forbidden. Thus, the figure of Durga embodies elements of strong ambivalence. The goddess, perceived as taking several different forms, is offered many animal sacrifices during the three central days of her worship. Blood sacrifice is an emotionally charged act for Bengalis; many meanings are represented in each sacrifice, some of them unconscious. The overt, culturally coded meanings of the sacrifices are contained in a Sanskrit myth known as "Chandi" (*Caṇḍī*) or "The Exaltation of the Goddess" (*Devī Māhāt-mya*), a portion of the *Markandeya Purana*. This myth provides in verbal form the overall structure of the ritual of Durga worship; in it the goddess repeatedly engages and destroys the leading demons (*asuras*) who have conquered heaven from the gods (*devas*). She is drawn into battle each time by the posturing and megalomanic boasting of demons who alternately wish to possess her, as the goddess of unmatched beauty, and to destroy her, as the sole threat to their control of heaven. Each animal sacrifice during the ritual symbolizes her destruction of a demon army or champion.[4]

Shitala (Śītalā), "The Cool One," as she is catachrestically named, goddess of diseases and especially of smallpox, is the preeminent mother goddess of the Mahishyas. Whereas Durga is worshiped in the autumn, Shitala is worshiped in the spring; whereas Durga is worshiped separately in each high caste house, Shitala is worshiped collectively by the village or "country." Durga is always anthropomorphic and clearly benign; Shitala is often a crude stone of dubious mien. Durga is married to Shiva and has four divine children; Shitala may be represented as a married woman, but her husband is unknown and she is childless. The splendor of Shitala's worship is strictly limited by the ability of the usually poor agricultural and laboring families to contribute in cash or kind. Moreover, cooperation is often difficult to gain where factionalism is rife and no one's motives are above suspicion. It is the goddess herself and the urgent necessity of worshiping her during the proper season that bring divided villagers together and restore lost unity. The Bengali word for spring, *basanta*, is also the most commonly used term for smallpox. Thus, behind the obligatory timing of her worship is a threat of punishment as well as the promise of common well-being.

25. Men of a Kayastha clan sacrifice a goat to Durga. They shout *jay ma!* (Victory Mother!) as the immolator, a man of the Blacksmith caste, severs the goat's neck with a single stroke from a sacrificial blade. A second blade is visible at the lower right.
*(Photograph by Ralph W. Nicholas)*

There is a formulaic description of Shitala in Sanskrit, but most of her mythology is in the Bengali language.[5] She is described in her myths as, in true form, a very beautiful maiden, but she spends most of her time in the guise of a haggard, witchlike Brahman widow. Her principal courtier is the horrendous, triple-headed Fever Demon (Jvarāsura), who goes about disguised as a young servant. She is also accompanied by a somewhat shadowy serving woman named Possessor of the Blood (Raktāvatī). Whenever Shitala is worshiped collectively by a village, the Cholera Goddess, Olabibi (who is a Muslim), is also worshiped.[6]

In broad outline, the myth of Shitala that is performed in the Kelomal villages consists of six segments or "dramas" (*pālā*).[7] In the first, she is born as a beautiful maiden from the cooled ashes of a sacrificial fire; the god Brahma names her "The Cool One" from the circumstances of her birth. Shiva gives her the Fever Demon as a servant, and she sets off to the kingdom of the god Indra to receive her first worship. She enters the royal court disguised as an ancient crone and is arrogantly treated, first by Indra, then by many other gods. Humiliated and in a great rage, Shitala orders the Fever Demon to take possession of their bodies; after the fever, smallpox erupts on their bodies. Shiva reveals to the afflicted gods that "this illness is caused by the wrath of Shitala." They then understand the true nature of the goddess and worship her with devotion; at once the pain and pustules disappear. Then Shitala proceeds to obtain worship from mortals.

In the second segment, Shitala appears to the king of Virata in a terrifying dream, and offers him all that life can give, as well as final release, if he worships her. She threatens him with the annihilation of his kingdom if he does not. The king, a devotee of Shiva, refuses to worship her. Infuriated, she assembles a vast army of diseases, including a separate detachment of poxes. The poxes are disguised as so many varieties of vegetable pulses. The Fever Demon places sacks of these appealing delicacies on the backs of bullocks. With the goddess on her mount, the ass, they hasten down the road to Virata.

The third drama concerns her encounter with a greedy toll collector who helps himself to the pox pulses, which he feeds to his seven sons. They, in turn, share them with the other boys of the village. When all the toll collector's sons have died horribly of smallpox, he and his wife prepare to bury themselves with the sons' bodies on the cremation ground. Shitala reveals herself to them at the last moment and says that she will revive the sons if the toll collector will worship her, which he gladly does. In order to avoid giving away her game, the goddess turns the boys' bodies into stone to wait for revivification until she has conquered Virata.

In the fourth and dramatically central segment of the narrative, she moves swiftly to punish the kingdom, selling pox pulses to the king and to his subjects in all of his markets. The kingdom is devastated. When the king's sons die, the king and and queen prepare to follow the course of the toll collector and his wife. But Shitala again appears and revives the dead sons. The royal preceptor praises the goddess

26. The goddess Shitala (*center*) receiving offerings during her annual worship in a village temple. At her left is Manasā, goddess of snakes, with the hood of a snake emerging from behind each shoulder. Seated on a lower level are two older images of these goddesses; Manasā wears a silver repoussé crown. Between them are the pot icons of the deities, established especially for their worship. One Brahman reads the verses of offering from a manual to insure against errors in their recitation by the second Brahman, who is making the offerings. *(Photograph by Ralph W. Nicholas)*

with an elaborate hymn, and she then restores life to the king's subjects. Thereafter, Shitala is worshiped throughout Virata.

In the fifth episode of the myth, a young, devoted merchant has a number of adventures while traveling to the southern Kingdom of Pakisa to bring back the golden pot originally used in the worship of Shitala. When the merchant returns to Virata, the king uses this pot in worship of Shitala.

A final, brief drama describes the obtaining of Shitala's worship in Gokul, the childhood habitation of Krishna.

The entire myth is referred to as the "Vigil Drama" (*Jāgaraṇa Pālā*). Singers take various parts in the several episodes, and the myth is performed as a cantata. (Once I saw a full operatic form with costumes and sets.) The drama continues through the night in front of the image of the goddess. The villagers obtain Shitala's blessing by remaining awake and attentive to the entire myth and its message about this mother who oscillates so often between rage and mercy, punishment and compassion.

Although practically the same version of the myth concerning Shitala's activities in the world of mortals is performed in conjunction with her worship in each village, she does not appear in any two villages in quite the same form. In five of the eight villages there are permanent images of Shitala; these receive regular daily worship as well as the special annual collective worship in the spring. Each of these five goddesses is most often referred to by villagers in an ambiguous expression (*grāmer mā*) that may mean either "mother of the village" or "mother belonging to the village." The three villages that presently lack such mothers nevertheless offer annual worship to Shitala. The following brief summary sketches the diversity of the forms and treatment of the goddess among closely linked villages.

In one village, Shitala has the form of an old, rather crude stone image, heavily coated with vermilion, that shares a temple with a ferocious form of Shiva and with the Bengali Snake Goddess (Manasā), both of whom receive worship and animal sacrifices when Shitala is worshiped. In the next village there are two images of the goddess, one a purchased modern brass figurine, and the other a stone roughly resembling a face and believed to have revealed herself in a village pond to a Vyasokta Brahman woman three generations ago. The two icons are worshiped as one and fed a cooked food offering including fresh fish curry. In a third village, which is on the southern boundary of the previous two, there are two figurines of Shitala (and two of the Snake Goddess) in a village temple. The older pottery image sits beneath a newer brass one installed by an upwardly mobile family as a means of establishing a new family name. This goddess eats a vegetarian diet.

In a fourth village the goddess has her own temple, in which pots representing the Fever Demon and the Bengali Tiger God (Daksina Raya) flank her brass image. She is said to accept animal sacrifices from individuals periodically during the year, but she receives only a fish in her annual collective worship. In the next village, the icon of the goddess is a pot that previously shared a temple belonging to the Snake Goddess. The temple is in disrepair and the Mahishya village headman has taken the deities' pots into his own household shrine, where they are worshiped daily by a Vyasokta Brahman who lives elsewhere. The annual village worship of Shitala is done at the Brahman's household temple. The northernmost Kelomal village has an image of the goddess, but no temple; so the goddess dwells in the temple of the Vyasokta Brahman who worships her. Families from this village send individual offerings to their goddess and there is no collective worship. The smallest of the villages has neither a temple nor a permanent image of Shitala, yet she is worshiped annually in a major collective ceremony. She and her attendants are established in the form of pots on the verandah of the Mahishya village headman's house.

The eighth village also has no permanent Shitala shrine but once came near to having one. The village headman there is not forceful and effective, and it is difficult to get villagers organized for a collective ceremony without strong leadership. Despite this problem, the annual worship of the goddess is done intermittently by the villagers. However, she receives worship every year in one household. An elderly Brahman of the Orissan order is head of a large, prosperous family in the village. He is a deed writer and is knowledgeable about land laws; he is also punctilious in ritual matters and contemptuous of the religious understandings of other villagers. It occurred to him some years ago that he might form a social benefice by establishing a Shitala temple for the village. He planned to donate a large part of his agricultural holdings to support the worship of the goddess, thereby obtaining a remission of taxes on the land. By declaring himself servant (sevāit) of the temple, he would receive considerable financial benefit in addition to religious merit. As he was preparing to do this, the goddess appeared to him in a dream and told him, in effect, that she did not approve of his motivation. Although he felt thenceforth unable to establish Shitala in the village, he thought it perilous to ignore the goddess. Therefore, he established her annual worship in his own house. He is basically inclined toward Vaishnavism and does not offer her animal sacrifices. However, the goddess is fed a fish curry—made not from the inferior variety of fish offered by Mahishyas, but from a large, expensive carp.

What can be concluded from this cursory review of the village mothers of Kelomal? First, it seems obvious that accidents of history and the motives of particular individuals in specific times, places, and circumstances have played a part in establishing the various goddesses. Second, villages have probably made some effort to create collective representations, emulating other villages while at the same time distinguishing themselves from them. Insofar as the villages have succeeded in establishing and maintaining village mothers, these are clearly differentiated from one another, even though they are all identified with Shitala. Third, there are important differences between the center and the periphery of the village cluster. The personality of the goddess is most strongly marked in the villages with high caste populations, where Shitala worship is close to the Durga worship of the Kayasthas; and the elaboration of Shitala worship is greater in the central villages than in the peripheral ones. These relatively trivial generalizations aside, the fact remains that it is always a mother goddess who identifies the ordinary cultivators of each village as a unity, but why a mother rather than any other possible kind of representation?

It is not possible to achieve a full and convincing cultural explanation of this phenomenon without examining much more of the religious understanding of the Mahishyas of Kelomal. I have not said anything about Shiva, the preeminent father and male fertilizer in the local pantheon. (There are Shiva temples in several of these villages.) Nor have I said anything about the other very significant goddesses —particularly Kali, Lakshmi, and Sarasvati—who are worshiped as mothers by most villagers, but who are not said to be the mothers of villages. The largest omission in this discussion has been the Vaishnava pantheon, centered on Krishna, Narayana, and Vishnu. Most of the Kelomal villagers—virtually all of the Mahishyas and many of the higher and lower castes—devote most of their regular religious attention to these deities. The number of people who profess to be preeminently goddess worshipers (*śākta*) is very small. At a sociological level, most of these villages are unified by a system in which, once each month, it is the turn of a different household to make a food offering to the village Vishnu temple. Enough food must be provided so that everyone in the village can share in the auspicious leftover food of the god (*prasāda*), and a quantity of it is carried to every house.

It may appear that I have biased the whole issue by focusing on a small part of a total system, thereby distorting the larger pattern. But this is not the way Bengalis think about the matter, for when a particular deity is being worshiped, all of the others recede into the background; they are not ignored or forgotten, but the deity before one at a particular time and place becomes the most high. When Shitala is being worshiped, there is no doubt that she is the foremost divinity.

The most fundamental mother of all, in the Bengali scheme of things, is the earth (*prthivi*) or the land (*bhūmi*), which is thought of as giving birth to all the most important things in the mortal world, including food and people. The earth is a very productive symbol of maternity. She is believed to menstruate for three days in the spring (*ambuvācī*), during which time men are forbidden to use their plows or to dig in the earth. Following this flow, the rains begin and men should dig and plow and plant their seeds, which the goddess then rears in the womb of her fields (*kṣetra*), providing the food that nourishes men's bodies. Like many symbols in Bengali culture, the earth may be seen as progressively encompassing or as divisible yet whole. Thus, one may worship a particular image of a deity in one place and satisfy that deity wholly even while others are doing the same thing elsewhere with equivalent effect. So, too, the earth of a particular village may be regarded as whole and complete in itself, or as a part of the encompassing earth of Bengal, or even all of India. Persons born of the same mother are considered to be closely related because they shared her womb. Similarly, persons born of the same village are considered to be closely related because they share the earth of that village. Thus, the unity and common concern with one another's well-being that fellow villagers should have is expressed in the maternal symbol of the earth of their village.[8] This is a very important part of the cultural explanation of the cult of the village mothers in Bengal, but is not the whole of it.

The goddess Shitala, even though her image is often regarded as consubstantial with the earth of a particular village, does not symbolize the birth-giving aspect of motherhood; other deities are worshiped for barrenness or successful delivery. Nor does she symbolize authority and protection, as does Durga, seen as vanquisher of the demons who wrested control of heaven from the gods. On the contrary, Shitala's mythology depicts her as invariably accompanied by the grotesque Fever Demon, whom she treats with the greatest affection, as if he were her own son. She punishes virtuous kings who are worshipers of Shiva or Vishnu and destroys peaceable kingdoms whose only fault is ignorance of her worship. She tempts fallible persons, and especially mischievous children, with irresistible delicacies, which then break out on their bodies as horrifying and fatal poxes. In the end, people are able to recognize the great goddess behind these terrifying manifestations. When they worship her, she sets the kingdom right again and restores the dead to life. The myth and ritual of Shitala make it possible for people to recognize the "grace of the Mother" (*māyer dayā*) even in their own suffering. Less explicitly, Shitala reminds Bengalis that the mother who gave them birth is also a punisher, sometimes with sudden and inexplicable rage. Petulant behavior, met on one day with indulgence, might evoke a beating and a screaming fit on the next.

Infectious disease may be an apt symbol of maternal punishment: it often seems to strike arbitrarily, laying low the righteous, ignoring sinners, and breaking out in epidemic rampages. However, it seems likely that there is also a specific historical connection between the founding of these villages, about two centuries ago, and outbreaks of contagious diseases, among which a severe form of smallpox may have been most fatal.[9] This unprecedented experience of devastating epidemics seems to have been a focus for religious creativity as well as practical action. Whereas the other Bengali mother goddesses, such as the Snake Goddess and Chandi (a much more complex and generalized mother), are well established in myths written down before the seventeenth century, the first known manuscript of a Shitala myth was not written until about A.D. 1690. Then there was a hiatus until about 1750 when suddenly half a dozen versions were composed within a few years. The rapid growth of interest in Shitala, evidenced by this large number of texts of her myth written in the mid-eighteenth century, was probably motivated by epidemics that swept lower deltaic western Bengal during these years. The longest, most detailed, of these texts, summarized earlier in this article, was written in a village only a few miles from Kelomal, and the others were all composed in the lower part of West Bengal. It would be a mistake, however, to think of Shitala as a localized Little Traditional goddess. She is known throughout Indo-Aryan-speaking India under the same name; and village tutelaries under various names, all associated with contagious and epidemic diseases, appear also throughout Dravidian India.[10]

Some verses from the "Salutation of Shitala" illustrate the complex and condensed character of this maternal figure. After saluting her divinity and her resplendent beauty, the poet says:

Whomsoever you look at, Mother, from the corner of your right eye, attains paradise merely at that hint. Whoever you look at with your left eye loses existence, and no one remains to light the lamp of his lineage.

With you, your handmaiden Possessor of the Blood; you travel on your special vehicle, the ass, with the Fever Demon and all the poxes in attendance.

. . . . . . . . . . . . . . . . . . . . . . . . . . . . . . . . . . . . . . . . . . . . . . . . . . . . . . . . . .

Oh, Mother of the Universe, Bestower of Life, Controller of Diseases, Daughter of the Ordainer [Brahmā], remove all obstacles and destroy all enemies.[11]

Even when she is perceived as Controller of Diseases, she remains capable of deliverance as well as destruction. She is the Supreme Mother of the Universe and Bestower of Life even while she is engaged in teaching humans of her grace by giving them horrible diseases. According to the tenets of Bengali culture, punishment is also a form of parental love.

# Notes

1. Fieldwork in Kelomal was made possible by a Fulbright-Hays Senior Research Fellowship. A grant from the Office of International Programs at Michigan State University enabled me to return to Kelomal in 1970 for the special autumnal ceremonies of Durga, Chandi, Lakshmi, and Kali. I am grateful to Raymond Fogelson and Ronald Inden for a critical reading of this manuscript, and to fellow panelists and discussants at the session of the 1975 American Anthropological Association meeting that dealt with mother worship for contributions to its final form.

2. In the nineteenth century this caste was most often designated Kaibartta; it included both cultivators and fishermen. Around the turn of the century the cultivators ceased giving daughters in marriage to fishermen and began referring to themselves as Mahishya, a name indicative of Shudra origins superior to those of the Kaibarttas. There are now two distinct castes, and the fishermen call themselves Rajbangshi, "Of Royal Clan."

3. Although it has its roots in the Mughal period, the zamindari (zamin-dār = "land-holder") system is a product of British revenue administration. To simplify somewhat, a zamindar was responsible for the collection of taxes from a group of villages and for the annual payment of a fixed sum to the government. Such persons were usually high caste Hindus and filled a "royal" role in local society.

4. Pargiter made a complete English translation of the Mārkaṇḍeya Purāṇa. There are several translations of the "Caṇḍī" portion of this Purana; the copiously annotated one by Agrawala (Devī Māhātmyam), which includes the full Sanskrit text, is useful. Although the myth is read aloud as part of the

worship of the goddess, the procedures of worship are contained in manuals (*paddhati*) derived from three other Puranas, the *Devī*, *Kālikā*, and *Vṛhan-nandīkeśvara*. It is also customary in certain households to include a reading of a sixteenth-century Bengali myth of the goddess, the *Kavikankana-Caṇḍī* composed by Mukundarāma.

5. A discussion of Shitala mythology and translations of two versions of her myth are available in Nicholas and Sarkar, "The Fever Demon." See also Bang, "The Smallpox Goddess."

6. I have presented a brief discussion of Olābibi and her mythology in "Śītalā and the Art of Printing."

7. This is an eighteenth-century text composed by Nityānanda Cakravartī, who lived only a few miles from Kelomal. His version, much more detailed than any of the others, was printed in Calcutta in 1878 and is still in print (*Bṛhat Śītalā Maṅgal*).

8. This is a brief summary of a complex symbol. For a fuller discussion see Inden and Nicholas, *Kinship in Bengali Culture*.

9. Although I have not yet been able to document this contention fully, Sarkar and I have shown that the printing of Shitala's myth first took place during a great malaria epidemic in the nineteenth century ("The Fever Demon").

10. For north India see Freed and Freed, "Two Mother Goddess Cere-monies"; for Nepal see Nepali, *The Newars*; for central India see Babb, *The Divine Hierarchy*; for Rajasthan see Carstairs, "Patterns of Religious Obser-vance"; for Punjab see Singh, "Religion in Daleke"; for Malwa see Mathur, "The Meaning of Hinduism"; for Gujarat see Naik, "Religion of the Anāvils"; for Nagpur District, Maharashtra, see Junghare, "Songs of Shitala." For a village in Poona District, however, Orenstein discusses the worship of a smallpox goddess called "Marai" (*Gaon*, p. 199). This name is similar to that of Mariamma, the most common name of the smallpox goddess in Tamil country, according to Whitehead, *Village Gods of South India*, pp. 31, 32. He found a Śītalamma in Telugu country, but she was identified there as a water goddess (p. 23).

11. Translated from Cakravartī, *Śītalā Maṅgal*, pp. 13, 14.

# Bibliography

Agrawala, Vasudeva S., trans. *Devī-Māhātmyam: The Glorification of the Great Goddess*. Varanasi: All-India Kashiraj Trust, 1963.

Babb, Lawrence A. *The Divine Hierarchy: Popular Hinduism in Central India*. New York: Columbia University Press, 1975.

Bang, B. G. "Current Concepts of the Smallpox Goddess Sitala in Parts of West Bengal." *Man in India* 53 (1973): 79–104.

Cakravartī, Nityānanda. *Bṛhat Śītala Maṅgal bā Śītalār Jāgaraṇ Pālā* [The great narrative of Shitala or Shitala's vigil drama]. Calcutta: Tarachand Das and Sons, 1968.

Carstairs, G. M. "Patterns of Religious Observance in Three Villages of Rajasthan." In *Aspects of Religion in Indian Society*, edited by L. P. Vidyarthi, pp. 59–113. Meerut: Kedar Nath Ram Nath, 1961.

Freed, Ruth S., and Freed, Stanley A. "Two Mother Goddess Ceremonies of Delhi State in the Great and Little Traditions." *Southwestern Journal of Anthropology* 18 (1962): 246–77.

Inden, Ronald B., and Nicholas, Ralph W. *Kinship in Bengali Culture*. Chicago: University of Chicago Press, 1977.

Junghare, Indira Y. "Songs of the Goddess Shitala: Religio-Cultural and Linguistic Features." *Man in India* 55 (1975): 298–316.

Mathur, K. S. "The Meaning of Hinduism in a Malwa Village." In *Aspects of Religion in Indian Society*, edited by L. P. Vidyarthi, pp. 114–28. Meerut: Kedar Nath Ram Nath, 1961.

Naik, T. B. "Religion of the Anāvils of Surat." In *Traditional India: Structure and Change*, edited by Milton Singer, pp. 183–90. Philadelphia: American Folklore Society, 1959.

Nepali, G. S. *The Newars*. Bombay: United Asia Publications, 1965.

Nicholas, Ralph W. "Śītalā and the Art of Printing." In *Mass Culture, Language and Arts in India*, edited by Mahadeo Apte. Bombay: Popular Prakashan, 1978.

———, and Sarkar, Aditi Nath. "The Fever Demon and the Census Commissioner: Śītalā Mythology in Eighteenth and Nineteenth Century Bengal." In *Bengal: Studies in Literature, Society and History*, edited by Marvin Davis, pp. 3–33. Asian Studies Center Occasional Papers, South Asia Series No. 27. East Lansing: Michigan State University, 1976.

Orenstein, Henry. *Gaon: Conflict and Cohesion in an Indian Village*. Princeton, N.J.: Princeton University Press, 1965.

Pargiter, F. Eden, trans. *Mārkaṇḍeya Purāṇa*. Calcutta: The Asiatic Society, 1904.

Singh, Indera Pal. "Religion in Daleke: A Sikh Village." In *Aspects of Religion in Indian Society*, edited by L. P. Vidyarthi, pp. 191–219. Meerut: Kedar Nath Ram Nath, 1961.

Whitehead, Henry. *The Village Gods of South India*. Calcutta: Association Press, 1921.

# 10

## The Goddess Chandi
## as an Agent of Change
### by James J. Preston

The role of the goddess in eastern India was once to serve as a tutelary deity supporting the local rajas. In recent years the fall of the nobility has produced significant changes in the style of worship, particularly in urban centers where the goddess is largely patronized by the rising middle classes. This study is concerned with functional transformations of the mother goddess, a key symbol of modern Hinduism. The flexibility of Indian mother worship as a vehicle for modernization is illustrated through an analysis of religious and social change in a growing temple in Orissa's largest city.[1]

## Religious Change in India

Modernization in India does not necessarily depend on the development of completely new institutions. Religious changes have taken place for thousands of years within the context of ancient Indian traditions.[2] Although it must be admitted that temples and village-wide festivals have tended to reinforce conservative themes in Indian society, these same institutions have also acted as media for the emergence of important social and religious changes. Hinduism is not an unchanging system of traditionalism; nor should conservative elements obscure more liberal trends.[3]

At certain crucial points in Indian history new sects have emerged to cope with pressures toward social reform. Sectarian Hinduism often revolved around a central holy person who reinterpreted religious traditions.[4] In the sixth century B.C., Buddhism, Jainism, and other smaller sects developed with the rise of the merchant classes.[5]

Again, in the medieval period, the powerful Bhakti cults arose, incorporating large numbers of lower castes and poor people in an India-wide movement that stressed the love of God, rather than ritualism, and employed regional languages instead of Sanskrit as a religious medium.[6]

In the nineteenth and early twentieth centuries several important religious reformers sought to reinterpret Hinduism. These individuals looked for ways to integrate scriptural Hinduism with the new political and nationalistic consciousness that was developing, especially among the middle classes. Ram Mohan Roy, Aurobindo, Vivekenanda, Tagore, Gandhi, and others tried to bridge the gap between social inequities and conservative life-styles reinforced by the Great Tradition.

It seems that whenever there has been sufficient dissonance between social and religious traditions in India, reformers have managed to reincorporate splintered segments back into the mainstream. This process of reinterpretation does not necessarily involve an individual reformer. Owing to the wide variety of symbolic media it is possible for people to choose one cluster of rituals in place of another without creating new traditions.

The process of religious change has not ceased in modern India. New cults, along with more subtle shifts from one ritual emphasis to another, continue to evolve.[7] There also have been, and continue to be, religious and political groups that could be classified as revitalization movements, seeking a return to some sort of social and ritual purity that once existed in the past.[8]

Religious change in modern India does not occur in isolated social institutions alone. It is multifaceted, complex, and wide-ranging. M. N. Srinivas illustrates this point eloquently when he observes:

> The significant changes occurring in the triad of institutions—caste, family system, and village community—have resulted in Hinduism becoming, to some extent, "free floating." But this again is only a part of the story. New agencies have emerged to provide a structure for reinterpreted Hinduism. These agencies are still somewhat fluid and emergent. They are, on the one hand, such new institutions as the Ramakrishna Mission and Arya Samaj and, on the other, old sects and monasteries which are trying to adjust themselves to the new circumstances, and in that process are undergoing change.[9]

In the last hundred years there has been an active relationship between state governments and temples as the Hindu Religious Endowment Commissions have expanded their jurisdictions.[10] These state government agencies have been granted legal powers to regulate and oversee the management of larger temples and monastic institutions in many parts of India. Despite the fact that India has a constitutionally defined secular government, several states are radically altering the administrations of religious institutions.[11]

Reviewing the several microstudies completed to date, it appears that there are at least three perspectives on change in religious institutions. Temples are perceived by social scientists as (1) collapsing, (2) maintaining the status quo, or (3) acting as agents of modernization. This variance is best explained, not so much by research bias, as by the fact that these studies have been carried out in quite different pockets of social reality.

This essay is concerned with the role of Indian mother worship as a focus of social and religious change.[12] Here it is argued that under certain circumstances goddess worship may act as a focal point for modernization. This is true particularly in those cities where westernization is minimal and the normal stresses of urbanization and status seeking are compounded by new structural relations among castes, classes, and modern social institutions. The role of mother worship in modernization is illustrated here with data collected by the author in an urban goddess temple during a twelve-month study conducted in Orissa, India, from 1972 to 1973.[13]

## Chandi and the Rajas of Orissa

When the rajas of Orissa lost political power after India gained independence in 1948, many Chandi festivals either were attenuated or disappeared altogether.[14] No longer did the goddess attract allegiance to the local raja. Over the years many goddess temples faced financial crisis as the rajas withdrew their traditional patronage. In some temples allegiance to the nobility was shifted to local political parties, and attempts were made to revitalize earlier secondary functions of these temples, such as resolving disputes and acting as centers of healing.[15]

In some goddess temples rituals were reformed so that they were brought more into the mainstream of classical Hinduism. An example of such reform is the case of animal sacrifice, which was abandoned in many temples to attract the support of higher castes, who were pushing for vegetarian reforms. If full Sanskritization was not possible, owing to the power of a large number of non-Brahman priests, compromises resulted in the compartmentalization of rituals. Thus, several temples in Orissa today depict the goddess as a vegetarian for special occasions during part of the year, although she remains non-vegetarian during the rest of the ritual cycle.[16] Some of these temples have been either partially or fully Sanskritized, but others have mustered support from lower castes, with continuation of animal sacrifice and the revitalization of non-Sanskritic themes as a result.[17]

Before the rajas of Orissa were divested of their political powers, many of them were supported by tutelary goddesses.[18] These female deities were associated with the founding of the raja's kingdom in legends portraying his successful conquest and right of sovereignty over local tribal peoples. Thus, the raja's tutelary goddess was a composite of numerous tribal goddesses who became amalgamated and absorbed into the protective service of the royal household.

Often the temple was located several miles from the palace, because the goddess was believed to be so powerful that it would be risky for the royal family to live near her. It is clear, however, that in certain instances this distance was maintained because the goddess was originally a tribal deity adopted by the raja and was therefore considered to be somewhat dangerous. A specially carved Hinduized sculpture of the tribal goddess was frequently kept within the palace itself.[19] Although the goddess was worshiped by Brahman priests in the palace temple, non-Brahman priests worshiped her several miles away in a temple built at her place of origin.[20]

Before Independence many of the rajas of Orissa took part in an annual ceremony that included army maneuvers meant to display the military strength of the ruler and his tutelary goddess. At that time weapons were exhibited, along with the royal sword and other regalia, all of which were dedicated to the goddess. The raja would go to the temple and make offerings. From there the royal family was followed by a particular caste of soldiers to the parade grounds, which were usually located near the palace.[21]

The ceremony at the parade grounds would culminate in target practice exercises. In some places the raja would take part in these: at the conclusion of the event he was expected to hit a target, and then aim his arrows in all the directions of the compass to demonstrate his sovereign power over the territory. After this, drums were beaten and fireworks set off to show his enemies symbolically that there was no chance for them to violate his domain. The whole ceremony was thus a display of the authority of the raja, reinforced through military maneuvers with the sanction of the goddess—great defender of the king and his people

One of the rajas of Orissa interviewed in 1973 described the significance of this form of goddess worship in his kingdom:

> In those days [before Independence] the raja was supported by his Chandi [goddess]. . . . I would go to the parade grounds where there was a standard which was a wooden fish hung up on a piece of string. For the last fifty years it has been a custom in my family for the raja to shoot the fish down with a rifle. My own father introduced an innovation to include more precision shooting. The challenge was to cut the string with a perfect shot, so that the wooden fish would fall to the ground. This was done at night from a distance of about seventy-five yards with the fish lit up by a petromax lamp.
>
> It was spectacular when the fish went down and the string was cut. Everyone was happy and the crowd would applaud enthusiastically. All of this was considered an auspicious sign that it would be a good year. . . . After this event the goddess would leave to visit various important goddess shrines throughout India. She was sent off with the blessings of the raja and the people.[22]
>
> I have managed to cut the string in the first shot many times, but this ceremony is kept in abeyance today. It is no longer performed.

At some point in history these tribal deities were allied to the Sanskritic form of the goddess Durga and ultimately linked with the state deity, Lord Jagannath, at a higher level. Thus, through a "universalization" of the Little Tradition, these goddesses became partially Sanskritized and tied some of the indigenous tribal peoples to a feudal lord, who in turn paid allegiance to the most powerful raja at Puri, patron of Lord Jagannath.[23]

Since Independence this hierarchical structure has largely dissolved, and the goddesses of Orissa no longer act as protectors of the nobility. Many vestigial rites of mother worship, however, can be traced to this earlier integrating function of the goddess. Nor is there any evidence to suggest that worship of the goddess is disappearing because of the decline of her previous role. Mother worship has instead taken other forms and continues to flourish, but with new patrons and through different media.

Some of the goddess temples that survived the immediate political and social changes after Independence suffered from serious economic difficulties owing to land fragmentation and dwindling support from the royal purse.[24] Other temples have managed to modernize their economies, implement ritual reforms, and further relate the local goddess to the growing popularity of mother worship celebrated in the Bengali style imported from Calcutta. This change is particularly evident in the two largest urban centers of Orissa.

## The Rise of Durga Worship in Cuttack

Milton Singer has demonstrated that there is no sharp distinction between Hinduism and modernization in his study of religion in the city of Madras.[25] Srinivas took a similar position when he suggested that changes in Indian urban religion involve something more than secularization.[26] He illustrated this point with the changing character of the Dasahara festival that was associated with the royal family of Mysore before Independence. The Dasahara festival has not been secularized, but has instead shifted to an emphasis on celebrating the birth of Basava, founder of the dominant Lingayat sect, which has risen to power in state politics. This example demonstrates the capacity for dropping certain old customs when they are no longer valid and replacing them with other, already established traditions. Neither secularization nor the rise of a new religious movement is necessary to fill the vacuum left by the decline of a single style of celebration.

A similar case can be drawn from data collected in Orissa's urban centers with the popular rise of Durga worship as celebrated in the Bengali style. James Freeman records this religious change in Bhubaneswar, Orissa's capital city:

> Another new development for Bhubaneswar is the dramatic rise
> of Durga Puja activities. The festival of the goddess Durga, which
> occurs usually in late September or early October, is one of the
> most important festivals of the state of Bengal and its principal city,
> Calcutta. It is also widely celebrated in the Orissan city of Cuttack,
> some twenty miles north of Bhubaneswar. In 1950 and 1962 Durga
> Puja was a small festival in Bhubaneswar celebrated primarily by a
> few Bengali residents. . . . By 1971 Durga Puja had become one of
> the big events of the festival year.[27]

In the city of Cuttack, which is the largest commercial center of Orissa (population over 200,000), Durga Puja has become the most widely celebrated festival. Each year it attracts thousands of people from surrounding districts.[28]

The Durga festival is not primarily temple centered; instead, it involves considerable street ritual. More than a hundred scenes containing life-size statues of the goddess Durga and other deities are constructed in the various parts of Cuttack. Several castes make the statues, using special clays taken from the Mahanadi River. It takes weeks to build these elaborate scenes, found along the main commercial arteries of the city and in the small neighborhood enclaves. They are beautiful, intricate, and sometimes costly. Four types of interest groups pool their money to purchase them: caste associations, neighborhood committees, merchants, and students. Sometimes a single wealthy individual will have one constructed.

Durga Puja lasts for sixteen days in Cuttack. The festival builds to a crescendo on the final three days, when there is much festivity, gift exchange, and finally a large procession lasting most of the day. The statues are carried through the streets of the city by lower castes hired especially for this purpose. At one point all the statues are gathered in a central bazaar, where they are judged for their beauty and intricacy. This contest brings considerable prestige to the particular interest group that wins. The procession then continues to the rivers bordering the city, and one by one the statues are thrown into the waters, to the accompaniment of cheering from the crowds. By this time there is dancing and singing throughout the city.

The impact of Durga Puja on the economy of the city is important. Many commercial enterprises make most of their income for the year during the last three days of the festival. This is because thousands of rupees are spent in exchanging gifts: saris are given to young girls, sweetmeats and special curries are purchased at temples and in neighborhood shops, and people buy different ornaments associated with the holidays.

Though Durga Puja is celebrated mostly with street ritual, people also attend several goddess temples. The most frequented of these is the temple of Chandi, a small structure located some distance from the heart of the commercial center. This temple is an important focus of Cuttack's religious life because in recent years the goddess here has become the presiding deity of the city.

Each evening during Durga Puja the goddess in Chandi temple is dressed in one of her sixteen aspects. Thousands of visitors crowd into the temple to pay their respects. The ritual reaches a series of peaks on the final three nights of the festival. On the first of these nights the deity is dressed as Saraswati, the goddess of learning. Approximately four hundred goats are sacrificed to Chandi, who takes the form of Kali on the second night. Finally, on the last night of the celebration, the goddess is dressed as Durga. This form of the deity represents the conqueror of the Buffalo Demon, who is victorious over the forces of evil. Thus the goddess remains the defender of her people—but no longer at the service of the raja.

What has happened to bring about this recent popularization of goddess worship in Orissa? Are there psychological, socioeconomic, and religious factors contributing to these transformations in the style of goddess worship? These questions may be partially answered by a more detailed study of Chandi's role in Cuttack.

## The Goddess as an Agent of Change

The notion that Hinduism is resistant to modernization has been refuted by many students of Indian civilization.[29] Freeman lucidly states the argument in support of the complementarity between modernity and tradition in India: "This author's study, like . . . Singer's (1966:55–67; 1972:245–414) questions any hypotheses which claim that (1) traditional worldviews are necessarily incompatible with rapidly changing and modernizing social environments, or that (2) modernization—at least in its relatively early phases—necessarily produces secularization."[30]

The city of Cuttack has been a commercial center for hundreds of years, despite its isolation between two rivers that remained without a passable bridge until very recently. On several occasions, Cuttack has been the capital of Orissa because of its strategic position as a fortress. Even today the city has little modern industry. Numerous small cottage industries, and several large businesses, many of them owned by merchants from Bengal, Rajasthan, and Gujarat, have opened in recent years. Gradually these establishments have become prosperous.

A little over a hundred years ago one of the rajas from a nearby kingdom who periodically stayed at his urban palace in Cuttack founded Chandi Temple as a place of worship for his family. At that time the temple was completely supported by the raja's family, who granted a small amount of land to the Brahman assigned to worship the goddess. The deity was housed in a modest mud structure near a quiet intersection some distance from the heart of the city. The raja's family had the privilege of using this semipublic temple as they saw fit, and the raja had complete control of the temple's budget. Chandi was no more than an urban counterpart of the goddess the raja's family worshiped in their rural kingdom.

This small temple was only one of many religious institutions in Cuttack. At that time it enjoyed no special notoriety, nor was it heavily attended. The goddess was an urban reminder of the raja's rural power. Temple services depended on the whim of his family. If they were in the city during a large festival, the temple would be closed whenever they wanted to worship there privately. Chandi's primary function was still to serve as defender of the raja's sovereignty.

Cuttack changed over the years. Independence weakened royal patronage and the temple became more publicly oriented. As in other parts of India, many higher castes lost some of their power and prestige.[31] Gradually the rich local merchants started patronizing Chandi Temple. The raja's support was no longer needed. Serious conflicts over temple management surfaced, and the Hindu Religious Endowment Commission stepped in to settle disputes between the Brahman priests and the raja. In 1968 the raja's family lost all financial and ritual control over the temple. Chandi was no longer the raja's defender or personal family deity.

Bengali influence has increased in Cuttack since the early nineteenth century.[32] In 1803 two-thirds of the bankrupt zamindari lands were purchased by Bengalis during an auction held in Calcutta.[33] Consequently, numerous Bengali customs were learned and brought home.

The Bengali style of worshiping the goddess was only one of many new influences that gradually entered Chandi Temple. The family of priests who were in charge of worshiping the goddess looked increasingly toward Calcutta for ritual models to develop the popularity of the temple among local Bengali patrons. Gradually the Bengali style of Durga worship gained momentum as the chief festival of Cuttack, making Chandi Temple increasingly important as a focus of public worship. When Independence came and the raja's patronage weakened, Chandi's role shifted from defender of the sovereign to patron goddess of an emerging urban elite. Thousands of rupees were poured into Chandi's treasury by the rich. The mud structure was torn down and a new cement temple was constructed. Tiles were laid in the courtyard. The once-empty intersection outside became crowded with small shops competing for business from the thousands of worshipers who started pouring into the temple.

In 1969 the Orissa Hindu Religious Endowments Commission established a system of auctions for licenses to temple concessions as a device to increase the temple's income. This led to intense competition among merchants who sought prestige and large profits from holding these licenses. (These small shops include a flower stall, two sweetmeat shops, a ghee lamp stand, and a barbershop located inside the temple premises.) By 1973, Chandi Temple had more than sufficient income to meet the demands of a swelling attendance that had reached nearly two thousand people per day. Plans were being made to spend the profits by increasing the temple's landholdings, building a lodge for pilgrims, and starting a religious school to train priests in the tradition of goddess worship.

Chandi Temple has shown an amazing ability to adapt to the modern commercial economy of Cuttack. No longer is it dependent on the raja's support. Now able to generate its own income, it is today what I call an "urban commercial temple."[34] Unlike the land-based temples located in rural Orissa, which rely on dwindling economic support from tenant farmers, Chandi Temple has become a self-sustaining religious institution—part of the ritual network of Cuttack's commercial life.

Why has this happened to Chandi and not to other temples in Cuttack?[35] There is no single reason. A combination of factors has opened Chandi Temple to modernization. Certainly the removal of the raja, increased patronage from the merchant classes, and the introduction of standardized management policies by the Endowment Commission have played a part in developing the temple into a vibrant religious institution. However, more important than all these is the role Chandi Temple plays in the growing citywide focus on mother worship during Durga Puja.

## Psychological Dimensions of Goddess Worship

Since 1970, Durga Puja has rapidly expanded in Cuttack. This popular increase in mother worship, particularly evident in urban centers, has its psychological component. Interviews conducted in Cuttack reveal how individuals relate to this recent development.[36] Perhaps most interesting is how the goddess helps people to resolve new problems arising from rapid urbanization.

People who move to Cuttack from the villages do not totally abandon their traditional life-styles.[37] Still, they must face new pressures resulting from lessened reliance on caste and kin, and the need for conformity with unfamiliar occupational and neighborhood groups.

As Srinivas notes: "Urban life sets up its own pressures, and a man's daily routine, his place of residence, the times of his meals, are influenced more by his job than by caste and religion."[38] People often adjust to these new urban requirements by compartmentalizing their lives and rearranging the role that tradition played in the village so that it complements city life.[39]

An important function of the goddess in Cuttack is to help the devotee alleviate stresses resulting from competition, alienation, and dislocations associated with urban life. This is seen at the end of the day in the temple, when people call out to Mother Chandi with tears in their eyes as they unburden themselves. One man expressed it as follows: "This is our soul. When a man falls down he cries out *ma* [mother]. We do not utter the name of the father when in trouble. At that time we turn to the mother."

The word *ma* is repeated to bring the goddess into the worshiper's consciousness. The recitation of her name is a source of peace to many who turn to her in their personal turmoil. "When I face trouble," said one person, "I feel sorrow. I call the goddess. And I know then that I am being helped." To some she is the gateway to the more distant father: "If we worship the mother, then we can get to the father." Those devotees who worship the goddess exclusively believe she is more powerful than a male deity.

Not only does Chandi fulfill the traditional function of healer, she is also expected to answer many of the other needs of devotees. People do not hesitate to ask the goddess to grant their wishes. Money, new jobs, and good health are typical requests from hundreds of worshipers who flock to her daily asking for their personal desires to be granted. Students pray to pass their examinations. Others ask for promotions, "good luck" in money matters, or a chance to travel to distant relatives.

As the stresses of modern life and the need for more cash, material goods, and opportunities for upward mobility increase, people turn more to the goddesses who have protected them for centuries from hostile forces like disease, famine, and flood. Durga, for example, is the slayer of the Buffalo-headed Demon. She represents the conquest of good over evil and promises hope where there is doubt and despair.

The new religious celebrations in Orissa's urban centers do not constitute a distinct break with the past. Even though the goddess Chandi is no longer at the service of the raja, she continues to fulfill the role of protectress of the people. Instead of narrowing her functions, modernization seems to have widened them as people seek her aid in their various adjustments to the demands of urban life. The goddess also articulates with the world of modern politics. Any serious politician must include visits to the religious shrines of Cuttack as part of his election campaign.

Singer argues convincingly that modernization does not pose a dilemma requiring a rejection of either modern or traditional culture: "The problem faced by traditional societies is how to continue their normal cultural metabolism, that is, how to continue converting the events of history into assimilable cultural traditions."[40] The case of Chandi Temple illustrates this continuing process of cultural metabolism at work in modern India. Today in Orissa the goddess symbolizes not only the continuity of an ancient tradition, but also the growing prosperity and expansion of India's commercial life.

Chandi is thus an agent of change for many of the people of Cuttack. She offers new forms of worship fitted to the urban climate, a sense of stability in the midst of change, and a link to the past. The temple where the goddess is housed is no longer a quiet place for the pious, but a vibrant hub of city life where there is much commercial activity. It is a place for relieving tensions, a place where people who do not have common family ties or caste affiliations can meet, and a focal point for the growing Durga Puja tradition.

## Conclusion

There is nothing incompatible between modern and traditional cultures in India. Indeed, "traditionalism" may become a major instrument of change.[41] As K. Ishwaran suggests, "India can experience her own unique pattern of modernization."[42] A radical break with the past is not necessary; nor is there any "life-negating" element in Hinduism that denies the materialism of a burgeoning society. "The quest for spiritual riches was always affected by a quest for temporal riches, for power, for the pleasures of the senses."[43]

Mother worship is one of many avenues for religious change in Orissa. The goddess is part of a larger world view capable of integrating fragments of the past with new social relations among castes, classes, and interest groups. This is a complex process, and not all goddess temples have managed to translate local traditions into the modern idiom. A recent survey of patterns of mother worship in Orissa reveals a significant variation in styles of religious change.[44]

One thing is certain. Profound religious changes are taking place today throughout India. Donald Smith suggests: "Hinduism is being infused with a modern outlook and a new sense of social responsibility. This is a religious reformation of a fundamental nature."[45] Despite the various degrees and types of religious change noted here, we should not be blinded to broad reforms that seem to be sweeping across the whole spectrum of urban and rural Hinduism. Particularly important in this connection is the standardization of Hindu law through legislation.

Mother worship is one thread in a complex process of modernization. It has been demonstrated that the goddess Chandi is a viable instrument for reinterpreting Hinduism. Thus, as an agent of change, the goddess emerges with new dignity from her previous role as a tutelary deity of the raja. Chandi is transformed into a goddess of the new India—commercialized, but still sacred—at once both modern and traditional.

# Notes

1. I am grateful to Professor Cora Du Bois for helpful suggestions in preparing this essay.
2. Basham, *Ancient Indian Culture*, p. 36.
3. Ashby, *Modern Trends*, p. 119.
4. Ibid., p. 78.
5. Basham, *Ancient Indian Culture*, p. 32.
6. Srinivas, *Social Change*, pp. 25, 76.
7. Several new cults have been noted in recent years. Among these the Aurobindo/Sri Ma sect and the Satya Sai Baba movement are of particular interest because they tend to attract followers from different social backgrounds. I conducted a brief survey of these two movements in Cuttack during 1973, finding that the Aurobindo/Sri Ma sect attracted mostly intellectuals and government officials, whereas the Sai Baba cult was patronized largely by educated lower castes and by merchants.
8. In the nineteenth century the Arya Samaj looked back to the Vedic period "to purge contemporary Hinduism of evil accretions in thought and practice" (Ashby, *Modern Trends*, p. 34). The Jan Sangh is a political party formed in 1951, which advocates a platform supporting a return to traditional Hinduism and Hindi as the only official all-India language (Elder, *Indian Civilization*, p. 430).
9. Srinivas, *Social Change*, p. 142.
10. For a full report of corruption, management problems, and suggested new directions for the development of Hindu temples see Aiyar, *Endowments Commission*.

11. Srinivas, *Social Change*, p. 144.

12. Anthropological studies of mother worship in India are scattered throughout the literature. This topic has received little systematic attention, despite the fact that mother goddess cults appear to have deep historical roots reaching back as far as the Indus Valley civilization (Chattopadhyaya, *Evolution of Hindu Sects*, pp. 150–70).

13. A cautionary note is appropriate here. Though the data from Chandi Temple in Orissa reflect certain *unique* characteristics of the institution and its setting, they are also a rich source of information about broader trends and issues throughout India. Dimock states this relationship of the part to the whole as follows: "Each part of India is in some sense a microcosm of the whole subcontinent; each part is also in some sense a unique and individual culture" (*Place of the Hidden Moon*, p. 29).

14. There were twenty-six semiindependent feudatory states in Orissa during British rule.

15. See Preston, *Cult of the Goddess*.

16. I gathered this information in a brief survey conducted on fourteen goddess temples of coastal Orissa (Preston, "Goddess Temples in Orissa").

17. For a discussion of the role of goddesses in Madras state see Stein, "Goddess Temples," pp. 22–25. For an elaboration on sacrifice and caste affiliation see Kulke, "Religious Cults," p. 20.

18. L. K. Mahapatra, "Gods, Kings."

19. Kulke, "Religious Cults," p. 14.

20. Goddess temples were usually associated with a sacred geography and frequently located near rivers, on mountain tops, or in valleys.

21. The soldiers who served the rajas of Orissa were known as Paiks. According to Mathab, "The Paik system was a very old institution in Orissa. The Paiks had constituted the standing army of the independent kings of Orissa all along. They lived as cultivators with the land granted to them free of rent by the kings and they were called upon to fight whenever necessary" (*The History of Orissa*, p. 437).

22. A similar instance of the goddess traveling throughout the country is found in Poona, where the goddess Bolai is considered a huntress who "sets out on a two-month hunting tour in winter, symbolized by a palanquin procession at the beginning and the end" (Kosambi, *Myth and Reality*, pp. 89, 90).

23. See L. K. Mahapatra, "Gods, Kings."

24. This is also true of many other temples that were supported by the royalty: goddess temples were not the only ones to suffer economic difficulties from the withdrawal of royal patronage.

25. Singer, *Great Tradition*.

26. Srinivas, *Social Change*, p. 129.

27. Freeman, "Religious Change," p. 129.

28. Preston, "Aspects of Change."

29. See Freeman, "Religious Change"; Singer, *Great Tradition*; Srinivas, *Social Change*; Basham, *Ancient Indian Culture*; Ashby, *Modern Trends*; and

Preston, *Cult of the Goddess*.

30. Freeman, "Religious Change," p. 131.

31. Srinivas, *Social Change*, p. 21.

32. Under British rule, Orissa was part of Bengal until it was made a separate and independent state in 1936.

33. Mathab, *The History of Orissa*, pp. 434, 435.

34. Preston, "Aspects of Change."

35. Government figures indicate that there are approximately forty temples in Cuttack, twelve of which are goddess temples. (This information was supplied personally by Sri Nilamani Senapati, ICS, editor of the *Gazeteer of Orissa*.)

36. Preston, "Aspects of Change," pp. 102–35.

37. Vatuk questions the validity of the simplisitc notions that urbanization in India results in weakened family ties or that it isolates individuals who were once rural inhabitants (*Kinship and Urbanization*).

38. Srinivas, *Social Change*, p. 123.

39. Singer, *Great Tradition*, p. 320.

40. Ibid., p. 406.

41. Ibid., p. 384.

42. Ishwaran, *Change and Continuity*, p. 11.

43. Basham, *Ancient Indian Culture*, p. 37.

44. Preston, "Goddess Temples in Orissa."

45. Smith, *India as a Secular State*, p. 251.

# Bibliography

Aiyar, C. P. *Report of the Hindu Religious Endowments Commission, 1960–1962*. New Delhi: Government of India Press, 1962.

Ashby, Philip H. *Modern Trends in Hinduism*. New York: Columbia University Press, 1974.

Bang, B. G. "Current Concepts of the Smallpox Goddess Sitala in Parts of West Bengal." *Man in India* 53 (1973): 79–104.

Barber, Bernard. "Social Mobility in Hindu India." In *Social Mobility in the Caste System in India*, edited by James Silverberg, pp. 18–35. The Hague: Mouton Publishers, 1968.

Basham, A. L. *Aspects of Ancient Indian Culture*. New York: Asia Publishing House, 1966.

Bharati, Agehananda. "Hinduism and Modernization." In *Religion and Change in Contemporary Asia*, edited by Robert F. Spencer, pp. 67–104. Minneapolis: University of Minnesota Press, 1971.

———. *The Tantric Tradition*. Garden City, N.Y.: Doubleday, 1965.

Bhattacharyya, N. N. *The Indian Mother Goddess*. Calcutta: R. D. Press, 1971.

Bruteau, Beatrice. "The Image of the Virgin-Mother." In *Women and Religion*, edited by Judith Plaskow and Joan Romero, pp. 93–165. Missoula, Mont.: The Scholars Press, 1974.

Chattopadhyaya, Sudhakar. *Evolution of Hindu Sects*. New Delhi: Munshiram Manoharlal Oriental Publishers, 1970.

Clothey, Fred. "Pilgrimage Centers in the Tamil Cultus of Murukan." *Journal of the American Academy of Religion* 40 (1972): 72–95.

Das, G. S. "History of Cuttack." *Orissa Historical Research Journal* 3 (1955): 187–214.

Dimock, Edward. *The Place of the Hidden Moon*. Chicago: University of Chicago Press, 1966.

Elder, Joseph. *Lectures in Indian Civilization*. Dubuque, Iowa: Kendall/Hunt Publishing Co., 1970.

Freeman, James. "Religious Change in a Hindu Pilgrimage Center." *Review of Religious Research* 16 (1975): 124–33.

Government of Orissa. *The Orissa Hindu Religious Endowments Act, 1969*. Cuttack: Cuttack Law Times, 1970.

Ishwaran, K. *Change and Continuity in India's Villages*. New York: Columbia University Press, 1970.

Jha, Makhan. *The Sacred Complex in Janakpur*. Allahabad: United Publishers, 1971.

Kosambi, D. D. *Myth and Reality: Studies in the Formation of Indian Culture*. Bombay: Popular Prakashan, 1962.

Kulke, H. "Religious Cults and Royal Authority: The Case of the Chiefs of Orissa." Ms. University of Heidelberg, 1972.

Loomis, Charles. *Socio-Economic Change and the Religious Factor in India*. New Delhi: East-West Press, 1969.

Mahapatra, L. K. "Gods, Kings and the Caste System in India." In *Community, Self, and Identity*, edited by Bhabagrahi Misra and James Preston, pp. 7–27. The Hague: Mouton Publishers, 1978.

Mahapatra Manamohan. "The Badu: A Service-Caste at the Lingaraj Temple at Bhubaneswar." *Contributions to Asian Studies* 3 (1973): 96–108.

———. "Lingaraj Temple: Its Structure and Change." Ph.D. dissertation, Utkal University, Orissa, India, 1971.

Mathab, Harekrushna. *The History of Orissa*. Vol. 2. Cuttack: Prajatantra Press, 1960.

Moddie, A. D. *The Brahmanical Culture and Modernity*. New York: Asia Publishing House, 1968.

O'Malley, L. S. S. *Bengal District Gazeteers: Cuttack*. Calcutta: The Bengal Secretariat Book Depot, 1906.

Patnaik, Nityananda. "Puri: Impact of Socio-Economic Changes on a Religious Complex." *Economic Weekly* 15 (1963): 1361–62.

Preston, James. "Aspects of Change in an Indian Temple: Chandi of Cuttack, Orissa." Ph.D. Dissertation, The Hartford Seminary Foundation, 1974.

———. *Cult of the Goddess*. New Delhi: Vikas Publishers, 1980.

———. "Goddess Temples in Orissa." In *Religion in Modern India*, edited by

Giri Raj Gupta. New Delhi: Vikas Publishers, in press.

Singer, Milton. *When a Great Tradition Modernizes*. New York: Praeger Publishers, 1972.

Sircar, D. C. "The Sakta Pithas." *Journal of the Royal Asiatic Society of Bengal* 14 (1948): 1–80.

Smith, Donald E. *India as a Secular State*. Princeton, N.J.: Princeton University Press, 1963.

―――. *South Asian Politics and Religion*. Princeton, N.J.: Princeton University Press, 1966.

Srinivas, M. N. *Social Change in Modern India*. Berkeley: University of California Press, 1966.

Stein, Burton. "Devi Shrines and Folk Hinduism in Medieval Tamilnad." In *Studies in the Language and Culture of South Asia*, edited by Edwin Gerow and Margery Lang, pp. 75–90. Seattle: University of Washington Press, 1973.

―――. "Goddess Temples in Tamil Country, 1300–1750 A.D." Unpublished paper, Conference on Religion in South India, Chicago, 1974.

Vatuk, Sylvia. *Kinship and Urbanization*. Berkeley: University of California Press, 1972.

Vidyarthi, L. P. *The Sacred Complex in Hindu Gaya*. New York: Asia Publishing House, 1961.

Woodroofe, Sir John. *Shakti and Shakta*. Madras: Ganesh and Company, 1929.

# 11

## Pox and the Terror of Childlessness: Images and Ideas of the Smallpox Goddess in a North Indian Village
### by Pauline Kolenda

This study is concerned with the folk imagery, theory, and rites for the prevention and cure of smallpox among the villagers of Khalapur in northern India.[1] Khalapur is located in western Uttar Pradesh, about one hundred miles north of Delhi.[2] This village, with a population of approximately 5,000, is dominated by Rajputs (numbering around 2,400) who own and control almost all the land. The next largest caste is the untouchable Chamars, with about 600 members. They are landless agricultural laborers (formerly Leather Workers—a highly defiling material in the Hindu view—hence their untouchability). The Chamars do much of the agricultural work for the Rajput landlords. Next in size are the Brahman priests, Baniya merchants, and Sweepers (untouchables), each numbering a few hundred persons. Then there are a plethora of small craft and service castes, composed of such groups as Goldsmiths, Carpenters, Washermen, Water Carriers, Barbers, Shoemakers (untouchables), Weavers, and Potters. Some additional castes, such as the Gosains and Jogis, are associated with particular Hindu religious sects.

About 10 percent of Khalapur villagers are Muslim. All the rest are Hindu. However, the area was under Muslim rule from Delhi for almost a thousand years; so Khalapur Hinduism absorbed some Muslim elements, such as the worship of the village *Pir* (Muslim saint). Associated with a large tomb on the northern side of the village, the *Pir* is considered to be the most powerful local deity. His predominance in the sacred realm perhaps reflects the old dominance of Muslim emperors in the secular realm.

There are two other gods in Khalapur of power almost equal to that of the *Pir*. Both of these are male deities: Lord Shiva, located in a small village temple; and the earth godling, Bhumiya, whose small shrine is located on the western outskirts of the village. Villagers also recognize an impersonal absolute above these three deities, known as Bhagwan, which is not worshiped directly, but from which all lesser powers derive.

There are many lesser deities, both male and female. Some of the males are hero godlings, such as the five Rajput brothers who were warriors under the Hindu ruler, Prithvi Raj (A.D. 1191). These are worshiped by the Sweepers.[3] The more than one hundred goddesses found in Khalapur can be classified into four types. First, there are those connected with the great goddess Kali, associated with epidemics, catastrophes, and destruction. Second are goddesses connected with smallpox, including Shitala ("The Cool One"), Ujali ("The White Lady"), Sedhu (an attendant of Shitala), Kanti (who causes swellings in the neck), Mahamai (who brings about large poxes), and Chhotimai (who causes small poxes). Third, there are goddesses associated with calendrical festivals based on Hindu legends or related to life-cycle rites. Fourth are the benign earth goddesses like Dharti Mata. Except for the latter, all the goddesses anger readily when neglected—that is, if they are not regularly offered food, drink, clothing, and shelter. Below the hero godlings and goddesses are various ghosts and sprites, associated with water and fields.[4]

Mother Pox belongs to a middle rank in the local hierarchy of supernatural powers. She and the other goddesses are vaguely subordinate to the three high male deities in both power and rank. One could hope to call upon the power of one of these gods to counteract the power of a mother goddess.

Scholars have found that the pantheons of local gods in India differ in degrees of purity, just like local hierarchies of castes.[5] High gods accept only vegetarian offerings made by high caste "pure" priests, whereas the lowest gods accept animal sacrifices or meat offered by middle caste or untouchable "impure" priests. The three most important pox goddesses in Khalapur are ranked in the same way. The goddess Ujali in her shrine to the southeast of the village is served by a Brahman priest and receives only vegetarian offerings; Shitala and her attendant, Sedhu, in their shrines to the northwest of the village, are offered hens and pigs, as well as vegetarian foods, and are served by untouchable Sweepers. The Chamars have their own separate shrine to Ujali and some other disease goddesses, located to the northeast of the village. Ujali is also called the Village Mother (*Gaon*

*Mata*), the Big Mother (*Mahamai* or *Baramai*), and She of the Hills (*Paharon*). I will not be concerned here with the differences in detail among these pox mothers.

## Mother Pox in the Imaginative Universe of Khalapur

This article is a "thick description"[6] of the images and ideas of smallpox among Khalapur villagers. Michael Fischer has defined "thick description" as "the elaboration of a cultural image by the anthropologist according to what he thinks he knows about the culture."[7] My assumption is that there is an imaginative universe in the subculture of Khalapur that contains ideas and images appearing in a variety of contexts.

Drawing upon such images and ideas may be the only way in which people lacking scientific medicine can treat illnesses. They develop "cures" that meet their needs for relief from anxiety and intellectual understanding of the phenomenon. As Claude Lévi-Strauss has said with respect to the application of a woodpecker's beak as a cure for toothache among the Siberian Iakoute: "The real question is not whether the touch of a woodpecker's beak does in fact cure toothache. It is rather whether there is a point of view from which a woodpecker's beak and a man's tooth can be seen as going together (the use of this congruity for therapeutic purposes being only one of its possible uses), and whether some initial order can be introduced into the universe by means of these groups."[8]

Rituals are often the acting out of a myth, or at least a myth is an explanation of a rite. But with the *mata* (Mother Pox), there is no myth—at least none known to the Khalapur villagers. The image must be inferred from the ritualized behavior. It is as though one heard only the words, "This is my body and blood . . . ," and had to fill in the context and infer what sort of figure might have made such a pronouncement on the basis of knowledge of the relevant culture.

In India the master image of pox is of a hot, angry, capricious, and deadly mother.[9] Why is she imagined like this? Because there is no explanatory myth it is necessary to rely on an analysis of the north Indian cultural context to understand images of pox. When a disease becomes the focus for imagination, there are both stimulants and constraints upon it, because the images, to be intellectually satisfying, must fit the empirical symptoms and stages of progression in the disease itself. There are a set of cues to which metaphors must be fitted. For example, Laura Bohannan found that, among the Tiv of Nigeria, the image for smallpox is water. The metaphor of water suggests that the pustules are like water drops. The Tiv also seem to recognize the contagious character of smallpox, as is reflected in their belief that the victim can cause smallpox in others, and in their custom of burning the hut of a sick person and purifying the victim's bed after death or cure. Their assumption that smallpox is originally caused by a witch, on the other hand, derives not from the empirical features of the disease, but from a general witchcraft complex.[10]

The depiction of Mother Pox in India matches the characteristics of the disease. The abusive, destructive pustules, along with the high fever, suggest anger. The seeming arbitrariness of recovery or death reflects the irrational volatility of the deity's rage.

The smallpox season occurs in the hot months of April and May, just before the arrival of the heavy monsoon. The victims are mostly children.[11] Although some mothers in Khalapur accept vaccination available from the community development worker, most fear that Mother Pox will be angered by such an effort to exclude her. Villagers thus believe that the disease is more likely to appear on a vaccinated child because Mother Pox will take revenge. For this reason considerable effort is made to please the goddess in different ways to prevent her from claiming a child. One method of appeasing Mother Pox is through ritual offerings.

## Mother Pox as a Receiver of Prestations

Indian society is strongly characterized by hierarchy. It is a basic principle in the organization of joint family, patrilineage, caste, and intercaste relationships.[12] Caste hierarchy is expressed primarily in the *jajmani* system, a pattern of intercaste exchange and cooperation whereby priestly, servant, and artisan castes provide services and products to one another and to high caste landed client families; the clients are called *jajmans*. This system has been found to operate in almost all parts of India.[13] It is a system of prestations, the action of paying in cash or service what is due by custom.[14] In Khalapur, the *jajmani* system was still operative during the 1950s. The typical pattern is for Brahman household priests, artisans, and servants to give commodities and services as prestations in return for fixed portions of grain after harvest, along with other foods and clothing from each *jajman* family.

Through the *jajmani* system lower castes absorb the ritual pollution of higher castes (from bodily wastes). Thus, in this system the Barber is a ritual specialist, since he is involved in the process of reducing pollution by removing hair and finger- and toenails for his clients. Similarly, the Sweeper woman absorbs pollution by cleaning up excrement from latrines or cattle yards.

Susan Wadley suggests that relations between a *jajman* and his servant are homologous with those between worshiper and deity; for the worshiper removes the deity's pollution, just as the servant removes his *jajman's* pollution.[15] Ursula Sharma also suggests that "there are obvious parallels . . . between the way a low caste man treats a high caste man and the way a worshiper treats the deity he worships."[16] G. M. Carstairs makes this same point with respect to the similarity between the way gods and government officials are treated.[17]

Deference to an honored figure—whether a high caste *jajman*, an official, a guru, or a deity—involves an etiquette of deferential address, even obsequious flattery, and lavish hospitality. This is accomplished through feasting the honored one, providing for his needs, and winning favor by satisfying his desires. Because mother goddesses are powerful figures, they are honored, offered lavish hospitality, flattered, even bribed, because the intention is to fend them off, keep them away, or if they are already too close, to remove them to a safe distance. They are morally indifferent. There is no idea that smallpox is a punishment for bad behavior, though some may say that serious illness and often death are part of a person's Karma (one's lot in life related to behavior in a past life). Still, this is not the dominant note in Khalapur.[18] Instead, villagers gingerly try to cope with a capricious, unpredictable, and dissatisfied female who causes serious illness and even death in her attempt to please herself. Theories of illness as punishment for sin—except for the "sin" of neglecting to make offerings to the godlings—are not prevalent in Khalapur.

The efforts made to fend off Mother Pox take the form of offerings or gestures of obeisance to the deity. Her name should be uttered at the moment of birth, and handfuls of grain should be promised to her during birth ceremonies. If such amenities are forgotten there is danger that she might strike back. Mothers make vows to Mother Pox to protect children. Many children wear charm necklaces, which include a coin for Mother Pox. Presumably the money is offered to her after the child has survived to a certain age (one-and-a-half or six-and-a-half or older). The hair of a newborn infant may also be shaved and presented as an offering at a shrine of Mother Pox.

Besides these rites, there are weekly offerings. On Mondays, mothers (especially of sons) give flour, oil, and salt to their family's Sweeper woman in order to protect the children from pox. In this ritual the Sweeper seems to be a medium. The food prepared with flour, oil, and salt given to the Sweeper woman is fed symbolically to the goddess.

Just before the hot season in March when pox is most virulent, pots called *dogharas* ("two pots") are placed on rooftops. They contain water and offerings like sugar puff candies, cloves, and *pan* leaves for chewing. The idea of the *doghara* offering is that the goddess will cool herself and enjoy the contents of the pots. She might even reside in them for a time. The hope is that after having cooled herself, the goddess will move on to some other place. These pots are most likely to be placed on rooftops by families whose children have just recovered from pox, or by their worried neighbors.

Another preventive measure is the annual worship at each of the three shrines devoted to Mother Pox, located in fields southeast, northwest, and northeast of the village. Different sections of the village worship at separate shrines, the one to the northeast belonging only to Chamars. The shrines are constructed in blocks of brick with pointed tops, varying from twelve inches to ten feet in height. They contain no images, but each has an indented niche at its base in which offerings are placed. Typical offerings to Mother Pox include sugar candy puffs, fried sweet cakes, rice and wheat puddings, boiled rice with *dal* sauce, hens, and clay pots. Various items may be promised to the goddess in return for her departure from a sick child. At one annual ceremony, the Sweepers are recipients of offerings made to Sedhu Mai, the guardian of goddess Shitala. Many headcoverings, an important part of a woman's daily dress, are offered; these have been promised at the time of a child's sickness. Blood sacrifices of piglets are also offered by untouchable Chamars. Some Sweeper boys wave chickens over the heads of worshipers in order to absorb any *mata* (Mother Pox) that clings to the women as they depart for home. Shaved hair from a baby may also be offered, along with some sweet cakes. A Barber explained, "The offerings are given to protect men and boys and everyone from smallpox, and to protect animals from disease."[19] So Mother Pox is treated like other superiors. She is honored with gifts lavished upon her.

From fear of her anger, one always speaks respectfully in the presence of the victim upon whom she resides. One must never complain,

27. The *dogharas* placed on rooftops by women as temporary residences and cooling places for Mother Pox. It is believed that the goddess rests and cools herself in the *dogharas* and then moves on. Such temporary abodes for Mother Pox are used as devices by which families hope to prevent the disease from entering their homes. *(Photographed in Khalapur by J. Michael Mahar)*

but should acclaim the benefits of her visit. For example, a mother attending her eight-year-old daughter who had pox was heard to say clearly and loudly, so that the goddess could hear, "Whenever the Mother appears, it does some good. Of course, the Honored Lady will take care of her [the sick child]." Similarly, a *siana* ("curer") commented as he left the child's sickroom after performing a cooling rite, "It is good the Mother is visiting. Having the Mother will be useful to her [the sick child]."

One of the first things done when the pox appears is to touch a coin to the sick child's forehead, vowing to the goddess that the money will be spent in offerings on her annual feast day. Such offerings might be made either at a shrine in Khalapur or elsewhere. Popular pilgrimage places for Mother Pox are at Raewala and Kankhal, villages near the important Hindu center at Hardwar. One might also promise to provide a place for the goddess to reside. For instance, the shrine on the northwest edge of the village was refurbished because a Rajput woman whose son was ill with pox promised to give the deity a place to live if her son survived.

## The Three Stages of Smallpox

The villagers of Khalapur conceive of smallpox in three stages.

*Stage one.* At first the sick person is ill with fever and bedridden. Because the diagnosis of the disease is unclear, it is common to have *jhars* performed. This process involves a curer who waves a wet broom or *nim* branch over the patient's face while saying *mantras* (powerful words). This rite combines a cooling effect with the power of the *mantra* to counteract the disease on the patient.[20] After this rite is performed, offerings of cooked food and other things may be touched to the victim's body. These items are then carried off to the wasteland or to a pond. It is hoped that whatever is causing the illness will be attracted away by the food and follow along out of the village.

*Stage two.* Next the poxes appear. Curing rites should not be performed once Mother Pox has made her presence known, because she is insulted by them and may cause the "shadow." The patient may recover after eight or ten days when the pustules have dried.

*Stage three.* In some cases, the disease progresses to a more serious stage, when the skin darkens and the person may lose his sight, voice, or hearing. This last stage is referred to as the "shadow," and is believed to be caused by the anger of Mother Pox at having been defiled or insulted. The patient is unlikely to recover once the shadow has fallen. However, a very powerful *siana* might be able to lift the shadow, leaving only a lighter layer of pox on the patient. There is great risk in having a curing rite performed by even a powerful *siana*. If the rite is not powerful enough, the *mata* may merely become more angry and complete her destruction.

The shadow may also fall upon the victim if annual worship of Mother Pox takes place at one of her shrines while someone in the worshipers' community has pox. The goddess is angered by this. She also is made jealous and angry by signs of joy and festivity, such as a person wearing new clothes or a pregnant woman.[21] Certain items protect the patient from the shadow, including branches of the sacred *nim* tree (*melia azadirachta*),[22] various snares or protective boundary items such as an acacia branch with a spider web in it, human hairs wrapped around the victim's hand, and sacred thread (like that worn by Brahmans) wrapped around a brick and placed under the sickbed, or stretched between two stakes at the door to the sickroom.

## Mother Pox as a Goddess in a Temple

Mother Pox is the illness itself. The victim is possessed by the deity[23] and treated like her image. The sickroom becomes the temple of Mother Pox, who manifests herself in the rash and pustules on the victim. The latter are called "pearls" and are viewed as the mother's teeth. The mother is "on" the sick person, devouring him.

The rendering of offerings that makes up normal Hindu worship is called *puja*. This is the most frequent means of communicating with the nonempirical. Lawrence Babb has called *puja* the "bedrock" of Hinduism.[24] He specifies its two essential features as (1) the creation of a zone of purity within which the deity may be approached, and (2) a food transaction. The food is presented to the god, who eats it. Then the *prashad* (food that has been defiled by the god's eating of it) is returned to the worshipers, who are benefited by consuming it.

I would add another essential feature of the *puja*, namely, the use of a transmitting medium that takes food and other offerings to the supernatural. Water may act as a medium to carry food or other offerings to a spirit or deity. Thus, a Hindu worshiper places offerings to his ancestors in a river or ocean. The medium may also be a person or an animal. One feeds a Brahman, an unmarried girl, or a cow—all considered to be pure. The medium for Mother Pox is a black dog. One may offer a cool drink of *sharbat* to a black dog in order to "cool" the deity.

The sickroom where pox has broken out becomes a temple. The therapies performed there are *pujas* to a temple goddess. The deity in a temple continually receives services and offerings. Above all, a supernatural wants a residence, a place to stay.[25] Then he or she desires food, drink, clothing, cooling baths, and so on. These needs of the deity are recognized in the worship of gods, godlings, and ghosts both in the most humble forms of worship and in the great temples of Hinduism. Perhaps the only major deviation from a temple paradigm in the smallpox sickroom is the deadly and polluting nature of the disease. The worshipers desire this deity to depart and take up her residence elsewhere.

The trick for those caring for the smallpox victim is to persuade the goddess to leave the sick person. It is difficult, given that she is readily insulted. Because Mother Pox is hot, one tries to get her to leave through measures calculated to "cool" her. The function of the *dogharas* described earlier is to cool the goddess before she takes up residence upon some victim. Once she *has* appeared on a person, the nursing relative may "cool the door" by pouring water on either side of the main doorway to the house.[26] Thus, Mother Pox, desiring to be cooled by the water, is lured out of the room to the doorway. Then the sick child's mother, carrying sweet cakes, leads the goddess from the doorway to her shrine out in the fields. The child's mother hopes that Mother Pox will stay at her shrine, away from the child. These sweets offered to the deity are usually received by a Sweeper woman, who is so polluted and poor that she may eat the *prashad* of the polluted smallpox goddess.

To cool Mother Pox, a clay pot of water is placed under the patient's cot, with another containing rice and sugar, near the doorway. The sick child may be bathed with the water from the pot under the bed, in order to cool the *mata* "on" the child. It is changed daily and the used water is poured out in the direction of the hills to the north, in hopes that the goddess will return to the place from which she came.

The child's mother also may cool the goddess by washing one of the shrines on the edge of the village. The patient is fed cooling foods, such as fruits—grapes, bananas, or oranges. Hot foods like fowl, fish, or pork are not offered. Mother Pox likes "cool" feast foods, such as the various kinds of sweet cakes and puddings, rice, curries, and *dal* made by village women for special occasions. But one should not fry near her place of residence, nor use spices, because these would make the food hot.

The villagers speak of three kinds of offerings prepared to tempt the goddess to leave the patient. The *ghahena* offering involves a paper palanquin, upon which seven kinds of sweets, flowers, and vermillion powder (used as a cosmetic) have been heaped. The palanquin is waved over the sick child as Mother Pox "on" the child is invited to go for an outing. Then the palanquin is taken out toward the hills where it is hoped the deity will go. A similar offering is the *alufa*, a combination of seven kinds of sweets, bangle bracelets, fried cakes, and an egg. This may be taken to a shrine of the goddess Shitala. A third offering is the *patroli*, made of seven leaves of the milkweed or pipal tree, woven together to form a plate. This plate is spread with *lapsi*, a favorite pudding of children and of Mother

28. Village women bathing a triple shrine that includes a shrine to Mother Pox. Such bathing cools the hot mother goddesses. *(Photograph by Pat Hitchcock)*

Shitala. The *patroli* is placed near a pond, which is considered to be a cool place for the goddess.

Only men, who are conceived to be purer as a sex than women, may risk taking offerings to the fields. Such a dangerous venture is only undertaken by the responsible male leaders of the community. Anyone who meets the procession is in danger, especially if he asks where it is headed, for then the *mata* may attach herself to the inquirer. For instance, one of the elders of the Sweeper community in Khalapur was reported to have been stricken and killed by the goddess because he had passed close by such a procession.

Another dimension of the rites of offering to Mother Pox has to do with strict rules to maintain the purity of places of worship. In Hindu temples, purity is ensured by keeping polluting persons at a distance from the *murti* ("image of the deity"). Usually only the bathed, freshly clothed, fasting priest can actually touch the *murti* or come within a few feet of it. Menstruating women, people suffering from either birth or death pollution, and especially untouchables are excluded. In Hindu household worship, also, the priest or other officiant, the worshipers, the deity, and the offering must all be pure. For the priest and worshipers, this requires bathing, fresh clothing, fasting, and possibly remaining continent. To ensure the deity's purity, the *murti* is bathed, the site is coated with cowdung, and shoes and other leather items are prohibited. The food offering is pure if the cook has bathed and the hearth has been freshly coated with cowdung before preparation. Later the leftover remains of the *prashad* should be immersed in running water, lest they be made impure by contact with some form of pollution as they lie waste.[27]

The shrines of Mother Pox at Khalapur are located in the fields, which are considered to be cleaner than the residential area of the village, away from animal and human defilement. During a case of smallpox there is great concern for the purity of the sickroom. The cot and patient's clothing are changed frequently. The patient is kept clear of women who are menstruating, or in *sutak* ("childbirth pollution") or *patak* ("death pollution"). If any of these defiling conditions prevail, it is believed that the shadow will fall. The shadow is a metaphor for pollution. It may also be caused by washing clothes or bathing near the patient. Probably the dirtied water from such activity is the polluting agent.

All these rites can be understood as those appropriate to a Hindu temple housing an empowered *murti*. A goddess resides on the patient in the sickroom. Mother Pox wants to be cooled just as other gods do, particularly Lord Shiva and the goddess Lakshmi. So one provides her with bathing vessels and cooling foods. One speaks respectfully in her presence and keeps her image and "temple" pure by bathing the patient, and by excluding those who might pollute the sanctum. Just as one does not cook in a temple, food is never prepared in a sickroom. Like the temple deity who is taken for an occasional outing, the goddess is invited to ride in a palanquin, or offered feast foods, along with cosmetics, clothing, flowers, perfumes, and bangles—all items used to adorn a *murti* in a temple—and is also promised offerings to be made in the future. The sickroom is the temple of the smallpox goddess.

## Mother Pox and the Shadow as Pollution

Impurity in Indian culture is "the irruption of the biological into social life."[28] In the Hindu concept of pollution, any waste product of the human body is defiling. Death itself is polluting.[29]

The distinctions between temporary and permanent pollution, and between self- and external pollution are useful.[30] A person becomes temporarily self-polluted by defecation, urination, or sexual intercourse. Women are temporarily self-polluted by menstruation and childbirth. One is temporarily, but externally, polluted by contact with a lower caste person, or by the death of a member of one's family or patrilineage. Those whose traditional work requires them to deal with bodily excretions are permanently self-polluted—they have inherited their defilement.

Pox itself is a form of temporary external pollution.[31] This is indicated by the custom of having to purify the sick person after the illness is over. At that time the victim is sprinkled with a *nim* branch dipped in water in a rite called *chhinta*.

The concept of the shadow as the most serious stage of smallpox can be explained as Mother Pox's anger at being defiled. But it can also be understood as a form of compound pollution, the effects of which are far greater than simple single pollution. Compound pollution occurs when an individual who already suffers a defilement has added an external act of pollution. The ancient Hindu law books that specify rituals of purification require much more severe rites in the instance of compound pollution than in that of single, simple pollution. The penances are much greater than they would be if the penances for two or more types of pollution were simply added together. Henry Orenstein writes about compound pollution as follows:

> In general, it appears that if one has polluting contacts with others while in self-pollution, the result is not as if one "stain" were simply added to another; rather one is much more defiled. According to Samvarta . . . , for example if someone touches a Chandala, he must bathe, but if he does so while he, the subject, has the leavings of food in his mouth, he must live on a highly restricted diet for six nights. . . . By itself, purification after eating involves a relatively simple rite and no austerity. The two defilements jointly do not add up to an ascetic diet for six nights. . . . Yama . . . requires a moderate penance for a woman who touches a Chandala but a severe one if she does so while menstruating. . . . Again, menstruation alone merely requires

bathing afterwards, hence simple addition of "stains" cannot be involved. Ushanas . . . stipulates that one must bathe after touching a Chandala, and later adds that if this occurs while one is defecating or urinating, purity is not attained until one has undergone a three-day fast.[32]

This same ancient principle operates in conceptions about small-pox. Compounded pollution is far worse than single, simple pollution. Pox is itself a form of pollution. When additional pollution is laid on it, the result for the smallpox victim is far worse than it would be from either form of pollution separately, or even from the separate effects added together. Hence the deadliness of the shadow.

## Mother Pox as a Barren Woman

It has been pointed out by several scholars that the female deity in Hinduism seems to be malevolent and destructive when she is un-married or uncontrolled by a male deity.[33] Louis Dumont notes, however, that even though mated, Parvati, the consort of Lord Shiva, is unable to bear children in the normal way. She is barren. As such, she curses other goddesses with sterility.[34] With respect to Shitala, the north Indian smallpox goddess, A. L. Basham points out that mother goddesses "were never thoroughly incorporated into the mythological scheme, or provided with husbands."[35]

Mother Pox lacks a mate. Thus, she is barren and behaves like a woman who yearns for a child. The titles of the Pox Goddess, such as *mata* or *mai* (both meaning "mother"), are ironic, because she is op-posite of a nurturing mother. Khalapur villagers use a similar irony in their worship of *pitars* ("fathers"). These are men among their patri-lineal ancestors who never had a son. Thus, *pitars* are really "failed fathers," just as *matas* are "failed mothers." The fate of being sterile, or childless, or unable to procreate a son is so terrible that one never admits it openly. It is assumed that among ghosts of the dead, or among other supernaturals, it is the sonless and the childless who cause great trouble.

Descent groups in Khalapur are patrilineal, and residence after marriage is patrilocal. Usually women marry at a young age out of their natal village into a husband's household, which is made up almost entirely of strangers. Women are not allowed to own houses or land, although they have a right to security for life support from their husband's minimal patrilineage. A de facto divorce may be obtained by returning a wife to her parental home if after a reasonable time (two years or so) she has failed to bear children. There is rigid segregation of the sexes, females being largely limited to women's quarters, men having their own separate clubhouses in which to sleep and spend their leisure. At all times a woman's head must be covered and her face hidden from view in the presence of men older than her husband. She seldom sees her husband except during his visits to her room at night. Nor is she fully accepted in her husband's family until she has borne a child—preferably a son. A daughter is better than no children at all; it is sons, however, who are the true reward of motherhood.[36]

Infant mortality is high in Khalapur. More than half of the babies born do not reach the end of their first year. The anger and envy of childless women is recognized in many ways. For instance, when a charcoal brazier set one of our tents ablaze, a barber caste woman told us that she suspected the fire had been set by a barren woman. In the past, she claimed, there had been many such arsonists who were barren women.

*Sianas* ("curers") are said to tell despairing women who have some degree of self-control to transfer their barrenness to another woman's house by putting a handmark of white rice paint on her door. The theme of a woman stealing another's child by destroying it is expressed in Khalapur in a number of ways, of which the mother goddess cult is only one. A childless woman is suspected of having an evil eye. She should never praise another woman's child, lest she betray her own envy. An evil eye may kill a child, and it is believed that somehow the woman with the evil eye will get the child.[37] In one instance, a Muslim medical specialist told a Chamar woman that her baby's gradual decline in health was caused by some other woman, who had secretly nursed it. One may also put color in another woman's clothing or cut up or burn her clothing in order to get her child.

A woman's fear of losing a child through the ill will of envious barren females is reflected in a strong belief in the malevolent ghosts of childless women (*chuRails*).[38] Though Khalapur villagers are familiar with the classical Hindu concepts of Karma ("fate"), *sansara* ("rebirth"), and *mukti* ("spiritual liberation"), women place much greater reliance on the folk beliefs associated with the ghosts of unfulfilled persons who died suddenly.[39] Ghosts love birth, death, and menstrual pollution. Because they are attracted by the smell of blood discharge when a birth takes place, protective measures must be taken against them. For example, a knife is put near the new mother's head, and *nim* branches are hung over the doorway to keep ghosts away.

There are various measures taken to protect babies, especially boys, from the envy of these malevolent ghosts. Mothers have the noses of their boys pierced so they look like girls, who are not preferred by ghosts. It is common to protect babies with necklaces of charms to fend off ghosts and to induce the protection of various benevolent deities.

A woman who has suffered a miscarriage and wishes to carry through a successful pregnancy also may wear a *tabij* ("locket"). Miscarriages are often attributed to female ghosts, usually those of the husband's brother's wives or other close marital female relatives, or to water sprites. These ghosts often appear in dreams. Khalapur women report a typical dream involving two women and a man. In the dream, the man has sexual relations with the dreamer, while the two women destroy the fetus in the dreamer's womb. The *tabij* repels the destructive trio, and consequently preserves the fetus in the womb. It contains sharp things like needles, strong smelling elements such as saffron, musk, and cloves, and powerful items like tiger whiskers. The power of protection embodied in the locket is established by the *siana*, who has attained his power from a tutelary deity, such as the Khalapur *pir* ("saint"). The magical efficacy in the locket may be destroyed by the shadow, or by exposure to untouchables or to the pollution associated with birth, menstruation, and death. The power of the *pir* or godling vanishes from the locket if the shadow falls upon it. Then the wearer is once again open to the attacks of ghosts and the evil eye. The godling in the locket must be kept pure, because this is a tiny residence for the deity, like the temple or sickroom.

Why is pox called a mother? In what way is she motherly? The answer is this: she is not a mother, but longs to be one—just as barren and childless women, both living and deceased, want to be mothers.

## Heat, Anger, and Danger among Women

The social stigma of barrenness means that a childless woman is likely to be terrified and then angry about her future status. Anger is heat, which is associated in Hindu thought with "feminine malevolence and divine power."[40] Brenda Beck attributes the heat of the south Indian smallpox goddess to her chastity.⁴¹ Such imagery is also consistent with the idea of Mother Pox, the barren, unmarried goddess who is hot because she is both divine and abstinent.

Anger and passion are connected with women in the Hindu theory of temperament. Thus, the quality of *rajas* ("passion") literally means menstrual impurity,⁴² revealing an ancient connection between passion (including anger) and female impurity. This is consistent with the Hindu worship of *shakti* (power or energy as a feminine force), which is usually symbolized by fierceness.⁴³ *Shakti* is personified as the consort of Lord Shiva, who is passive, serene, and wise. Morris Opler has connected the Hindu female principle with disease goddesses like Shitala: "In Indian philosophical thought, the highest manifestation of spirituality—perfect serenity and absence of desire —is considered to be a male attribute. The striving and activity that result in creation and change are attributed to female energy, or *shakti*. This insures life and mobility; by the same token it initiates a lapse from perfection and therefore ultimate sorrow. The female principle is always disturbing; the godlings of disease are invariably goddesses."⁴⁴

In the Hindu view the male's retention of semen contributes to his strength, whereas sexual intercourse weakens him both physically and spiritually. Thus, the Hindu attitude toward women is ambivalent. According to Carstairs:

> Sexual love is considered the keenest pleasure known to the senses; but it is felt to be destructive to a man's physical and spiritual well-being. Women are powerful, demanding, seductive—and ultimately destructive. On the plane of creative phantasy, everyone worships the Mataji, the Goddess, who is a protective mother to those who prostrate themselves before her in abject supplication, but who is depicted as a sort of demon . . . any woman whose demands one has refused is liable to be feared as a witch who may exact terrible reprisals.⁴⁵

In Hindu thought, there is an active feminine principle of energy and disturbance, and a more passive masculine principle of spirituality and quietude. To emulate these philosophical ideals, men should conquer their sexual desires, but women need not do so: men see women as oversexed, seductive, demanding, powerful, and dangerous.

Edward Harper notes that women in a Brahman community in Karnataka are viewed as dangerous. This point brings us back to social organization from the philosophical-religious domain. He explains the view of women as dangerous as a result of the low status of women in a strongly patrilineal society. Men project an expectation of resentment and a desire to retaliate upon women, an expectation powered by their own hidden guilt.[46]

Mother Pox as a social category is treated much like women in north Indian village culture. She is feared because of her voracious desires, as are childless or barren women, who are terrified about their low status. This terror may turn into anger, resentment, deceit, and retaliation.


## Binary Oppositions and Denial

There are contrasts in the images of Mother Pox presented here. She is both superior and inferior, goddess and rejected woman (barren and easily angered). She must be kept free from pollution within her sickroom temple; yet ironically she is the source of pollution herself. Why these oppositions—pure/impure, goddess/barren woman?

The answer lies in the helplessness and hopelessness of people faced with the real unmediated situation of smallpox. Although there are preventive measures like variolation and vaccination, there is no cure for smallpox, even in the storehouse of modern medicine.[47] Culture mediates between the terror of a deadly disease and its all-too-realistic symptoms. The cultural response involves denial and innovation. As Clifford Geertz suggests, the religious response for people faced with the "dumb senselessness of intense or inexorable pain" is "to deny that there are inexplicable events," to formulate "by means of symbols . . . an image of the world which will account for, and even celebrate" such deadly incomprehensibles.[48] Thus, helplessness is denied by rites designed to carry the malady away. One denies the impurity of this biological irruption by making it as pure as possible. In her presence, one denies—by making her a goddess —that one sees Mother Pox at base as like other angry, envious, retaliating barren women.

Faced with a hopeless, destructive situation, people search for cultural images to fit it, just as the French handyman (*bricoleur*) patches and repairs with whatever comes to mind.[49] Just as Australian aborigines use the species and aspects of nature "to think with" in their totemism,[50] so north Indian villagers use aspects of the female role to fit the nature of smallpox. They think about the cure for pox and attempt to control it by using the principles of the Hindu pollution concept. They appease the power of the disease just as they appease human powers—the power of those in high dominant caste or official position—by granting it high status—here, the status of a goddess, with all the perquisites thereof. Throughout Indian history those with military might were given high caste rank as *Kshatriyas*, second only to Brahmans.[51] The granting to pox of the high status of goddess is consistent with a Hindu pattern of satisfying powerful beings by giving them high rank.

The smallpox goddess rites are imaginative solutions, formulated and integrated into a broader religious frame involving the same general principles—the image of women as energetic, powerful, disturbing, and dangerous; the principle of purity and pollution; the personification of power in gods. With such integration, the rites take on a "persuasive authority,"[52] as they are validated by a consensus of the people in meeting the crisis of smallpox. An incomprehensible, helpless, hopeless situation—the chaos that is a case of smallpox—is now manageable.

# Notes

1. I owe thanks to Russell Reid for references on the epidemiology of smallpox, and to A. N. Srivastava, Rae Michaels, Terry Prewitt, and Konstantin Kolenda, as well as the editor of this collection, James Preston, for reading drafts of this article and making helpful suggestions for its improvement.

2. I conducted ethnographic fieldwork in Khalapur village between October 1954 and June 1956, working closely with untouchable Sweepers, so that the data presented here are drawn from their reports. I have also used field data collected by Jack Planalp, Leigh Minturn, J. Michael Mahar, Usha Bhagat, Saubhagya Taneja, and R. Prakash Rao. The beliefs and ideas about smallpox described here are held generally in Khalapur. See Hitchcock, "The Martial Rajput"; and Minturn and Hitchcock, *The Rajputs of Khalapur*.

3. Kolenda, "Relations of a Bhangi Cult."

4. Although there is some suggestion that elsewhere Hindu villagers see Shitala as a manifestation of Kali or Durga (consort of the great Hindu god, Shiva), this is not the case in Khalapur. See Freed and Freed, "Two Mother Goddess Ceremonies." For a similar hierarchy of gods in another north Indian village see Wadley, *Shakti*.

5. See Sharma, "Village Hinduism"; Dumont, *Hierarchy and Marriage Alliance*; and Harper, "A Hindu Village Pantheon."

6. See Geertz, "Thick Description."

7. Fischer, "Interpretive Anthropology," p. 403.

8. Lévi-Strauss, *The Savage Mind*, p. 9.

9. Mother Pox is universal in India, most often being called Shitala ("The Cool One") in north India and Mariamman ("Mother of Death or Rain") in south India. See Monier-Williams, *Brahmanism and Hinduism*. In south India, Mariamman is commonly a village guardian. See Dumont, "A Folk Deity of Tamil Nad"; Harper, "Fear and the Status of Women"; Bean, "Meanings of *amma*"; and Beck, "Colour and Heat." As a guardian and a pox deity, she has both a benevolent and a malevolent aspect. Her benevolence is lacking in Khalapur, because other gods and goddesses—such as Bhumiya and Dharti Mata—are benevolent. Nor is the Pox Mother balanced with or married to a male deity, as Dumont described for a south Indian village ("A Folk Deity of Tamil Nad").

10. Bowen, *Return to Laughter*, pp. 244–50.

11. Children are not the only victims of smallpox. However, according to an epidemiologist, "In densely populated areas where smallpox is still endemic and primary vaccination does not cover a substantial proportion of infants, a large proportion of cases will occur among young children" (Deutschmann, "The Ecology of Small Pox," p. 8).

12. Dumont, *Homo Hierarchicus*.

13. See Beidelman, *The Jajmani System*; and Kolenda, "The Hindu Jajmani System."

14. Dumont, *Hierarchy and Marriage Alliance*, p. 30.

15. Wadley, *Shakti*, p. 182.

16. Sharma, "Village Hinduism," p. 18.

17. Carstairs, *The Twice-Born*, p. 94.

18. Ishwaran reports that in a Karnataka village a smallpox epidemic was "regarded as a sign of the sinfulness of the entire community," and that to these villagers "all diseases are essentially sinful" (*Shivpura*, p. 104).

19. For a more detailed description of the annual worship of Shitala among village women in north India see Freed and Freed, "Two Mother Goddess Ceremonies," pp. 262–68.

20. Beck also speaks of a watery branch used for cooling the smallpox victim in western Tamilnadu, south India ("Colour and Heat," pp. 559, 561).

21. Also see Babb, *The Divine Hierarchy*, p. 73.

22. Khalapur villagers say that the *nim* tree is effective against the shadow because it is bitter. Babb describes the leaves of the *nim* tree as "proverbially cold" (*The Divine Hierarchy*, p. 139). In Bengal branches of *nim* leaves are hung over the door of the house of a smallpox victim so passersby can pay respect to Shitala (Bang, "Current Concepts of the Smallpox Goddess," p. 84). In south India the color green is considered to be "cool," and the green substances used in rituals are primarily leafy branches (Beck, "Colour and Heat," pp. 559, 561).

23. Also see Monier-Williams, *Brahmanism and Hinduism*, p. 228; Carstairs, *The Twice-Born*, p. 83; Freed and Freed, "Two Mother Goddess Ceremonies," p. 248; Bang, "Current Concepts of the Smallpox Goddess," p. 83; and Babb, *The Divine Hierarchy*, pp. 129, 227.

24. Babb, *The Divine Hierarchy*, p. 33.
25. Also see Wadley, *Shakti*, pp. 145, 146.
26. Also see Freed and Freed, "Two Mother Goddess Ceremonies," p. 267.
27. Sharma, "Village Hinduism," pp. 12–17.
28. Dumont, *Homo Hierarchicus*, p. 61.
29. Stevenson, "Status Evaluation."
30. Orenstein, "Hindu Sacred Law"; Stevenson, "Status Evaluation."
31. Also see Blunt, *Caste System of Northern India*, p. 99.
32. Orenstein, "Hindu Sacred Law," p. 28. Samvarta, Yama, and Ushanas are legal authorities; Chandalas are untouchables.
33. See Beck, "Colour and Heat"; Babb, "Marriage and Malevolence," pp. 141, 143, 150, and *The Divine Hierarchy*, pp. 222–26; Wadley, *Shakti*, pp. 26–38, 121; and Bean, "Meanings of *amma*," pp. 323, 326.
34. Dumont, "World Renunciation," p. 39.
35. Basham, *The Wonder That Was India*, p. 316.
36. Babb (*The Divine Hierarchy*, p. 76) and Bean ("Meanings of *amma*," pp. 325–37) refer to the importance of childbearing for the status of Indian women.
37. On the evil eye in India, see Maloney, *The Evil Eye*.
38. For other references to *chuRails* see Wadley, *Shakti*, p. 55; Babb, "Marriage and Malevolence," p. 144; and Monier-Williams, *Brahmanism and Hinduism*, p. 229.
39. See Kolenda, "Religious Anxiety," p. 76.
40. Babb, *The Divine Hierarchy*, pp. 175, 176.
41. Beck, "Colour and Heat," pp. 553–63.
42. Zimmer, *Philosophies of India*, p. 296.
43. Bharati, *The Tantric Tradition*, p. 216.
44. Opler, "The Themal Approach," p. 221.
45. Carstairs, *The Twice-Born*, pp. 156, 157.
46. Harper, "Fear and the Status of Women."
47. Henderson, "The Eradication of Smallpox."
48. Geertz, "Religion as a Cultural System," p. 108.
49. Lévi-Strauss, *The Savage Mind*, pp. 16–22.
50. Lévi-Strauss, *Totemism*.
51. See Kolenda, *Caste in Contemporary India*; and Srinivas, "Mobility in the Caste System."
52. Geertz, "Religion as a Cultural System," p. 112.

# Bibliography

Babb, Lawrence A. *The Divine Hierarchy: Popular Hinduism in Central India*. New York: Columbia University Press, 1975.

————. "Marriage and Malevolence: The Uses of Sexual Opposition in a Hindu Pantheon." *Ethnology* 9 (1970): 137–48.

Bang, B. G. "Current Concepts of the Smallpox Goddess Sitala in Parts of West Bengal." *Man in India* 53 (1973): 79–104.

Basham, A. L. *The Wonder That Was India*. New York: Grove Press, 1954.

Bean, Susan S. "Referential and Indexical Meanings of *amma* in Kannada: Mother, Woman, Goddess, Pox and Help!" *Journal of Anthropological Research* 31 (1975): 313–30.

Beck, Brenda. "Colour and Heat in South Indian Ritual." *Man* 4 (1969): 553–72.

Beidelman, Thomas O. *A Comparative Analysis of the Jajmani System*. Locust Valley, N.Y.: J. J. Augustin, Publisher, 1959.

Bharati, Agehananda. *The Tantric Tradition*. London: Rider and Co., 1965.

Blunt, E. A. H. *The Caste System of Northern India*. Delhi: S. Chand and Co., 1931.

Bowen, Elenore Smith. *Return to Laughter*. Garden City, N.Y.: Doubleday, 1964.

Carstairs, G. M. *The Twice-Born: A Study of a Community of High Caste Hindus*. London: Hogarth Press, 1957.

Crooke, William. *Religion and Folklore of Northern India*. London: Oxford University Press, 1926.

Deutschmann, Z. "The Ecology of Smallpox." In *Studies in Disease Ecology*, edited by M. May, pp. 1–13. New York: Hafner Publishing Co., 1961.

Dumont, Louis. *Hierarchy and Marriage Alliance in South Indian Kinship*. London: Occasional Papers of the Royal Anthropological Institute, no. 12, 1957.

————. "A Structural Definition of a Folk Deity of Tamil Nad: Aiyanar, the Lord." In *Religion/Politics and History in India*, edited by Louis Dumont, pp. 20–32. The Hague: Mouton Publishers, 1970.

————. *Homo Hierarchicus: An Essay on the Caste System*. Chicago: University of Chicago Press, 1970.

————. "World Renunciation in Indian Religions." In *Religion/Politics and History in India*, edited by Louis Dumont, pp. 33–60. The Hague: Mouton Publishers, 1970.

Fischer, Michael. "Interpretive Anthropology." *Reviews in Anthropology* 4 (1977): 391–404.

Freed, Ruth S., and Freed, Stanley A. "Two Mother Goddess Ceremonies of Delhi State in the Great and Little Traditions." *Southwestern Journal of Anthropology* 18 (1962): 246–77.

Geertz, Clifford. "Religion as a Cultural System." In Clifford Geertz, *The Interpretation of Cultures*, pp. 87–125. New York: Basic Books, 1973.

————. "Thick Description: Toward an Interpretive Theory of Culture." In Clifford Geertz, *The Interpretation of Cultures*, pp. 3–30. New York: Basic Books, 1973.

Harper, Edward B. "Fear and the Status of Women." *Southwestern Journal of*

*Anthropology* 25 (1969): 81–95.

———. "A Hindu Village Pantheon." *Southwestern Journal of Anthropology* 15 (1959): 227–34.

———. "Ritual Pollution as an Integrator of Caste and Religion." In *Religion in South Asia*, edited by Edward Harper, pp. 151–96. Seattle: University of Washington Press, 1964.

Henderson, Donald A. "The Eradication of Smallpox." *Scientific American* 235 (1976): 25–33.

Hitchcock, John T. "The Idea of the Martial Rajput." *Journal of American Folklore* 71 (1958): 11–31.

Hutton, J. H. *Caste in India*. 4th ed. London: Oxford University Press, 1963.

Ishwaran, K. *Shivpura*. London: Routledge and Kegan Paul, 1968.

Khare, R. S. "Folk Medicine in a North Indian Village." *Human Organization* 22 (1963): 11–31.

Kolenda, Pauline. *Caste in Contemporary India: Beyond Organic Solidarity*. Menlo Park, Calif.: Benjamin/Cummings Publishers, 1978.

———. "The Functional Relations of a Bhangi Cult." *Anthropologist*. Special vol. edited by S. C. Tiwari (Delhi University, Department of Anthropology). 2 (1968): 22–35.

———. "Religious Anxiety and Hindu Fate." In *Religion in South Asia*, edited by Edward Harper, pp. 71–81. Seattle: University of Washington Press, 1964.

———. "Toward a Model of the Hindu Jajmani System." *Human Organization* 22 (1963): 11–31.

Lévi-Strauss, Claude. *The Savage Mind*. Chicago: University of Chicago Press, 1966.

———. *Totemism*. Boston: Beacon Press, 1963.

Mahar, Pauline. "A Multiple-Scaling Technique for Caste Ranking." *Man in India* 39 (1958): 127–47.

Maloney, Clarence, ed. *The Evil Eye*. New York: Columbia University Press, 1976.

Minturn, Leigh, and Hitchcock, John T. *The Rajputs of Khalapur, India*. New York: John Wiley and Sons, 1966.

Monier-Williams, Monier. *Brahmanism and Hinduism*. London: John Murray, 1887.

O'Malley, L. S. S. *Popular Hinduism: The Religion of the Masses*. Cambridge: Cambridge University Press, 1933.

Opler, Morris E. "The Themal Approach in Cultural Anthropology and Its Application to North Indian Data." *Southwestern Journal of Anthropology* 24 (1968): 215–27.

Orenstein, Henry. "Logical Congruence in Hindu Sacred Law: Another Interpretation." *Contributions to Indian Sociology* 4 (1970): 22–35.

Sharma, Ursula M. "The Problem of Village Hinduism: 'Fragmentation' and Integration." *Contributions to Indian Sociology* 4 (1970): 1–21.

Srinivas, M. N. "Mobility in the Caste System." In *Structure and Change in*

*Indian Society*, edited by Milton Singer and Bernard Cohn, pp. 189–200. Chicago: Aldine Publishers, 1968.

Stevenson, H. N. C. "Status Evaluation in the Hindu Caste System." *Journal of the Royal Anthropological Institute* 4 (1954): 45–65.

Wadley, Susan Snow. *Shakti*. Series in Social, Cultural, and Linguistic Anthropology, no. 2. Chicago: University of Chicago, 1975.

Wilkins, W. J. *Hindu Mythology*. Calcutta: Rupa and Co., 1975.

Wiser, William. *The Hindu Jajmani System*. Lucknow: Lucknow Publishing House, 1936.

Zimmer, Heinrich. *Myths and Symbols in Indian Art and Civilization*. Edited by Joseph Campbell. New York: Harper and Row, 1946.

———. *Philosophies of India*. New York: Meridian Books, 1956.

# 12

## The Milk Overflowing Ceremony in Sri Lanka

### by A. J. Weeramunda

One of the most pervasive rites in the villages of Sri Lanka is the milk overflowing ceremony (*kiri ithirilla*) performed to avert illness or bring good fortune to villagers. In its most elementary form the ceremony involves the boiling of coconut milk in an earthen pot until it begins to overflow. An elaborate version of this rite is performed in Mulgama, a single-caste, Buddhist village in Sri Lanka's Western Province.[1]

The milk overflowing ceremony is a form of mother worship that centers on a symbol, milk, rather than on a specific goddess. Pattini, who is the sole female divinity in the pantheon of Sinhalese villagers, is only remotely connected with the ceremony. This may be because she lacks the nurturant and maternal attributes of most goddesses found elsewhere in South Asia, such as Shitala in India. Sinhalese villagers do not invoke Pattini to make barren women fertile or to bring desired sons. Through special ceremonies (*madu*), villagers appease the anger of the goddess, which is manifested in the form of disease and drought. Folk mythology portrays Pattini as a defeminized goddess who aspires to become a man in a future birth. It is thus suggested here that mother worship in rural Sinhalese society takes the symbolic form of nurturance rather than the typical personification of this theme found in other parts of the world. This view is substantiated by an examination of both the secular and the ritual meanings that Sinhalese villagers attach to milk.

29. Boiling milk in the *kiri ithirilla* ceremony.
(*Photograph by A. J. Weeramunda*)

## Symbol and Goddess

The symbol of milk and the goddess Pattini stand for opposing sets of meanings in Sinhalese folk ideology. This opposition may stem from the fact that worship of the goddess is of foreign origin.[2] In contrast, the rites and beliefs surrounding the efficacious qualities of milk are indigenous to rural Sri Lanka. This is evidenced by the wide variety of cultural contexts in which milk is featured.

In the kinship ideology of the Sinhalese people milk symbolizes the bond between mother and child.[3] Milk is the mother's blood, which has been transformed by her body heat as she suckles the child. Milk symbolizes warmth, nurturance, and security. It is similar to semen, which is the father's blood transformed during sexual intercourse. However, though blood is changed by each parent, milk and semen have radically different cultural attributes. In the Sinhalese folk taxonomy, semen possesses properties present in "hot foods," such as beef and mangoes. It is believed that an excessive intake of either "hot" or "cold" foods causes a loss of equilibrium in the human body that results in disease. Villagers do not consider mother's milk to be either hot or cold; it thus symbolizes bodily equilibrium. Rice, cow milk, and coconut milk used in the milk overflowing ceremony are classified as neutral foods.

Kinship relations reveal the crucial interplay between these symbols of maternity and the inheritance of property. Ideally, a child inherits equally from both parents, despite the fact that he may live outside his village of birth. However, because the village is organized along lines of patrilineal inheritance, women generally leave to take up residence in the villages of their husbands. Thus, local women who marry leave their rightful shares of paternal property in their natal villages. This means that a man may inherit land in his mother's village of birth, but never be able to use it because it will remain in the hands of his mother's brothers. Despite the ideal of equal inheritance from both sides of the family, a man rarely uses the property he inherits from his mother.

Maternal inheritance, symbolized by mother's milk, operates at another level to tie together groups of kin located in different villages. Though the inheritance of property tends to be governed by patrilineal relations that isolate villages from one another, maternal ties represent a more enduring bond, which links them together. Through cross-cousin marriage, which is the ideal marriage among Sinhalese, a man is able to claim some of the wealth from his mother's side of the family.[4] Marriage ties are, therefore, a means of extending one's links to other villages. In this way, a villager is able to claim his portion of the harvest of his maternal kin as compensation for his mother's share in her parental estate. Another way of recreating this bond is for a man to send his own children to be cared for or adopted by his maternal kin.

Mother's milk also relates to the Sinhalese classification of flora. There is a category known as "milk trees" (*kiri gas*), so termed because they exude a milky sap when their bark is pierced. Members of this category include the peepul (*bo*), ironwood (*na*), banyan (*nuga*), and jak (*kos*) trees.[5] Besides giving ample shade to the weary traveler, these trees occupy an important place in ritual and religious symbolism. Villagers regard their milky sap as symbolic of mother's milk. The peepul is sacred to Buddhists, as it is the tree under which Gautama Buddha attained enlightenment. Ironwood and banyan trees have also been associated with the worship of nature goddesses among the ancient Sinhalese.[6] Village curers use leaves of the jak tree to hold offerings of chicken blood to appease the wrath of demons and other impure spirits. In all these ritual contexts, one finds the identification of milk with an all-encompassing and protective principle.

Milk is also present in many other Sinhalese ceremonies as an ingredient in the basic ritual meal. It may be recalled that both coconut milk and rice are neutral foods like mother's milk. The milk rice consumed by villagers is associated with ideas of nurturance. For example, village ceremonies for propitiating the goddess Pattini end with an event known as "the donation of food to the gods" (*deviyange dane*). During this rite, members of different castes, both high and low, participate by sitting together at the same level to share milk rice, sweets, and fruits. Gananath Obeyesekere has shown how this commensal meal represents a horizontal, unifying principle that counteracts the divisive, vertical relations among castes.[7] A ritual widely practiced in the village of Mulgama is the "donation of food to the milk mothers" (*kiri ammale dane*). In the ceremony, each household offers milk rice to a group of seven women who have given birth to children. Villagers regard this as a highly meritorious act that can increase the material well-being of a household. Finally, all auspicious events, such as the celebration of the Sinhala New Year, feature the preparation and eating of milk rice by household members.

The goddess Pattini stands in sharp contrast to the ideas of nurturance attached to mother's milk. There are two reasons for this. In the first place, Pattini shares certain aggressive characteristics with her Indian counterparts, the goddesses Kali and Durga. These include a vindictive quality causing the goddess to express herself through calamities affecting village society as a whole. Another feature of Pattini is her Buddhist nature. As a "Buddhicized goddess," she is committed to the goals and ideals of a Buddhist ascetic. Sinhalese myth pictures her meditating on a barren hill, aspiring to be reborn as a male in order to achieve Buddhahood. A female cannot attain this state in Buddhist theology. Pattini's asceticism is also evident in her relationship with her consort. Whenever sexual desires arose in him, she would surround herself with a wall of fire and force him to turn to prostitutes for release. Finally, the opposition between the non-maternal goddess and the nurturant symbol of milk is clearly brought out in Pattini's life history. When her consort, Palanga (an Indian prince), was put to death by royal decree because of accusations that he had stolen an ankle bracelet, Pattini had the king's city burned to ashes. She accomplished this by casting her left breast to the ground. Thus, unlike mothers' breasts, which nurture and sustain life, Pattini's breasts create fire and destruction.

## Milk as Mythical Charter

In the myth providing the charter for the milk overflowing ceremony, milk symbolizes an egalitarian principle that transcends social hierarchy. This myth is concerned with a god called Mangara who is capable of either causing or curing cattle diseases. The myth also explores the ways in which the social order can dissolve into chaos and provides a method to reestablish proper harmony. The theme of order is illustrated at the beginning of the narrative as a harmonious relationship between man and animal, both equally sharing a common resource. Chaos results from a violation of this arrangement, which brings about "pollution" in the form of bloodshed and death. The restoration of order takes place when people heat blood and change it into milk. The myth was narrated as follows by a man from the village of Mulgama.

> A certain king of the city of Kitalvara (in India) owned many buffaloes. One buffalo cow shared its teats equally with the king's infant son and her own calf. One day the prince took all the cow's milk for himself, at which the calf became very angry with the prince.
>
> Years later when the calf died, it was reborn because of its hatred as a spirit (*gevalaya*). It went to Sri Lanka and took up residence in a golden banyan tree where hung a gigantic golden honeycomb. When the prince died, he was reborn in another palace in the province of Maya (in India). The court astrologers predicted at the birth of the prince that he would be gored to death by a buffalo in his nineteenth year. The prince did not know of this prediction. On reaching this age, he decided to go to Sri Lanka with a large retinue.

After they landed on the island, it was decided to leave two men at the landing place while the rest explored the interior. Soon they came upon the golden banyan tree and seeing the gigantic honeycomb, attacked it with their weapons, opened it, and ate the honey. This made the spirit in the tree furious at the prince.

In revenge, the spirit took possession of a wild buffalo and gored the prince and his men to death. Only the two men left behind were unharmed.

After waiting some time, the two men went in search of the prince and coming upon the gory scene, they wept. Sakra, king of the gods, heard the weeping of the two men and appeared as a hermit who instructed them to perform a milk overflowing ceremony in honor of the Sun God and to sprinkle the milk on the dead. Having no utensils for this rite, the two men caught and killed the spirit-possessed buffalo. They used different parts of the buffalo to construct an altar; its skull served as a pot and its blood was used as the liquid to be heated. They then searched for turmeric (*kaha*), which could purify anything that had been polluted.[8] They found a turmeric plot belonging to the goddess Pattini, who denied them entry because they had come in contact with the pollution of death. They took the turmeric by force, and the "contaminated" plot became infested with worms.[9]

Consequently, the two men performed the milk overflowing ceremony. After heating it, the blood was changed into milk; this they sprinkled on the dead men and the remains of the buffalo. The prince, his men, and the buffalo arose as if they'd merely been sleeping.

## Myth and Social Structure

The mythical transformation of blood into milk, of pollution into purity, and of death into life provides the basis for the villager's belief in the efficacious qualities of the milk overflowing ceremony. The efficacy of symbol and ceremony are also tied to the fact that they portray a world order that does not exist in reality. The myth portrays this order as a harmonious coexistence among beings who enjoy a common resource equally. The actual social order is characterized by a system of hierarchic relations governing kinship and property.

Mulgama is an agricultural village of about two thousand people. Although they are all of the same caste and religion, there has developed considerable heterogeneity in kinship status among them. Roughly three categories of persons make up the village. First there are the "citizens" (*game minissu*), who trace their patrilineal descent to Mulgama's founding father, Loku Appu. They indicate this by prefixing Loku Appu's surname to their personal names. Although citizens comprise only 10 percent of the total population, they hold the highest rank and their claim to the use of village land is superior to all others. The second level in the social hierarchy is the "naturalized citizens" (my term), who are descendents of men who married women from Loku Appu's village and settled down in it. They also attach the surname of Loku Appu to their own names. They constitute 40 percent of the total population and are considered inferior to "citizens" because they trace their lineage through women. This hierarchical theme rests on a cultural assumption that patrilineal ties are superior to matrilineal ties; it is thus more prestigious to derive residence and property rights through fathers than through mothers. The remaining 50 percent of the population are called "outsiders" (*pita minissu*); they are relatives by marriage of either real or naturalized citizens, but they have not adopted the surname of Loku Appu. They form the lowest level in this kinship hierarchy.

As the increasing population pressures of Mulgama limit its natural resources, some citizens have taken advantage of their position in the hierarchy to redistribute the land unequally among themselves, naturalized citizens, and outsiders. There is no judicial body within the village to protect the property rights of the dispossessed villagers, and few have the cash to seek legal assistance elsewhere. Afflicted villagers express their conflict in ideological terms, stating that they are the victims of sorcery committed by unknown relatives, the evil influences of spirits of the dead, and the anger of the gods.

The milk overflowing ceremony can be interpreted as a ritual compensation for this inequality. First, milk, as symbolic of the nurturant mother, stands for the matrilineal ties through which naturalized citizens and outsiders have usually inherited land. In essence, kinship mothers have given them land in much the same way as a mother nourishes her child with milk. Ritually, the ceremony is a reaffirmation of these ties. Secondly, the ritual mother is neutral, in comparison to the inferior status of matrilineal ties. Thirdly, in the ritual enactment of the prince and the calf who shared teats, there is a symbolic breakdown of this kinship hierarchy. For if milk is blood, then the prince and the calf are blood relations. Although the prince is actually an adopted child of the buffalo cow, he and the calf obtain sustenance from the same source equally in much the same way as villagers ideally share land. Finally, if this balance is lost, it will be restored at a later time in accordance with the Buddhist concept of Karma. Thus, the prince and the calf can right the imbalance in subsequent births. This would apply particularly to those villagers who have lost their property rights.

## The Ceremony

In 1972 a special milk overflowing ceremony was performed at the home of a man named Karthelis, a naturalized citizen whose mother inherited land in the village of Mulgama. Karthelis's mother gave this land as dowry to her daughter, leaving her son only a small portion of garden land for his residence. The dowry in land was later sold to the village headman despite Karthelis's attempts to buy it. Thus, Karthelis felt that he and his family were deprived of a means of livelihood because of his mother's actions.

The milk overflowing ceremony was held in connection with a serious illness. It seems that Karthelis had gone to bathe in the river, where he claimed to have seen a human corpse floating downstream in a bamboo receptacle containing offerings to demons. Villagers living upstream had cast the receptacle into the river, which is the custom for disposing of offerings of this kind. When Karthelis returned home he developed a high fever. His concerned family rushed him to a local hospital. Because the doctors were unable to help, the family summoned a village exorcist, who performed the standard cure of tying charmed threads on the sick man.[10] Karthelis recovered soon thereafter. The exorcist had advised the family to perform an elaborate version of the milk overflowing ceremony as an expression of gratitude to the supernaturals, including the gods, demons, and spirits of the dead whose aid he had solicited during the preliminary curing rite.

The milk overflowing ceremony was only the final episode in a more complex ritual known as the *Gopalu Samayama*, which took place in the courtyard of the home of Karthelis. The exorcists performing the ritual had constructed various altars for the supernaturals who were invoked. First, through mime, dramatic dialogue, and song, they enacted the various episodes of the milk myth, including the voyage of the prince, the discovery of the banyan tree, the eating of the honeycomb, the attack of the buffalo, and the slaughter of the prince and his retinue. The milk overflowing ceremony began as a dramatization of the mythical event by which the prince and retinue were raised from the dead.

In contrast to the theatricality of the major portion of the ritual, the chief exorcist performed the milk overflowing ceremony in simple and subdued tones. He brought an image of the buffalo in front of Karthelis and placed a small wooden board on it. Then he piled some fresh earth on the board, leveled the earth, and made a fireplace with three stones. Next, an earthen pot containing coconut milk was placed on the stones and lit from beneath. While the milk heated, the exorcist recited the myth of the god Mangara, including a description of his fetal development and birth. When the milk started boiling, a few pieces of turmeric were placed in the pot and the milk was allowed to overflow until it reached the flames beneath it. At this point, recitation stopped and milk was sprinkled on the altars of all the major deities. Then Karthelis was asked to be receptive to the benefits of the ceremony.

This rite derives power from the simplicity of its performance. It mobilizes a variety of meanings and values in one concrete symbol, milk. The heating symbolizes a transformation of mother's blood into nurturant milk. The act of allowing the milk to overflow the boundaries of the earthen pot signifies both its abundant nature and its power to overcome and transcend man-made definitions. Finally, the ceremony invokes the nurturant qualities of milk for humans and supernaturals, and signifies these qualities by the act of spreading the milk on the altars of the deities.

## Conclusion

I have focused on milk as a central symbol in a Sinhalese religious ceremony, examining the ceremony as a symbolic form of mother worship because it invokes the nurturance of human mothers as a means of bringing health and well-being to mankind. Health is understood among devotees to mean both the equilibrium of an individual's body and integrative relations among kinsmen who make up the body politic of the village community. Thus, at one end of a continuum of meaning, the symbol milk stands for the biological tie between mother and child and the sustenance a child obtains from this relationship. In the cultural scheme of Sinhalese rural society, mother's milk is the ultimate form of nourishment, because it has neither the hot nor the cold properties present in most other foods.

At the other end of the continuum, it stands for the integration of all kinsmen as human beings regardless of hierarchical relationships: it links kinsmen matrilaterally, biologically, and therefore equally.

Why is mother worship in rural Sinhalese society expressed as milk rather than through goddess imagery? First, this more abstract ceremony bridges several dimensions of mother symbolism quite effectively. Milk stands for the nurturant quality of the human mother, the sap of milk trees, matrilineal kinship bonds, bodily health, and an egalitarian principle underlying the very nature of human existence. Whereas the symbol of milk is rooted in social concerns, the goddess is removed from them. The ideals that the goddess Pattini represents are not those of villagers, but those of orthodox Buddhism, which advocates the liberation of the individual from the fetters of society. Pattini meditates upon a barren hill in the manner of a Buddhist ascetic. She represents not a mother, but a female striving to become a male in some future birth in order to achieve Buddhahood. She is unwilling to be "contaminated" by sexual intercourse with her consort or by the pollution of death and bloodshed, which are part of human living. When she does intervene in human affairs, it is as a punitive agent causing epidemics and drought.

Secondly, the values embodied in the symbol of milk are "positive," or psychologically reinforcing, when compared with the destructive nature of the goddess. Thus, ideas of nurturance, integral kin relations, equilibrium, and harmony associated with the symbol form an appropriate environment for curing and for symbolically integrating the disenfranchised individual into his society. In this sense, the milk overflowing ceremony is a special form of mother worship that stresses the life-sustaining attributes of human mothers rather than the emulation of Buddha reflected in the goddess.

Finally, this approach to mother worship has continued to be popular among Sinhalese villagers, whereas rituals in honor of the goddess are performed less frequently than they were at the turn of the century. This may be due to government-run health and vaccination programs, which have effectively eroded infectious diseases, the major source of power for the goddess Pattini. Through these programs villagers are beginning to understand the Western biological conception of disease.

The continued use of natural religious symbols, such as milk, does not necessarily imply a decline in the worship of all supernaturals among the Sinhalese villagers. Obeyesekere has examined how certain Sinhalese deities have assumed national importance, because large numbers of people seek their aid to fulfill needs that the secular political order cannot or does not satisfy.[11] However, it may be noted that the needs these deities fill are specific in nature, such as passing an examination, curing an illness, or obtaining a job or political position. The analysis of the milk overflowing ceremony reveals how a ritual symbol like milk meets needs of a different kind. In the state of alienation experienced by Karthelis, the need was for a principle that encompasses the individual and reintegrates him into society. Milk, as a symbol of mother worship, answers this need totally.

# Notes

1. The research on which this study is based was conducted from 1971 to 1972 while I was attached to the academic staff of the University of Sri Lanka, Peradeniya. I am grateful to several colleagues for their comments and criticisms in preparing this article. I thank, in particular, James Preston and Phillip Staniford for the direction they have given me. The responsibility for opinions expressed here is entirely mine.

2. The origin of Pattini is debatable. According to Nevill (*Sinhala Verse*) and Wirz (*Healing in Ceylon*), Pattini has had several incarnations, of which her south Indian birth is the final one. All her previous births took place in Sri Lanka. I emphasize her south Indian birth because this is the image by which she is presently worshiped in Sri Lanka. This cult was brought from south India to Sri Lanka by Gajabahu, a Sinhalese king who ruled from A.D. 174 to 196 (Raghavan, "The Pattini Cult").

3. Yalman, *Under the Bo Tree*.

4. In cross-cousin marriage a man marries his mother's brother's daughter or his father's sister's daughter. Only by marrying the former, however, will a man be able to claim his mother's inheritance in her natal village.

5. The botanical terms for these are *ficus, religiosa, messua ferrea, ficus benghalensis,* and *artocarpus intergritola,* respectively. It should be noted that not all milk-bearing trees are sacred. For example, rubber and breadfruit trees serve no ritual purpose. On the other hand, most sacred trees do not have practical uses, such as fruit or timber. The jack tree is an exception.

6. These trees were associated with the worship of Kiri Amma (literally, "Milk Mother"), a nature goddess of great antiquity no longer prevalent in Sri Lanka. It is quite likely that this goddess was replaced by the Pattini cult.

7. Obeyesekere, "Sinhalese Ritual."

8. Turmeric is a plant belonging to the ginger family. It is mixed in water and used in Sinhalese rituals as an agent of purification because it is believed to be a disinfectant. Powdered turmeric is used in the preparation of curries.

9. Although it is questionable how two humans could accomplish the defeat of a deity, perhaps the event symbolizes Pattini's loss of power in the

context of the milk overflowing ceremony.

10. Wirz, *Healing in Ceylon*, p. 83.

11. Obeyesekere, "Religious Symbolism."

## Bibliography

Nevill, Hugh. *Sinhala Verse*. Ceylon National Museums Manuscript Series, vol. 4. Colombo: Government Press, 1954.

Obeyesekere, Gananath. "Religious Symbolism and Political Change in Ceylon." In *The Two Wheels of the Dhamma: Essays on the Theravada Tradition in India and Ceylon*, edited by B. Smith, pp. 58–78. Chambersburg, Pa.: American Academy of Religious Studies, no. 3, 1972.

————. "The Structure of Sinhalese Ritual." *Ceylon Journal of Social and Historical Studies* 1 (1958): 192–202.

Raghavan, M. D. *The Pattini Cult as a Socio-religious Institution*. Ethnological Survey of Ceylon, no. 3. Colombo: The National Museum, 1951.

Wirz, Paul. *Exorcism and the Art of Healing in Ceylon*. Leiden: E. J. Brill, 1954.

Yalman, Nur. *Under the Bo Tree*. Berkeley: University of California Press, 1967.

# FOUR

The Divine Feminine
in Southeast Asia
and Africa

# 13

# Rangda the Witch
## by Philip Frick McKean

### Religion in the Republic of Indonesia

In the cultural multiplicity constituting the contemporary nation of Indonesia, a variety of religious expressions have been so intermingled and recombined that there now exists a paradigmatic form of religious pluralism. Yet the variety has not vitiated the strength of religion in Indonesia. As the Republic emerged from colonialism and entered the formative years of independence under President Sukarno (and beginning in 1966 under the "New Order" proclaimed by Suharto), the importance of religious belief and expression was regularly reiterated. The constitution is based on "Five Principles," one of which affirms "belief in Almighty God." Are there forms of worship in this young nation that emphasize the sacred power of the mother?

On the surface mother worship—that is, forms of ritual and religiosity connected with female forms and characteristics—is notably absent in modern Indonesia, particularly in the populous, garish, and bustling urban areas such as Jakarta. It is the *male* political leaders, military officers, and business tycoons who dominate in contemporary Indonesia; and it is the religious traditions in which masculine persons are believed to reveal the divine, namely, Islam and Christianity, that have come to dominate the formal conceptions of the sacred in most of the ancient islands of the Indies.

The religious forms that first gained official endorsement and recognition by Indonesia's Ministry of Religion were "world religions," such as Christianity and Islam, which had developed nationwide networks during the independence struggle and which claimed adherents in several population centers. In constructing a modern Indonesian state the efficiency, organization, and usefulness of all institutions have been stressed in every sector, from the agencies planning for economic development to the military and civil bureaucracies. There has been increasing insistence by the state on those values connected with the orderly, the reasonable, and the urbane. Scholars of religious change, following Max Weber's lead, have described this transformation as the "rationalization" of religion.[1] The movement toward such values in Indonesia has been documented, especially among Islamic reformers and urban Christians.[2] The efforts of Balinese intellectuals to formalize and disseminate widely the syncretic traditional religion of the island were spearheaded by a council of Hindu reformers, called the Parisada Hindu Dharma.[3] This council attempted during the 1960s to legitimize the ancient religious expressions of Hinduism and Buddhism and was rewarded through official recognition by the Ministry of Religion and the establishment of Hindu Dharma branches in every province of the nation.[4]

But along with the movement toward religious rationality and ecumenism in modern Indonesia goes a counter-trend. Participants adhere to a practice that is at once more ancient, parochial, and ritually celebrated than theologically defined. It is expressed in the *adat* or customary law of the outer islands of Sumatra, Sulawesi, and Kalimantan, and is seen in Java among traditional villagers performing the ritual feast called *slametan*.[5] In Bali the form of religion called "animism" (spirit worship) by early anthropologists is still found linked to the periodicity of the seasons, to the life cycle, and preeminently to the celebrations associated with the temple complex.[6] This autochthonous religion is intertwined with the spread of Hinduism and Buddhism. It finds expression in the cockfight and the *ketjak* performance (also known as the Monkey Dance), as well as in rites of passage such as the tooth filing of adolescents and funerals for the dead. One of the most dramatic enactments of the rituals to which Balinese continue to devote themselves is the confrontation between two powerful deities, Rangda and Barong. These masked characters seem to be the antithesis of the rationality that modern Indonesians embrace, for their appearance is marked by magic and sacrifice, trance and psychic convolution. In this article, I first describe the traditional rituals in which Rangda and Barong figure prominently, including the ways in which these rites have been transformed and employed by the Balinese tourist industry. Finally, I analyze why these particular cultural creations continue to speak to contemporary Balinese, as well as to other Indonesians and international visitors.[7]

## The Traditional Barong and Rangda

Descriptions of Rangda ("witch") and Barong ("dragon") are frequent in ethnologies about Bali.[8] But no verbal description can capture and communicate fully the sights and sounds, the movements and moods portrayed when the two characters appear in the midst of Balinese audiences. To eyes and ears trained in the West, the cast may seem stereotyped and the tale repetitive, but the performance has a force and power to turn observers into terrified, deeply moved believers in the uncanny, arcane wonder of the drama. What are the more significant attributes of Rangda and Barong as noted by ethnographers watching this drama in prerevolutionary Bali?

Barong is thought by some scholars to be linked to the Chinese dragons or to the class of "protective animals," such as lions; both are widely found in Southeast Asia, and so tracing Barong's history is difficult.[9] *Barong*, when used by Balinese, means *Barong keket*, or "lord of the forest." Barong appears with a massive, feather-covered body behind a wooden mask with prominent bulging eyes, an arched tail, and pointed ears. Beneath the "skin" two men dance, positioned fore and aft as in a circus horse. The "head dancer" operates his jaws, which are hinged to provide a champing sound. Mead writes vividly of Barong:

> The *barong* is a magnificent beast mask, worn by two men
> who give it a most engaging, lifelike quality, prancing with soft,
> tripping, carefully synchronized steps to maintain the four-footed
> illusion. The *barong* may be either white or black, his hair coat made
> of various kinds of vegetable fiber, or rarely of crow feathers
> specially sent by the gods. His great mask is of wood, with a
> moveable lower jaw . . . protruding round eyes painted "so as to
> live" as the people say. His legs—actually the legs of the men
> inside the mask, cut with the illusion perfectly maintained by the
> delicate pawing, the mincing prance of the dancers—are decked
> out in long striped trousers.
>
> The rare and most sacred *barong* can command offerings and
> entertainment from one village after another, on the strength of
> their power to heal and to consecrate holy water which brings
> cleanliness and blessing. Most *barongs*, although treated with
> reverence, are said by the people to be made for enjoyment.[10]

There are other kinds of Barongs, with faces of tigers, boars, and elephants, but the Barong keket is ubiquitous in southern Bali, and may be seen with his followers in dozens of villages during the annual celebration of Galungan. The dragon may never touch the ground, and so is always carried, suspended on poles, or hung from the temple roof. Barong is seen by the Balinese as a protecting and beneficent beast, warding off disease and magically induced plagues or misfortune. The dragon is always counterposed with Rangda (the witch), for between these two figures are enacted central motifs in Balinese cosmology and religion.

*Rangda* means "widow." She is associated with the death of her husband and death in general. Rangda is linked in the thought of Balinese, from university leaders to rice farmers, with the terrible and fearful power of divine origin. A Hindu deity, in this case Shiva, is manifested in an angry, destructive, and vengeful state through his consort Durga. Statues in Bali of the goddess Durga have an appearance closely corresponding to the masks of Rangda regularly seen in village drama—tangled black hair, long fingernails, pendulous breasts, hairy legs, flowing tongue between terrible fangs, protruding eyes, flames emanating from around her eyes and mouth to underscore her consuming, fiery passion. When Rangda is portrayed on a stage, she slowly emerges through a cloth curtain, showing herself first in the shaking of her unnaturally elongated fingernails. Then follows the grotesque face, half concealed by a white cloth held in one hand, embossed with magical signs and verses in archaic Balinese. Rangda is always danced by a man, for otherwise, said one village leader, "she would be too powerful, even for Barong to overcome, and might destroy all of Bali." Rangda leaps forward in awkward stylized bounds, looking left and right, shaking her white cloth, and emitting terrible shrieks of hysterical laughter, throwing her head and hands up and back until she is nearly doubled over backwards, as her unkempt hair sweeps the ground. In some dramatic sequences, a story entitled the *Tjalon Arang* is enacted. In this tale the witch represents a legendary woman in east Java who became angry at the refusal of the son of the royal house to court her beautiful daughter. Enraged by this slight, she received permission from the goddess Durga to destroy the land, and enlisted disciples (*sisias*) who learned her magic and brought pestilence on the kingdom, eating corpses and unleashing the power of lesser evil beings (*layaks*) on the populace. At last the king learned her secret and, through the wisdom and guile of a saintly mystic, was able to counteract the plagues and death.

When Barong appears on stage he exchanges taunts with Rangda and the two creatures move to opposite ends of the cleared stage. Then a group of men, followers of Barong, who are stripped to the

30. A scene from the Barong-Rangda performance for tourists.
Here Rangda the Witch is laughing while her helpers gather around.
*(Photographed in Batubulan, Bali, in 1971 by Philip F. McKean)*

waist and armed with Balinese daggers (*kris*), leap to their feet and
attempt to stab the witch. They approach her from the rear, but as she
swings to face them, they fall back, unable to force their daggers to
penetrate her. They retreat, and then advance when she turns away
from them. Again they fall back on the ground as she swings around
to gaze on them, until at last she leaves the arena. Then, in trance, the
men turn their daggers on themselves, stabbing at their chests in
paroxysms of leaping, grunting, and screaming until they are dis-
armed by their fellows who are not in a state of trance. Finally the
men are calmed by holy water sprinkled and incense wafted into their
faces by attending priests; meanwhile, Barong moves among them,
clattering his jaws in reassurance.[11]

These encounters between Barong and Rangda are scheduled at

night, and may last for several hours, with many auxiliary dancing scenes, comic relief, and orchestra (gamelan) selections. In November 1970, a *Tjalon Arang* performance at the village of Pandjar, near suburban Sanglah (Denpasar), began at 10:00 P.M. and continued until 4:00 A.M. Elaborate preparations had been made at the site, with an enclosed "stage" walled off by bamboo, an entrance platform for Rangda rising 40 or 50 feet off to one side of a performance area in front of a temple, electric lights strung from a canopy of rattan and bamboo, and several hundred chairs arranged for spectators. Villagers were charged, Rp 20, 50, or 100 (5 to 25 cents), and as usual dozens of children lined the perimeter of the performance area. The tale of *Tjalon Arang* was interspersed with side plots of animals and demons, courtly intrigues, and priestly magic, so that when Rangda at last descended from her tower it was nearly dawn, and the children were sleeping. They all awoke when the followers of Barong went into trance and attacked Rangda. At this time others in the audience also went into trance, including several young women, an army officer, and an usher; after attempting to stab themselves with a *kris* they were calmed by a Barong who appeared quickly for a few minutes. They recovered their normal appearance after receiving holy water. The crowds went home as dawn lit the sky.

At the village of Kuta, located only three kilometers from the international airport and near a swimming beach popular among young tourists, the Barong and Rangda ceremonies were performed periodically during the 1970–71 rainy season (between December and April) when cholera had taken four lives in the vicinity. During this period the appearance of Rangda and Barong was a regular event, occurring nightly for several weeks. The performance was said to be for the purpose of exorcising disease-bearing spirits, and was produced on the main street of the village without special decorations, but with a small orchestra accompanying the dancers. The plot was stripped to its elemental structure. Rarely did persons other than the anticipated men (followers of Barong) fall into trance, and within two hours the ceremony was normally concluded. The area surrounding Kuta had become a popular low-cost residential area for young travelers from Australia, America, and Europe who often looked on, along with occasional tourists, but no effort was made to collect money or give tourists special places to view the ritual. They were simply spectators at the drama that had its own raison d'être according to the beliefs of the Balinese.

In March 1971 a new Barong had been fashioned at Side Karya, a village between Kuta and Denpasar. I was invited to attend the initial performance by friends who were playing in the orchestra. Early in the evening we gathered with townspeople around a clearing in front of the temple associated with death (*pura dalem*), which was decorated with a few banners of cloth and bamboo. The lengthy preliminaries included dancing by disciples of Rangda and Barong who were dressed in a variety of masks and costumes. Rangda arrived, danced briefly, then temporarily retired to the temple courtyard. Then it was Barong's turn; his mask had been carved of special wood, and the feathery covering was snowy white with shiny mirrors. Several teams of dancers began to move. Villagers debated which team had the proper characteristics of authenticity and liveliness (*hidup*) and therefore should have the privilege of performing in the future. The Barong danced for two hours, prancing and cavorting in a half-playful, half-fearsome manner, until all contestants had been offered an opportunity to allow themselves to be "entered" by Barong's spirit. This performance ended with only two persons entering trance, but at the close of the ceremony the temple priest began to sprinkle holy water not only on the entranced, but also on all the villagers. By that time it was midnight. Fellow spectators explained that it was a "successful" ritual, indicating pleasure that the new Barong was so full of spirit that it had brought beneficence to the place.

Along with these locally produced dramas of Barong and Rangda, the state-operated radio station in the city of Denpasar (Radio Republik Indonesia) had a well-known music and dance troupe that often performed the *Tjalon Arang*, including tours to surrounding villages and towns. One night during this period this group was at Bandjar Kadja, a hamlet in the village of Sesetan, just about 300 meters from our house. The stage for the performance had been set outside a small temple. Tickets were sold, attracting 2,500 persons from the neighboring villages. For five hours these "professional" dancers enacted the tale of *Tjalon Arang* with magnificent costumes and music. But the conclusion was rather anticlimactic, for Rangda made only a perfunctory appearance, as did Barong, and no one fell into trance. Our neighbors were somewhat disappointed and said that the actors were "without life" (*kurang hidup*), perhaps from too many performances or because proper offerings had not been made by the villagers or actors.

These descriptions indicate the variety and ubiquity of Barong and Rangda in their "natural" setting, and provide a basis for comparison as we turn to the tourist performances they have inspired.

## The Tourist Version of Rangda and Barong

*Singapadu*

In the village of Singapadu is the royal residence of an old man named Tjakorda Oka. He is the originator of the "tourist Barong" drama. In May 1971, Tjakorda Oka gathered with a dozen members of his family to describe how he happened to produce what has become one of the most famous performances viewed by visitors. Before 1930 the village had a resplendent Barong and especially sacred Rangda, famous for their magical religious power. Agents of the Dutch colonial government asked him, as a political leader of the group responsible for these symbols of the divine, to allow them to travel to the Paris Colonial Exposition in 1930, representing Balinese culture. He refused to allow them to go, but agreed to arrange for another set of images to be fabricated and for a troupe from the village to attend. Preparing for the trip included carving new masks and making costumes. But from the beginning, Tjakorda Oka said that he did not plan to have this Barong and Rangda sanctified by special offerings or treated with the awe appropriately expressed toward the sacred Barong and Rangda. He also wove into the dance a story from the Hindu epic *Mahabharata*, portraying how Dewi Kunti, the mother of the five Pandava brothers, tried to sacrifice her stepdaughter, but was herself killed. This suffering stepdaughter theme (*Kunti-yadnaya*) is recurrent in Bali. Tjakorda Oka said that he thought it would be understood by "foreigners" and would help them to see that evil, personified by Rangda, is universal, not found just in Bali.

The story was told by masked characters reciting speeches, posing, and miming as heroes, clowns, villains, and animals, in a style of drama known as *topeng*. The whole performance was introduced by two beautifully clad young girls dancing a *legong*, a classical dance normally seen in another context. The "tourist" drama reached a climax as Barong and Rangda confronted each other. Followers of Barong simulated entering trance, and were revived by a priest sprinkling holy water after they had attacked themselves with their *kris*.

Tjakorda Oka said that in the 1930s after the special troupe had returned from Paris, where they had made Bali "the most famous island in the world," they were often visited by tourists, and a few taxis brought tourists for weekly performances. This practice ceased during the Japanese occupation, and then resumed in the late 1940s. Sukarno brought international guests in the 1950s, and by 1970 the special troupe was performing four times a week with an average of

31. Rangda mask, shown with Tjakorda Oka, who developed the
program for tourists. This cultural innovator prepared the Barong
and Rangda performances for the Paris Exposition and for tourists
visiting Bali in the 1930s. *(Photograph by Philip F. McKean)*

two hundred spectators weekly. All performers came from the hamlet
of Bandjar Tunguan in the village of Singapadu, which included members of Tjakorda Oka's family. A total of fifty persons were actively
involved in the production: thirty gamelan musicians, ten *kris* dancers,
five leading actors, and five decorators. Each family unit in the hamlet
was represented, and proceeds from the performance—after about
half of the profits were set aside for temple repair, expansion, and
ceremonies for the hamlet inhabitants—were divided equally.

The sacred Rangda and Barong seldom appear in public ceremonies
during festivals now; they remain in the temple and receive offerings
(*sadjen*). Tjakorda Oka acknowledged that the trance dancers for the
"tourist Barong" do not enter real states of trance. However, these
same dancers often continue to go into trance when rituals at temple
ceremonies are held.

According to Tjakorda Oka and other members of his family, the presence of tourists is helpful and has had a good economic effect on the village. Not only does it provide cash income for members of the hamlet, but neighboring hamlets are able to make many sales of their carvings when tourists stop to see the dance. He estimated that there are 1,500 carvers in the village of Singapadu, at least one in every family, who seek to avoid the shopkeepers in the provincial capital of Denpasar and in the beach hotels because they pay much less for carvings.

## Batubulan

As in Singapadu, the Barong and Rangda performance in the village of Batubulan is also performed for tourists. It is held during the morning for approximately one hour, three times a week. One kilometer closer to Denpasar, the Batubulan group has an imposing temple (*pererepan*, or "place of keeping"), which was built in 1967 and was ceremonially dedicated to Barong and Rangda. I attended this performance several times with my family and with tourists or friends before I realized that one of the advanced students in anthropology at Udayana University was a native of Batubulan and that he often represented his family as an organizer and producer of the Barong performances. The student, Wayan Geria, kindly arranged for interviews with leaders of the group. From them I learned that there was, in the 1930s, an autochthonous Barong and Rangda who danced at the annual ceremony called Galungan and occasionally at local temple festivals. Tourists, on their way from the mountains began to watch; two or three sedans a week arrived, with about a dozen people. Sometimes the resident European artist Walter Spies would commission Barong and Rangda dances for his friends, making special offerings and giving sums of money to the hamlet. After interruption by the war and revolution, the villagers again performed for tourists in the 1950s; they had little success, however, because the performance at Singapadu was the favorite of Sukarno. Few tour agents asked the group from Batubulan to perform until 1967, when the Hotel Bali Beach and Nitour (the Indonesian National Tour Agency) requested them to give Barong and Rangda performances four times a week, in return for Rp 7,000 (about U.S. $20) for each performance. By 1971 the group was giving daily performances, but had parted company with the former tour agents, who would not agree to new contract terms. In 1971 the group received a base of Rp 7,000 for the first thirty-

five tourists, then half the profit over that base. Tickets were sold for
Rp 500 ($1.50), and the performers could usually earn Rp 10,000–
15,000 for each performance, even after one-quarter of the total income
was returned to guides and taxi drivers as a kickback (see Table 1).

Table 1 *Attendance and Income at the*
*Batubulan Tourist Performances of Barong and Rangda*

| Date | Number of Performances | Total Persons Paying Admission | Income (In Rupiah) to Hamlet |
|------|------------------------|-------------------------------|------------------------------|
| December 1970 | 18 | 947 | 205,930 |
| March 1971 | 17 | 912 | 195,200 |
| May 1971 | 28 | 718 | 216,000 |
| June 1971 | 28 | 632 | 164,000 |

Note: U.S. $1.00 = Rp 375.

The Batubulan performers consist of 110 family groups, each of
which sends a representative to prepare the grounds, make decorations, dance, or serve as a proxy. These 110 families come from
two complete hamlet (*bandjar*) groups: one from Bandjar Denjalan
(64 households participate) and one from Bandjar Batu (46 households); families from all the caste levels are represented. The leaders,
who are elected for a fixed term, serving three or four years at most,
do not receive more profit than any of the other family groups. Each
family was said to earn indirectly about Rp 80 daily for its presence, at
a time when the wages of a farmhand were Rp 50 and those of a
semiskilled laborer Rp 200 for a day's work. During 1970–71 this
income was made available to the two hamlets for five purposes: (1)
equipment and repairs needed for performances—costumes, chairs,
decorations; (2) loans to sick or poor families; (3) village temple festivals; (4) taxes for communal village development programs; and (5)
the purchase of goods for each participating family. Bicycles, at a cost
of about Rp 15,000 each (U.S. $40), were being purchased for each of
the 110 family groups during 1970 and 1971.
The leaders of the Sekeha Barong Dendjalan, as this corporate

group of 110 families from two hamlets calls itself, were concerned that performing daily was becoming too difficult for persons who had heavy responsibilities as farmers. The hamlets would be hard pressed to plant and harvest properly during those two normally busy seasons, and the production would be likely to drop. Then the families would have to use income from tourism to buy rice, and that would be bad—a sign to neighbors that they were lazy or stupid farmers. The leaders of the "tourist drama" insisted that a healthy Balinese adult should be caring for rice fields, his fighting cocks, and his musical, artistic, or ritual obligations, and invest only a minimum of his energies in tourist dramas. Yet the tension between desire for profits and an ideal life-style remained unresolved.

After the Barong and Rangda performance became popular with tourists at Batubulan, there was a diminished interest in using it for ritual occasions. When ceremonies were to be scheduled at the local temples, there were different performances because, it was said, the hamlet was understandably bored with Rangda and Barong, and did not want to have them for either entertainment or religious veneration. When once-sacred forms become commonplace and commercial, their power to transcend and transform human experience appears to be diminished. The Balinese, like the early Israelites, may find it impossible to become overly familiar with the sacred realm, discovering that the symbols of divine power cannot become items of commerce in everyday life without losing some of their authority. But because there are a variety of alternate symbols appropriate for worship, there is little danger that the Balinese will want for symbolic performances that they can consider sacred. If a form such as the Monkey Dance (*ketjak*) becomes commercialized in one village, then villagers may turn to *Tjalon Arang* for their temple festival, or vice versa. Yet where they have not been commercialized, the figures of Rangda and Barong remain in favor as symbolic portrayers of a religious belief in sharp contrast to the orderly and bureaucratic rationality sought elsewhere in modern Indonesia. Why this continues to be the case deserves analysis.

## Conclusion

I have shown that although Rangda and Barong have become popular among tourists, they have also remained central to indigenous Balinese temple festivals. If we are to understand why the ritual, now described by generations of ethnographers, retains its central place, we could turn to a number of explanations. Indeed, the history of explanations of the ceremony composes a kind of microhistory of ethnology, for they range from psychocultural to phenomenological. Tempting though it is to accept one or another, and then close off further thought about the ritual, I would claim that for full appreciation of Rangda and Barong, one analytical model alone cannot suffice; for as truly authentic symbols, they are greater than the conceptual frameworks analysts construct. Surely there is truth in viewing Rangda as the Great Mother, who can be compared to other harmful, devouring women, such as Medusa or Isis. Erich Neumann stokes these interpretive fires with such crosscultural observations as this:

> The open womb is the devouring symbol of the uroboric mother, especially when connected with phallic symbols. The gnashing mouth of the Medusa with its boar's tusks betrays these features most plainly, while the protruding tongue is obviously connected with the phallus. The snapping—i.e. castrating—womb appears as the jaws of hell and the serpents writhing around Medusa's head are not personalistic—pubic hairs—but aggressive phallic elements characterizing the fearful element of the uroboric womb.[12]

And there is also truth in John S. Lansing's phenomenological account of Barong as representing the playful or innocent, in contrast to the aged, corpselike and corpse-loving Rangda. Thus the Hindu categories of purity and pollution are enacted in the dance.[13] But along with these explanations there are at least two more that seem to go hand in hand with psychological and folk interpretations.

*The Ritual as an Economic Event*

In the villages of Batubulan and Singapadu there is evidence that the people are maximizing their cultural resources by attracting tourists. They are able to improve their hamlet buildings, distribute gifts and offerings, buy bicycles, and profit from other tourist-related activities (such as carving and vending), thereby bringing new cash into their pockets. The use of religion is, from the folk point of view, extremely functional, contributing to the growth and economic health of the community. Magic and music serve not only to honor the gods, but also to entertain paying guests. Ritual performance thus becomes a commodity, as surely as paintings by Wyeth are a commodity auctioned off in the galleries of New York, or the music of the Boston Symphony is sold at Tanglewood Concerts. Yet the Balinese do not want to become so specialized in this form of entrepreneurial petty capitalism that they lose their multiple connections to other endeavors, such as tending the rice fields, building temples, or participating in recreational clubs. If they maintain these diverse economic behaviors, they are not likely to become completely dependent on tourism, and become just a "culture factory" turning out dance, music, and the arts for international travelers. Complete "rationalization" of this religious ritual would encourage such a trend, but as we have noticed, there are countervailing values that balance such tendencies.

That Rangda and Barong do speak across the distances separating cultures is demonstrated by the reception they receive among tourists. Viewers easily accept the role of the widow, the mourning, vengeful, aging woman, as dangerous or evil. They find it easy to associate Rangda with remembrances of Halloween witches, or with the cackling crones in Macbeth mixing poisonous brews with magical potions intended to pollute and kill enemies. The analogies between Rangda and caricatured female followers of the Evil One in the Euro-American tradition are clear enough, and enable tourists as well as anthropologists and psychologists to appreciate Rangda and Barong as potent forces. They see the performance as a "good show," and applaud because of their enthusiasm for a dramatic confrontation that extends beyond the limits of Balinese culture. To appreciate Rangda and Barong the tourist does not require a consciousness that the "widow" may be a collective representation of the ambiguous role played by all mothers, who simultaneously give and then withdraw pleasure, as Margaret Mead's Freudian analysis of the drama would have it.[14] Nor does Rangda have to remind tourists that a widow may be symbolically paired with death by the demise of her lover-husband, or represent a combination of unfulfilled sexual desires and waning fertility. Though these may be implied in the figure of the deity, all the tourist needs to know is that an evil female is coming on stage, and is being met by opposition, in the form of Barong.

### The Ritual as a Paradigm of Contemporary Conflicts

As more new wealth, promise of economic development, and complicated national political forces become present in Bali, the hope of progress from the "planned economy" and "modern bureaucracy" become at once tantalizing and frustrating. In only a generation the

Balinese have experienced occupation by Japanese invaders, revolution, and then civil strife and massacre within the nation-state. The political process has not been one that conforms to the logical, ideal systems proclaimed in Jakarta. Rather, it has been full of intrigue, surprise, and guile, as factions have jockeyed for power: first one political party cooperates with another; then they turn against each other, as ideologies, personalities, and internal or external issues intervene to create a volatile mix within Indonesian political life. These experiences have engendered in Bali an atmosphere of order and fear, corruption and purity of motives, uncertainty about election processes but certainty about the increasing economic divisions between the few wealthy urbanites and the majority of poor farmers, laborers, and underemployed traders. Clifford Geertz expressed this political situation in Indonesia as follows:

> Organizing a cultural hodgepodge into a workable polity is more than a matter of inventing a promiscuous civil religion to blunt its variety. It required either the establishment of political institutions within which opposing groups can safely contend, or the elimination of all groups but one from the political stage. Neither of these, so far, has been more than marginally effected in Indonesia; the country has been as incapable of totalitarianism as it has of constitutionalism. Rather, almost every institution in the society— army, bureaucracy, court, university, press, party, religion, village —has been swept by great tremors of ideological passion which seems to have neither end nor direction.[15]

In the midst of such sociopolitical tension, such wavering of intention, such difficulties in managing to bring economic satisfaction to the multitudes, a ritual has been preserved expressing these profound contradictions. Rangda and Barong intentionally recreate a cosmic tension, which brings into vivid focus the conflicts known to exist among the groups that compose Balinese and Indonesian society. Rangda and Barong may be read not only as a paradigm of the classic antagonism between male and female, adult and young, good and evil, life and death, but also as an expression of the social tensions that become exacerbated as the old order is neither replaced nor removed. This tension is not, of course, restricted to Indonesia alone; conflicts between generations and classes, male and female roles, and parties and ethnic associations may be found in all nations moving away from traditional structures of band, tribe, or feudal organization.[16] In Bali, where the move into the modern nation-state is recent and abrupt, where the traditional culture has been so firmly rooted, and where the promise of modernization is immediately obvious through the presence of automobiles, hotels, and airplanes constructed to serve tourists, the conflicts are immense as well as intense. Whenever Barong and Rangda dance they reflect an accurate picture of political, economic, and social life experienced by a Balinese audience, and provide a structure—rational beyond the limits of logic—which serves to make the conflict manageable, if not terminal. Thus the ritual continues and, in surviving, may make more sense than the shallow planning of bureaucrats and managers. The mother who is also widow, the one who represents the beginning and end of fertility and of life, dances on. Such is the power of religion to plumb the reality of human existence and to surprise even social scientists by the accuracy of its statement about the human condition—composed of both hope and fear, suffering and affection, boredom and ecstasy, life and death, male and female.

## Notes

1. See Weber, *The Protestant Ethic*; and Gerth and Mills, *From Max Weber*.
2. See Geertz, *Peddlers and Princes*; Peacock, "Muslim Reform in Indonesia"; and Simatupang, *Christian Service*.
3. Geertz, "Internal Conversion."
4. *Proceedings and Decisions of the II Congress*.
5. See Geertz, *The Religion of Java*; and Jay, *Javanese Villagers*.
6. For detailed descriptions of Balinese rituals, see Goris, *Bali*; Swellengrebel, *Bali*; Belo, *Traditional Balinese Culture*; Geertz, *The Interpretation of Cultures* (especially the articles entitled "Person, Time and Conduct in Bali" and "Deep Play: Notes on the Balinese Cockfight"); Hooykaas, *Agama Tirtha*; McKean, "From Purity to Pollution?"; and Zoete and Spies, *Dance and Drama*.
7. The research for this paper was conducted during 1970 and 1971 with the support of NIMH Training Fellowship #3 FO1 MH47221-0151, CUAN U.S. Department of Health, Education and Welfare, administered by Brown University. Writing was encouraged by a Hampshire College Faculty Research Grant. I am grateful to Robert R. Jay, George L. Hicks, Philip E. Leis, Dwight B. Heath, Gloria Davis, Eric Crystal, Stephen Lansing, Deborah McKean, Judith Hudson, and A. B. Hudson for comment on drafts; to Dr. I. Gusti Ngurah Bagus and his colleagues and staff at the Bali Museum and Udayana University; to Dr. Koentjaraningrat and the Indonesian Institute of Science (LIPI); to Nyoman Rembang, Wayan Geria, and other villagers of Batubulan, Singapadu, and Sesetan; and to my "nuclear" and "extended" families for their many kindnesses. To typists Franciska Duda, Bette White,

Bobbie Belliveau, and Jeanette Berube, my thanks for their interest, patience, and care.

8. The most complete descriptions of Rangda, "the witch," are found in Mead, "The Strolling Players"; Bateson and Mead, *Balinese Character*; Lansing, *Evil*; Belo, *Bali*; and Zoete and Spies, *Dance and Drama*. The 16-mm film *Trance and Dance in Bali* by Bateson and Mead (Audiovisual Center, University of California, Berkeley) depicts the ceremony as it was performed in the 1930s.

9. Belo, *Bali*; Zoete and Spies, *Dance and Drama*, p. 95.

10. Mead quoted in Belo, *Traditional Balinese Culture*, pp. 137, 139.

11. See Zoete and Spies (*Dance and Drama*, pp. 116–22) and Bateson and Mead (*Balinese Character*, pp. 164–71) for prewar descriptions of the Barong and Rangda they witnessed.

12. Neumann, *Origins and History of Consciousness*, p. 87.

13. Lansing, *Evil*, pp. 75–85.

14. Bateson and Mead, *Balinese Character*, pp. 29–39.

15. Geertz, "The Politics of Meaning," p. 323.

16. The study of conflict by social scientists has a long history of analysis; not only Marx but also Simmel wrote on the topic of conflict and claimed that it served to unite as well as to divide: ". . . a certain amount of discord, inner divergence, and outer controversy, is organically tied up with the very elements that ultimately hold the group together" (Simmel, *Conflict*, p. 18). The place of conflict in social analysis has been reemphasized by Gluckman, *Custom and Conflict*; and Dahrendorf, *Class and Class Conflict* and *The Theory of Society*.

# Bibliography

Baal, J. van, ed. *Bali: Further Studies in Life, Thought and Ritual*. Amsterdam: W. van Hoeve, 1969.

Bateson, Gregory, and Mead, Margaret. *Balinese Character*. New York: New York Academy of Sciences, 1942.

Belo, Jane. *Bali: Rangda and Barong*. Seattle: University of Washington Press, 1949.

_____. *Traditional Balinese Culture*. New York: Columbia University Press, 1970.

Dahrendorf, R. *Class and Class Conflict in Industrial Society*. Stanford, Calif.: Stanford University Press, 1957.

_____. *Essays in the Theory of Society*. Stanford, Calif.: Stanford University Press, 1968.

Geertz, Clifford. "Internal Conversion in Balinese Religion." In *Malayan and Indonesian Studies*, edited by John Bastin and H. Roolvink, pp. 282–302. Oxford: Oxford University Press, Clarendon Press, 1964.

————. *The Interpretation of Cultures*. New York: Basic Books, 1973.

————. *Peddlers and Princes*. Chicago: University of Chicago Press, 1963.

————. "The Politics of Meaning." In *Culture and Politics in Indonesia*, edited by C. Holt and B. Anderson, pp. 319–36. Ithaca, N.Y.: Cornell University Press, 1972.

————. *The Religion of Java*. Glencoe, Ill.: Free Press, 1960.

Gerth, H. H., and Mills, C. W., eds. *From Max Weber*, New York: Oxford University Press, 1946.

Gluckman, Max. *Custom and Conflict in Africa*. Oxford: Blocklell, 1956.

Goris, R. *Bali: Cults and Customs*. Jakarta: Government of Indonesia, Ministry of Education and Culture, [1955].

Hooykaas, Christiaan. *Agama Tirtha: Five Studies in Hindu-Balinese Religion*. Amsterdam: Noord-Hollandsche, 1963.

Jay, Robert R. *Javanese Villagers*. Cambridge, Mass.: MIT Press, 1969.

Lansing, John S. *Evil in the Morning of the World*. Ann Arbor: Center for South and Southeast Asian Studies, University of Michigan, 1974.

McKean, Philip F. "From Purity to Pollution? The Balinese *Ketjak* (Monkey Dance) as Symbolic Form in Transition." In *The Imagination of Reality: Essays in Southeast Asian Coherence Systems*, edited by A. L. Becker and Aram Yengoyan, pp. 293–302. Norwood, N.J.: ABLEX Publishing Corp., 1979.

Mead, Margaret. "The Strolling Players in the Mountains of Bali." *Natural History* 43 (1939): 17–26.

Neumann, Erich. *The Origins and History of Consciousness*. Princeton, N.J.: Princeton University Press, 1973.

Peacock, James. *Indonesia: An Anthropological Perspective*. Pacific Palisades, Calif.: Goodyear Publishing Co., 1973.

————. *Rites of Modernization*. Chicago: University of Chicago Press, 1968.

*Proceedings and Decisions of the II Congress: Hindu Religion in the Five Year Plan*. Denpasar: Parisada Hindu Dharma, 1970.

Simatupang, Tahi Bonar. *Christian Service in the Revolution*. Singapore: East Asian Christian Conference, 1962.

Simmel, George. *Conflict: The Web of Group Affiliations*. Glencoe, Ill.: Free Press, 1955.

Swellengrebel, J., ed. *Bali: Studies in Life, Thought and Ritual*. The Hague: Van Hoeve, 1960.

Weber, Max. *The Protestant Ethic and the Spirit of Capitalism*. London: Allen and Unwin, 1930.

Zoete, Beryl de, and Spies, Walter. *Dance and Drama in Bali*. London: Faber and Faber, 1952.

# 14

# The Great Goddess Today
# in Burma and Thailand:
# An Exploration of Her Symbolic Relevance
# to Monastic and Female Roles
by John P. Ferguson

That the Great Goddess exists at all in Burma and Thailand may be denied by many in and out of both countries. This essay is devoted to suggesting that she is very much present and may furthermore be in evidence throughout all Theravada Buddhist societies. Evidence is taken not only from the usual orthodox texts but also, more importantly for an anthropologist, from the popular religion of the people as they practice their beliefs. The approach taken delves into speculations on historical origins and also deals with popular literature and art as valid sources for the investigation of religious symbols. Patterns traced here may, furthermore, be useful for thinking about other Southeast Asian cultures and societies.

The reader is warned that this approach is eclectic, arbitrary to a great degree, and very tentative at this point. The model to be proposed has proven invaluable in actual fieldwork, and it is offered as one researcher's hypothesis or meditation mandala for others who might be fascinated by religious symbols in complex societies.[1] At the center of this mandala, I suggest, is the Great Goddess, for it is in response to her that I believe Theravada Buddhism has developed its revolutionary arrangement of symbols. To understand why the Great Goddess is the still point at the center of the active Theravada Buddhist world, it is necessary to consider the historical factors of the symbolic climate in India, where the religion first developed.

As is well known, the Indian religions developed the symbols of the Great Goddess to an unparalleled degree. What the Buddhists see as attachment to the sensuality of this world is epitomized in her many forms and states. She is, among many things, mother, lover, fecundity, eroticism, and, of course, the great "maw" that swallows all living creatures and vegetation in the end.[2] Inescapable in her hold upon all creatures, she is the Earth Mother of infinite aspects, whose moods inspire both the tenderness of mother toward child and the lust for the blood of sacrifices. Often indifferent to source, her fertility is activated by bull deities of the sky or serpents from the deep. She pours forth from her womb an endless mass of beings who will become attached deeply to a world that they cruelly will be forced to quit.[3] To the Buddhist the Great Goddess is a veritable matron of suffering, the primal cause of all mankind's troubles. She makes us love her more than we should.

The Buddha preaches his message in India to a society portrayed as all too infatuated with worldly getting and begetting. His advice is nonattachment, symbolized by his emancipation from worldly desire and by the monastic life lived by his followers. His life, as popularly told in Burma and Thailand, can be seen as a bold rejection of the Great Goddess, but in the Buddhist refutation of the feminine lies many a hidden tribute as well—a negative validation. So well has the Great Goddess attached her followers to herself that the Buddha merely *assumes* the existence of family love, sexuality, fascination with politics, joy in finery, playfulness, intoxicants, and all the other well-worn human habits of then and now. The message is told clearly through the popular symbolism of the Buddha's life.[4]

Impregnating his own mother, Maya, with the time-honored earth symbol of the lotus, the Buddha-to-be commits himself to the mire of earthly existence. Maya, whose name significantly means "illusion," dies after seven days and departs for one of the many-layered heavens that rise in higher and higher spirituality above this world. Her son, Prince Siddhartha, who will become the Buddha, is raised by his mother's sister, who is taken to wife by Siddhartha's royal "father." Siddhartha thus is not raised by his real mother, nor was he his father's son; yet he is said to be in the lineage of a solar dynasty represented by his father. Destined to become a king, Siddhartha marries, has a son, Rahula (whose name means "bond" or "attachment"), but leaves both wife and son for the ascetic's quest for release from such concerns. It is clear that Siddhartha is no jaundiced hater of this world; he loved his father and his wife, and realized that he would also love his son if he stayed. His great departure to the ascetic life is a renunciation of not what he hates but what he loves too much. This point is the key to the model being proposed here: there is a positive valorization of the world of the Great Goddess at the very moment the Theravada Buddhist rejects it. It is almost as though the Buddhist fears the effects of a lesson taught too well by the Goddess. The middle path of moderation preached by the Buddha is not at all a simple rejection but a complex compromise.

In Burma and Thailand the process of the Enlightenment itself, as popularly portrayed in statuary and mural form, reveals the nature of this compromise, because both the Earth Mother and the serpent of the deep play key roles.[5] When it is not yet certain that his quest will be achieved, the Buddha-to-be floats his alms bowl in a river. The bowl mysteriously floats upstream, where it sinks, descending to the depths and settling on top of the three bowls already there from the three previous Buddhas of the present era. The sound that the bowl makes there awakens a dozing serpent, or Naga, who is king of this underwater realm. From this moment on, the Buddha-to-be has both blessings and protection from this ancient symbolic mate of the Great Goddess.[6] The Naga, living in his jeweled palaces under the water, is most certainly the controller of the fertile waters that are desperately needed to make the fields grow. For reasons that will become clear later, the Naga king knows that the Buddha and his monks will serve in a revolutionary way the same function as those beings who once were sacrificed to him and to the Great Goddess so that the fertile waters upon the earth could be released. When the enlightened Buddha is later sitting under a tree during a terrible rain storm, the Naga king comes from the deep, coils his body about the Buddha, and spreads his cobra hood above to shield him from the deluge. Statues of this scene are popular throughout Southeast Asia. To interpret the scene as the support of the new "son" by the old husband of the Great Goddess seems to fit well in terms of iconographic consistency and popular belief that has long related serpents and life-giving rains.

The Goddess herself is also not absent from the events of the Buddha's Enlightenment. Actually she makes it all possible. At the crisis point, the Buddha-to-be, on a throne under his Bodhi tree, is challenged by his archenemy Mara, the god of desire and illusion. Mara demands proof that under the Bodhi tree is sitting a being who deserves to be there. If no evidence can be brought forth, then Mara and his armies will sweep the imposter away. The Buddha-to-be, in response to the challenge, places his right hand upon his knee and touches the earth, asking Mother Earth to bear witness to the meritorious deeds of his previous lives that qualify him for Enlightenment. In one version (based upon Pali sources), found mainly in Burma, the

Earth Goddess roars in response from the deep below, making such a fearsome sound that Mara and his armies flee in terror, leaving the Buddha-to-be alone in the quiet necessary to achieve his coming enlightenment.[7] In the more popular version, seen particularly in murals of Burma and Thailand, the Earth Goddess herself appears before the throne.[8] From her long hair she wrings a flood of water that symbolizes the meritorious deeds done by the Buddha-to-be in all his previous lives on earth. So great is the flood that it wipes away Mara and all his armies. The Enlightenment is thereby assured by the timely intervention of the Great Goddess herself.[9]

Explanation of this dramatic event involves the central notion of merit in Theravada Buddhism. Merit is obtained by giving to Buddhism, such as by feeding monks, donating a monastery, or paying respect to the Buddha, the scriptures, or the monkhood.[10] At rituals, when meritorious giving has been completed, water blessed by the attending monks is poured by lay people into the ground so that the merit, now symbolized by the water, seeps down into the earth, eventually to reach those serving time in the hells below. Such merit, particularly when shared with the dead, accrues to one's overall cosmic record kept in the heavens. Yet the Earth Mother herself also keeps the record, as noted in the account of the Buddha's Enlightenment. It is she who retains the water in her hair, available for the coming Buddhas when they too must face the challengers.

Statues of the Earth Mother wringing her hair are common throughout Burma and Thailand and the scene of her flooding the armies of Mara is a popular mural theme as well. Most important, however, is the fact that the most common form of the Buddha image in both countries is the earth-touching pose (see Figure 32), with the right hand touching the realm of the Great Goddess, calling upon her to validate the latest claimant to her ancient throne, which in many accounts rises magically out of the earth itself to support the soon-to-be-enlightened one. It seems reasonable to interpret these iconographic statements as a clear tribute to the feminine soil out of which Theravada Buddhism has so luxuriously grown over the millenia.

Once the Buddhists had claimed the support of both the Great Goddess and her Naga spouse, the field was not yet theirs, for there were many other masculine rivals in the Indian and Southeast Asian religious world who claimed the people's loyalty. The most serious competitor, of course, was Shiva, the time-honored spouse of the Great Goddess in all her forms.[11] It was Shiva to whom many Indian ascetics turned for inspiration, but Buddhist monks, from the start, had to differentiate themselves from these world renouncers. The

32. The Buddha is portrayed in the earth-touching position as the central image behind the altar at Wat Chetawan, Chiangmai. The image is done in the Burmese style. The robe draped over the image is part of a *kathin* merit-making ritual.
*(Photograph by Christine B. Johannsen)*

Buddha, in shaping his monkhood, condemned harsh, life-denying asceticism that involved nakedness, deliberate self-torture, complete isolation from society, and sexual rituals. The first serious disruption of the monkhood was caused by Devadatta's attempt to make the severities of the forest monks' way of life the norm for the entire monkhood. The Buddha had a vision of a middle way that brought the monks more directly into contact with the laity in reciprocal relationships. His monks were to be seen in villages and towns as healthy, neat, well-disciplined, but compassionate symbols of the Buddha himself, not emaciated, unkempt, and individualistic fugitives from forest hermitages. In Theravada Buddhism, the monkhood has always contained a spectrum of ascetic practices that include the severe self-denying forest ascetics at one extreme, contrasted with the urbane and literate city monks at the other, with the village monks somewhere in between.[12] To maintain this type of monkhood, Theravada societies have stressed the supportive role of housewives in making it all possible.

Whereas the severe ascetics of the Shaivite tradition coopted the extremist roles of self-denial in the forests or fed the divine aspirations of many Southeast Asian rulers with esoteric court fertility rituals, as in Khmer and Javanese kingdoms, the Theravada monks based their tradition upon an everyday symbiotic relationship with the householders. Ideally, Theravada monks walk their daily rounds to receive food from the housewives, who thereby receive merit for their giving. Each son is encouraged to emulate Siddhartha and dress up as a prince who forsakes all to enter the monastery in the famous novice initiation ceremony. The merit for first entrance to the monkhood significantly accrues to the boy's mother. Even as a son renounces his mother to join the monks, he pays tribute to her suffering for him in childbirth and her care in raising him. Once again the ritual of renouncing affirms the value of what is being renounced.

Even more significant is the fact that males enter and leave the monkhood at will. They are seldom permanent renouncers of the realms of the Goddess. A few stay on as lifetime monks, but the majority enter only for the three-month rainy season, or for even shorter periods. A male who has not been in the monkhood is traditionally seen as "raw" or "crude" by females. Ex-monks, it is often said, make much better husbands, for they have learned how to control themselves. The 227 rules that have to be kept in the monkhood are severe. Rather than break them, one should leave. The challenge is always there for all males to test their powers of self-control. Upon those who can master themselves and live as monks, the society lavishes both love and profound respect. Such voluntary sacrifice of normal male desires is the highest form of human behavior in these societies. So much is very clear. But the widespread custom of joining the monkhood for the duration of the rainy season suggests that something more symbolic may be involved.

It may be merely coincidental with slack labor periods that males who choose to become temporary monks pick the period when the rains fall upon the newly planted rice and come out of the monasteries to become farmers again at harvest time when labor demands are greatest. Such an explanation is traditional. Yet there is reason to see the timing as part of a much deeper and more meaningful statement. In the whole of southern Asia, the fertility of the crops was often ensured by sacrifice of things dear to the people. Vegetation rituals were developed that included human sacrifice and dismemberment for burial in the fields, animal sacrifice with blood poured into the ground for the Earth Goddess, and various planting and harvesting dramas to please the goddess with gifts and kind words.[13] Theravada Buddhism evolved in the midst of such ancient beliefs and practices. It is not impossible that the self-denying monks sequestered in their compounds for the growing season were a revolutionary substitute for the ancient sacrifices to the goddess.

If such a hypothesis is correct, then the monks of Theravada Buddhism can be seen as silently but dramatically sacrificing, not their bodies or their blood, but their desires. Their rainy season retreat, in effect, became a behavioral alternative to Shaivite and Brahmanistic fertility rituals.[14] Each male member of Theravada society could thereby make his own personal contribution. As faithful models of the Buddha himself, such monks today are surrounded by symbols of the original serpent father, who, it will be remembered, gave his support from the start. In Burma and Thailand, huge snakes or *nagas* are represented as serpentine gates or railings at most monasteries and temples. One enters the building or grounds by walking between the ancient symbols of the mate of the Goddess. In Thailand, even the finials on monastery roofs are in the shape of brightly colored *nagas*. At shrines honoring the Buddha's footprints, *nagas* encircle the place where the Buddha is said to have stepped, and they release the nearby rivers and spring waters as acts of devotion to the Buddha. In Thai ordination rituals, novices are actually called *nags*, and their shaved heads are watered from troughs shaped like serpents.[15] *Nagas* twine about pillars that support temple roofs, frame Buddhist murals, hold up monastic fans, rise up behind Buddha images, and, in general, permeate the monastic world. Their insistent ubiquity forces one to assign them more than a residual symbolic valence. In brief, they can be seen as reminders of the original relationship between the Naga king and the Buddha which initiated the model of self-control as a substitute for sacrifice. The Goddess, it could be said, has been happy with the innovation, as the rainy season retreat has produced rice in abundance for thousands of years.

When the period of the rainy season withdrawal is complete, the Burmese celebrate with an impressive festival of lights that illuminates the world so that the Buddha may see his way clearly as he returns from the heavens.[16] It is said he has been up in the heavens for the duration of the rainy season so that he could preach to his mother Maya and other deities, such as Indra and Brahma, who assembled there to hear him.[17] It is surely significant that the Buddha is said to be with his mother when the rice is growing. The sequestered monks on earth can therefore be said to be with the goddess in a similar sense. The withdrawal of both the Buddha and his living monks to the realms of the mother as a new form of sacrifice serves to release the fertile waters controlled by the Naga earth father, and the ancient bargain is annually consummated. Thus, it is perfectly logical for monks in Thailand to bless rice seed before the next planting.[18]

The model being proposed here is basically a simple one. The Great Goddess, seen particularly as the Earth Mother, needs the fertile waters of her serpent Naga husband (the earth father) in order to bring forth her agrarian abundance. The serpent, however, will not release the waters unless human beings give something precious to him. In the place of traditional sacrifices to the Goddess and the Naga, the Theravada monks offer their exemplary self-denial. The complex Theravada world has been developed from this basic structural relationship. Other ideologies and rituals remained as competitors, but the Buddhists incorporated their competition within a hierarchical symbolic system that gave ascendancy to the Buddha's teachings, to which all competing deities were said to subscribe. So male oriented is this hierarchy of symbolic forms that one is often led to ignore the Goddess and the Naga at its very foundations.

As the Theravada Buddhists have increased their hold upon the people's minds and imaginations, there have been fewer and fewer competitors in the form of Shaivite ascetics, Brahmanical priests, followers of Vishnu, or blood sacrifice cults to the Goddess. The royal plowing ritual in Thailand (formerly performed in Burma also), the hill tribe buffalo sacrifices, and the folk rituals for the Rice Goddess are among the few survivals in terms of actual rituals still performed. In murals of the royal plowing ceremony, the Earth Goddess is often shown emerging from the fresh furrow made by the Thai king as he symbolically initiates the planting season; and in traditional Brahmanistic Thai rituals,[19] water was scattered on the earth by the king's minister to honor her. In Burma, during the traditional Kachin sacrifices of buffalo by the chiefs, parts of the animal are buried in a circular area dedicated to Shadip, the Earth Goddess.[20] Though they are on the wane, rituals to honor the Thai Rice Goddess are still observed, and white flags symbolizing her pregnancy can occasionally still be seen fluttering over green paddy fields. Evidence for the existence of the goddess today is mainly found in the form of verbal and iconographic symbols that reflect ancient struggles with other religions.[21] In these symbols one can trace the means by which Theravada Buddhists substituted giving to an actual, living monkhood as an alternative to propitiating imaginary deities through mysterious rituals. All competing gods, including the goddess herself, were systematically made inferior to monks in the Buddhist world view.

In Theravada Buddhist cosmology the earth is at the center, with Mount Meru's peak rising up from the world to touch the lowest heavens (see Figure 33). Below the earth are the layered hells. In the realms above, layer after layer of heavens, filled with beings we might mistakenly think of as "gods," rise higher and higher in increasing spirituality and nonmateriality until at the highest level there is nothing at all—the sublime, full emptiness of Nirvana, the ultimate goal of the good Buddhist. Inhabiting these heavens are beings such as Indra, Mara, and Brahma, who may look like gods in the western sense but are merely human beings who are temporarily being rewarded for meritorious lives.[22] All such "gods" must be reborn on earth eventually in order to try again. To be born human in the realm of the Goddess is thus the ultimate condition in which one has the best chance of achieving Nirvana. Even more specifically, one should seek to be reborn as a man, for only men have the opportunity to become monks, who are closer to Nirvana than any of the deities cramming the heavens above. To be a deity in a sensual heaven is still, after all, to be in the clutches of the Goddess, and to escape her is the whole point of the sequence of rebirths. The only final release is Nirvana. There one is at last free of females forever.

Within this cosmic vision of shuttling forms of being, we find that the competing Hindu deities have been made into died-in-the-wool Buddhists. Brahmas, complete with four heads, are bodiless forms of pure thought in the highest of the heavens. Mara (the Hindu god of love and desire) is found in the highest of the sensual heavens, where he plots his campaign against all those who try to renounce attach-

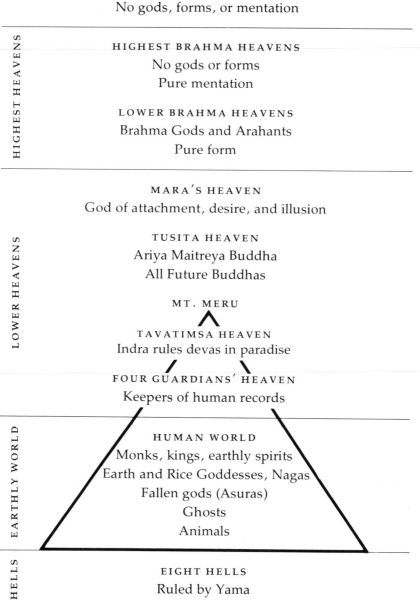

**NIRVANA**
No gods, forms, or mentation

HIGHEST HEAVENS

**HIGHEST BRAHMA HEAVENS**
No gods or forms
Pure mentation

**LOWER BRAHMA HEAVENS**
Brahma Gods and Arahants
Pure form

**MARA'S HEAVEN**
God of attachment, desire, and illusion

LOWER HEAVENS

**TUSITA HEAVEN**
Ariya Maitreya Buddha
All Future Buddhas

**MT. MERU**

**TAVATIMSA HEAVEN**
Indra rules devas in paradise

**FOUR GUARDIANS' HEAVEN**
Keepers of human records

EARTHLY WORLD

**HUMAN WORLD**
Monks, kings, earthly spirits
Earth and Rice Goddesses, Nagas
Fallen gods (Asuras)
Ghosts
Animals

HELLS

**EIGHT HELLS**
Ruled by Yama

33. Simplified outline of Theravada Buddhist cosmology.

ment to the realm of the Goddess. Indra, or Sakka, once the king of the gods, is transformed into a ruler of a lower sensual heaven or paradise that is only two layers above the earth. There he watches over the progress of Buddhism and helps the faithful (particularly good rulers) whenever he can. In the lowest heaven are the four guardians of the cardinal points, who keep the formal records of human behavior and control the four sides of Mount Meru, where live many fabulous beings and creatures. These are the main deities in a medieval cosmology that still is a vital part of Buddhist literature and art today in Burma and Thailand. These main gods are male. The whole purpose of the hierarchy is to stress the religious superiority of the masculine state, which is equated with the potential for higher and higher mentation. Females, by definition, are attached hopelessly to sensuality and the earthly state.[23] The best a woman can hope for is rebirth as a man.

We find in Burma, particularly, a further dimension to the divine hierarchy in the form of thirty-seven heavenly or "inner" *nats* ("spiritual beings").[24] A list of the first nine, in order of descending importance, follows:

1–4. The Four Guardians
5. Indra
6. Shiva
7. Ganesa (son of Shiva)
8. Sandi (alias Chandi, Kali, etc.—wife of Shiva)
9. Saraswati (wife of Vishnu or Brahma)

The first five gods, as already noted, fulfill Buddhist functions in their proper heavens. Shiva is portrayed as patron of the hermits.[25] When the Buddha visited heaven, Shiva is said to have followed after the *arahants* (almost-enlightened monks) in the train of beings doing honor to Buddha. Ganesa, the elephant-headed son of Shiva, is associated with a wide variety of Buddhist water festivals that come before —and seem designed to produce—the monsoons that cause the rice to grow. Other stories about Ganesa in Burma show him as a rival of his father and Vishnu, as well as a favorite of his mother, Sandi; and he is said to have lost his human head as a result of such family tensions. Sandi, the Great Goddess herself—she of many names—is said to have once been a rather violent deity, but she is now the benign guardian of the world and controller of events there. She is said to have followed the train of adoring spirits who honored the Buddha when he visited his mother in the heavens. Finally, Saraswati is portrayed as riding the *hintha* (the mount of Vishnu) and holding the Buddhist scriptures, which she guards and causes people to respect. She also inspires scholars and urges them on to moral excellence.

Close inspection of the Burmese literature on the *nats* reveals the operation of a characteristic of hierarchies in general. Louis Dumont has noted that whereas Westerners tend to "approve or exclude," the people of India have agreed upon a code that ranks and separates but *includes* all in a hierarchy as it does so.[26] Analysis of the Burmese Theravada Buddhist cosmology indicates that it includes rival religious symbols of the past and present, ranked though they may be below the supreme symbol of the Buddha. Thus, not only Shiva but his whole family are retained in the *nat* hierarchy; the record of past victories over rival religious symbols and their accompanying beliefs is thereby preserved. As time allows Theravada Buddhism to permeate the symbols of the entire society, the hierarchy of *nats* becomes more a historical record of syncretism than a mirror of contemporary beliefs.

A brief survey of the first nine of the heavenly *nats* shows clearly how the Hindu gods have become transformed into minor Buddhist functionaries. They exist to honor Buddhism and to absorb whatever Hindu loyalties might exist in the populace. They are pale reflections of their Hindu selves. Even the Great Goddess may ride her fearsome lion, but in one of her ten hands she holds a Buddhist rosary. In the case of Vishnu, only his wife is granted a place among the thirty-seven *nats*. He himself is preserved only as an icon outside the hierarchy, without meaning or function. Theravada Buddhist symbolization thus consistently promotes the Buddha's message of the ideal male renunciation of the goddess and all the deities associated with her. It is, however, a tribute to her power over the minds of the people that she still survives at all in the hierarchy of Buddhist symbols.

Theravada Buddhism, it would seem, built its religious edifice upon a preexisting structure in which worship of the Goddess was fundamental.[27] It honored her by the strength of its rejection. So vital to this point of view was the promotion of male spirituality that even the institution of nuns, reputedly allowed by the Buddha during his lifetime, has long since faded into oblivion. Today there are no orthodox nuns because the teacher-pupil lineages died out soon after the Buddha's death, if, indeed there ever were nuns on a par with monks. Today in Burma and Thailand there are nuns, but they cannot be ordained except by a monk, and they do not receive, by and large, the same respect accorded to the monks. In recent years, it was reported to me that a Rangoon monk who proposed admission of nuns into the Sangha (the official monkhood) was practically run out of Burma by angry Buddhists. In Thailand the nuns one sees exist in a somewhat unorthodox limbo at the edge of things, and are usually somewhat eccentric individual ascetics eking out an existence at pilgrimage centers. Only in Rangoon did I find a large, disciplined nunnery that was well supported by the local population. There may be a direct relationship between a slackening of orthodoxy among the male monks and the growth of nunneries in urban areas. Most certainly, however, over the long history of Theravada Buddhism, female ascetics have been assigned a minor role as brown-robed hermits or almost as kitchen servants in large monasteries. The glory of emulation of the Buddha's renunciation of the Goddess has primarily fallen to the males.

All this might lead one to expect to find a society in Burma and Thailand in which the religious promotion of male spirituality and the teaching of female sensuality has produced a paradise for male chauvinists. The opposite, of course, is true. Though the male may claim to be spiritually superior, insisting on deference from women, in reality he does not command either on the home front or in the society at large.[28] Southeast Asian women are among the world's most liberated females, and in Burma, particularly, they hold a power that is awesome to behold.[29] We thus are faced with a still more striking tribute to the power of the Goddess.

So great is the confidence of the women that it seems they are quite happy to allow the males their quest for a place in the other worlds above. Women in Burma can divorce men when they wish. They control much of the nation's material wealth. They can and do inherit equally with their brothers. They are often more active in business ventures than are the more meditative males. Many have owned and run large business enterprises. They are the main supporters of the monkhood through food and funds, and they predominate at religious rituals. They retain the loyalty and affection of their daughters, whereas males often lose their sons in the attempt to tell them what to do. In essence, the females, as one woman vividly explained to me, are well content to let the males go first in the forest. "Let them meet the snakes first," she said. When asked about the loss of the breadwinner, should he enter the monkhood, the same Burmese woman replied, "Let him go! There is nothing he can do about the place that a good Burmese woman cannot do as well. We can take care of ourselves." Such is the spirit of Burmese women.

The situation for Thailand is much the same, although less commented upon by Western and Thai observers alike. As noted by

A. Thomas Kirsch, Thai women play a vital role in commercial activities, at least to the degree that the ubiquitous Chinese network of business relationships allows the Thai any room to expand.[30] Thai women can inherit equally with males. They control much of the family's money flow, are active in politics (the mayor of a large northern city was a female), and can divorce their husbands without much trouble. They work with men in the fields, often run their own small shops, support the monkhood vigorously, and appear socially with the grace, confidence, and directness of essentially free souls. In these matters they resemble their Burmese counterparts, but there are differences also. Many Thai women have come under the influence of Western feminist movements and speak up boldly to attack traditional male attitudes and roles, particularly in the areas of legal and ethical rights in marriage (including multiple ones), divorce, jobs, educational opportunities, and even the exclusion of females from the formal Buddhist monastic order. Modern coeducational university life has challenged the chaperone system that has coexisted with a relatively open prostitution establishment. For more and more Thai women, living in Western countries to earn college degrees has become a reality, and these women return home with fresh challenges to traditional Thai ways. Despite these strains from a greater Western influence in Thailand than in Burma, Thai women in general seem as ebullient under Theravada Buddhism as the Burmese. Burmese and Thai women have been hardly damped by a symbolic religious system that has put them down consistently for centuries.

One ponders about the significance of such matters. The same puzzling contrast is evident in other areas of Burmese and Thai society. The religion stresses the suffering and wretchedness of sensuality, but the Burmese and Thai are famous for their sense of humor and their capacity for lighthearted fun. The religion extols the renouncing of family, but the Burmese and Thai love their kin and live in close proximity to each other in all kinds of extended families. The religion urges a turning toward Nirvana, but the Burmese and Thai seem to live life with a fullhearted relish that impresses all who know them. Quite obviously the male-female situation is part of a larger phenomenon that involves the total effect of a religion like Theravada Buddhism upon daily living.

The only explanation that seems to help make some sense out of the situation, as far as I can understand it, is to consider Theravada Buddhism as a profound commentary upon what might happen to a people if adoration of the Great Goddess and her world were allowed to proceed too enthusiastically to excess. To prevent excesses, the

Buddha preached his middle path. The basic assumption was apparently that, left unchecked, the followers of the Goddess would burn themselves out with sensual, materialist surrender to her enticements. Only moderation and denial could bring to the people a true happiness not based upon the false goal of sensual satiation as the ultimate human experience.[31] Only by observation of the personal denial of an exemplary body of monks could the people realize the existence of a visible alternative to overindulgence. Theravada Buddhism has never siphoned off too many males into its revolutionary world view: the majority of males remain in the clutches of the Goddess. Yet there is always the option of the monastic retreat if life loses its zest and meaning. The monkhood, instead of dampening the spirits of society, exists as a perpetual source of revitalization. Its revolutionary powers to regenerate have passed far beyond those needed to ensure a good rice crop. Today it offers even a modernizing society the precious option of a meaningful contrast. The more the Goddess offers everyone an electronic and materialistic embrace, the more vital it is for Theravada societies to retain a monkhood that shuns her advances. Western society, with its rapidly secularizing clergy, may have cause for concern. It is as though people of the West are convinced that the Goddess is so benign and her serpent spouse so dormant that any form of sacrifice is anachronistic folly. Theravada societies seem to caution us strongly to think more profoundly on the matter.

# Notes

1. Fieldwork that indirectly contributed data for this article was done primarily in the Chiangmai area of northern Thailand, with occasional travel in Burma, in 1973 and 1974. Gratitude is due the NDFL Title VI program, the London-Cornell Project, and the Cornell Southeast Asia Program for funding the field study. Thanks are also rendered to the American Council of Learned Societies for a postdoctoral fellowship that has helped to continue the analysis of Theravada Buddhist cosmology and symbols.

2. Campbell, *Primitive Mythology*, pp. 70, 71.

3. For a general discussion of the many symbolic roles played by the Goddess, see particularly Eliade, *Comparative Religion*, pp. 239–366; Neumann, *The Great Mother*; von Cles-Reden, *Realm of the Great Goddess*; and Campbell, *The Masks of God*. More specific attention to her role in India is found in Basham, *The Wonder That Was India*, pp. 311, 312; Zimmer, "Indian World Mother" and *Myths and Symbols*; and Campbell, *Oriental Mythology*, pp. 147–97. Zimmer, *Art of Indian Asia*, pp. 68–168, treats the Indian and

Southeast Asian aspects of the iconography of the Goddess.

4. The best English version of the life of the Buddha as told in Burma is in Bigandet, *Legend of Gaudama*; also useful is Zanabivamsa, *Illustrated History*. Useful sources for the Thai interpretations are U.S. Information Service, *Life of the Buddha*; and Vajirananavarorasa, *Life of the Buddha*. For an overview see Thomas, *Life of Buddha*.

5. Ferguson and Johannsen, "Modern Buddhist Murals."

6. For discussion of the relationship between serpent symbolism and the Goddess see particularly Campbell, *Occidental Mythology*, pp. 9–41, and *The Mythic Image*, pp. 281–301. Also see Eliade, *Comparative Religion*, pp. 163–71. The serpent's control of the life-giving waters in the Indian account of Indra and the Vritra is analyzed by Campbell, *Oriental Mythology*, pp. 182–89. Wales theorizes on the significance of the *naga* in prehistoric Southeast Asia (*Siamese State Ceremonies*, pp. 130–49). For Thailand, see Tambiah, *Buddhism and the Spirit Cults*, pp. 113, 173–75; and for Burma see Htin Aung, *Folk Elements*, pp. 109–13.

7. Bigandet, *Legend of Gaudama*, pp. 61, 62.

8. U.S. Information Service, *Life of the Buddha*, pp. 68, 69.

9. In Burma the Earth Goddess is known as Wa.thunda.yei (Judson, *Burmese-English Dictionary*, p. 962). Duroiselle explores the textual and legendary aspects of her nature ("Wathundaye"). In Thailand she is known as Thorani (L. M. Hanks, "Merit and Power," p. 127; Ferguson and Johannsen, "Modern Buddhist Murals," pp. 650, 651).

10. L. M. Hanks, "Merit and Power"; Keyes, "The Power of Merit."

11. Coedès, *The Indianized States*, p. 23.

12. Ferguson, "The Symbolic Dimensions."

13. The archetypal form of human sacrifice for the crops is described by Denyer for the Nagas in northwest Burma (*Dawn on the Kachin Hills*, pp. 58, 59). For a discussion of the animal sacrifices, or "feasts of merit," among the hill tribes of Southeast Asia, see Kirsch, "Feasting." Rituals to honor Mae Phosop, the Rice Goddess, and Thorani, the Earth Goddess, performed most often in traditional Thailand, are described by Kaufman, *Bangkhuad*, pp. 204–7; de Young, *Village Life*, pp. 141–46; and Anuman Rajadhon, *Loy Kathong*, pp. 11–14, 23–25, 38–49. A specific discussion of belief and ritual for northeast Thailand is given by Tambiah, *Buddhism and the Spirit Cults*, pp. 351–66. Available evidence for Burma (Nash, *The Golden Road*, p. 176; Mendelson, "Field Notes") and northern Thailand (personal observation) would seem to indicate that elaborate rituals to the Rice Goddess (as distinct from the Earth Goddess) either were never very popular or died out earlier than in central and northeast Thailand.

14. Htin Aung, *Folk Elements*, p. 121.

15. Anuman Rajadhon, *Life and Ritual*, p. 73; Tambiah, *Buddhism and the Spirit Cults*, pp. 103–13.

16. In actuality, rituals in Burma and Thailand at the end of the rainy season do not always explicitly celebrate the Buddha's return from the heavens. What Scott calls the Burmese "Tawadeintha Feast" does commemorate the

event, complete with a welcoming hundred-foot-long paper *naga*, but the ritual does not stress pagoda lighting (*The Burman*, pp. 328–33). Spiro describes the archetypal ritual for Burma, which he calls "Thadin:jut," or the First Festival of Lights, when pagodas are lighted to celebrate the event (*Buddhism and Society*, pp. 225, 226). Fytche describes a similar ritual (*Burma, Past and Present*, pp. 90, 91), as does Htin Aung (*Folk Elements*, pp. 80, 81).

Thai explanations for the Loi Kratong light festival stress non-Buddhist elements, such as the Goddess of Water (Ganga), royal innovations, or Brahmanistic concerns (Manich Jumsai, *Understanding Thai Buddhism*, pp. 59–68; Anuman Rajadhon, *Loy Kathong*, pp. 3–12).

In both countries lights floated in rivers after the end of the rainy season are part of rituals that deal with an *arahant* (almost-enlightened monk) who controls storms that could ruin temple festivals. For Thai details, see Tambiah, *Buddhism and the Spirit Cults*, pp. 160–78. For Burma see Duroiselle, "Popular Saints," pp. 23–25; Scott, *The Burman*, pp. 228, 229; and Qoun: Maun, *Qashin*.

As noted by Tambiah, the end of the rainy season is celebrated variously in the different regions of Thailand, combining the festival of lights, the reenactment of the Buddha's descent from heaven, by having a procession of monks or a Buddha image descend from a hill, or giving gifts of robes (*kathin*) (*Buddhism and the Spirit Cults*, pp. 157–60). In Burma commemoration of the Buddha's descent, *kathin*, and floating lights down rivers to the *arahant* Qu.pa.gou' seem to be retained as separate ritual occasions.

17. Bigandet, *Legend of Gaudama*, pp. 136–41.

18. See Kaufman, *Bangkhuad*, p. 205; and Blanchard, *Thailand*, p. 107.

19. Wales, *Siamese State Ceremonies*, p. 257.

20. Carrapiett, *The Kachin Tribes*, p. 79.

21. For example, Wales notes how the Earth Goddess Dhavani was portrayed in ancient Thai rituals as waiting upon Shiva (*Siamese State Ceremonies*, p. 250), and Mendelson records a November ritual at the end of the rainy season for a *nat* or spirit called Pounmagyi, whom farmers propitiated with food offerings to ensure a bounteous harvest ("Field Notes"). Informants identified Pounmagyi as "Kali yokini," i.e., the Great Goddess Kali, wife of Shiva.

22. In Theravada Buddhism there are many Brahmas inhabiting the upper heavens.

23. Except for Maya, the mother of the Gautama Buddha, who is portrayed as living a rather saintly life, females in heaven are traditionally described as sensual companions of handsome princes living in grand palaces, as adoring queens, or as playful musicians, dancers, or rejoicing flower throwers. Females do not seem to be reborn in the highest heavens at all.

24. In Thailand there are also many lesser deities, including Shiva, Brahma, Vishnu, Ganesa, Asuras, and other *devas* ("heavenly spirits"), as well as a host of lesser beings from legend, folklore, and such sources as the Jatakas or the Ramayana (Manich Jumsai, *Understanding Thai Buddhism*, pp. 44–52). There are also numerous nature spirits, place guardians, and, of course,

ghosts. All these supramundane beings, however, seem less systematized in Thailand than in Burma, where hierarchy is more evident. The most useful Burmese source on the inner *nats* is Hpou: Ca:, *37 min:*.

25. Sein Hpei notes that Shiva is the patron of the Kassapa hermits (*Pu Ya* 9, pp. 115, 116). In iconography, Shiva wears the tiger skin and the hair in the knotted fashion, so typical of the forest hermits who have always played a contrapuntal role to the Theravada monks. It is possible that severe ascetics, such as the Kassapa hermits of the Buddha's time, have been Shaivite rivals aligned with Earth Goddess (Kali, Sandi, etc.) beliefs since the beginning of Theravada Buddhism. This would suggest that the defeat of Shiva as a symbol adversely affected the Goddess as well.

26. Dumont, *Homo Hierarchicus*, p. 191.

27. The nature of prehistoric religion in Southeast Asia remains largely a matter of creative conjecture, of course, as archeology has yet to be funded adequately to uncover the needed evidence. Writers like Wales can work out theories on the importance of the earth as a deity (*Prehistory and Religion*, pp. 128–48), but only future archeological discoveries will confirm or dispute present notions. This essay proposes, through analysis of symbols, the preeminence of the Goddess before Buddhism, but the reader is warned that the archeological evidence simply is not yet available to resolve the matter.

28. It should also be noted that the antifeminine viewpoint is primarily launched in books and sermons by monks, often for the purpose of strengthening the monkhood's resistance to the legendary temptations of women. Secular males in Burma and Thailand seem as fascinated by female charms as men anywhere, with the romantic spirit almost a national tradition in both countries. The lack of feminist movements in Burma would seem to speak to a certain satisfaction with what women have achieved (Mi Mi Khaing, "Golden Land," p. 111, and *Burmese Family*, p. 149; Mya Sein, "The Women of Burma").

29. Hall, *Soul of a People*, pp. 169–211.

30. Kirsch, "Buddhist Values."

31. Thai monks, in viewing with regret the inroads of modern media upon traditional attitudes, said that people possessed by movies, television, transistor radios, popular photo magazines, and stereos had "hot minds" instead of the "cool minds" long felt to be exemplary.

# Bibliography

Anuman Rajadhon, Phya. *Life and Ritual in Old Siam*. New Haven, Conn.: Human Relations Area Files, 1961.

———. *Loy Kathong and Songkran Festival*. Bangkok: National Culture Institute, 1950.

Basham, A. L. *The Wonder That Was India*. New York: Grove Press, 1954.

Bigandet, P. *The Life or Legend of Gaudama the Buddha of the Burmese*. Rangoon: Pegu Press, 1858.

Blanchard, Wendell et al. *Thailand: Its People, Its Society, Its Culture*. New Haven, Conn.: Human Relations Area Files, 1958.

Campbell, Joseph. *The Masks of God: Occidental Mythology*. New York: Viking Press, 1964.

_____. *The Masks of God: Oriental Mythology*. New York: Viking Press, 1962.

_____. *The Masks of God: Primitive Mythology*. New York: Viking Press, 1959.

_____. *The Mythic Image*. Princeton, N.J.: Princeton University Press, 1974.

Carrapiett, William J. S. *The Kachin Tribes of Burma*. Rangoon: Superintendent Government Printing and Stationery, 1929.

Coedès, G. *The Indianized States of Southeast Asia*. Honolulu: East-West Center, 1964.

Denyer, C. H. *Dawn on the Kachin Hills*. London: Bible Churchmen's Missionary Society, 1927.

de Young, John E. *Village Life in Modern Thailand*. Berkeley: University of California Press, 1958.

Dumont, Louis. *Homo Hierarchicus: An Essay on the Caste System*. Chicago: University of Chicago Press, 1970.

Duroiselle, M. Charles. "Popular Saints in Burma." In *Report of the Superintendent, Archaeological Survey, Burma, for the Year Ending 31st March 1923*, pp. 22–26. Simla: Government of India Press, 1924.

_____. "Wathundaye, the Earth-Goddess of Burma." In *Annual Report of the Archaeological Survey of India, 1921–22*, pp. 14–17. Simla: Government of India Press, 1924.

Eliade, Mircea. *Patterns in Comparative Religion*. New York: Sheed and Ward, 1958.

Ferguson, John P. "The Symbolic Dimensions of the Burmese Sangha." Ph.D. dissertation, Cornell University, 1975.

_____, and Johannsen, Christina B. "Modern Buddhist Murals in Northern Thailand: A Study of Religious Symbols and Meaning." *American Ethnologist* 3 (1976): 645–69.

Fytche, Albert. *Burma, Past and Present: With Personal Reminiscences of the Country*. Vols. 1 and 2. London: C. Kegan Paul, 1878.

Gutman, Pamela. "The Ancient Coinage of Southeast Asia." *Journal of the Siam Society* 66 (1978): 8–21.

Hall, H. Fielding. *The Soul of a People*. London: Macmillan, 1905.

Hanks, Jane. *Maternity and Its Rituals in Bang Chan*. Cornell University, Southeast Asia Program Data Paper no. 51. Ithaca, N.Y.: Cornell University Press, 1963.

Hanks, Lucien M. "Merit and Power in the Thai Social Order." *American Anthropologist* 64 (1962): 1247–61.

Hpou: Ca:, Qu:. *37 Min:* [The 37 Nats]. Rangoon: Qu: Hci'Hswei, Myan Ma. Goun Yei, 1973.

Htin Aung, Maung. *Folk Elements in Burmese Buddhism*. London: Oxford University Press, 1962.

Judson, Adoniram. *Burmese-English Dictionary*. Rangoon: Baptist Board of Publications, 1953.

Kaufman, H. K. *Bangkhuad, a Community Study in Thailand*. New York: J. J. Augustus, 1960.

Keyes, Charles F. "The Power of Merit." *Visakha Puja*, 1973, pp. 95–102.

Kirsch, A. Thomas. "Buddhist Values and Thai Sex-Roles." Mimeographed. 1965.

————. "Feasting and Social Oscillation." Cornell University, Southeast Asia Program Data Paper no. 92. Ithaca, N.Y.: Cornell University Press, 1973.

Manich Jumsai, M. L. *Understanding Thai Buddhism: Being a Compendium of Information of Buddhism as Professed in Thailand*. Bangkok: Chalermit Press, 1971.

Mendelson, E. Michael. "Field Notes." Mendelson Papers, 1958–59. Private collection, John P. Ferguson.

Mi Mi Khaing, Daw. *Burmese Family*. Bloomington: Indiana University Press, 1962.

————. "People of the Golden Land: Burmese Character and Customs." *Atlantic Monthly* 201 (1958): 107–12.

Mya Sein, Daw. "The Women of Burma." *Atlantic Monthly* 201 (1958): 122–25.

Nash, Manning. *The Golden Road to Modernity*. New York: John Wiley, 1965.

Neumann, Erich. *The Great Mother: An Analysis of the Archetype*. Princeton, N.J.: Princeton University Press, 1963.

Qoun: Maun, Qu:. *Qashin Qu.pa.gou'* [The revered Upagote]. Rangoon: Pei.thu mei' hswei Press, n.d.

Scott, James George. *The Burman: His Life and Notions*. New York: W. W. Norton, 1963.

Sein Hpei, Qu:. *Pu Ya 9 Hsu Pu Zo Nei: Sa Tan:* [How to worship the 9 Buddhas]. Rangoon: Book Shop of Qu: Pyain, n.d.

Spiro, Melford E. *Buddhism and Society: A Great Tradition and Its Burmese Vicissitudes*. New York: Harper and Row, 1970.

Tambiah, S. *Buddhism and the Spirit Cults in North-East Thailand*. Cambridge: Cambridge University Press, 1970.

Thomas, Edward J. *The Life of Buddha as Legend and History*. 3d ed. London: Routledge and Kegan Paul, 1949.

U.S. Information Service. *The Life of the Buddha according to Thai Temple Painting*. Bangkok: United States Information Service, 1967.

Vajirananavarorasa, H.R.H. Prince. *Life of the Buddha*. Bks. 1, 2, and 3. Bangkok: Mahamakut Educational Society, Buddhist University, n.d.

von Cles-Reden, Sibylle. *The Realm of the Great Goddess: The Story of the Megalith Builders*. Englewood Cliffs, N.J.: Prentice-Hall, 1962.

Wales, H. G. Quaritch. *Prehistory and Religion in Southeast Asia*. London: Bernard Quaritch, 1957.

————. *Siamese State Ceremonies*. London: Bernard Quaritch, 1931.

Zanabivamsa, Aggamahapandita Venerable. *Illustrated History of Buddhism*. Rangoon: Young Men's Buddhist Association, 1951.

Zimmer, Heinrich. *The Art of Indian Asia*. Edited by Joseph Campbell. Vols. 1 and 2. New York: Pantheon Books, 1955.

_____. "The Indian World Mother." In *The Mystic Vision*. Vol. 6 of *Papers from the Eranos Yearbooks*, edited by Joseph Campbell. Princeton, N.J.: Princeton University Press, 1969.

_____. *Myths and Symbols in Indian Art and Civilization*. Edited by Joseph Campbell. New York: Harper and Row, 1946.

# 15

## Mother Earth:
## The Great Goddess
## of West Africa
### by Daniel F. McCall

*Griaule has taught us to mistrust
the simplicity of appearances in
African culture*[1]

The title of this article is assertive because what it proclaims has
not been generally recognized.[2] Most writers on West African religions have mentioned an earth deity, but they have underplayed its
maternal quality, left unclear its relation to others in the pantheon, or,
after mere reference to its existence, given disproportionate attention
to a sky god and minor deities and spirits.[3]

In order to make discussion manageable in a brief format, attention
is here confined to the eastern Upper Guinea rain forest.[4] Emphasis is
on three peoples, the Akan, Yoruba, and Ibo, each of which is a term
for a language and cultural grouping: Akan consists of Akuapim,
Ashanti, Baule Brong, Fanti, and others; more than a score of kingdoms are comprised within Yorubaland; and there are five major
divisions of Ibo.

## Society and Religion in Durkheim's Theory

If one takes the Durkheimian view that the form of religion is a
reflection of the type of society,[5] one would expect that in addition to
a male god, a mother goddess would be significant in Akan theology:
the highest political office is bifurcated into a male and female seg-

ment, *ohene* ("king") and *ohema* (awkwardly translated as "queen mother"), the former taking precedence in military and diplomatic matters, the latter preeminent in ritual. Succession to male political office, from kingship down to minor chieftaincies, is via matrilineal relationships, as are also descent and inheritance.[6]

Maintaining the same Durkheimian perspective, one would expect Yoruba religion to contrast sharply with that of Akan, because the patrilineal pattern prevails among the Yoruba in descent, inheritance, and succession. The king might have an *iyalode* ("queen of the ladies"), but she does not have the same influence as an Akan *ohema*. In Yoruba commoner families, mothers are at the disadvantage of being considered "outsiders" in the extended patrilineal households of their husbands. Thus, following Durkheim's concept, one would not expect to find a mother goddess; yet she is more prominent here than among the Akan. The goddess Onile ("owner of the earth") is worshiped by all but is especially the deity of Ogboni, a "secret society" that has considerable influence, even over the Yoruba king. Known also, in some areas, as Oduduwa, this goddess is recognized as the ancestress of all human beings, as well as creatrix of the world. She is portrayed in art as a mother with a child.[7]

The social organization of the Ibo (or Igbo) people falls more or less midway between those of the Akan and the Yoruba, insofar as gender roles are concerned. Kingship is foreign to Ibo culture. Some Ibo groups have patrilineal descent, but Ibo wives are less dominated by the husband's patrilineage than is the case among the Yoruba. Also, some Ibo groups are matrilineal or have double descent systems. Ibo society has little development of hierarchical statuses, and is often characterized as essentially egalitarian. This relative lack of a superordination system also applies in a general way to gender roles. In general, women are under few restrictions that do not also apply to men. They have wider latitude of independent action than Yoruba women, but—lacking any female political office comparable to *ohema*—they have fewer opportunities for public influence than Akan women. Therefore, following Durkheim's theory, we would expect Ibo religion to have a balance of supernatural power between a father god and a mother goddess. Instead, we find a flourishing Earth Mother cult, more prominent than among either the Akan or Yoruba cultures. For instance, temples that honor Ale (or Ala), the Earth Goddess, have larger-than-life-size sculptures portraying her with children. Often she holds a big yam knife, ambivalent symbol of agricultural bounty and of retribution and death. Various natural, social, or mythological creatures of Ale's world are portrayed, all—

and the building, too—constructed of her own substance: earth, or mud. In some Ibo regions, Earth has priority over Sky in cosmology, and here Sky may be conceptualized as feminine. There are explicit statements concerning the maternal nature of the Earth Goddess. She is considered capable of withholding harvest if her laws are not obeyed. All this adds up to a virtual monopoly of cosmic and chthonic forces in the hands of a mother goddess.[8]

Predictions of the character of religion on the basis of social organization, in keeping with Durkheim's theory, is relatively accurate in the case of the Akan, but misleading with respect to Yoruba and Ibo cultures. It must be admitted that local variations in each of the ethnicities are a complicating factor, but they do not account for the unexpected elements found in these religions. For example, the vigor of the Yoruba mother goddess could not have been predicted by looking at social organization alone. One would have predicted an egalitarian balance of male and female deities for the Ibo, but one finds among some groups, on the contrary, an unmarried mother goddess reigning supreme. Even in the case of the Akan one would have expected to find more weight given to the mother goddess, because they are matrilineal and have an influential female political office.

The purpose of demonstrating the lack of fit, in these cases, with Durkheim's theory is not to refute his arguments, but to point out that West African societies are not blank sheets on which to impose a simple formula. In actuality, each society has a developmental past that must be understood if modern ethnographies are to make sense. In fact, the principle that Durkheim discovered is clearly at work if we take into consideration archeological evidence of a Neolithic basis for recent West African societies, along with the nature of Neolithic religion. The various earth mother cults among the Akan, Yoruba, and Ibo (and other West African peoples) are remnants of the Neolithic religion, truncated and modified by later influences, in the Durkheimian manner. In other words, within theology there is a conservation of concepts, appropriate to earlier stages of a society's development, as well as those reflecting its contemporary form, but both the older and the newer beliefs are explicable as reflections of social organization.[9]

What I have added to Durkheim's findings is a diachronic perspective. Because Durkheim based his discussion on Australian societies that had not experienced a "Neolithic revolution," he failed to allow for such changes in his general statement. Malinowski recognized change, but assumed that the accommodation of myth to newer conditions would wipe out the older conceptions. His statement on the "mythic charter" of society is a half-truth that has misled many later anthropologists. The corollary proposed here stresses the special conditions of social evolution and the tendency of religious belief systems to resist jettisoning outmoded but familiar and revered notions. The purpose here, however, is not to pursue theory except where necessary to unravel the history of the cults of Mother Earth in West Africa.[10]

## The Neolithic in West Africa

In the rain forest occupied by the Akan, Yoruba, and Ibo peoples, ground and polished axes have been found, some of which are dated to the third millenium B.C. Pollen studies reveal no large-scale clearings in the forest, however, until the first millenium B.C. It is clear that both the knowledge of how to make these Neolithic tools and the concept of cultivating plants came to the forest dwellers from the grasslands. These grassland farmers were in turn the recipients of technology and ideas from other, still more distant, Neolithic peoples. Some authorities favor a route westward from the Upper Nile Valley. Another likely route is via North Africa and the western Sahara before it became a desert again a couple of millenia B.C. Whichever route this diffusion followed, most scholars agree that the source was Southwest Asia. Significantly, the diffusion of Neolithic ideas had spread far west of Egypt three thousand years before the pharoahs. This means that the cultural influences carried by such a movement were those of the *primary* Neolithic. Thus, the Stone Age farming cultures of West Africa began prior to the onset of the metal ages in Mesopotamia and Egypt and could not have been affected by early ideologies of kingship and other notions that developed as a result of the "urban revolution."[11]

## Religion in the Primary Neolithic

There was a "strong underlying uniformity" in primary Neolithic cultures throughout the wide extent of their distribution, a uniformity "reflected in their religious forms." A mother goddess "held sway" over the primary Neolithic cultures, and her aspect as an earth goddess "came to the fore." This goddess had little if any supernatural competition at that time; it was only later, after the "urban revolution," that, as male rulers and priests became powerful, "the status of the goddess in all her manifestations" was lowered. It is important to stress that the high gods of the ancient civilizations emerged only with the "urban revolution." In other words, the day of the Sky God had not yet come in primary Neolithic times. Religion in the primary Neolithic was a reflection à la Durkheim of the society: the basic social institution was the matriclan, and "land would generally have descended in the female line."[12]

The goddess of the primary Neolithic had a number of epiphanies or symbols. One of these was the dove. Another was the lion (or lioness), and the domesticated animals it might prey upon: the pig, goat, and cow. The serpent was also a companion. The tree was a major symbol of the goddess. The moon and the planet Venus were epiphanies. In addition, the goddess was represented by the color black and the number three. The range and combination of attributes has been compared to the litany of the "Beatitudes" associated with Mary, Mother of God, in the Roman Catholic church. Taken together they represent all segments of the universe of a farming community. Therefore, Mother Nature would be a more accurate appellation than Mother Earth, for, in fact, earth was only one, though a central one, of her manifestations. Many of the other symbols relate directly to earth. Black is the color of fertile soil (barren soils are lighter). Serpents burrow intimately in the earth, and all animals and even birds are dependent on the earth. The tree is the climax of vegetation growing from the body of the earth. But some symbols may be multivocal: the bird may be Mother Earth's messenger, the lion a reminder of her destructive powers. Female symbolism was not lacking: the moon has a menstrual rhythm, timing the menstrual flow of women and measuring the seasons.[13]

A similar *cluster* of these associations with an earth goddess in West Africa might suggest the presence of the ancient Southwest Asian goddess. Although resemblance between isolated traits in different regions is not an adequate foundation for an argument of diffusion, a cluster of traits organized in the same relationships, that is, a culture complex, found in two or more regions is much more likely to indicate some kind of historical connection.[14]

## Possible Primary Neolithic Religious Traits in West Africa

Diffusion along the route of transmission from Southwest Asia to West Africa must have involved a number of local syncretisms that would tend to disguise the origins. Yet diffusion of Neolithic religion has been traced from Southwest Asia to the British Isles (an even greater distance). We may hope, then, to follow a route that is somewhat shorter. In the European case, an amplitude of archeological data provided a basis of evidence closer in time to the period of diffusion, but in West Africa, where excavations have been fewer, we have to rely mainly on survival of cultural forms in the living communities; and because cultural change never ceases, we must recognize that modern ethnographic evidence is not qualitatively comparable to archeological evidence. Nevertheless, ethnographic data can be used in historical reconstruction. Two considerations provide a basis of feasibility: first, religious systems of thought tend to be conservative; and second, after the diffusion of agriculture and Neolithic ideas, the desiccation of the Sahara region created an obstacle to the succeeding wave of diffusion, that of the technology and ideology of the "urban revolution." West Africa received its Neolithic input at about the same time as western Europe, but was a millenium behind in getting iron technology. (In West Africa the period between did not include a Bronze Age.) The Yoruba were the earliest of the peoples of the eastern Upper Guinea rain forest who were affected by iron weapons (and implements), along with "urban" ideas such as kingship. This was no earlier than A.D. 500 and perhaps a bit later. The Akan survived for additional centuries before they felt the impact of state-building intruders. The Ibo, for the most part, escaped having the essential form of their society changed, though they did acquire iron tools.[15]

We have seen that the Akan, Yoruba, and Ibo have an earth goddess. Now we must determine if this goddess has any of the specific attributes of the ancient Southwest Asian Neolithic goddess. The number three is a good place to begin, because numbers are abstractions of quantity, and neither three nor any other quantity is an obvious feature of a nature deity. Three is the special number of the Ogboni society, which is devoted to the Yoruba earth cult, and thus is the numerical sign of the goddess Onile. Among the Akan, three is considered to be a lucky number. But more than luck is involved, because the number nine, the triple of three, is dangerous—not merely unlucky. I suggest that behind this attribution of danger is the common concept that when any supernatural power is intensified there is too much potency for mortals; therefore, three times three is to be avoided by human beings. One source specifies that the luck of three derives from the Earth Goddess. It is clear that threeness is associated with the goddess in the eastern Upper Guinea forest in modern times, just as it was with the Southwest Asian goddess in antiquity. In a midpoint between these regions, the Saharan Fezzan, in southern Libya, the number three connotes femininity but is not now associated with divinity. Here and in other localities in North Africa, three and its designated femininity contrast with four, which represents masculinity. In the western Sudan, these number symbols of the sexes have been reversed so that three represents masculinity and four femininity. This reversal was effected by the Mande people, who built the Mali empire; it had such widespread influence that many other West African peoples have adopted the Mande set of symbols. The fact that the symbol three works just as well either way shows how arbitrary it is. Thus, to find an arbitrary "three goddess" in both the ancient Near East and the eastern Upper Guinea forest, thousands of miles apart, suggests the likelihood of diffusion because, as A. L. Kroeber pointed out, diffusion can more easily be shown in the case of arbitrary than in the case of logical associations.[16]

To move from number symbolism to color symbolism, we find that the very name of the Yoruba Earth Goddess, Oduduwa, means the "Black One." For the Akan culture, the evidence is oblique. Alfred Ellis was told of a black goddess, whom he does not name, but there is every likelihood that she is Asase. Robert Rattray was puzzled by the name *Asase ne abuo* ("the earth and its rocks") for a textile design, the warp of which was entirely of black threads and the weft of green. The signature of Asase is in these colors, her black earth and green vegetation.[17]

Neither of these realms of symbolism, numerology and color spectra, is as prominent as that of the tree, which was much more developed in ancient Near Eastern religion. Charles Meek wrote that among the Ibo, "the symbols of the deity are usually a tree with a pottery dish which served as a receptacle for offerings." This deity he specified as Ale, the Earth Goddess, adding that she is regarded as "the owner of men, whether dead or alive." Percy Talbot gives us the additional information that one tree, called *offor-na-obochi*, was considered to be the oldest tree in the land, having been brought there by Ale. He also tells us that sticks cut from this tree have a special power: every head of a dwelling compound has such a stick "to ward off all bad things." A person guilty of an offense must cut such a stick and place it on Ale's shrine.[18]

In the Yoruba myth of creation, the goddess is surrounded by several mythemes that are suggestive of Southwest Asia. She is accompanied by a dove and, after causing the dry land to come into being, plants a tree at the navel of the earth. It is the oil palm, which is very important in Yoruba nutrition and ritual.[19]

Among the Akan, the tree symbolism has been obscured by expansion of the Sky God cult, which has taken over some attributes of the goddess. That the cult of Nyame, the Sky God, has appropriated the tree of Asase, the Earth Goddess, is suggested by the fact that a shrine made of a tree is called *Nyame dua* ("Nyame's tree") by the Akan, but the same type of shrine among the Ibo is the property of Ale. The word "tree" appears in an appellation of deity, which H. Evans says is "half-way between a personal name and a 'praise-name.'" This appellation is Twereduampon ("if you lean on a tree—*dua*—you do not fall"). Evans was discussing Nyame, to whom the quasi-praise-name is sometimes given, but on the same page he has a quotation of a prayer to Asase, the Earth, and the name Twereduampon appears! Thus, the tree praise-name was used for Asase as well as for Nyame, and like the tree shrine was probably originally hers alone.[20]

Thus far, we have some evidence for an arbitrary symbol, three, and two symbols, black and tree, which are essentially chthonic. It would strengthen the argument if we could add one of the celestial symbols. Among the Akan, the planet Venus is related to the earth cult in a curious way. The Akan have the "planetary week." In this system each day is considered to be under the influence of one of seven planets, considered as deities. The planatary week originated in Southwest Asia with the goddess Ishtar as the sole female deity among the seven. She is considered by Assyriologists to be the continuation into historic times of the old Neolithic goddess. The Romans identified her with their goddess Venus, the Germanic peoples with Freya (hence Friday), and it would seem that the Akan have equated her with Asase. One day out of the week the earth "rests" and no one may farm; this day of rest for most of the Akan is Friday, though the Ashanti dedicate Thursday to the earth. Today, however, there is no mention of planetary deities, and Johann Christaller used the term "genii" to refer to the spiritual forces that rule the days. In any event, the presence of the system of the planetary week implies an association of the Earth Goddess and the planet Venus.[21]

The difficulty is the chronology: the development of the planetary week was a Hellenistic refinement of older Mesopotamian ideas, and its diffusion to North Africa did not occur until about A.D. 200. This system must have reached the Akan much later. We do not know whether the goddess Asase was associated with the planet before the planetary week arrived. The Akan are the only people in West Africa who now have an indigenous form of the planetary week. The Yoruba do recognize Venus: it is the only celestial body other than the sun and the moon for which a specific name is used. Unfortunately, on presently available evidence, we cannot say whether this cognizance of the planet ever fit into the earth cult. At the moment, we cannot go further with the question of Venus for lack of data.[22]

We should take the Akan week as a salutary warning of the danger of misreading the antiquity of evidence in investigations of this nature. The planetary week could not have reached the Sudan until after A.D. 200 (but probably before 700) and reached Guinea perhaps some centuries later. If the association of Venus with the Akan earth cult is due *only* to this calendrical system, the whole thing is post-Neolithic.[23]

A case that is made especially complicated by the transformations of time and culture change is the symbology of the serpent. In many ancient cults the serpent was the familiar of a goddess. Male associations, which are most likely later developments, are also mentioned in early documents. Modern writers seem to have difficulty in seeing snakes without the overtones of phallic or Freudian symbolism. A coiled snake, modeled in mud, in relief on an Ibo temple wall is exactly the same in design (with the head projecting from the center of the coils to the outer circumference) as in an Akan representation. The association with the goddess is certain, but no one seems to have elicited any account of what is conceptualized in these sculptures.[24]

Because all our symbols are subject to the ambiguities introduced by reinterpretation over time (as well as the ambiguity that is at the heart of symbolizing), we will not add to creditability by prolonging the discussion of our list of symbols; what is needed is evidence of another kind. We have drawn largely from myths and the verbal aspects of religion; we will turn now to ritual, which has also a symbolic component, but is basically action rather than speech.

Kwesi Dickson argues that "Akan religion does not exhibit traits commonly associated with fertility cults." He cites Eastwood's studies, which epitomize fertility cults as having, among other traits, "ritual nuptials" and other sexual rites, "for it was believed that in some way human fertility would be reflected in the fertility of the land." For the Akan, which is all that Dickson was concerned with, this criticism is trenchant, but in the wider regional context—if we accept some common underlying cultural stratum for the area—we do find evidence of ritual sexual license. At Ado, a principal place for the worship of Oduduwa (the Yoruba Earth Goddess), it was reported in the nineteenth century that sexual license was part of the cult activities. The Fon, who are bordered by the Akan on the west and the Yoruba on the east, had what seems to have amounted to a temple prostitute cult associated with a serpent deity. Shortly after colonial administration was set up, these fertility rituals either became less open or disappeared. Probably they had already been suppressed among the Akan by precontact influences within West Africa, which were as hostile to the earth cult as was Christianity in the subsequent period.[25]

## History of West African Religion: A Proposed Reconstruction

During the primary Neolithic period, the elements of a food-producing economy were carried into the Nile Valley, North Africa, and the present area of the Sahara (then largely a grassland). This economy was accompanied by the type of social organization and religion that had become integrated into a functionally interrelated culture complex in Southwest Asia. By at least 1000 B.C. this complex penetrated the eastern Upper Guinea forested coastlands. These forest food producers depended on a locally domesticated species of yam and on the grains (sorghum and millet) that had earlier been domesticated in the Savanna to the north (before wheat and barley were finally lost in the gradual spread of grain cultivation into the tropics). At that time matriclans were the only existing social institution through which some political cohesiveness could be achieved. Centralized authority was still quite limited. Worship focused on the Earth Goddess. Any other deity that may have existed, such as a "yam spirit," "farm god," "bush god," or water, rock, tree, and rain or firmament spirits, was subordinate to her.

After this Neolithic society had thrived for many centuries, wielders of iron weapons conquered some of the forest farmers and set up the capital of their kingdom at the spot where the principal shrine of the Earth Goddess (in that area) had been located. The conquerors took over the highest priestly office of the goddess, imposed a cult of a male god, and manipulated myth to reduce the status of the goddess and enhance that of their own god. This was the first Yoruba kingdom, Ife, from which the others claimed to derive their dynasties. This conquest occurred sometime between the fifth and ninth centuries A.D. Some cultural influences stemming eventually from the Mediterranean area came with this invasion, as evidenced by metallurgical technology and the "fish-legged" figure motif. Yoruba culture is the result of a merger of the Yoruba-speaking Neolithic farmers with Iron age invaders, modified by later external contacts via trade, and internal growth and innovation.[26]

Kingdoms were founded among the Yoruba before Islamic influence was a factor that might affect forms and ideas. The basic form of Akan kingship is likewise pre-Islamic and was probably brought to the edge of the forest region by the Mande who at that time had not yet become Moslem. Later trade with Moslem Mande brought Islamic proselytization to the Brong and the Ashanti. The River God, Tano, was modified to become a receptacle of Islamic ideas. Friday, which is the day of special prayer for Moslems, became the day of respect for Tano, and this deity took on other characteristics suggestive of Moslem influence. The Friday cult of Tano is the only one that forbids the ritual participation of women. It was the conflict between the worship of misogynist Tano and that of the goddess Asase that caused the move of her day (in Ashanti) to Thursday, and it is the atmosphere created by the conflict between these cults that has fostered obscuration of Asase's attributes and eminence.[27]

On the whole, Akan kingdoms are as indifferent to Moslem concepts as are the Yoruba kingdoms; but both peoples, having kingdoms, were inevitably involved in regional interstate systems of diplomacy, war, and trade. Therefore, to some extent they were open to the flow of cultural influence coming from more distant states. Essentially this meant that their northward networks were connections to the Islamic world, just as their southern ones, after the fifteenth century, were maritime and European. Both of these outside linkages would have brought attitudes that were loath to grant cognizance to the cult of the Earth Goddess and the social and cultural value system that was part of this religion.

The tension between kingship and earth worship was present from the introduction of the concept of kingship to West Africa. Horses and metal weapons, as accoutrements of the warriors of the kings, were not permitted to be brought into the locality of an earth shrine.[28] The Ogboni society (Yoruba earth cult organization) has an uneasy relationship of competition and complementarity with kings. The opposition between kingship and the earth cult in West Africa is the old antagonism of the two revolutions, the Neolithic and the urban, with the second always striving to transform the first. The events in the early contact of the forces of the urban revolution and those of a

Neolithic society tend to set up in each ethnic area a pattern by which continuing conflict can be mediated—and thus later influences channeled—but each locality will have its own pecularities. The urban forces may arrive as military conquerors (as happened to the Yoruba) and set up a kingdom. Or they may arrive peacefully as traders (as seems to have been the Akan experience) and stimulate the creation of local kingdoms. Or, again, they may arrive as itinerant smiths, without sufficient force or wealth to effect the establishment of kingship, but still succeed in introducing some of their social and religious ideology; the last type fits the Ibo case.

In Yorubaland, the Neolithic heritage was protected as much as possible by the Ogboni society, which emerged in the politics of the early Ife kingdom as the autochtonous community of Earth Goddess worshipers, now entrenched against the pressure of new male deity cults introduced and favored by the conquering king and his men. In that remote time there were only a few enclaves of kingship in the West African grassland and no others yet in the forest. The Ife kings were willing to make compromises with the then-prevalent forces of Neolithic religion, and thus a considerable amount of Neolithic mythology was given some sanction, though not without attempts to reinterpret it.

In the Akan area, kingdoms were created at certain trading entrepôts only slightly earlier than the spread of Islamic influence. As Muslim merchants came to dominate the trade, they were much more confident in their ability to prevail than the first Ife kings had been, and less willing to give recognition to a supreme goddess. It is due to this ambience that the symbols of the Akan goddess, Asase, have become more muted than those of the Yoruba goddess, Onile, or of the Ibo goddess, Ale.

Only in two peripheral areas, on the north and the west, were the Ibo directly affected by attempts to establish kingdoms. Neither of these intrusive efforts had a lasting political success, but they were not without ideological influence. Nonetheless, the principal means of conversion in Iboland from the Neolithic earth cult to the urban Sky God cult was persuasion, and insofar as it was accomplished, this was achieved by smiths. The absence of royal authority accounts for the survival of a more pristine form of Neolithic religion in certain Ibo areas than elsewhere in the region we have surveyed.[29]

In all cases, whether kingship came early or late or not at all, whether Islamic influence was present in a strong or weak form or not at all, there was indirect contact with kingdoms through trade and the network of smiths, whose guild generally enjoyed protection even in times of war. The area in which a Neolithic type of religion persisted became ever more diminished as time went on and the character of the outside influence became more and more consistently patrilineal in the social sphere and patriarchial in the religious sphere, so that the original cults of the Earth Goddess suffered a persistent attrition.

What has been attempted here is comparable to what Sir William Jones in the eighteenth century essayed in his "On the Gods of Greece, Italy, and India," and some of his words will stand us in good stead:

> We cannot justly conclude, by arguments preceding the proof of facts, that one idolatrous people must have borrowed their deities, rites, and tenets from another; since Gods of all shapes and dimensions may be formed by the boundless powers of imagination, or by the frauds and follies of men, in countries never connected; but when features of resemblance, too strong to have been accidental, are observable in different systems of polytheism, without fancy or prejudice to colour them and improve the likeness, we can scarce help believing, that some connection has immemorially subsisted between the several nations, who have adopted them.[30]

That Sir William's demonstration be judged creditable does not, of course, make mine convincing; his comparisons were more detailed and the time depth of the relationships shallower, as well as falling within a single language family (the Indo-European, which he had discovered); yet the "features of resemblance" set out above deserve scrutiny and consideration.

## Conclusion

The relationship that Durkheim saw between society and religion is not apparent in the West African religions surveyed above if one takes a static view of them, but a historical perspective brings out what the static view obscured. However, the reconstruction of religious history for this area is a scarcely explored field. The problems of applying to a nonliterate area techniques used elsewhere in the comparative study of religion and history of religions are considerable. What is presented here can be no more than a set of working hypotheses to be assessed by other scholars. The emphasis of this article has not been to use history to prove theory but rather to use theory to help order the data for historical reconstruction.

The implication of my investigation is that West Africa is an integral part of a single (though complex and areally dispersed) cultural tradition that began with the development of food-producing societies in Southwest Asia about ten millenia ago and has since affected most of the Old World. Almost everywhere these early cultural forms are overlain with a second phase of diffusion, this time of urban influences, which began spreading from the same Southwest Asian locus about five thousand years ago. Africans participated in the Neolithic revolution and contributed to it, domesticating millet, sorghum, the oil palm, the African yam, and other crops. They accommodated the Neolithic religion to their social and natural environment, utilizing the artistic and mythopoetic qualities for which Africans are justly famous, but the modifications they innovated are within the range of variation found in the wider extent of Neolithic societies throughout the Old World. The rain forest, being an obstacle to the carriers of the subsequent metal-age technology and ideology, eventually became in effect a refuge area for the lingering remnants of the Neolithic religion—a survival that had already been prolonged by the intervention of the Sahara.

If other scholars agree that this framework is valid, there will have to be a reexamination and reinterpretation of African religions; and, where still possible, more fieldwork is needed before Islam and Christianity further submerge the ancient African faiths.

## Notes

1. Paques, *L'Arbre cosmique*, p. 8.

2. The thesis presented here is sketched as an overview, leaving particular points to be argued more extensively in a later publication, now tentatively titled "West Africa and the Eurasian Ecumene." Since 1962, when I presented a still-unpublished paper—"West African Religions"—I have touched on the problem in several papers, notably "Culture Map," "The Hornbill and Analogous Forms," "Mud Sculpture," and others cited below.

3. For example, even a gifted ethnographer like Rattray could write, "The Ashanti regard the Sky and the Earth as their two great deities" (*Ashanti*, p. 214), and then have eleven pages on which reference is made to Asase, the Earth Goddess, whereas fifty-two pages have reference to Nyame, "the Supreme Being, or Sky-God." There is a chapter devoted to the Sky God but

none to the Earth Goddess, and two subsequent volumes of his ethnography do not redress the balance. He does substantiate that she is the ultimate mother (ibid., p. 214; *Ashanti Law*, p. 343; *Religion and Art*, p. 162), and that she is the source of all bounty (*Ashanti Law*, pp. 242, 243). Offerings are made to her (*Ashanti*, p. 52), and she requires moral behavior and has the power to punish offenders (ibid., pp. 225, 226).

In contrast, Manoukian (*Akan and Ga-Adagme Peoples*) makes no mention of Asase, the Akan Earth Goddess. Likewise, Forde (*The Yoruba-Speaking Peoples*) makes no mention of Onile (or Oduduwa), the Yoruba Earth Goddess. It has been more difficult to ignore Ale (or Ala or Ane), the Ibo Earth Goddess, because she is so prominent, but she is often given brief and inadequate mention. However, Talbot, in several works, and a few others have presented a fuller depiction. And Zwernemann (*Die Erde in Vorstellungswelt*) gives a sensitive survey of all of West Africa.

4. Parrinder (*West African Religion*) adopted this geographical delimitation without giving any rationale for it as a region. It is only the eastern half of one of Herskovits's culture areas, though he refers to it as a "focal" area in *Myth of the Negro Past* (pp. 79, 80). Murdock makes the Akan (Twi), with the Ewe and a few other small populations, a separate province of the "the Yam belt" (*Africa*, map 13, p. 223, and chap. 32); in general he follows fairly closely Baumann's culture provinces (personal communication). Zwernemann (*Die Erde in Vorstellungswelt*) includes in his *Ostliche Oberguineakuste* just the area I have delimited, but extends it slightly further eastward, which is culturally as well as ecologically defensible but runs into the problem of accounting for the culture history of the so-called Semi-Bantu peoples.

5. Durkheim, *Elementary Forms*, passim, esp. pp. 241 ff. To quote Benoit-Smüllyan, ". . . the fundamental idea of Durkheim's *Les formes elementaires de la vie religieuse* is that religion is entirely a 'social thing.' This involves two distinct theses: first, that religious ideas and practices refer to or symbolize the social group, and second, that association is the generating source, or efficient cause, of religious experience" ("Sociologism," p. 514). We are concerned here only with the first thesis. And use of Durkheim's theory does not imply that Max Weber's rather different interpretation is rejected: there are different contexts, so that on the whole they supplement each other.

6. McCall, "Queen, Queen Mother." See Rattray, *Ashanti Law*, chap. 11, and *Ashanti*, p. 106.

7. Morton-Williams, "Cosmology of the Oyo-Yoruba"; McCall, "The Marvelous Chicken."

8. Early references to the temple of Ale, known as Mbari ("decorated") Houses, are collected in Forde and Jones, *Ibo and Ibibio-Speaking Peoples*; later work by Cole appears in various issues of the journal *African Arts*. Descent systems are explicated in Ottenberg, *Double Descent*; and Nyugbe, *Ohoffia*. Other aspects of Ibo society are described in Henderson, *The King in Every Man*; Ischei, *History of the Igbo People*; Uchendu, *The Igbo*; and Neaher, *Bronzes of Southern Nigeria*.

9. The antihistorical bias of Radcliffe-Brown and others has lost ground in anthropology, especially since Evans-Pritchard's Marrett Lecture (1950), which foreshadowed his *Anthropology and History*. That bias never prevailed in American anthropology; see Kroeber, *An Anthropologist Looks at History*.

10. Malinowski, "Myth in Primitive Psychology." Malinowski's debt to Durkheim for this concept has been obscured: see McCall, "Malinowski."

11. Aliman, *The Prehistory of Africa*; Forde-Johnston, *Neolithic Cultures*; Davies, *West Africa*; Clark, *The Prehistory of Africa* p. 205 (for quoted dates); Mauny, *Les Siècles obscurs*, chap. 2, esp. p. 50; McCall, "Culture Map" (on routes of agricultural diffusion). Murdock (*Africa*) and Diop (*African Origin*) do not accept a non-African source, but archeological evidence demolishes both of these theories. Huard (*Le Sahara*) is the source of the phrase "3000 years before the pharoahs." The "primary Neolithic" is that time period from the beginning of food production to the beginning of political state organization; those societies which persisted in a Neolithic condition subsequent to that time are part of the "secondary Neolithic." The importance of making the distinction is that all secondary Neolithic societies may have been influenced by the diffusion of ideas from urban societies. The classic statement of the characteristics of Neolithic and urban societies is Childe, *Man Makes Himself*.

12. Hawkes and Woolley, *Prehistory*, pp. 264, 343, 350.

13. Campbell, *Primitive Mythology*, p. 139 (for a comparison to the litany of Mary); Hawkes and Woolley, *Prehistory*, p. 338 (and fig. 55c for the dove); McCall, "The Prevalence of Lions"; James, *The Tree of Life*, p. 163. Nowhere are all these symbols drawn together in one discussion; that will be attempted in the work promised in n. 2.

14. Kroeber, *Anthropology*.

15. Crawford, *The Eye Goddess*.

16. Williams, "Iconology"; Morton-Williams, "Cosmology of the Oyo-Yoruba"; Meyerowitz, *The Akan*, p. 28; my field notes, 1952; Paques, *L'Arbre cosmique*; Dieterlin, *La Religion bambara*. The Grebo of Liberia, the Lobi of the Ivory Coast and Upper Volta, and the Birifor of northern Ghana, I can testify from my own investigations, follow the Mande pattern of number/gender symbolism.

17. Ellis, *The Yoruba Speaking Peoples*, p. 41, and *The Tshi-Speaking Peoples*, p. 62. "The chief god resides in the Adanse Hills. It is represented as female, black in color and monstrous in size" (Ellis, *The Tshi-Speaking Peoples*, p. 62). He probably refers to a sculpture of her; he does not specify that she is an earth goddess, but as Ashanti traditions claim an origin in Adanse, identifying the Adanse chief deity with Asase is not unreasonable (Rattray, *Religion and Art*, p. 238, fig. 127).

18. Meek, *Law and Authority*, p. 21; Talbot, *Tribes of the Niger Delta*.

19. McCall, "The Marvelous Chicken."

20. Rattray, *Ashanti*, p. 142, fig. 52; Evans, "The Akan Doctrine of God," p. 248.

21. McCall, "The Akan Planetary Week"; Christaller, *Dictionary* (see Asase,

A'fuwa, Yaa, and Appendix B III); Williamson, *Akan Religion*, p. 88. In 1975, I was told that western Akan groups also observed Friday as Asase's day.

22. Colson, *The Week*; Ojo, *Yoruba Culture*.

23. The planetary week must have diffused south from North Africa before the advent of Islam.

24. La Barre has a very sophisticated discussion of the problem (*They Shall Take Up Serpents*, pp. 62, 75, 76); he suggests "body-image symbolizing." Phallic connotations of snakes do not necessarily deny association with the goddess, but may indicate an aspect of service to her. See also Holas, *Animaux*, pp. 96, 97; and Herbert Cole, Mbari slides, set of 50, available from Professor Cole, Department of Art, University of California, Santa Barbara.

25. Dickson, Introduction, p. xvii. Note the identical forms in Akan and Ibo tree shrines and coiled snake sculptures; Ibo *ale*, earth and earth goddess, and Yoruba *ile* and *on-ile*, earth and earth goddess ("owner of the earth"), are linguistic cognates. Ashanti and Ibo have the same caution in placing something abruptly on the earth, out of respect for the goddess (Ellis, *The Ewe-Speaking Peoples*, pp. 139 ff.). Crowther in the latter half of the nineteenth century described the rites of Ado.

26. Fraser, "The Fish-Legged Figure"; Williams, "Metal Work" (on smelting furnace distribution).

27. The character of Tano is quite complex; see Rattray's ethnography (all 3 vols.). I have a half-written article on the problem ("The Great God Tano").

28. Goody, *Technology*.

29. Shaw, *Igbo-Ukwu*; Stevenson, *Population and Political Systems*.

30. Jones, *Asiatick Researches*, p. 319.

# Bibliography

Aliman, Henriette. *The Prehistory of Africa*. Paris, 1955. English trans. London: Hutchinson, 1957.

Barnes, Harry Elmer, ed. *An Introduction to the History of Sociology*. Chicago: University of Chicago Press, 1948.

Baumann, Hermann. Personal communication, 1964.

Benoit-Smüllyan, Emile. "The Sociologism of Emile Durkheim and His School." In *An Introduction to the History of Sociology*, edited by Harry Barnes, pp. 499–537. Chicago: University of Chicago Press, 1948.

Biobaku, Saburi Oladeni, ed. *Sources of Yoruba History*. New York and London: Oxford University Press, 1973.

Campbell, Joseph. *The Masks of God: Primitive Mythology*. New York: Viking Press, 1959.

Childe, Vere Gordon. *Man Makes Himself*. London: Watts, 1941.

Christaller, Rev. Johann Gottlieb. *Dictionary of the Asante and Fante Language called Tshi (Twi)*. 2d ed. Basel: Evangelical Missionary Society, 1933.

Clark, John Desmond. *The Prehistory of Africa*. New York: Praeger, 1970.
Cole, Herbert. "Art as a Verb in Iboland." *African Arts*, Autumn 1969, pp. 34–41.
_____. "Mbari Is a Dance." *African Arts*, Summer 1969, pp. 42–51.
_____. "Mbari Is Life." *African Arts*, Spring 1969, pp. 8–17.
Colson, F. H. *The Week*. London: Cambridge University Press, 1926.
Crawford, Osbert Guy Stanhope. *The Eye Goddess*. London: Phoenix House, 1957.
Danguah, Joseph Boakye. *The Akan Idea of God*. 1944. 2d ed. London: Cass, 1968.
Davies, Oliver. *West Africa before the Europeans*. London: Methuen, 1967.
Dickson, Kwesi. Introduction to *The Akan Idea of God*, by Joseph Danguah. 1944. 2d ed. London: Cass, 1968.
Dieterlin, Germaine. *Essai sur la religion bambara*. Paris: Presses Universitaires de France, 1950.
Diop, Cheik Anta. *The African Origin of Civilization: Myth or Reality*. Translated by Mercer Cook. New York: L. Hill, 1974.
Durkheim, Emile. *The Elementary Forms of the Religious Life*. Glencoe, Ill.: Free Press, 1954.
Ellis, Alfred Burden. *The Ewe-Speaking Peoples of the Slave Coast*. London: Chapman and Hall, 1890.
_____. *The Tshi-Speaking Peoples of the Gold Coast in West Africa*. London: Chapman and Hall, 1887.
_____. *The Yoruba-Speaking Peoples of the Slave Coast in West Africa*. Oosterhout, Netherlands: Anthropological Publications, 1894.
Evans, H. "The Akan Doctrine of God." In *African Ideas of God*, edited by E. W. Smith, pp. 241–259. London: Edinburgh House, 1950.
Evans-Pritchard, Evan. *Anthropology and History*. Manchester: Manchester University Press, 1961.
Forde, Cyril Darryl. *The Yoruba-Speaking Peoples of South-Western Nigeria*. London: International African Institute, 1951.
_____, and Jones, G. I. *The Ibo and Ibibio-Speaking Peoples of Southeastern Nigeria*. London: International African Institute, 1950.
Forde-Johnston, James. *Neolithic Cultures of North Africa*. Liverpool: Liverpool University Press, 1959.
Fraser, Douglas. "The Fish-Legged Figure in Benin and Yoruba Art." In *African Art and Leadership*, by Douglas Fraser and Herbert Cole, pp. 261–94. Madison: University of Wisconsin Press, 1972.
_____, and Cole, Herbert. *African Art and Leadership*. Madison: University of Wisconsin Press, 1972.
Goody, John Rankine. *Technology, Tradition and the State in Africa*. London: Oxford University Press, 1971.
Hawkes, Jacquetta, and Woolley, Sir Leonard. *Prehistory and the Beginnings of Civilization*. New York: UNESCO Press, 1963.
Henderson, Richard. *The King in Every Man*. New Haven: Yale University Press, 1972.

Herskovits, Melville Jean. *The Human Factor in Changing Africa*. New York: Alfred A. Knopf, 1962.

———. *The Myth of the Negro Past*. 2d ed. Boston: Beacon Press, 1958.

Holas, Bohomil. *Animaux dans la sculture ivorienne*. Paris: P. Greunthner, 1969.

Huard, Paul. *Le Sahara avant le desert*. Paris: Arthaud, 1970.

Ischei, Elizabeth. *A History of the Igbo People*. London, 1976.

James, Edwin Oliver. *The Tree of Life*. Leiden: E. J. Brill, 1966.

Jones, Sir William. *Asiatick Researches*. In *The Works of Sir William Jones*, edited by Lord Teignmouth. London: J. Stockdale and J. Walker, 1807.

Kroeber, Alfred Louis. *An Anthropologist Looks at History*. Berkeley: University of California Press, 1963.

———. *Anthropology*. New York: Harcourt, Brace, 1948.

La Barre, Weston. *They Shall Take Up Serpents*. Minneapolis: University of Minnesota Press, 1962.

McCall, Daniel Francis. "The Akan Planetary Week." Unpublished paper, American Society for Ethnohistory, 1966. To be incorporated into "West Africa and the Eurasian Ecumene."

———. "Culture Map and Time-Profile of the Mande." In *Papers on the Manding*, edited by Carleton Hodge, pp. 27–98. Bloomington: Indiana University Press, 1971.

———. "The Great God Tano." Unfinished MS.

———. "Historical Implications in West African Religions." Unpublished paper, Colloquium on African History, African Studies Center, Boston University, 1962.

———. "The Hornbill and Analogous Forms in West African Sculpture." In *African Images*, edited by Daniel McCall and Edna Bay, pp. 268–324. New York: Africana Publishers, 1975.

———. "Malinowski: An Ideological Portrait." Unfinished Ms.

———. "The Marvelous Chicken and Its Companion in Yoruba Myth and Art." *Paideuma* 24 (1978).

———. "Mud Sculpture: Flesh of Mother Earth?" Unpublished paper, African Studies Association meetings, 1976 (copies available from ASA, Brandeis University, Waltham, Mass.).

———. "The Prevalence of Lions." *Paideuma* 19/20 (1973/74): 130–45.

———. "Queen, Queen Mother, Princess and Great Wife: Female Political Office in African Traditional States." Unpublished paper, Northeastern Anthropological Association meetings, 1966. To be incorporated into "West Africa and the Eurasion Ecumene."

———. "West Africa and the Eurasian Ecumene." Unfinished MS.

Malinowski, Bronislaw. *Magic, Science and Religion*. Garden City, N.Y.: Doubleday, 1954.

Manoukian, Madelaine. *Akan and Ga-Adagme Peoples of the Gold Coast*. London: International African Institute, 1950.

Mauny, Raymond. *Les Siècles obscurs de L'Afrique noire*. Paris: Fayard, 1971.

Meek, Charles Kingsley. *Law and Authority in a Nigerian Tribe*. London: Oxford University Press, 1937.

Meyerowitz, Eva. *The Akan of Ghana*. London: Faber and Faber, 1958.

Morton-Williams, Peter. "An Outline of the Cosmology and the Cult Organization of the Oyo-Yoruba." *Africa* 34, no. 3 (1964): 243–61.

Murdock, George Peter. *Africa: Its Peoples and Their Culture History*. New York: McGraw-Hill, 1959.

Neaher, Nancy. *Bronzes of Southern Nigeria and Igbo Metal-smithing Traditions*. Ann Arbor: University of Michigan Microfilms, 1976.

Nyugbe, P. O. *Ohoffia: A Matrilineal Ibo People*. London: Oxford University Press, 1974.

Ojo, Afolabi. *Yoruba Culture*. London: University of London Press, 1966.

Ottenberg, Simon. *Double Descent in an African Society*. Seattle: University of Washington Press, 1968.

Paques, Viviana. *L'Arbre cosmique dans la pensée populaire et dans la vie quotidienne du Nord-ost Africaine*. Paris: Presses Universitaires du France, 1964.

Parrinder, Edward Geoffrey. *West African Religion*. 2d ed. London: Epworth, 1961.

Radcliffe-Brown, Alfred Reginald. *Structure and Function in Primitive Society*. Glencoe, Ill.: Free Press, 1952.

Rattray, Robert Sutherland. *Ashanti*. Oxford: Oxford University Press, Clarendon Press, 1923.

———. *Ashanti Law and Constitution*. Oxford: Oxford University Press, Clarendon Press, 1929.

———. *Religion and Art in Ashanti*. Oxford: Oxford University Press, Clarendon Press, 1927.

Shaw, Thurston. *Igbo-Ukwu*. Evanston: Northwestern University Press, 1970.

Smith, Edwin William, ed. *African Ideas of God*. London: Edinburgh House, 1950.

Stevenson, Robert. *Population and Political Systems in Tropical Africa*. New York: Columbia University Press, 1968.

Talbot, Percy Amaury. *The Tribes of the Niger Delta*. London: Sheldon Press, 1932.

Uchendu, Victor. *The Igbo of Southeastern Nigeria*. New York: Holt, Rinehart and Winston, 1965.

Williams, Denis. "Art in Metal." In *Sources of Yoruba History*, edited by Saburi O. Biobaku, pp. 140–64. London: Oxford University Press, 1973.

———. "Iconology of the Yoruba *Edam Ogboni*." *Africa* 34, no. 2 (1964): 139–66.

Williamson, S. G. *Akan Religion and the Christian Faith*. Legon: University of Ghana Press, 1965.

Zwernemann, Jurgen. *Die Erde in Vorstellungswelt und Kultpraktiken des Sudanischen Völker*. Berlin: D. Reimer, 1968.

# Conclusion:
# New Perspectives on Mother Worship
## by James J. Preston

### Early Theories

In the nineteenth and early twentieth centuries a number of historians, psychologists, and anthropologists advanced elaborate schemes designed to explain the worship of female deities. Yet none of these theories were adequate as explanatory devices; they were based on armchair speculations and were heavily burdened with biases about human nature. Consequently, the topic of mother worship fell into obscurity. But with the contemporary changing role of women in world cultures, along with resurgent studies of symbolism and religious cults, a new interest in the phenomenon has emerged.

Recent improvements in anthropological field techniques have produced refined data previously unavailable to scholars. Also, there is a clearer understanding today of how symbolic forms relate to specific cultural contexts. These new developments have stimulated some scholars to construct crosscultural hypotheses to explain worldwide patterns of religious behavior. A marked resurgence of interest in the connections between culture and symbolic forms is becoming evident.[1] Therefore, the time is ripe for a *new* comparative perspective on key themes in world religions.[2]

This focus on universal religious themes was once a major interest of social scientists. Early theories proposed by great figures like Freud, Tylor, Morgan, and Durkheim need to be examined and reformulated to fit the large amount of data on religion that has been gathered through decades of intensive fieldwork. Mother worship is a major theme in world religions that demands a theoretical framework built on adequate sources of crosscultural data. This volume of essays on the subject is offered as a first step toward rekindling the kind of scholarly dialogue necessary to produce a new synthesis.

Difficult questions are raised by reopening the topic of mother worship. Fortunately, today we are largely free from many of the problems faced by the early comparative evolutionists. For instance, we no longer seek a unilinear evolutionary scale with clear stages in which to place goddess cults. Nor do we need to find a place or time of origin for the phenomenon. Some nineteenth-century cultural evolutionists postulated an early matriarchal social order, reasoning that the general predominance of women in society was reflected in a parallel set of relationships among the deities. Thus, female deities should be found wherever matriarchal social organization is manifested. The idea that the first period of human history was matriarchal, vigorously advanced by J. J. Bachofen and others, has been almost universally discredited.[3] But this notion still persists in current popular writings about goddess worship. It is unfortunate that authors of such writings ignore the evidence against this misleading assumption about early cultural evolution. In a brilliant essay, Carolyn Fleuhr-Lobban discusses the preconceptions that have clouded the argument for a matriarchate. These include the following:

> First, there is the assumption that the presence of female deities and female figures in ancient myth and symbol is evidence for a historical epoch of mother-rule or matriarchy. Bachofen originated this idea, and Engels utilized it in his formulations. Second, there is the assumption that matrilineal societies are survivals of a prior matriarchal era. Morgan arrived at this conclusion, and Engels did not take a different view. Third, there is the assumption of a natural and necessary relationship between matrilineality and matriarchy. All these assumptions are unwarranted.[4]

The majority of British and American anthropologists totally reject any notion of the priority of matriarchal social organization. Humans evolved for millions of years in small bands as hunter-gatherers who stressed equality among members. And though there was not absolute equality between men and women among hunter-gatherers, "women cannot be considered matriarchs or men patriarchs."[5] Such social differentiation could occur only in class-ranked societies, which first emerged with agriculture about ten thousand years ago. Furthermore, even in the few contemporary groups with matrilineal social organization, power remains in the hands of males (usually the mother's brother). Thus, the assumption that matriarchy was a general stage in culture history that preceded patriarchy is totally unfounded and misleading. According to Rudiger Schott this whole issue can be put to final rest: "I suggest that the matriarchate be given a decent burial in the cemetery of anthropological figments together with the 'aboriginal horde,' 'group marriage,' and 'primeval promiscuity.'"[6]

Bachofen's work on mother worship, nevertheless, must not be taken lightly. His mistake was common among nineteenth-century scholars who used legends and folklore as sources of evidence for historical stages of cultural evolution. Bachofen thought folk culture preserved the collective memory of people. Thus, legends become in their transformations "a living expression of the stages in a people's development, and for the skillful observer, a faithful reflection of all the periods in the life of that people."[7] Robert Briffault spent his life constructing a theory of mother worship based on evidence similar to that employed by Bachofen.[8] Despite serious inaccuracies in their theories, at least these scholars were not afraid to engage in bold speculation. Though social science theory must proceed cautiously and with meticulous attention to gaps in the data, it becomes impotent without the construction of grand-scale theoretical frameworks for explaining significant variants of human nature. The mid-twentieth century was bankrupt of such theory construction, but a new epoch has dawned. We are now capable of developing relatively sophisticated generalizations about human nature grounded in several decades of firsthand field research.

The most common error emanating from the works of Bachofen and Briffault is found also among other scholars writing at the turn of the century. This is the idea that religious symbolism is an epiphenomenon, a mere projection of psychological or social realities. Thus, if women have low status in a particular society, the same pattern will be echoed at the level of ideology in the relative position of gods to goddesses. Recently, Marina Warner has attacked this erroneous, but persistent, remnant of social and psychological determinism: "There is no logical equivalence in any society between exalted female objects of worship and a high position for women."[9] There can be no doubt that symbolic forms, such as deities, are somewhat *shaped* by life experiences and conceived in familiar terms. But the ideological realm cannot be explained simply as a projection of other domains of human experience. Though ideology is informed by social and psychological factors, it has an independent, self-perpetuating mode that resists reductionist interpretations. It is impossible to predict the types of deities in a religious system from an analysis of social structure or the personalities of individuals found in a particular culture. The presence of powerful goddesses in a religious pantheon rarely reflects anything about the role of females in that particular society. The idea that religion is a derived, secondary institution is simplistic and naive.

Psychologists have also contributed significantly to theories about mother worship. Freud suggested that goddess worship stems from unconscious fantasies shared by all people. In his opinion devotion to female deities represents an infantile desire for reunification with the mother. Raphael Patai summarizes this Freudian view of the psychological components of mother worship: "The Freudian position on the goddess is that she represents that stage in the early development of the human individual in which the mother appears to the child as the all-powerful source of both gratification and deprivation. The goddess is a mother figure whose qualities are universal because they stem from unconscious fantasies common to all peoples from time immemorial, which have their primary source in the infantile mind."[10] The child repudiates the father's role in procreation and longs for a pure, virginal mother.

Jung goes a step further by invoking an archetypal feminine principle to explain mother worship. This innate universal archetype combines both positive and negative attributes, forming complementary and interlocking components in the human psyche. Jung's contribution is significant because it incorporates the rich symbolism represented both in the great world religions and among primitive peoples. Unfortunately, Jung ignores the cultural contexts of the mass of symbols he musters to prove his contention of a universal feminine archetype. He treats symbols as though they were floating, disconnected entities separated from sociocultural realities. This shallow treatment of the phenomenon weakens the potential force of his perceptive and largely intuitive insights about mother symbolism. Erich Neumann is the chief proponent of the Jungian interpretation of goddess symbolism.[11] His classic book *The Great Mother* is the most comprehensive treatment of the feminine aspects of divinity. Unfortunately, Neumann merely extends the paper-thin, semimystical interpretations of Jung, his mentor.

Such great minds must be admired for their attempt to place this enigmatic phenomenon in a meaningful framework. But their theories are disconcertingly unidimensional, offering few insights about social, environmental, and economic variables that impinge upon mother worship. Human behavior cannot be reduced to innate principles, infantile fantasies, or archetypes. And even though the psychological roots of mother worship may be universal, generalizations on such a grand scale as those proposed by nineteenth-century scholars were premature. It is evident from the studies presented in this volume that the phenomenon is more complex and problematic than previously assumed. Early theorists were asking questions that led them astray from the most important issues surrounding mother worship. Instead of explaining the adoration of female deities by employing convenient innate principles lodged in the human psyche, these early scholars should have been probing into the great multiplicity of the phenomenon to understand *how* mother worship is perpetuated and *why* this form of religious expression is utilized in place of others when there is a wide range of modes for expressing religious impulses.

Perhaps the questions asked today about mother worship are less ambitious than those advanced by scholars at the turn of the century. Yet, in some ways, the new questions are more focused and fundamental to our understanding of human nature. The whole framework of knowledge about man has shifted. We know that ecological factors must be taken into account in any matter concerning human evolution. It is imperative, therefore, to inquire how ecological conditions contribute to sustaining, giving rise to, or inhibiting the development of mother worship. Also, how do we explain the paradoxes associated with female sacred images: that they appear motherly, nurturant, and protective under some conditions, but become instruments of destruction, terror, and death in others?[12] And there is no reason to ignore an evolutionary perspective on mother worship just because Bachofen, and others, made the error of associating it with matriarchy. We must continue to probe into the role of goddess symbolism in the evolution of religion. This time the questions should be more specific. Instead of suggesting a psychic unity for man, with predetermined stages of evolution, it is more appropriate to consider the role of mother worship in the development of specific religious systems. Under what conditions does mother worship emerge and flourish, or recede into the background? We should be concerned also about how this phenomenon relates to human needs. Is goddess worship particularly suited to persons experiencing special life crisis problems? Perhaps the most important question has to do with the symbolic process itself; that is, how do symbolic systems unfold and evolve to become increasingly more complex forms? What stimulates or inhibits this evolution of symbols? And what role does mother worship play in speaking to human consciousness about the nature of divinity?

The questions proposed above are not exhaustive. Each culture area presents the reader with another facet of mother worship, providing, it is hoped, a broad range of problems to be integrated eventually in a larger theoretical framework. Each study presented here has contributed a unique perspective on the topic. Goddesses are multivariant and retain strong cultural differences contributing to the parochial needs of individuals. Yet significant common refrains can be abstracted from data on mother deities in diverse religious and cultural contexts.

## Common Patterns of Mother Worship in World Cultures

The most striking feature of mother worship is its antiquity as established in the archaeological record.[13] Fertility goddesses were the first deities formally worshiped by human beings. Patai observes the ubiquity of such mother images in prehistory:

> They stood by the cradle of Homo Sapiens, and testified to his earliest known appearance in Europe, some thirty to forty thousand years ago, as evidenced by the discovery in Aurignacian deposits of statuettes of nude women with enormous breasts and buttocks and protruding abdomens. These figurines, representing in a highly stylized and exaggerated form women in an advanced stage of pregnancy, are usually referred to as paleolithic Venuses . . . and are generally regarded by students of prehistory as having had religious significance.[14]

Similar goddess figures have been found throughout Europe, western Asia and the Middle East. There has been much speculation about their meaning. Usually, Venuses are interpreted as part of a widespread fertility cult that disappeared after the Ice Age and then re-emerged during the Neolithic. These later Neolithic goddesses were unmistakably related to a well-established cult of Mother Earth, taking various forms in different places, and associated with the development of agriculture. Goddesses were worshiped in the earliest civilizations of Sumer, Egypt, and the Indus Valley. They were part of an equation between the fertility of earth, the pregnancy of women, and the divine feminine principle represented in elaborate pantheons of deities.[15] For instance, the ancient Near Eastern goddess Astarte was widely worshiped as a fertility deity by the Hebrews. (The name Astarte means "womb.")[16] This ancient fertility function of the goddess remains active in folk religion throughout the world. In India, women still turn to goddesses to attain pregnancy. South Asian earth mothers link the fecundity of crops with the fertile human womb.

Corn mother dolls are still placed in fields by some European peasants and American Indians.

Most goddesses, wherever they are found, are connected in some way to motherhood, the bearing of children, and, in many cases, a principle of purity symbolized by virginity. This nurturant characteristic of female deities is highly visible in the studies included in this volume. Even goddesses not *directly* associated with motherhood are connected to the nurturant function through other deities. This is often the case in pantheons of deities that include numerous goddesses; for instance, in complex pantheons where feminine functions are divided and specialized among several sister deities the nurturant function may be represented by only one of the divinities. A striking example of the nurturant quality of a goddess is the Canaanite Asherah. She was the wet nurse of the gods, who "suckled even human princes."[17] Similarly, in the ancient Hindu Vedic tradition a theme common to all Indo-European peoples emerged, in which sky father impregnated earth mother with rain; her offspring became the gods.[18] But it is rare for female deities to be nurturant alone; they also have nonnurturant qualities. Certain Hindu goddesses, such as Saraswati and Kali, are associated largely with nonnurturant aspects of divinity. Saraswati is the goddess of learning, worshiped primarily by students. Kali combats demons and often receives animal sacrifices to quench her thirst for blood. Yet these two goddesses are addressed as *ma* ("mother") by devotees because Hindu female deities represent different manifestations of one all-embracing Great Goddess, the Divine Mother, who represents both creative and destructive aspects of divinity. Even the Virgin Mary displays a "motherly aggression against those who threaten her young."[19] Thus, despite certain nonnurturant attributes, female divinities display a universal nurturant quality and are conceived by devotees as "mother" no matter how little the motherly aspect is emphasized at the abstract theological level of the Great Tradition. In folk religion female deities are "mothers" with both nurturant and nonnurturant qualities.

Another universal characteristic of mother worship is ambivalence. Female deities are fraught with paradox, combining such opposites as love and anger, trust and terror, forgiveness and vengeance. In this volume the Indian goddesses Shitala and Kali and the Christian Madonna of the Arch display such opposites and the consequent ambivalence elicited in their devotees. Neumann explains the negative and positive attributes of goddesses by asserting the existence of three forms of the Great Mother archetype: (1) the good mother, (2) the terrible mother, and (3) the good-bad mother. The Great Mother is the divine vessel—the central symbol of life—equated with women and the human body. Neumann insists that the image of the divine feminine is universal and deeply embedded in the human psyche.[20] It is not necessary to invoke an innate archetype to explain the widespread ambivalence represented in goddess worship. Even conceding Neumann's thesis that the Great Goddess is a central life symbol, it is impossible to classify the many manifestations of the goddess in one of these three binary oppositions. Mother worship is more complex than Neumann would have us believe. As evidenced in this volume, goddesses are multifaceted phenomena, integrating a wide range of human experiences and aspirations. The Christian madonna, for instance, would be impossible to fit neatly into Neumann's scheme. She may be simultaneously "good mother," "terrible mother," even "good-bad mother" to devotees. The madonna is a polymorphic sacred image, combining certain characteristics in some settings and others elsewhere. She integrates maternal and life-giving qualities, while also symbolizing a focus for witness to the teachings of Christ. Mary is intercessor through her special access to her son. She may be perceived as an exemplary devotee, a symbol of purity, the protectress of human communities, or Queen of Heaven.[21] In some cases she takes only one of these forms. Occasionally she combines qualities associated with pagan goddesses, as in the case of Saint Brigid and the Madonna of the Arch. The madonna is a powerful focus of pilgrimage and miracle. The polymorphous feature of female divinities is the very factor that defies classification in a simple scheme like that proposed by Neumann. Indeed, if it were not for the great range of possible forms potential among goddesses, they would not be so frequently utilized as instruments of syncretism, fusing older modes of religious expression with new styles of worship.

To devotees, mother goddesses universally display a defensive function, protecting people from natural disasters or hazards associated with a particular occupation. In Spain, for instance, Our Lady of Macarena in Andalusia is protectress of bullfighters. The Virgin of Copacabana, patroness of Bolivia, protects fishermen from storms on Lake Titicaca.[22] Pilgrimage to Marian shrines has been associated with disasters such as famine, plague, flood, and blight. Victor Turner and Edith Turner note this significant role of the madonna figure as a source of refuge from disasters:

> In patrilineal, patrimonial, and patriarchal social systems, attachments through women . . . come to stand for the seamless unity of

the whole community, its *prima materia*, so to speak—as against the association of paternity and, by extension, masculinity, with property, law, the delimitation and demarcation of rights and duties, the rules of succession to high office; that is, parceling out and division of all kinds, "pattern" against "matter." Thus Mary is purity, totality, protection against law, who pleads with her divine Son to show sinners mercy rather than punish them according to their just deserts. Mary is a sanctuary, a refuge, a source of remedies.[23]

This protective aspect of the divine feminine extends beyond the danger of natural disasters or hazardous occupations; it also includes protection from enemies who threaten the often fragile fabric of human communities. When people unite to combat a common enemy, goddesses act as symbols of integration. In many parts of the world female deities incorporate people of different races, religions, and language groups under a single symbolic banner. Once again, Roman Catholicism affords appropriate examples. Tutelary madonna figures are found in South America, Europe, Asia, and Africa; and some madonnas, like the dark Virgin of Guadalupe, protectress of Mexico, have symbolic power for representing international levels of human community. By papal decree, the Virgin of Guadalupe has transcended her Mexican cultural identity to become Empress of the Americas.[24] In Bolivia the Virgin of Copacabana represents the collective ethnicity of her people.[25] Poland offers a famous instance of how a madonna can unify the national identity of an oppressed people:

The Polish nation attributes its very existence to the help of
the Virgin of Czestochowa. The veneration of the picture of the
Madonna is the expression of the Polish nation's faith and gratitude. . . . After the partition of Poland between Austria, Prussia,
and Russia the Polish people, although divided into three different
states under foreign domination, remained undivided in their
faithfulness to Mary, Queen of Poland. In every Polish church there
was and there still is a reproduction of the Madonna of
Czestochowa.[26]

In this volume the goddess Kannagi of south India has a similar function. She is the master symbol and focal point of Tamil culture. This integrative, protective aspect of female deities has its darker side. Although at one level motherhood is widely associated with community and "mystical nationalism," it also may act as a divisive force, perpetuating parochialism, regionalism, and fragmentation.[27]

In this volume, Campbell illustrates such divisiveness in the conflict between two major virgins—Guadalupe and Remedios—who became identified with opposing forces in the Mexican War of Independence. Like other female sacred images found throughout the world, Mary is venerated as protectress at different levels of social organization, such as neighborhood, village, city, state, or region. And these levels may be either brought into opposition or unified through mother symbolism.

Everywhere sacred mother figures are associated with the advent and resolution of human problems. Most noteworthy in this connection is their role in the cause or cure of disease. Often miracle traditions are built around divine healings, associated with pilgrimage shrines famous for miraculous cures. In India, the goddess Shitala, when angered (see Kolenda and Nicholas in this volume), can *cause* smallpox, not just cure it. She must be cooled through appropriate offerings if the devotee is to be healed. People both fear and adore Shitala because she affects their health and fortune. The great Christian pilgrimage centers at Lourdes (1858) and Fatima (1917) are famous for the manifestation of the divine mother on earth to cure the ills of mankind.

One of the most intriguing, yet somewhat perplexing, problems related to mother deities is their frequent manifestations as virgins. How is it possible to conceive of a goddess as simultaneously *both* virgin and mother? This apparent "contradiction" exists in both Hinduism and Christianity. Paul Hershman's skillful analysis of goddess worship in the Punjab (India) concurs with Pandian's study in this volume, by explaining the dual symbolism of virginity and motherhood as a symbolic expression of spiritual purity:

> Punjabis themselves are aware that there is an uncomfortable juxtaposition in their beliefs concerning female sexuality and motherhood, but it is only the anthropologist who can pose a "contradiction" between the negative values of female sexuality and the positive values of maternal fertility. To the Punjabi these ideas are contextually separate and apart. Similarly I have been careful to entitle this essay "Virgin and Mother" and not "Virgin-Mother." The Mother goddess whom the Punjabis worship is not a "virgin-mother," she is a virgin *and* a mother: the Punjabis conceive of the goddess in some contexts as a virgin and others as a mother, but they never bring the two together to form a contradiction of which they themselves would be aware. . . .
> . . . In Punjabi ritual the symbols of the goddess who is both

virgin and mother, and the cow that is both animal and "human,"
do not so much synthesize contradictory values through their
anomalous character, but instead maintain the separateness of
those values while highlighting their proximity to one another.[28]

Hershman offers a key to the apparent contradiction of the female
deity as both mother and virgin: the virginity of a goddess is a symbolic statement of her spiritual purity, not to be taken literally or
confused with human sexuality. The divine mother should not be
understood as a mere projection of human motherhood. In many
societies the process of giving birth, with its associated blood and
placenta, is considered to be a polluting event that requires the practice of elaborate taboos for women. The divine mother gives birth and
sustains life, but does not usually become polluted by by these events.
She is the source of *all* life, the ultimate spark of being itself, involved
directly in human affairs, yet always transcendent because she is
divine. Ancient Near Eastern goddesses, like Inanna, Ishtar, and
Anath, combined the traits of chastity, promiscuity, motherliness,
and bloodthirstiness. These virgin deities were associated with fertility, love, and war; they were at once promiscuous and virginal. The
paradoxical unity of chastity and active sexuality in the same mother
goddess, so characteristic in the Near East, becomes a paradigm for
the later emergence of the Virgin Mary figure in Christianity.[29] This
combination of opposites should be no surprise to students of religion. Deities are supernatural beings not to be judged in human
terms. It is their capacity both to transcend and to penetrate into the
everyday life of communities that gives these divine figures a special
power and influence in human affairs. Edmund Leach expresses this
same point in an eloquent discussion of "virgin birth," suggesting
that virginity has a metaphorical rather than a literal meaning for
devotees:

> Now in its Christian context the myth of the Virgin Birth does
> *not* imply ignorance of the facts of physiological paternity. On the
> contrary, it serves to reinforce the dogma that the Virgin's child
> is the son of God. . . . It is plain . . . that Christians who say that
> they "believe" in the doctrine of the Virgin Birth or in the closely
> related doctrine of the Immaculate Conception are not ordinarily
> arguing from a position of ignorance; on the contrary these are
> doctrines of extreme philosophical sophistication.[30]

So far we have noted how mother goddesses are associated with
(1) the fertility of both crops and human beings, (2) the bearing of

children and nurturance, (3) the expression of human ambivalence, (4) protection from natural disasters, (5) mediation between humans and more distant male divinities, (6) justice, (7) ethnic identity, (8) healing, (9) spiritual purity, and (10) punishment. But mother deities are polymorphous. They have many more characteristics than those noted in this volume. Often goddesses spring organically out of nature and become associated with mountains, rivers, volcanoes, the sun or moon. Also, a mother goddess may become a receptacle for suffering, as she weeps for the sorrows of mankind.[31] In India, virgin girls may be worshiped as incarnations of the goddess; or the deity may take the form of the cow, mother of man.[32] In some parts of the world goddesses are intermediaries, consorts, or followers of a male deity. Sometimes the goddess is preeminent, mother of the gods, self-generated. At other times she requires blood, even human sacrifice, to be sustained. As Earth Mother, she may even menstruate, as in the case of the Hindu goddess Khamakya. In Arctic and Siberian religions the goddess is Mother of the Animals, who releases game, the source of food, or holds it back if she is dissatisfied.[33] The Virgin of Guadalupe is not only a symbol of national unity; she also relates to the private needs of individuals suffering from the terrors of death. She soothes Mexican villagers, who drink a milky sap (of the Maguey) called "Virgin's milk." A bottle of this liquor is placed in the coffins of dead children believed to be nursed on the Virgin's milk in the heavenly Garden of Flowers until they can be weaned.[34] Thus, mother goddesses as organic, self-generated deities become ubiquitous, polymorphic, and deeply entwined at all levels in the everyday events of human life.

## The Divine Feminine and Human Nature

A significant issue remains to be resolved: what is the relationship of the *symbols* of mother to the *empirical cultural reality* of mothers? None of the articles in this volume address this matter directly, but it is clear after reviewing them that mother symbolism is *not* a simple reflection of the cultural role of mothers or females in general. The Virgin of Guadalupe may be dark skinned like her Indian devotees, but in no way does she behave like a passive feminine figure in a world where males express what they consider to be their "rightful dominance" as expressed in the concept of machismo. Instead, in this context she is an idealized "model" of motherhood that transcends the ordinary dimensions of everyday life. Motherhood at this magnified macro-level takes on properties different from those of motherhood found at the microlevel of empirical reality. Yet in other contexts there may be a clear pattern of imitation of the deity, as in eastern India, where women behave as though they themselves were menstruating during the three days when the Earth Mother menstruates. But this imitation of the deity does not occur with all mother goddesses. Kali is a blood-thirsty Hindu deity who demands sacrifices, displays fury, and stands on the corpse of Lord Shiva. If anything, such symbolism represents an *inverse* relationship between the human empirical reality of moth-erhood and a more idealized concept of maternity that includes war-fare and bloodshed as part of the maternal function.

A crosscultural review of mother worship yields at least four types of relationship between motherhood as conceived at the symbolic level and motherhood as lived in empirical reality. Mother deities may be (1) reflections of sociocultural realities, (2) models to be imi-tated by humans, (3) opposites inversely related to their human coun-terparts, or (4) idealized extensions of motherhood as conceived and practiced in empirical reality. The same goddess symbol may be em-ployed in several of the ways noted above at different times and in various circumstances. An additional factor is also at work here. It is important to differentiate between levels of analysis. There is, for instance, a universal theological dimension of the Virgin Mary as established by the Roman ecclesia. This level transcends specific cul-tural contexts. There are also regional and local variants that may employ different formulas for conceiving of the relationship between the symbol and the empirical reality.

A more interesting question than the one of distinctions between symbols of mother and the actual role of mothers in specific cultures is why some religions repress or seem to omit mother symbolism. Of the great world religions mother deities appear to be either conspicu-ously absent or at least little emphasized in Theravada Buddhism, Judaism, Islam, and certain denominations of Protestant Christianity. Ferguson's article illustrates how mother symbolism can be repressed and latent within a religious tradition, as in the case of Burmese and Thai variants of Buddhism. Patai exposes the strong roots of goddess worship in Judaism, illustrating how the later Judaic tradition be-comes purged of mother symbolism. According to this scholar the powerful father symbolism in the God of Judaism was accompanied by a latent feminine element taking several intriguing shapes at vari-ous phases of Jewish history. This female aspect of Judaism reemerged during the Kabbalistic era and in Hassidism, then "disappeared from the Jewish God-concept to leave it centered upon a strictly monotheistic, spiritual, and non-corporeal but nevertheless masculine, godhead."[35] We know that at least one Protestant denomination refers to the supreme deity as "mother-father": Christian Science (founded by a woman). But divine motherhood is little emphasized among most Protestants. What could be the reason for this omission? Is it deliberate? And is it not curious that "women's rights" are stressed mostly in secular societies with strong Protestant backgrounds? Issues like these can be resolved only with further research.

Feminists have observed this general absence of feminine symbolism in Western religions like Judaism, Christianity, and Islam.[36] Yet some have overstated their cases by generalizing too widely on this issue. We have already noted the latent feminine symbolism in Judaism. And it is inaccurate to say that Christianity has purged itself of the divine feminine. In the Catholic tradition such symbolism not only exists, it thrives. Thus, the conspicuous absence of feminine symbolism is attributed more accurately to Islam and certain branches of Protestantism. According to Rita Gross this absence of bisexual symbolism is linked to the repression of women in Western societies: "It is undeniable that the male symbolism of deity has been a major contributor to the exclusion of women from positions of respect or authority in Western society and religion."[37] This is a simplistic explanation for the style of a particular theology. The relationship of symbol to society is far too complex for such facile conclusions. Each religion needs to be analyzed separately with full attention to cultural variations. For instance, to speculate that Protestant denominations omit feminine symbolism because of an attempt to exclude women from power overlooks other equally plausible explanations. Protestants deliberately streamlined their theologies to create a clear separation from Roman Catholicism. The Virgin Mary was one of the first icons to go in the iconoclasm of the Reformation. This explanation for the relative lack of female symbolism among Protestants is more feasible than that proposed by Gross. Feminist arguments on this issue will be more forceful and convincing if they avoid generalizations that suggest a necessary linkage between goddess symbolism and the social roles of women. No doubt there is a connection between ideology and social roles, but an understanding of one level does not predict the nature of the other. We have seen how nineteenth-century scholars fell into this trap and consequently became lost in a confusing set of misleading theories.

It is hoped that this volume has contributed in some small way to correcting the errors of those who came before. New issues are raised by current scholarship on mother worship. Some of these issues are biased by contemporary social and methodological problems. It is impossible, even undesirable, for us to avoid the questions that arise out of our present social conditions. All scholarship is somewhat colored by the central issues of a particular era. It is to be hoped, however, that we have learned something new since the nineteenth century, when mother worship was a flourishing topic of scholarship. The firsthand data of field researchers presents us with exciting new avenues of investigation.

Mother worship remains vital today as a form of religious experience, even in highly secularized societies. We know that the most popular pilgrimage shrines in Christianity are those devoted to Mary, and numerous Marian shrines have been established throughout the world in recent years.[38] Indeed, it appears that Marian apparitions are part of an emerging "Catholic millenarianism."[39]

Several essays in this volume discuss the role of mother deities as media for change (Preston, McKean, and Pandian). Despite the variety of goddesses in different cultural settings, all have one thing in common; they are *syncretic* aspects of divinity, cementing gaps between older and newer forms of religion. Female deities connect folk and classical religious traditions, while integrating seemingly disparate, even incongruous, religious themes. For this reason they often evoke ambivalence among devotees. The sacred mother, as we have seen in this volume, can act as protectress, source of ethnic identity, and nurturant healer. She is also capable of stirring the deepest levels of the religious imagination by focusing human terror and assisting in its resolution. Ambivalence, awe, and terror are linked together at the most fundamental level of the human experience.

What is this deeper element calling forth human ambivalence and resonating throughout the world in the form of mother worship? What is this mixture of terror and calm lurking in the shadows of our prehistory and persisting even in modern industrialized man? Humans are vulnerable beings. Our elaborate civilizations are but recent experiments in a long evolutionary process. Mother worship is an ancient reminder for humans of their vulnerability and their earlier dependency on the earth; for we continue to be, in the words of W. H. Auden, "children afraid of the night." Everywhere the divine mother is a focus for this profound insecurity at the root of the human experience. The more earthy aspects of mother worship, such as blood sacrifice, possession trances, and various forms of self-torture, continue to reemerge over and again, despite continuous attempts by the world's great religions to exorcise them.

A final question must be posed: why this new interest in mother worship, both at the popular level and among scholars? What does this return to a topic that once preoccupied religion specialists tell us about our present world? Could it be we have come to realize the limits of Western science, particularly when it comes to understanding the human imagination? A profound exercise of the imagination is at the root of the mother goddess phenomenon, creating a multitude of forms to express something mysterious at the heart of human experience. The creation of sacred images is perhaps the most awesome act available to man. Icons are constructed and destroyed, displaying the fundamental insight that divinity is both seen and unseen. This is the mystery that challenges humans to continue to perfect and refine their relationship to something beyond and within them, something that can never be fully comprehended. Throughout the world mother goddesses have been associated with the coexistence of two fundamental processes—*iconicity* (the creation of sacred images) and *iconoclasm* (the destruction of such images). According to the Turners, these two dynamic processes have become detached in the great historical religions, iconicity being associated with certain theological positions and iconoclasm with others. In Christianity, Marianism is the "epitome of iconicity" and "contra-Marianism is the most extreme form of iconoclasm," dividing Catholics and Protestants.[40] Is the resurgent interest in female sacred images perhaps an index of our discontent with "'male' iconoclasm, technical progress, bureaucratization, the conquest by reason of all natural vehicles?"[41]

There is something even more fundamental about our fascination with mother worship. Modern industrialized people are uprooted, lonely, severed from the earth. The mother goddess figure represents a metaphorical image of *primacy*. It is probably no accident that female deities were the earliest human representations of divinity, for in each of us is a memory of that time of perfect bonding between mother and child. This is the most fundamental organic relationship possible for human beings. Modern man seeks a sense of intimacy in his loneliness and desolation. Despite radical attempts to be independent, self reliant, and manipulative, he is ever vulnerable to uncontrollable events like birth and death. Though he is ashamed of his dependency, even terrified of it, a return to a womblike state is always tempting. Thus, the mother/child relationship lurks as a remnant of sweet completion in the unconscious of moderns. The womb is a place of comfort and nurturance; it is *also* temporary. Our ambivalence about the symbols of this primary bond of mother with child is nothing new in human experience. But our current intellectual fascination

with motherhood and its divine manifestations is a secular ritualiza-
tion of something that will not go away. For mothers are places of
origin associated with beginnings, the process of metamorphosis,
and the eternal return. Ultimately, mother goddesses are symbols of
transformation, whatever shape they may take. Rebirth is the key
theme of the religious life, and mother deities are profound reminders
to us all of the primacy of the mother/infant bond—a source both of
stability and of change. In essence the mother worship phenomenon
is an attempt to recapture this primal experience by divinizing it and
thus enshrining it with a sense of meaning and sustenance available
for all humans, old and young alike.

# Notes

1. Turner, Foreword, p. 7.
2. For instance, what does recent fieldwork tell us about themes like
sacrifice, death, rebirth, and rites of passage? Maloney addresses himself to a
major theme of folk religion in his recent edited volume entitled *The Evil Eye*.
3. See Fluehr-Lobban, "Reappraisal of the Matriarchate."
4. Ibid., p. 343.
5. Ibid., p. 346.
6. Schott, "Comments," p. 354.
7. Bachofen, *Myth, Religion*, p. 75.
8. Briffault, *The Mothers*.
9. Warner, *Alone of All Her Sex*, p. 283.
10. Patai, *The Hebrew Goddess*, p. 3.
11. Neumann, *The Great Mother*.
12. I am grateful to members of the 1975 (San Francisco) American
Anthropological Association session on mother worship for calling my
attention to these questions. Particularly helpful were issues raised by our
discussants, Dr. James Freeman and Dr. Alan Sandstrom.
13. Marshack, "Ice Age Man," p. 41.
14. Patai, *The Hebrew Goddess*, p. 1.
15. Ashe, *The Virgin*, p. 14.
16. Patai, *The Hebrew Goddess*, p. 46.
17. Ibid., p. 20
18. Tyler, *India*, p. 45.
19. Turner and Turner, *Image and Pilgrimage*, p. 161.
20. Neumann, *The Great Mother*, p. 21.
21. Warner, *Alone of All Her Sex*, p. 103.
22. Aradi, *Shrines to Our Lady*, pp. 82, 158.
23. Turner and Turner, *Image and Pilgrimage*, p. 199.

24. Ibid., p. 93.
25. Lafaye, *Quetzalcoatl and Guadalupe*, p. 226.
26. Aradi, *Shrines to Our Lady*, pp. 63, 64.
27. Turner and Turner, *Image and Pilgrimage*, p. 64.
28. Hershman, "Virgin and Mother," p. 290.
29. See Patai, *The Hebrew Goddess*, pp. 153–60.
30. Leach, "Virgin Birth," pp. 42, 45.
31. The miraculous tears of the Virgin of Syracuse in Sicily are an example.
See Warner, *Alone of All Her Sex*, pp. 221, 222.
32. Hershman, "Virgin and Mother," pp. 269, 294.
33. Eliade, *Shamanism*, p. 294.
34. Madsen, quoted in Turner and Turner, *Image and Pilgrimage*, p. 102.
35. Patai, *The Hebrew Goddess*, p. 258.
36. Gross, "Hindu Female Deities," p. 270.
37. Ibid., p. 271.
38. Turner and Turner, *Image and Pilgrimage*, p. 148.
39. Ibid., p. 149.
40. Ibid., pp. 235, 236.
41. Ibid., p. 236.

# Bibliography

Aradi, Zsolt. *Shrines to Our Lady around the World*. New York: Farrar, Straus and Young, 1954.

Ashe, Geoffrey. *The Virgin*. London: Routledge and Kegan Paul, 1976.

Auden, W. H. "September 1, 1939." In *Immortal Poems of the English Language*, edited by Oscar Lewis, pp. 583–86. New York: Washington Square Press, 1952.

Avalon, Arthur. *Hymns to the Goddess*. Madras: Ganesh and Co., 1964.

Bachofen, J. J. *Myth, Religion, and Mother Right*. Princeton, N.J.: Princeton University Press, 1967.

Briffault, Robert. *The Mothers*. New York: Atheneum, 1977.

Campbell, Joseph. *The Masks of God: Primitive Mythology*. New York: Viking Press, 1959.

Eliade, Mircea. *Shamanism*. Princeton, N.J.: Princeton University Press, 1964.

Fluehr-Lobban, Carolyn. "A Marxist Reappraisal of the Matriarchate." *Current Anthropology* 20 (June 1979): 341–60.

Gross, Rita M. "Hindu Female Deities as a Resource for the Contemporary Rediscovery of the Goddess." *Journal of the American Academy of Religion* 46 (1978): 269–91.

Hershman, Paul. "Virgin and Mother." In *Symbols and Sentiments*, edited by I. M. Lewis, pp. 269–92. London: Academic Press, 1977.

James, E. O. *The Cult of the Mother Goddess*. New York: Praeger Publishers, 1959.

Lafaye, Jacque. *Quetzalcoatl and Guadalupe*. Translated by Benjamin Keen. Chicago: University of Chicago Press, 1974.

Leach, Edmund. "Virgin Birth." The Henry Myers Lecture. Cambridge University, King's College, 1966.

Madsen, William. *The Virgin's Children: Life in an Aztec Village Today*. Austin: University of Texas Press, 1960.

Maloney, Clarence, ed. *The Evil Eye*. New York: Columbia University Press, 1976.

Marshack, Alexander. "The Art and Symbols of Ice Age Man." *Human Nature* 1, no. 9 (Sept. 1978): 32–41.

Neumann, Erich. *The Great Mother: An Analysis of the Archetype*. Princeton, N.J.: Princeton University Press, 1955.

Patai, Raphael. *The Hebrew Goddess*. New York: Avon Books, 1967.

Schott, Rudiger. "Comments on Fluehr-Lobban." *Current Anthropology* 20 (June 1979): 354.

Trotter, Robert J. "God: She's Alive and Well." *Science News* 109, no. 7 (1976): 106–10.

_____. "Mother Worship's Old Saga." *San Francisco Chronicle*, May 9, 1976, pp. 16, 17.

Turner, Victor. Foreword to *Symbol and Conquest*, by Ronald Grimes, pp. 7–10. Ithaca, N.Y.: Cornell University Press, 1976.

_____, and Turner, Edith. *Image and Pilgrimage in Christian Culture*. New York: Columbia University Press, 1978.

Tyler, Stephen A. *India: An Anthropological Perspective*. Pacific Palisades, Calif.: Goodyear Publishing Co., 1973.

Warner, Marina. *Alone of All Her Sex: The Myth and the Cult of the Virgin Mary*. New York: Alfred A. Knopf, 1976.

# Contributors

Ena Campbell is research fellow in anthropology at the Institute of Jamaica, Kingston. She is a member of the Social History Project of the University of the West Indies and is presently conducting research on the Jamaican self-image. Her specialties include Caribbean ethnology, folklore and ethnohistory, symbolic anthropology, and social movements.

Stephen C. Cappannari was professor of psychiatry and anthropology and director of the Division of Human Behavior at Vanderbilt University School of Medicine. Shortly before his death, he received a joint appointment as professor of psychiatry and law at Vanderbilt. Professor Cappannari conducted research in Italy and authored articles that have appeared in *Scientific Monthly, American Sociological Review, Anthropological Quarterly, Journal of American Folklore,* and *American Anthropologist.*

John P. Ferguson is associate professor of anthropology at the State University of New York College at Cobleskill. He is coeditor of *Sangha and State in Burma* (with E. Michael Mendelson) and has published articles in the *American Ethnologist* and the *Journal of the Siam Society.* His main research interest is in religious symbolism both in Southeast Asia and among American Indians.

James M. Freeman is professor and chairman of the Department of Anthropology at San Jose State University. He is author of *Scarcity and Opportunity in an Indian Village* and *Untouchable: An Indian Life History.* His articles have appeared in numerous prestigious journals and books on a wide range of topics related to South Asia. Professor Freeman is particularly interested in the life history approach to ethnology and is presently preparing several South Asian life histories for publication.

Joanna Hubbs is associate professor of Russian history at Hampshire College. She has written several articles on women's roles and is presently completing a book entitled *Mother Russia*. Her special research interest is in the history of Russian culture.

Pauline Kolenda is professor of anthropology at the University of Houston. She is the author of *Caste in Contemporary India* and *Caste, Cult and Hierarchy*. Her articles have appeared in many scholarly books and journals, including *Man in India, Human Organization, Journal of South Asian Studies, Psychiatry, Contributions to Indian Sociology*, and *Current Anthropology*. She has conducted extensive field work in various parts of India. Her research interests include studies of kinship, family, caste, women, and South Asia.

Daniel F. McCall is professor of anthropology at Boston University. He has conducted extensive field work in Africa and has published numerous articles on African societies and culture history and a book entitled *Africa in Time Perspective*. His research interests include historical anthropology, Africa, and nineteenth-century American ethnology.

Philip Frick McKean has been associate professor and dean at Hampshire College. He has authored numerous articles on various aspects of contemporary Indonesian society.

Leonard W. Moss is professor of anthropology at Wayne State University. He has published numerous articles in such scholarly journals as the *American Sociological Review, Scientific Monthly, Human Organization, Journal of American Folklore*, and *American Anthropologist*. He is winner of several distinguished awards and is widely known for his expertise on Italian ethnography.

Ralph W. Nicholas is professor of anthropology at the University of Chicago. He is coauthor of *Kinship in Bengali Culture* (with Ronald Inden) and has published several papers on the goddess Shitala and on Hinduism in India. He is currently preparing a full-length study of religious observances among Hindus of rural Bengal.

Donál Ó Cathasaigh is professor of English at the State University of New York at Oneonta. He is coeditor of *The Irish Peasant, 1800–1916* (with Robert Rhodes), editor of *Irish-American Fiction*, and author of *Benedict Kiely*. His articles have appeared in numerous scholarly journals, including the *Journal of Human Relations, Education,* the *Mankind Quarterly,* and *Aquarius.* His research is mostly concerned with the development of Irish culture.

Jacob Pandian is professor of anthropology at California State University at Fullerton. He has published articles on various aspects of South Asia in *Man in India, Contributions to Asian Studies,* and *Ethnohistory.* His research interests span several subfields of anthropology, such as urban studies, religion, and South Asia.

James J. Preston is associate professor of anthropology at the State University of New York at Oneonta. He is coeditor of *Community, Self and Identity* (with B. Misra) and author of *Cult of the Goddess: Social and Religious Change in a Hindu Temple.* His articles have appeared in numerous edited volumes and journals. His research interests include the study of religious change in South Asia and the role of pilgrimage as a unifying force in the great world religions.

Alan R. Sandstrom is assistant professor of anthropology at Indiana University/Purdue University at Fort Wayne. He is the author of several papers on various aspects of Nahua culture and has conducted extensive field work in Mexico and Tibetan exile communities in northern India.

Tullio Tentori is professor of cultural anthropology at the University of Rome, Italy. He has been a member of the Italian Commission to UNESCO and director of the National Museum of Popular Art and Folklore of Italy. Professor Tentori's list of publications is extensive. He has published articles in numerous international books and journals. His research interests are wide in scope, with particular focus on the ethnology of Italy, peasant culture, and urban anthropology.

Edith Turner has conducted field work on religion in Africa, Europe, India, and Latin America. She is coeditor of *Primavera* and is a free-lance writer whose work has appeared in numerous literary and poetry journals.

Victor Turner is professor of anthropology at the University of Virginia. He has held several distinguished positions in anthropology and African studies at the University of Chicago, the University of Manchester, Cornell University, and Princeton University. Professor

Turner has been general editor of Cornell University Press's series Symbol, Myth, and Ritual. He is the author and editor of sixteen books, including such classics in the anthropology of religion as *The Forest of Symbols*, *The Ritual Process*, and *Dramas, Fields, and Metaphors*. He has contributed significantly to the study of ritual, pilgrimage, and metaphor in numerous articles published in books and journals.

A. J. Weeramunda is lecturer in sociology at Colombo University, Sri Lanka. He has published several articles on various aspects of Sinhalese kinship, demography, and religion. His present research interests include South Asia, religion, and rural development.

# Index